MARKETS OF PAIN

OPIUM, CAPITALISM, AND THE GLOBAL HISTORY OF PAINKILLERS

BENJAMIN ROBERT SIEGEL

OXFORD
UNIVERSITY PRESS

OXFORD
UNIVERSITY PRESS

Oxford University Press is a department of the University of Oxford.
It furthers the University's objective of excellence in research, scholarship,
and education by publishing worldwide. Oxford is a registered trade mark of
Oxford University Press in the UK and in certain other countries.

Published in the United States of America by Oxford University Press
198 Madison Avenue, New York, NY 10016, United States of America.

© Oxford University Press 2026

CIP data is on file at the Library of Congress.

ISBN 9780197527825

DOI: 10.1093/oso/9780197527825.001.0001

Printed by Marquis Book Printing, Canada

The manufacturer's authorized representative in the EU for product safety is
Oxford University Press España S.A. of Parque Empresarial San Fernando de Henares,
Avenida de Castilla, 2 – 28830 Madrid (www.oup.es/en or product.safety@oup.com).
OUP España S.A. also acts as importer into Spain of products made by the manufacturer.

Contents

Acknowledgments

Throughout a decade of work, this book was materially supported by the Boston University History Department, an American Council of Learned Societies Fellowship, a fellowship from the Boston University Center for the Humanities, and a grant from the Smithsonian Lemelson Center for the Study of Invention and Innovation. I spent a semester working on the project as a visiting fellow at the Program in Agrarian Studies at Yale University, thanks to the kind invitation of Kalyanakrishnan Sivaramakrishnan and the late James C. Scott, and discussed many of its animating themes in the Seeing and Not Seeing Seminar at Boston University, organized with great care and generosity by my colleague Jeffrey W. Rubin.

I had the opportunity to present this project in various states of progress during visits to Freie Universität Berlin, Harvard Medical School, Harvard University, Johns Hopkins University, Maharaja Ranjit Singh College, the Massachusetts Institute of Technology, Shanghai University, Syracuse University, the University of Basel, the University of Cambridge, the University of Wisconsin, Madison, and Yale University. I am grateful to Susan Branson, Ved Baruah, Nicola Gess, Kiran Kumbhar, Casey Lurtz, Tim Nunan, Mukesh Patidar, Harriet Ritvo, David G. Satin, Tehila Sasson, Mitra Sharafi, and Christy Thornton for their invitations to think through my research, and to Sophia Abbas, Sebastian Conrad, Lisa Mitchell, and Alyssa Paredes for particularly constructive thoughts at those presentations. During a book manuscript workshop held at Boston University and generously sponsored by the Department of History and the College of Arts & Sciences, I benefited from the unflinching feedback of Caroline Acker, Megan Black, David Herzberg, David Jones, and Gabriela Soto-Laveaga.

Year after year, my colleagues at Boston University have offered camaraderie, material support, and the most grounded of intellectual stimulation. My friends in the history department have taught me that teaching, research, and mentorship are never separate pursuits; I wish to particularly thank Betty Anderson, Brooke Blower, Arianne Chernock, Jilene Chua, Lou Ferleger, Phil Haberkern, Rui Hua, James Johnson, Deeana Klepper, James C. McCann, Eugenio Menegon, Alex Peri, Sarah Phillips, Andrew Robichaud, and Bruce Schulman. Like every other book produced in this department, this one would have been impossible if not for the indefatigable Cady Steinberg. Beyond my colleagues at 226 Bay State Road, Marié Abe, Michael Birenbaum Quintero, Rachel Brulé, Joanna Davidson, Joe Harris, Julie Klinger, Noora Lori, Rachel Nolan, and Kaija Schilde have all taught me how to confound bureaucracy in the service of getting our real work done.

If there are insights in this book, many owe to good conversations with younger scholars. Julia Fine and Tara Suri, world-class historians, each read early drafts of this book with characteristic intellectual rigor. Two of my graduate students at Boston University, Ayushi Chauhan and Niveditha Senthilvel, have inspired me in their pursuit of cutting-edge historiographic work on the environment, politics, and economics of modern India. I have also had the pleasure to work alongside and learn from superlative young scholars, including Fathimath Anan (Anu) Ahmed, Hafsa Arain, Cari Babitzke, Agnes Burt, Kristen Carey, Warren Dennis, Elizabeth Hameeteman, Jeanna Kinnebrew, Alyssa Kreikemeier, Rachel Monsey, Cole Parker, Pritika Sharma, Courteney Smith, Thomas Sojka, Lejiu Sun, Henry Tonks, Katie Wynn, Aixin Yi, and Chenguang Zhu. It has been a privilege to work with some exceptionally capable undergraduates, including Kaasinath Balagurunath, Margo Blank, Sadie Cowan, Crystal Luo, Ryan Metz, and Isha Pawar.

I am thankful for many other colleagues who have offered mentorship, friendship, and sage advice on this project. They include Sunil Amrith, Aditya Balasubramanian, Samuel Dolbee, David Engerman, Bérénice

Guyot-Réchard, Stefan Helmreich, Alma Igra, Elisabeth Leake, Prasannan Parthasarathi, Heather Paxson, Gyan Prakash, Jayita Sarkar, Taylor Sherman, and Nico Slate. Long after my time as a graduate fellow there, the Harvard Academy for International and Area Studies continues to be an important intellectual home; I am grateful to Kathleen Hoover, Bruce Jackan, Larry Winnie, and George Soroka for the enduring welcome. The legendary Susan Ferber has guided this project through several major revisions; I am immensely grateful for her steady hand and vision. I thank Brian Distelberg, Michael Dwyer, and Matt McAdam for their thoughts on early versions of this project.

In Turkey, I have benefited from the hospitality of many generous interlocutors and friends who helped me make sense of a new site of research. My thanks are due to Ömer Döndüren, Özlem Döndüren, Esra Kartal, Lokman Önsoy, and Gülşa, for their kindness in particular. In India, I am grateful for the long-standing friendship and support of Riham Hussain, Raghu Karnad, Anush Kapadia, Venkatesh T.T., and Maitri Gopalakrishna. I would like to thank those who made a bottom-up view of India's contemporary opium production possible: these include Chandra Prakash Goyal, Chief Controller of Factories at the Government Opium and Alkaloid Works, Asoka Raina, Manoj Kumar Singh of the Indian Police Service, and the families of Mandsaur town and district who spoke with me with great care and conviction about their work. I am grateful to the archivists and librarians who helped me find needles in haystacks in New Delhi, Sitamau, London, College Park, and Istanbul; I wish to offer particular thanks to Fatma Çolakoğlu of Salt Research in Istanbul and Alison Oswald of the Smithsonian Lemelson Center.

Books emerge best in a state of general psychological resilience. I offer gratitude to Dr. Deborah Greenman and Dr. Gil G. Noam for the work we have done together, without which this book and many more important things would have been harder to finish. Caffeine is also useful. I thank the steely baristas of Jamaica Plain's Brassica Cafe, Jadu, and Ula Cafe, as well those of Blue Tokai in Said-ul-Ajaib, New Delhi, and Yakın Kitabevi in İzmir for perfect places to work and to be distracted from work. In a noisy world, I am also grateful for quiet and for the thinking and reading spaces offered by the Biblioteca Civica U. Pozzoli in Lecco, the Boston Public Library, and the Cambridge Public Library.

Jamaica Plain is the greatest neighborhood in America; my thanks to Aziza Ahmed, Amy Cantor, Christian Dambolena, Sam Davis, Bonnie Delaune, Dave DiCiccio, Joanna Diana, Diana Doty, Keegan Dougherty, Emily Falconer, Pilar Garcia Trujillo, Cara Herbitter, Rosa Herrero de Andrés, Jason Jackson, Adina Koch, Carmel Levy, Xiomara Lorenzo, Mike Pinkham, Molly Phelan, Josh Resnick, Maggie Roth, Matt Shuman, Becky Silverstein, Naomi Sobel, Karti Subramanian, Nick Tracey, and Jaclyn Youngblood for making it so. My lunch club of vegan South Asianists and fellow travelers in Camberville—Richard Delacy, Namita Dharia, Aditya Nochur, Liza Oliver, and Josh Resnick—remains the most convivial and grounding force; may our culinary one-upmanship continue. Others in Boston—Harry Bullivant, Kristian Espiritu, Pete Fishman, Elisabeth Leake, Ariel Nierenberg, Jen Noble, and Prapti Verma—gleefully defy its staid reputation. Friends elsewhere have filled this last decade with joy, including Alessandro Angelini, Kalliope Amygdalou, Sam Asher, Yael Berda, Naor Ben-Yehoyada, Rachel Berger, Akiva Fishman, Morgan Day Frank, Tasha Eccles, Alessandro Iandolo, Radhika Jain, Jeff Kahn, Nachy Kanfer, Mary Kuhn, Nicole Labruto, Miriam Liebman, Jyothi Natarajan, Nejat Dinç, the memory of Philippa Hetherington, Naamah Paley, Nathan Pearson, Sarah Shortall, David Singerman, Josh Specht, Chiara Superti, Anand Vaidya, and David Watson.

I am most grateful to my family on both sides of the Atlantic, who remind me that kinship and love, like history, are done on scales grand and small. The Scaramelli, Corno, Betelli, and Ronchi families, Maria Corno most of all, have taught me Italian and have made Lombardy a second home. My aunts and cousins in Chicago and Madison—Pam Cohen, Noah Kalafut, Amy Novick, Pam Novick, and Eve-Lynn Siegel—and their families are steady, joyful anchors. My parents, David and Sharon Siegel, my brother, Joshua Siegel, and his family—Katie, Elliott, and Isla—are the loving foundation for all that I take on, no matter how far afield from Detroit. Caterina Scaramelli has lived and thought through every page of this book while writing her own more impressive ones; I am so grateful that it is the least of our shared ventures. My children, Danit Giulia Scaramelli and Nuri Samuele Scaramelli, are the greatest of these: in their delight in the world around them, they remind me that each of us deserves the tenderness and care to build our own. It is to my grandfather, Jack Cohen—world-class thinker and connoisseur of culture in all forms—that this book is dedicated. It remains a joy to share so much with him.

Introduction
Opium Wars

On a sweltering late August day in the bustling Indian town of Indore, ten thousand opium cultivators gathered to hear a lofty promise. The politician speaking, like most of the farmers, came from India's northern central plains, the Malwa and Mewar regions once ruled by formidable Rajput kings. He knew the crop they handled intimately. Members of his large family had lanced opium poppies in vast fields, cutting shallow grooves in the green downy capsules, barely letting the white latex ooze out before moving on to the next. They had scraped the dried gum with the sides of flat blades and had waited for it to dry, offering up small harvests to the state bureaucracy, which would eventually pay the amount that every family member agreed was too low. They, too, had known the temptation of smugglers who offered far greater rewards for a bit of their crop siphoned off discreetly, and had weighed this against the threat of daunting punishments.

The cultivators had all heard the rumors: they were worried that their industry was reaching its end. But the politician who had summoned them offered confident reassurance. The following season, he thundered, the government would vastly increase the number of licenses available to cultivators. It would offer new opportunities: loans and crop insurance, and the same concessions given to other important cash crops like tea, coffee, and jute. It would help them market their product, fetch higher prices, and move their opium to hungry markets overseas.

It mattered little that the politician was making promises he could not possibly fulfill. The legal landscape in places far away was shifting, and the market for Indian opium was in massive flux. Opium's remunerative destinations, at least the legal ones, were reduced. For the government in New Delhi, opium was a liability as much as a boon: vast amounts of it were moldering in government warehouses, more than it could possibly sell. The farmers, perhaps, knew some of this, but above the din, they nonetheless roared their approval.

Opium's uncertain future, its changing economics and legality, the lure of the black market, and the empty promises of politicians and bureaucrats had characterized the 1880s, a moment when opium's vast and profitable global market was coming into the crosshairs of a global movement for prohibition. But this speech was being given in 1981. The politician was India's finance minister, Sawai Singh Sisodia, and the shifting markets to which Indian opium was destined were not the ports of China and Southeast Asia, but largely the pharmaceutical manufacturers of the United States, who would process it into alkaloids for medicine.

Months after the launch of the space shuttle and MTV, in the year when AIDS was recognized and the personal computer was first sold, peasant cultivators in India were still enmeshed in the politics of opium, the quintessential crop of nineteenth-century empires. Their counterparts in the Golden Crescent of Afghanistan, Iran, and Pakistan and the Golden Triangle of Burma, Laos, and Thailand were scoring poppy for black-market heroin. But these farmers and a smaller number in Turkey were raising poppy crops in the service of producing medical alkaloids. Shipped to the United States and a few other destinations, their opium would be processed into codeine for cough syrup, morphine for hospital stays, and thebaine that could be transformed into any number of pills for pain relief.

This production was deeply anachronistic. Scraping opium gum by hand, Indian peasants were producing a commodity that was scarcely different from that which their forebears had made a century and a half earlier. Anywhere else poppy was cultivated licitly for pharmaceutical purposes, farmers plowed whole fields of poppy by tractors or combines, bathing the capsules and the first few inches of stalk in organic solvents to produce alkaloids directly, sidestepping the gum altogether. Only in India did farmers still carry out the laborious scraping and drying of gum favored elsewhere by heroin producers.

The Indian politician's promise, at the turn of the 1980s, came late in the day. Opium stood on the edge of profound transformation. The global system that had sustained it—forged in the mid-twentieth century through American regulatory power, international treaties, and the developmental ambitions of two post-imperial states, India and Turkey—was unraveling. New technologies, shifting agricultural methods, and evolving pharmaceutical markets were remaking the very foundations of the licit opium trade.

But opium had animated many other outsized visions in the twentieth century, long after the heyday of the imperial Asian opium trade was presumed to have passed. At the turn of the century, scientists working in India's opium bureaucracy worked to create opium better suited to Western medical needs, undeterred by growing calls for prohibition. In the 1930s, a radical Turkish socialist had urged the new republic to find new markets for Anatolian opium to underwrite its ambitious project of infrastructural modernization. In the 1950s, a charismatic Indian Narcotics Commissioner pitched Indian opium as a world-class product to executives at America's leading pharmaceutical firms. A Turkish prime minister wondered how high a price he could extract from American diplomats for banning opium's cultivation altogether. Even into the 1970s, an Indian horticulturalist—known until then for breeding roses—led an ambitious research program to reengineer India's poppy supply for the modern pharmaceutical age.

What held these visions together across decades and regimes was a shared conviction that opium, no matter the winnowing space for its legal production, could still serve as a tool for national development, political leverage, and economic value. In India and Turkey, opium was a privileged crop: more than any other agricultural product, it linked peasant labor to global capital, and domestic planning to international markets. For the Indian politician speaking in Indore, like many others, it seemed that this unruly and powerful substance might be harnessed again to serve the modern world.

◖◯◗

The modern world was built on the transformation of raw materials into systems of power: crops into capital, labor into expertise, and substances into commodities traded across empires and states. Few substances embodied these transformations more fully than opium. This book shows how, long after the collapse of the imperial opium empires, peasant producers in India and Turkey were essential in building a global pharmaceutical economy that linked agrarian labor, state power, scientific innovation, and international markets.

Over the past two decades, opioids have become synonymous with crisis—shorthand for the greed of pharmaceutical companies, the complexities of addiction, and the interlinked failures of public health and labor in the United States. But long before the emergence of the contemporary moment of crisis, there was a vast and global system of opioid production, built upon imperial structures and contested ideas about the future of labor, regulation, and medicine, which reshaped the modern world. Instead of following the US crisis of access and consumption, this book follows the people who grew pharmaceutical opium, the bureaucrats who sought to promote the commodity or regulate it, the companies who profited from its sale, and the shifting international rules that governed the product's trade.

Opium's centrality to the construction of empire and global capitalism in the long nineteenth century is well known: British, French, Dutch, and American merchants amassed fortunes by fueling addiction abroad, primarily in East and Southeast Asia. But opium did not vanish with the rise of international prohibition in the early twentieth century. As its derivatives like morphine and codeine grew increasingly central to modern pharmaceuticals, the crop underwrote late colonial and postcolonial development schemes in India and Turkey, tied rural labor to global pharmaceutical markets, and helped forge a regulatory order meant to control the world's supply of narcotic pain relief.

That order would also collapse. Quietly, unevenly, and often unnoticed, the infrastructure that once stabilized the global trade in licit opium came apart—just as demand for opioids surged again in the late twentieth century. The quest to replace morphine and codeine's useful properties with synthetic or partially synthetic substitutes began to yield useful results. The peasant production of opium in India and Turkey, laborious but politically valuable, lost much of its protected status, and a new mechanized form of production on the Australian island state of Tasmania captured much of the world market. The glut and crisis that followed in the United States was not an aberration. It was the wreckage of a global system of production that had governed the world's relationship to pain and its management for more than a century.

This story offers three new ways of seeing the global system of opioids and pain relief in the long twentieth century. First, it frames the story of opioids in the modern world not as one of sudden and isolated crisis in the United States but instead as one rooted in a long global infrastructure of production and supply. In recent years, journalistic accounts have foregrounded a set of real and profound distortions in access to and the overuse of opioids.[1] They follow Purdue Pharma's launch of OxyContin in 1996, when the Sackler family's aggressive marketing and misleading claims about this and other opioids' addiction potential led to the widespread use of opioid drugs for chronic pain conditions in the United States, where they had once been reserved for palliative care, surgery, and acute trauma.[2] They focus on American geography, and the movement of opioid drugs from Appalachia and other places "left behind" or "hollowed out" by changing structures of labor and family into major cities.[3]

Some of these stories have global elements. The confounding rise of fentanyl and other synthetic opioids—potent enough to be shipped in DHL envelopes even as the majority is trafficked from Mexico across the United States' southwestern land border—has brought attention to the global supply chain that brings illicit opioids and precursor chemicals from China to North America.[4] These stories show how the quintessential black market of the twentieth century—the global heroin market linking producers in Asia, the Middle East, and Latin America to consumers in Europe and the United States—has given way to a different global supply chain in the twenty-first. Mostly, however, these accounts focus on the uniqueness of American suffering. They foreground the grim milestone of a million opioid-related deaths that the United States reached in 2020, and the idea that these deaths might be seen as "deaths of despair": fatal outcomes driven by economic insecurity, social isolation, and the collapse of traditional working-class institutions.[5]

It is not necessary to minimize the scale of the US crisis to offer a radically different perspective on the massive distortion of the world's opioid supply. The contemporary world of opioid drugs has been structured and shaped by the legacy of imperial opium monopolies, the postcolonial politics of agricultural production and national development in India and Turkey, Cold War battles over pharmaceutical supplies, and US regulators' and companies' attempts to build dominance over global supply chains. Rather than starting in Appalachia or in a Connecticut boardroom, this book begins in colonial India and the Ottoman Empire, where poppy cultivation transformed into a tool of imperial statecraft. It shows how opium grew central to modern Turkey and postcolonial India's ideas of development and power, shaping bureaucracies and domestic politics alike. Seeing opium as a commodity central to modern state-building, international trade, and global pharmaceuticals shows how contemporary distortions are built upon a two-century architecture of labor, politics, and power.

Studies of opioid consumption, secondly, can be intimate, harrowing, and morally or politically charged. But a focus on consumption alone elides the world of production, cultivation, and marketing that produces these substances. While some opioids, and an increasing number of them, are made partially or wholly in a laboratory, this has been a slow and incomplete transformation over the course of the twentieth and twenty-first centuries. Since the emergence of modern pharmaceuticals in the late nineteenth century and until the closing decades of the twentieth, painkilling drugs have largely relied upon a singular agricultural product: the sap of the poppy, cultivated primarily in Asia and the

Eastern Mediterranean major by peasant producers. This story moves the production, marketing, and export of opium to the center of the history of global pharmaceutical opioids and the consolidation of state power in India, Turkey, and the United States.

From the late nineteenth to the early twenty-first centuries, millions of cultivators in Anatolia and north and central India have produced opium for pharmaceutical firms primarily located in the United States and Europe. Opium was rarely the only crop these peasant producers grew. In India, farmers grew it alongside wheat and rice, lentils, sugarcane, potatoes, and oilseeds. In Turkey, they planted it with wheat and barley, chickpeas and lentils, as well as olives, grapes, figs, apricots, and nuts. But in each place, the crop was uniquely central to the lives of its cultivators. Vital to the social and cultural worlds of both regions, opium could also be sold to black-market buyers, and governments often had practical and political reasons to turn a blind eye to those sales. Seeing the construction of the global opium order from the ground up, starting with the peasants who produced the crop, locates the history of opioids within particular histories of agriculture, development, and state formation. Locating the production of opium as a commodity in particular climates, cultural contexts, and regional political economies demonstrates how a particular kind of agricultural supply chain was rooted in highly localized forms of knowledge, labor organization, and ecological constraints.[6]

Peasants were not the only people whose work with opium helped forge that order. Bureaucrats, administrators, and agronomists all managed the work of cultivators and sought to coax better or more usable product from particular soils. Brokers forged particular relationships with farmers, politicians made political and actual capital from their engagement with opium cultivation, and pharmaceutical executives and regulators abroad worked to enact particular visions of production for modern medical use.[7] These diverse entanglements reveal a global narcotics economy shaped not simply by consumption or corporate greed, but by the intersecting motives, logics, and imperatives of agrarian labor, state authority, and transnational capitalism. The result was a global supply chain that brought together substance and commerce, science and culture, and developmental and political imperatives with global pharmaceutical demands. All global commodities bring together disparate ideas and practices. But some are substances whose extraction and circulation reorder bodies, landscapes, and political authority in particularly complex ways, tying the most intimate scales of life to the architecture of global commerce.[8] Tracing these potent connections makes visible the long and largely hidden infrastructure that built the modern world's reliance on opioids.

Finally, as those involved with the trade made divergent claims about opium's production and export, they built shifting ideas of what represented legitimate and illegitimate forms of narcotic production.[9] They attached those ideas to rapidly changing notions of what opioids—described as "opiates" until the 1960s—were. The processes of scientific discovery and political claim-making about what was legal and illegal were intertwined. As chemists broke opium into its constituent alkaloids and pharmacists transformed those compounds into new ones in the laboratory, bureaucrats and politicians worked to delineate medicine from vice, while positing a world where an essential agricultural product could be replaced entirely with synthetic substitutes. Each successive breakdown and reconstruction of opium into new compounds confounded regulators' hopes of simplicity and their search for an easily demarcated line between medical use and black-market contraband.[10]

From the early nineteenth century onwards, when its active components were first identified, opium was a substance in flux that could be used to different ends. The gum that was essential to modern medicine in its infancy was the same substance that Britain cultivated forcefully in India and sold to addicts in China. Bayer could process Anatolian opium into heroin, the first semisynthetic opioid, but underworld intermediaries could use the same crop to make heroin for recreational use in Marseille, Shanghai, and New York. Indian and Turkish nationalists made claims in international arenas about the value of their crops to modern pharmaceuticals while offering unofficial sanction to black markets, which were integral parts of regional political economies. Lawmakers in the United States put stock in plant breeding, briefly pinning their hopes on a poppy that could produce for pharmaceutical markets but not the underworld. More characteristic, however, was the emergence of new fully synthetic opioids like fentanyl, touted as potential replacements for poppy-derived opioids, but further confounding efforts to regulate their diversion. By the late twentieth century, a fragile architecture of control built through postcolonial politics, pharmaceutical research, and global politicking began to unravel under the weight of its own contradictions.

Opium's history is often told through the narrow lens of prohibition—a story of organized crime, smuggling, and the steady expansion of American efforts to stamp out its trade.[11] But behind the clash of American power and black-market actors lay vast networks of farmers, scientists, and diplomats bound together in a fragile system of international control that struggled to contain a substance constantly shifting form.[12] Centering India and Turkey, the twin pillars of licit global supply, in this story shows how the unstable boundary between medicine and vice became a site of political power, scientific ambition, and global contestation, long before and long after the familiar war on drugs took shape.

◖◉◗

Opium's global story begins with the plant itself. The latex drawn from its capsule carries alkaloids that block pain by mimicking the body's own ability to do so. This basic fact has sustained industries, shaped laws, and fueled illicit markets for more than two centuries. The term *opiate*, later *opioid*, describes the expanding set of substances built upon its chemistry, whether extracted from poppies or manufactured synthetically.

Opium is the sticky, resinous gum harvested from *Papaver somniferum*, a poppy that grows readily in most temperate climates. Its production is labor-intensive but requires only modest skill. The poppy blooms in shades of vermillion, parchment white, or blush pink. After the petals fall, a knobby green capsule remains, covered in fine down and topped with a fluted crown, its interior packed with delicate white seeds. Scoring the capsule's skin with a knife or pin releases a milky sap, which dries within hours into a murky brown gum. This gum, scraped off with the blunt edge of a knife, is acrid and bitter on the tongue, with a sharp whiff of ammonia. Once dried further, it can be swallowed in small balls, steeped into a bitter tea, or dissolved into tincture. The effects come quickly: lightheadedness, relaxed muscles, and a creeping euphoria. Smoked, as has long been common across Asia, opium delivers a deeper and more immediate stupor. These effects stem from its distinctive mix of active compounds, hypothesized for centuries but not fully identified until the nineteenth century.

The effects of opium have been known since antiquity, though the poppy was likely first domesticated for its oily, nutrient-rich seeds in Neolithic Europe. The earliest evidence of its cultivation comes from a cache near Rome dated to 5600–5500 BCE, alongside finds from later centuries in southern France and northeastern Spain.[13] Earlier claims that Sumerians cultivated opium now appear unlikely; instead, the plant spread eastward across Europe, acquiring symbolic roles in religious and ritual life within Minoan and Mycenaean cultures before reaching Asia Minor. Opium's painkilling and euphoric properties were recognized by the time the poppy had become established across the Eastern Mediterranean. The Greek word *opós*—a general term for plant sap—eventually narrowed to *ópion*, referring specifically to poppy sap, and from there entered Latin and nearly every subsequent language as *opium*.

The long overland and maritime trade routes of the Arab world carried opium eastward to China and India, where cultivators adopted it as both a social commodity and a tool of early medicine.[14] In Europe, opium largely disappeared during the first millennium, but by the Middle Ages it reemerged at the center of new medical practices. The *spongia somnifera*—a sponge soaked in various compounds and used as a crude anesthetic—may have drawn much of its limited effectiveness from opium alone.[15] Later, opium became more useful with the development of laudanum: a tincture made by dissolving powdered opium in alcohol. Long before the advent of scientific medicine, opium was one of the few reliable agents for easing pain and inducing sleep.

The opium poppy was quickly drawn into projects of state power and empire. Though it preferred dry climates, its tolerance for varied conditions made it easily transplantable across much of the world. Still, early European observers recognized that certain regions offered ideal climates and skilled labor capable of producing superior opium. Afyonkarahisar, a town in western Anatolia, was already known for its expertise; the very name Afyon referred to the substance itself. In 1513, after a failed assault on Aden, Portuguese viceroy Afonso de Albuquerque sent a captured opium cultivator back to Lisbon, urging the king to "order poppies of the Açores to be sown in all the fields of Portugal and command opium to be made."[16] Albuquerque proposed shipping Portuguese-grown opium to India to supply laborers there—an early vision of how imperial powers might reorder global opium production.

For all its potency, opium's inner workings remained a mystery until 1804, when German chemist Friedrich Sertürner isolated its active compound. Boiling eight ounces of opium with ammonia, he extracted a small quantity of grayish crystals. Sertürner tested the substance on dogs, rats, and eventually on himself to treat a toothache, gradually developing an addiction to the compound he named *morphium*, after the Greek god of sleep and dreams.[17] His discovery of opium's "soporific principle" marked the beginning of the alkaloid era—the systematic isolation of physiologically active compounds from plants. In the years that followed, chemists would extract caffeine, nicotine, cocaine, quinine, strychnine, and eventually hundreds and then thousands more alkaloids.

Morphine, as Sertürner's compound came to be known, was uniquely potent. By 1827, the German pharmacist Emanuel Merck was producing and marketing morphine from his Engel-Apotheke pharmacy in Darmstadt, laying the foundation for the German—and later American— pharmaceutical empire that would bear his name. Morphine's strength was both its appeal and its danger: the purified compound was far more powerful and reliable than raw opium, which was often adulterated during both production and trade. French chemists soon identified two additional active compounds in opium, naming them codeine and narcotine; a fourth, thebaine, followed shortly after.[18] Eventually, chemists would isolate more than eighty distinct alkaloids from the poppy's dark resin.

Since the fifteenth century, the word *opiate* in English had referred broadly to opium and other substances—mandrake, henbane, belladonna—that induced sleep or stupor. But by the late nineteenth century, growing chemical knowledge gave the term a new precision. In 1874, an English chemist boiled morphine with acetic anhydride, a relatively new reagent, producing diacetylmorphine—a "semisynthetic" compound created by chemically modifying an opium alkaloid. Marketed by several companies as a cough suppressant, it achieved its greatest commercial and black-market success under Bayer's trade name: heroin. In the early twentieth century, as the pharmaceutical and chemical industries expanded rapidly, a wave of new semisynthetic opiates followed. German chemists synthesized oxymorphone and oxycodone in 1914 and 1916; hydrocodone and hydromorphone soon followed.

The rapid development of semisynthetic drugs raised the prospect of even greater breakthroughs. By the 1920s, chemists and pharmacologists aimed to create painkillers that no longer depended on opium, combining the curative power of poppy alkaloids with reduced risk of addiction—by then well recognized. Researchers set out to produce "synthetic opium" or "synthetic morphine," and over time developed increasingly potent synthetic analgesics. Compounds like pentazocine, fentanyl, and carfentanil would astonish for their strength, but none could fully replace poppy-derived drugs.

By the early 1960s, researchers were positing that the body contained natural sites on which opioid drugs acted. This emerging line of inquiry led to both a semantic and scientific shift. A study at the National Institute of Mental Health Addiction Research Center, testing how morphine-addicted rats responded to etonitazene, a powerful synthetic analgesic, introduced a new term almost in passing. In a footnote, the authors proposed replacing *opiate* with *opioid* to describe "any chemical compound with morphine-like properties."[19] In the years that followed, teams in the United States and the United Kingdom worked to identify the brain receptors where these drugs exerted their effects. In 1973, researchers confirmed not only that such receptors existed, but also that the body produces its own "endogenous" opioids—now known as endorphins.[20]

As laboratory knowledge of opioid drugs advanced, so too did methods for extracting alkaloids from the opium poppy itself. In the late 1920s, a Hungarian chemist devised a novel but economically impractical process to extract morphine directly from dried poppy capsules and the upper stalks of the plant. Four decades later, improvements in processing made this approach viable, allowing countries to adopt the "poppy straw method" and eliminate the need to lance pods in the field. This technique proved better suited to the political and agricultural conditions of some countries than others, but the rise of poppy straw, and its easily transportable derivative, concentrate of poppy straw, expanded the scope of poppy-derived opioids alongside their synthetic and semi-synthetic counterparts.

Beneath the expanding category of opioids remains the physical reality of the poppy. Its cultivation and conversion into usable alkaloids shaped the political economies of states, the structures of global trade, and the shifting boundaries between legal markets and illicit circuits. However far laboratory science extended the pharmacological reach of opioids, the biological realities of the poppy and the labor required to unlock its chemistry remained at the center of struggles over production, regulation, and power.

The story begins in the nineteenth and early twentieth centuries, as opium was remade into a global commodity through its production and trade in British India and the Ottoman Empire. In both regions, the poppy shifted from a minor crop to a central pillar of imperial economies, shaping state power, fiscal systems, and international relations. By the early twentieth century, with global prohibition movements gathering force, opium's future as a freely traded commodity was under threat. Yet modernizers, administrators, and nationalists still saw new possibilities: a commodity that could meet medical demand and finance ambitious projects of development. These transformations unfolded within, and helped to constitute, the expanding architecture of global capitalism, agricultural modernization, and the bureaucracies that sought to divide licit trade from illicit markets.

In the nineteenth century, opium became the lynchpin of Britain's imperial economy in India. A state monopoly, enforced by a vast administrative apparatus, bound millions of peasant cultivators across Bihar, Bengal, and the country's northwest into the brutal, tightly regulated production of poppy. The government's factories at Patna and Ghazipur processed tens of thousands of chests annually, while British and Indian traders funneled the product into lucrative Asian markets, with the China trade at their center. To the west, in the region of Malwa, Indian princes, merchant families, and financiers carved out an alternate system of production that eluded British control. Branded as smugglers, these indigenous traders ultimately forced the colonial state to accommodate their thriving export networks.

As pressure mounted from transnational prohibitionists—including missionaries, women's activists, Indian social reformers, and early nationalists—the contradictions of this imperial system became harder to ignore. The Royal Commission on Opium, convened in 1893, exposed the coercion and economic hardship imposed on India's cultivators, even as it ultimately defended the trade as benign. Yet even as Chinese markets contracted, British administrators and Indian elites searched for new futures for the crop. Some envisioned Indian opium as a source of painkilling alkaloids for modern pharmaceuticals, experimenting with improved cultivation and extraction techniques at Ghazipur and Patna. Others defended opium's central place in India's vernacular medical cultures and household economies, where it remained a widely used remedy across castes, religions, and regions. For India's princely rulers, merchant dynasties, and creditor-moneylenders, opium revenues underwrote infrastructure, stabilized local power, and financed growing regional autonomy.

By the early twentieth century, the Indian opium economy stood at an uneasy crossroads: increasingly untenable as an imperial export but too embedded in the political economy, medicine, and social life of India to be easily dismantled. It was a dilemma shared, in different form, by the late Ottoman Empire as both systems faced the turbulent new global order emerging from two world wars.

In the Ottoman Empire, as in India, opium was remade into a global commodity over the course of the nineteenth century. Once valued primarily for its oil and seed, Anatolian poppy became a sought-after export as American merchants arrived in the Eastern Mediterranean, eager to supply China's expanding opium markets. In 1828, the Ottoman state briefly attempted to centralize control through the Yed'i Vahit monopoly, but British pressure forced its dissolution a decade later, leaving the trade in the hands of private intermediaries.

As demand from China declined, foreign merchants turned westward. Expanding pharmaceutical markets in Europe and the United States offered new outlets for Ottoman opium, prized for its reliable morphine content and consistent quality. During the era of the Tanzimat reforms, when the Ottoman state pursued sweeping administrative, legal, and fiscal reform, its administrators integrated opium cultivation into a broader program of agricultural modernization, seeking to stabilize the Empire's fragile finances and secure new revenues for an increasingly indebted state.

Unlike India's state monopoly, Turkey's opium trade continued to flow through a network of private brokers—primarily Armenian and Jewish merchants—who bridged Anatolian cultivators and foreign buyers. By the century's end, their role was gradually eclipsed as chemical assays, new forms of quality control, and direct relationships between American pharmaceutical firms and Turkish producers signaled a shifting global narcotics economy on the brink of transformation.

In the early twentieth century, the global opium economy was rebuilt under a new international order. As demand for medical opiates surged in Europe and the United States, geopolitical calculations kept poppy cultivation firmly rooted in the former imperial peripheries. In India and Turkey, newly assertive states seized this narrowing space, using their bureaucratic machinery to position themselves as indispensable suppliers to the pharmaceutical trade. For both, opium offered not just access to global markets, but served as a vital resource for financing national development and projecting economic sovereignty.

By the late eighteenth century, opium had become indispensable to American medicine, a remedy of first resort for a wide range of ailments. Yet despite rising demand, the United States remained fully reliant on imports, primarily from the Ottoman Empire. Throughout the nineteenth century, enterprising farmers, merchants, and scientists sought to establish programs of domestic cultivation, including serious proposals for large-scale plantations in the southwest in the years after the Civil War. All these efforts fell short: the fantasies of a self-sufficient opium industry that might meet its swelling needs at home yielded to the realities of a global supply chain.

This dependence molded the next phase of American pharmaceutical expansion. As German firms dominated global pharmaceutical production, American companies pursued a distinct business strategy, combining global botanical prospecting with aggressive marketing to capture a share of the growing global trade. At the same time, American missionaries and diplomats emerged as leaders in the global prohibition movement, casting opium as both a vital medicine and a dangerous vice. By the interwar years, the contradictions sharpened: scientists and industrialists sought to synthesize fully artificial substitutes that might sever the country's reliance on the poppy altogether. Yet even as laboratories advanced, opium remained irreplaceable and firmly entangled in the shifting geopolitics of the global pharmaceutical trade.

In the interwar years, Turkey and India moved to the center of a growing struggle over opium's future, each country torn between the crop's enduring economic importance at home and mounting demands for global prohibition abroad. Since the turn of the century, the global prohibition movement had cast opium as a threat to public health and international order. But for both governments, opium remained too valuable to abandon. It was an agricultural commodity that could still generate revenue, sustain rural labor, and fund ambitious projects of national development.

In Turkey, left-leaning economic modernizers within the new Kemalist regime imagined expanded opium sales as a way to pay for modern infrastructure and industrial growth. In India, princely rulers defended opium's central role in their regional economies and lobbied for continued cultivation as a lucrative source of revenue. Both visions clashed with the rising international consensus that sought to tighten control over narcotic production and limit opium's circulation. Yet even as their ambitions were constrained, Turkey and India adapted to the new regulatory landscape by building complex state bureaucracies capable of controlling, regulating, and legitimizing their opium industries.

Turkey's Narcotic Substances Monopoly, established in 1933, centralized control over the republic's cultivation and exports, presenting the state as a modern, disciplined actor capable of supplying the pharmaceutical needs of Western markets. India's administrators expanded its parallel system of licensing, oversight, and factory regulation, creating a flexible apparatus that could meet shifting global demand while maintaining state authority over production. These bureaucratic structures made both countries increasingly attractive to the United States, which, by the late 1930s was seeking stable international partners for its growing pharmaceutical industry. Under Harry Anslinger, the uncompromising commissioner who came to personify America's global war on drugs, the United States' Federal Bureau of Narcotics sought both to suppress illicit narcotics and to secure reliable supplies of licit opium. India and Turkey, with their tightly managed state systems, became central nodes in the emerging architecture of American-led global narcotics control.

In the postwar years, Indian and Turkish opium followed sharply divergent paths. As international drug control regimes hardened and American pharmaceutical interests expanded, India successfully transformed the colonial system it had inherited into a modernized, tightly regulated industry. Turkey, by contrast, struggled to reform its more loosely governed monopoly, leaving its opium sector increasingly vulnerable to international pressure.

In newly independent India, nationalist leaders wrestled with the tension between prohibitionist ideals and the fiscal importance of opium revenue. Indian civil servants transformed creaky colonial infrastructure into a centralized bureaucracy capable of meeting evolving international standards and expanding export capacity. They phased out the domestic "quasi-medical" opium market, established new regulatory bodies, and ratified international narcotics conventions. Even as political tensions strained broader Indo-American relations, Indian opium officials cultivated close ties with US regulators and pharmaceutical firms. By the late 1960s, India had become the world's dominant supplier of licit opium, and the United States was its largest and most reliable customer.

Turkey's trajectory was far less stable. Its Narcotic Substances Monopoly, hastily established in the 1930s, failed to fully contain diversion to the illicit market. Despite Ankara's repeated assurances of control, significant volumes of Turkish opium continued to feed the black-market heroin trade, particularly along the infamous "French Connection" pipeline into Western Europe and the United States. By the 1950s, American officials had grown increasingly frustrated with Turkey's inability to separate rural cultivation from illicit trafficking. Yet domestically, opium retained powerful cultural resonance in Anatolia—celebrated in rural economies, defended in political discourse, and romanticized in Turkish literature and film. By the middle of the 1960s, Turkish officials faced mounting calls from US diplomats to eliminate opium cultivation altogether.

In the final decades of the twentieth century, the global architecture of licit opium production began to unravel. From the early 1970s through the 1990s, the value of opium gum as an export commodity steadily eroded. Despite occasional shortfalls, production in India and Turkey increasingly outstripped what importing countries—above all, the United States—could absorb for pharmaceutical use. New technologies for processing poppy straw bypassed the labor-intensive work of scraping gum, while renewed hopes for synthetic substitutes once again threatened to render the plant obsolete. For India and Turkey's peasant producers, these shifts unfolded within sharply diverging political landscapes. India's state-run monopoly sought to maintain rural livelihoods through continued cultivation, while Turkish authorities, under sustained

American pressure, moved toward more radical restrictions. What had once been a highly protected global trade was quietly displaced by new modes of production, new technologies, and a pharmaceutical economy increasingly severed from the labor of the poppy field.

The 1970s marked a volatile turning point in the global politics of opium. As American drug control expanded its reach at home and abroad, the uneasy balance between pharmaceutical supply, agricultural production, and international diplomacy began to fracture. In Washington, policymakers increasingly envisioned a future without opium cultivation at all, betting—despite the reservations of many scientists—that synthetic substitutes would soon render the poppy obsolete.

Turkey was the first major battleground in this shifting landscape. In 1971, under heavy American pressure, Ankara imposed a nationwide ban on poppy cultivation. The economic consequences for Turkish farmers were significant, though Turkey's shrinking role in pharmaceutical markets had already weakened the industry's commercial footing. The ban proved politically unsustainable. Domestic protests forced Ankara to reverse course in 1974, reinstating cultivation under a newly regulated poppy straw system that sharply curtailed the diversion of raw opium to the black market.

The brief collapse of Turkish production forced American officials to confront a familiar dilemma. Fearing potential shortages, they revived long-dormant proposals for domestic cultivation, experimenting with a new poppy strain bred to minimize morphine content and eliminate the risk of diversion into heroin production. Backed by government agencies, pharmaceutical firms, and agricultural researchers, the plan briefly gathered momentum. But it soon ran aground on the broader imperatives of US foreign policy. The global management of narcotics remained deeply embedded in America's diplomatic relationships, where stable overseas supply chains offered greater leverage than domestic cultivation ever could.

In the aftermath of Turkey's retreat from opium production, India assumed a new centrality in the global licit opium trade. With few other reliable suppliers remaining, US officials leaned increasingly on India to meet the growing pharmaceutical demand of the world's largest opioid market. At home, as Indian authorities faced rising concerns over illicit diversion and heroin production, they deepened cooperation with American narcotics officials, linking domestic enforcement efforts to the broader stability of licit opium exports. But Indian negotiators grew frustrated: while US officials depended on Indian supply, they offered little assurance of long-term purchasing commitments.

India had become an outlier by the 1970s. While other producers had shifted to mechanized poppy straw processing, cultivation in central and northern India still relied on the manual scraping of gum. With tens of thousands of Indian families reliant on the crop, proposals to adopt the poppy straw method used elsewhere were politically untenable. Reducing cultivation risked triggering rural unrest and cutting off both licit and illicit income streams that anchored local economies and political networks.

In 1978, facing mounting stockpiles and declining prices, Indian officials sought to stabilize their position through long-term agreements with the United States. These negotiations helped to produce the "80-20 rule" in 1981, which guaranteed India and Turkey a combined 80 percent share of US narcotic raw material imports. On paper, the deal secured India's dominance. But beneath the surface, the agreement locked India's producers into an increasingly fragile position, preserving labor-intensive cultivation while global pharmaceutical markets moved toward more efficient, mechanized, and chemically advanced forms of opioid production.

By the 1990s, global opium production was entering a new era. In India, the crop still enjoyed political protection, but it had become increasingly irrelevant to the global pharmaceutical supply. In Tasmania, a once-marginal poppy industry seized the advantage. Working with multinational pharmaceutical companies, Tasmanian growers developed new poppy strains bred for the demands of modern drug manufacturing. The breakthrough came in 1996 with the release of the Norman poppy—high in thebaine, free of morphine, and nearly useless to illicit heroin producers. With the chemistry recast to serve pharmaceutical priorities, the risks of diversion were sharply reduced. Johnson & Johnson's international division capitalized on the innovation, pressing American regulators to loosen long-standing import quotas and open the US market to Tasmanian supply.

In Turkey, the shift registered only faintly; poppy cultivation had by then become a modest rural sideline. But in India, the consequences were profound. The country's elaborate system of manual gum scraping, once central to global pharmaceutical supply, was left stranded. The legal trade endured on paper, sustained by bureaucratic momentum and political sensitivities, but in practice had become a hollowed-out "zombie commodity," propped up by regulation but cut off from the global currents that once gave it value. As licit returns dwindled, black-market profits surged. In the Malwa-Mewar region, poppy cultivation was increasingly given over to informal power networks and illicit trafficking, even as the rest of India's economy raced ahead into new sectors. The labor of India's opium farmers, once tied to global commerce, was increasingly disconnected from the modern pharmaceutical economy they had once supplied.

By the century's end, the long chain that had once brought opium from peasant fields to global pharmaceutical markets had largely unraveled. New technologies, new geographies, and new forms of industrial control displaced the labor-intensive cultivation that had anchored India and Turkey's opium industries for generations. Across both countries, the farmers, traders, and administrators who had once stood at the center of a vital global trade were increasingly irrelevant to the industry they had sustained. Yet the long arc of licit opium shows how a single crop— bound up in empire, medicine, national development, and international regulation—could for generations serve as both an engine of global commerce and a flashpoint of political struggle.

◁○▷

On that August day in Indore in 1981, as farmers gathered to hear promises that politicians could not keep, the contradictions which had come to define the global opioid economy were at their apex. Indian cultivators still scraped poppy gum by hand, producing a raw material that was in some ways central to global pharmaceutical markets, even as those same markets contracted. Bureaucrats invoked development while nodding tacitly at smugglers' alternative rewards, American regulators worried about diversion, and US pharmaceutical firms remained reliant on the Indian and Turkish supply. This unstable configuration which brought together state control and rural labor, licit commerce and illicit markets, medical need and political calculation had been the architecture of the global opioid system for more than a century. Yet even as it was enshrined into law, it was nearing its end, collapsing under the weight of its own contradictions.

The contemporary American opioid crisis cannot be understood apart from this longer global history. Purdue Pharma's marketing campaigns, the surge in US prescribing, and the rise in overdose deaths emerged within a global system whose contradictions were already deeply entrenched. While the United States consumed ever greater volumes of opioids—accounting at one point for more than 80 percent of global morphine consumption—vast portions of the world's population remained unable to access even basic palliative care. The same commodity chain generated both extraordinary medical capacity and staggering global inequality. In the twentieth and twenty-first centuries, some patients died from excess, and others died in pain for lack of access.

These outcomes were not accidental. They were the result of two centuries of imperial consolidation, postcolonial development strategies, pharmaceutical innovation, and evolving regulatory regimes that together shaped where opium would be grown, how its alkaloids would be extracted, who controlled supply, and who received its benefits. The modern opioid economy was built in boardrooms and laboratories, and in poppy fields, administrative offices, and diplomatic negotiations that brought together peasant producers, bureaucrats, companies, and states. Each effort to draw a clear line between medical necessity and black-market danger—through regulation, breeding programs, or synthetic alternatives—exposed the fragility of that distinction.

This book reconstructs that global system. It begins with the peasant producers in India and Turkey whose labor sustained pharmaceutical markets, and follows the postcolonial bureaucracies that transformed colonial monopolies into instruments of national development. It examines how pharmaceutical companies in the United States and Europe, dependent on these supplies, helped stabilize—and later helped dismantle—the old system of licit cultivation. And it traces how new synthetic opioids like fentanyl ultimately bypassed the agricultural economy entirely, producing a global marketplace where old patterns of scarcity and excess now coexist in new forms.

The opioid crisis is not a uniquely American story. It is the product of a global infrastructure that, over two centuries, tied together agricultural labor, pharmaceutical science, state power, and medical care. The contradictions that defined its rise and management remain at the center of the global opioid system today. For two centuries, the effort to balance pain relief with political control has tied together farmers, firms, regulators, and states. The result is not simply a story of excess or absence, but a global economy in which the power to produce, regulate, and consume opioids has continually redrawn the boundaries between medicine, production, and politics.

PART I

The First Great Unraveling

I

A Trade Which Is Presumably Remunerative

If the three farmers were nervous, they tried hard not to show it. But Poonit Singh, Imri Singh, and Tilangi, who went by one name, made for an incongruous sight as they walked into the auditorium of Patna's College Hall on a January morning in 1894. Early that morning, the men had walked past the imposing walls of the city's opium factory—more of a glorified compound of warehouses, really—to wait for their turn to speak about the crop to which their lives and labor were inexorably bound.

The ten members of the Royal Commission on Opium present that morning—eight foreigners and two Indian men—had been charged with deciding the future of this industry, the bulwark of imperial finances which, after a century, had fallen into clear disrepute.[1] Only decades earlier, Britain's Indian opium trade had underwritten the dramatic expansion of the entire British Empire. It had made fortunes for the British East India Company, the Crown, and Indian merchants who had strong-armed a place for themselves within the Asian trade. The inter-Asian opium trade had snared millions of Indian cultivators into the production of opium by pressure, coercion, and force, and it had turned a once incidental commodity into a powerhouse export, with nearly sixty thousand chests leaving the ports of Calcutta and Bombay each year. Two devastating wars had been fought in the trade's name: to wrench open China for opium sales, Britain had bombarded Canton, battled Qing battalions, and razed the better part of the emperors' beloved summer palaces. In the end, opium had emerged as British India's second-largest source of government revenue, second only to the taxes collected on land itself.[2]

Outside Patna, eastward toward Bengal and westward into the country's central plains and its northwest, ten million peasants like Poonit Singh, Imri Singh, and Tilangi were still cultivating poppies and scoring their pods for sap, orienting their work and household management toward the production of opium. The product they proffered as an imperial commodity was also the source of cooking oil and animal feed, leaves for cooking and seeds to eat—and indeed, occasionally, a tea, tincture, or other preparation that helped to dull the pain of arduous labor.

But this once formidable regime had begun to crack. By the closing decades of the nineteenth century, a transnational network of prohibitionists—social reformers, missionaries, and women's activists— had put opium in the crosshairs, casting it as a venal industry that immiserated Chinese users and exploited Indian laborers. An early wave of Indian nationalists had lamented the unfair economics of the trade. Even staid administrators were conceding that the economics of opium had grown less favorable: India's roads and railways had improved, allowing for the easier movement of bulkier and perishable goods like rice, seeds for oil, jute, hides, and tea.[3] The modest constraints of a new Opium Act for India in 1878 had done little to quell the rising tide of metropolitan objections. So in 1893, this Commission had been put together to hear from those involved in or concerned with the opium trade about what its future might look like.[4]

That morning, before the three peasants walked into the room, the Commission's members had grilled three witnesses who spoke to a radical divergence over the crop and its merits. A missionary had argued forcefully that the crop had effected mass ruin. An indigo planter had defended the trade as profitable and cast opium's use as equally innocuous as beer or wine. An Indian lawyer had sidestepped the question of ethics, simply arguing that the price that the state monopoly offered to opium cultivators did not even cover their costs. Finally, the Commission was to hear from three cultivators themselves, one of only a few moments when, during imperial England's most exhaustive commission, peasants themselves were asked to weigh in.[5]

The interrogation started with technical questions—the cost of plowing opium and the amount of water the crop required, as well as the question of which cultivator took on what work. Before long, the conversation turned tense. "I lose by cultivation of the poppy," Tilangi stated through his interpreter, adding that he wished he could grow wheat, potatoes, or sugarcane instead. Why then, one member asked, did he continue growing it? "Because we are poor people, and it is the order of the Government that we should cultivate poppy." The "Government," Tilangi seemed to mean, were the low-level staffers of the Opium Agency, who threatened to uproot other crops were they to plant them. The other two men nodded their assent. Imri Singh added that he, too, lost money by cultivating poppy, but feared that those same staff would seize his land if he refused. Poonit Singh had experienced this force firsthand when, five years earlier, he had planted half his field with wheat, only to have an Opium Agency staffer uproot his wheat and insist upon poppy instead. This had been so upsetting that Poonit Singh had left cultivation altogether and gotten a job as a peon in an office.

The testimony that the Commission's members heard—that January morning and throughout their extensive tour of India—was head-spinning. *Zamindars* (hereditary landlords) defended the trade one moment, and surgeons and missionaries decried it the next. Even the testimony of the few peasants brought before the Commission reflected different understandings of the crop and its production. When, a month later, its members interrogated Patel Sheobaksh, a cultivator from Bundi State, he could only insist that opium was an excellent crop.[6] Its gum made healthy profits, to be sure, but Patel and his family could fry the leaves and spent capsules, use the oil for cooking, and press the spent seeds into cakes to feed livestock. The tea made for a relaxing digestive. Patel Soma Bin Udai Ram, who described himself as a "hereditary cultivator," attested that "no other produce can bring money so much as opium does."[7] His colleagues, he added, "respect the opium plant, because it keeps us happy and comfortable.... If our merciful monarch prohibits the growth of opium, it will be a death-blow to us, and we shall prefer death without it." Yet cultivators seemed to feel more free to lament opium's injuries in group petitions. In Ambala, a tehsil (subdistrict) of opium cultivators lamented that the taxes they paid on their land had been assessed while taking into account a generous potential opium profit.[8] "If cultivation is stopped," they complained, "we shall be ruined."

The eclectic, divergent views of even the small number of India's opium cultivators that the Royal Commission consulted in the closing decade of the nineteenth century spoke to the conundrum that the commodity represented after a century of expansion, consolidation, and formalization. Scorned by prohibitionists, opium still represented a potent economic and social force on the Indian subcontinent. Even if its traditional market in China was shrinking, the industry itself could not simply wither into oblivion. Opium was bound for a remaking as the contours of a new century came into view.

◖○◗

Opium, as medication and social lubricant, had long been a feature of precolonial India's agricultural economy. The *Ain-i-Akbari*, the Mughal Emperor Akbar's voluminous administrative record, described opium as one of North India's most important commercial crops in the sixteenth century; by the end of the seventeenth, the northern province of Bihar was India's foremost producer. For nearly a century, as Europeans expanded their commercial and then administrative purview in India, opium remained an important but not prepotent commodity.

Britons had not been the first to bring the crop into transnational trade; like so many other imperial contrivances, they merely perfected a practice piloted by their European rivals. In the middle of the seventeenth century, Dutch merchants had helped to make opium smoking fashionable among the upper classes of Batavia, their canal-lined colonial entrepôt on the island of Java.[9] Before long, the Dutch East India

Company was importing ever-larger quantities of opium from northern India to sell at a profit at its Southeast Asian trading posts, while reserving a certain amount to sell to Canton, in southern China. The Indian opium syndicates sold, in descending order of preference, to Dutch, British, and French traders, accruing heady profits for their work moving the crop to the coasts.[10]

By the 1760s, the fertile Indian provinces of Bengal and Bihar had come under the formal dominion of the East India Company, and the merchants of the British East India Company saw in the poppy—as in nearly everything else—the making of great riches. For about a decade, the Company, having pushed aside the indigenous syndicates, eschewed the work of collecting opium in favor of purchasing it from private merchants and traders, many of whom were also its own employees. In an era of impressive administrative scandal and corruption, these traders earned a reputation for exceptional debasement. Eager to maximize returns from the Company that would do the work of buying, marketing, and exporting it, private merchants stole harvests, threatened and extorted rural producers, and adulterated the wares they presented for purchase.

Scruples were not of concern to Company officials, but profits were, and a chaotic, poorly organized trade—along with a product of questionable quality—threatened a rising demand for opium from China. Over the next quarter century, the system grew increasingly routinized. In 1773, the Company put an end to the freewheeling opium trade, replacing it with a "contract" system: the Company claimed a monopoly over procurement and sales, and it licensed private contractors to advance cash to cultivators and collect each year's harvest. This system was a compromise: contracts, first obtained by private connection and then by auction, were only slightly more regular than the anarchic wheeling-and-dealing that had preceded it. But it inured the Company against the thorny questions of ecology, agrarian labor, and marketing into which it was not yet prepared to enter. Contractors, rather than formal agents of the Company, were tasked with negotiating how much opium a given plot of land "ought" to produce, or securing a *nuzzar*, or a bribe, from cultivators when they came up short.[11] By the turn of the nineteenth century, however, India's colonial administrators were more confident—even delusional in their ability to understand the workings of the country's agrarian production. In 1797, the East India Company replaced the intermediary contract system with an "agency system," a vast colonial apparatus of production and administration that would dominate North Indian rural life for much of the nineteenth century.

The agency system brought together ecology, rural production, and agrarian labor, and colonial economic life under the purview of a new Opium Department. Its basic premise was monopoly. Private cultivation of opium poppies was banned, and peasant cultivators were coerced into growing opium on designated plots of land under official licenses. Each year's raw opium output was to be sold in its entirety to the Company at prices set unilaterally each year, with severe punishments for noncompliance. Those who failed to deliver a crop were fined three times the amount of their initial advance. The Company offered cash advances to grow opium, but at prices that did not even cover rent, irrigation, seeds, and labor, to say nothing of the cut that middlemen and landlords took. If not quite bondage, the system represented a cruel agrarian exploitation, with no allowance for the many caprices of climate, blight, and soil.

The Opium Department was divided into two administrative units that divvied up the whole of northern British India's opium output, labeled as Bengal opium even though it encompassed production beyond that region's traditional boundaries. The Bihar Agency covered the productive regions of Bengal and Bihar, closer to Calcutta, while the Benares Agency was responsible for India's Northwest Provinces and Awadh, where a smaller volume of opium was produced in a much larger area. The regions of the fertile northern plain were administratively separate but knit together by the river traffic of the Ganges. The Benares Agency was headquartered in Ghazipur, a bustling, largely Muslim town several bends in the river downstream from Benares. A hundred miles closer to Calcutta, the Bihar Agency operated out of Bankipore, a suburb of the city of Patna. In each town, a lavishly paid Opium Agent oversaw the work of sub-agents, assistant sub-deputy agents, and finally, the Indian clerks who oversaw *kothis*, the smallest administrative units, which might still contain ten thousand to fifteen thousand individual poppy cultivators. Those clerks, paid poorly and by commission, worked as *gomastahs*, intermediaries who liaised between British sub-deputy agents and local Indian staff, and as *zilladars*. The *zilladars*, like so many ground troops of imperial administration, were the closest to matters of practical concern: they helped choose cultivators, assessed the agronomic worth of a plot of soil, monitored the growth of crops, weighed the final product, and arranged for its final delivery.

In Ghazipur and Patna, two giant "Sudder factories"—sprawling compounds with open-air processing, extensive storage warehouses, and administrative facilities—were the beating heart of each agency's operations. The compounds were immense. By the end of the nineteenth century, the Ghazipur factory employed 10 percent of the town's forty thousand inhabitants.[12] The production work inside the factories was careful and grueling but unsophisticated. Opium was dried into a

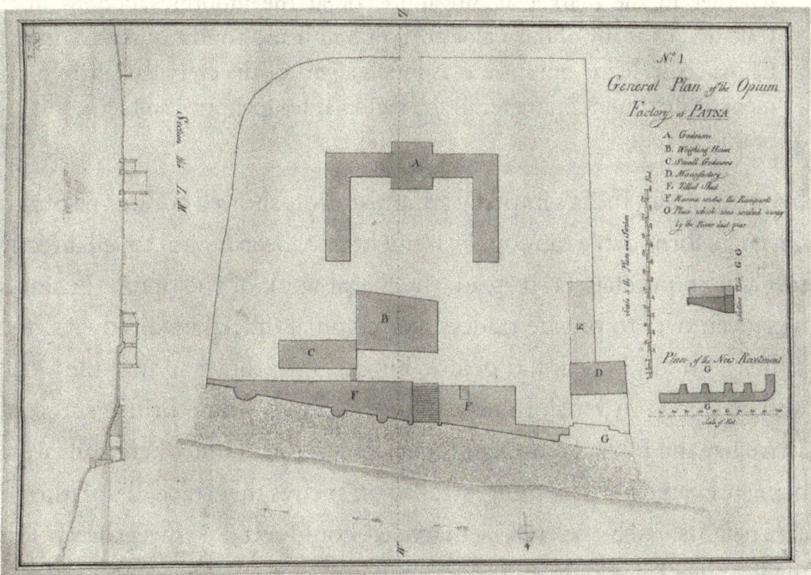

Figure 1.1 Map of the Patna opium factory in Bankipore, c. 1780. British Library.

standardized consistency, mixed together and shaped into 1.5 kilogram "cakes" with brass cups lined with leaves, and then left to dry further in the open air, before ultimately being packed into mango wood crates. Crates with sixty kilograms of opium—the industry's new standard unit of weight—were loaded onto speedy opium clippers for the short trip to Calcutta. The Government Opium Sale Room at No. 2 Bankshall Street was a stone's throw from the banks of the Hooghly River, the western distributary of the Ganges. Its auctions were staid, but the immense potential value of the crates stoked fierce fighting, double-dealing, and speculating among the representatives of trading housing who tendered bids. Both foreign and Indian firms could make fortunes from their work smuggling opium to China: among the early winners were the Scottish firm of Jardine & Matheson and the Parsi trader Nusserwanji Tata. No matter who moved it, the British Indian product was the ubiquitous gold standard for the commodity itself, a "brand name" of indisputable quality. Wherever a traveler went east of Suez, historian Carl Trocki writes,

> on any day he could pick up the local English language newspaper to discover the daily quotations for the prices of "Patna" or "Benares" opium; whether in the market at Singapore, or at the monthly auctions in Calcutta, or at any of the major ports of South and Southeast Asia or the China coast. Patna opium was as much a part of the every day environment of maritime commerce in the region as tea, pepper, gambier, copra or tin.[13]

In one domain, India's imperial administrators showed curious restraint. Given its formidable monopoly, it might have been logical to sell directly to Chinese purchasers. Instead, the illegal work of the opium business was given over to private traders. No colonial official involved with the industry in any way could delude himself into thinking that the work was anything but venal. In 1831, Julius Jeffreys, a young British surgeon, arrived at the Patna factory and marveled at the depot where balls were being prepared for packaging, stacked on shelves that reached unfathomable heights. Such a reserve, he marveled, could certainly meet the world's medical needs for morphine for decades to come.[14] The director of the magazine chortled at the surgeon's naïveté. "These stores of opium," he laughed, "have no such beneficent destination. It is all going to debauch the Chinese, and my duty is to maintain its smack as attractive to them as possible."

Over the course of sixty years, the industry had transformed from an incidental trade reliant on private merchants into a state-controlled monopoly that linked together Indian producers and Chinese consumers in different bonds of servitude. Britain's Indian opium was used to bring Chinese tea and silver to Britain, transferring Asian wealth to Europe while strengthening the foundation of imperial rule.[15] The Bihar and Benares agencies had become among the most prominent institutions in British India. What had begun with two understaffed offices was, by the 1820s, a web of a hundred divisional branches staffed by over 2,500 clerks, vested with the power to enforce the labor of countless Indian peasants. The monopoly was by no means as secure as its proponents insisted and was readily complicated by the caprices of ecology. The farther one traveled away from the core of the Bengal and Benares agencies, into regions such as Rangpore, Cooch Bihar, Assam, and Bhutan, the more small-scale cultivators could eke out opium crops from disturbed, post-flood landscapes, often with the tacit acceptance of Company officials.[16] In short, the production of opium, no less than indigo, cotton, or finished textiles, had been transformed from an unremarkable component of the precolonial North Indian landscape into a quintessential colonial commodity. Opium's ubiquity was apparent in both production and consumption. In 1813, the colonial government accepted what had long been apparent to its agents: that domestic opium consumption could not be effectively controlled in India. It opened licensed "excise shops" for domestic consumption that mushroomed across the North Indian and wider landscape over the following decades.

Opium—a longtime household remedy—was deployed with increasing frequency as a palliative for the pains wrought of its own cultivation.[17] A rich Hindustani lexicon was deployed to describe the crop's growth, cultivation, and use: words for the plant and the advances made to grow it, the cakes of poppy petal set aside, the instruments used to pierce and lance the pod, the coagulated gum, and the juice that the fresh opium left behind on rags and in pots.[18] New words were coined for the new modes of consuming opium; one, for instance, to describe the resin left behind in a well-used pipe as smoking came to supplant chewing and sipping. Most importantly, the fortunes being made for imperial administrators and merchant houses through the opium trade were stoking more powerful Indians to new forms of competition.

◖○◗

Since the late eighteenth century, the East India Company's officials had increasingly become aware that theirs was not the only opium industry functioning on the subcontinent. The central Indian region of Malwa, a flat and fertile tract of volcanic soil roughly the area of Austria, had long produced opium of high repute. Malwa opium was a prized remedy in neighboring regions.[19] By the 1790s, it was clear to Company officials that Malwa opium, produced and transported outside its monopoly agencies, was arriving in China by routes beyond the Calcutta auctions. It took some time for those officials to understand both the mechanisms and the scale of this alternate supply, but by the turn of the nineteenth century, they were aware that Malwa opium was being packed and sent to Goa and Surat, which was also an entrepôt for Egyptian opium imported and sold by Hindu, Muslim, and Jewish traders. Surat's prominence soon faded as the opium trade moved down the coast to the booming urban center of Bombay. From there, Malwa opium—alternately described as Bombay opium—was sold to Indian and Portuguese merchants for transshipment to China.

Bombay had been under British authority since the late seventeenth century. But that authority did not stretch meaningfully beyond its fort and a series of marshy islets that were connected as the city's trading role expanded. In 1803, officials banned the cultivation of poppy in all territories subject to its authority—a gesture with no practical consequence, given that those territories produced little, if any, opium. More significant was its concurrent ban on the export of opium from any ports

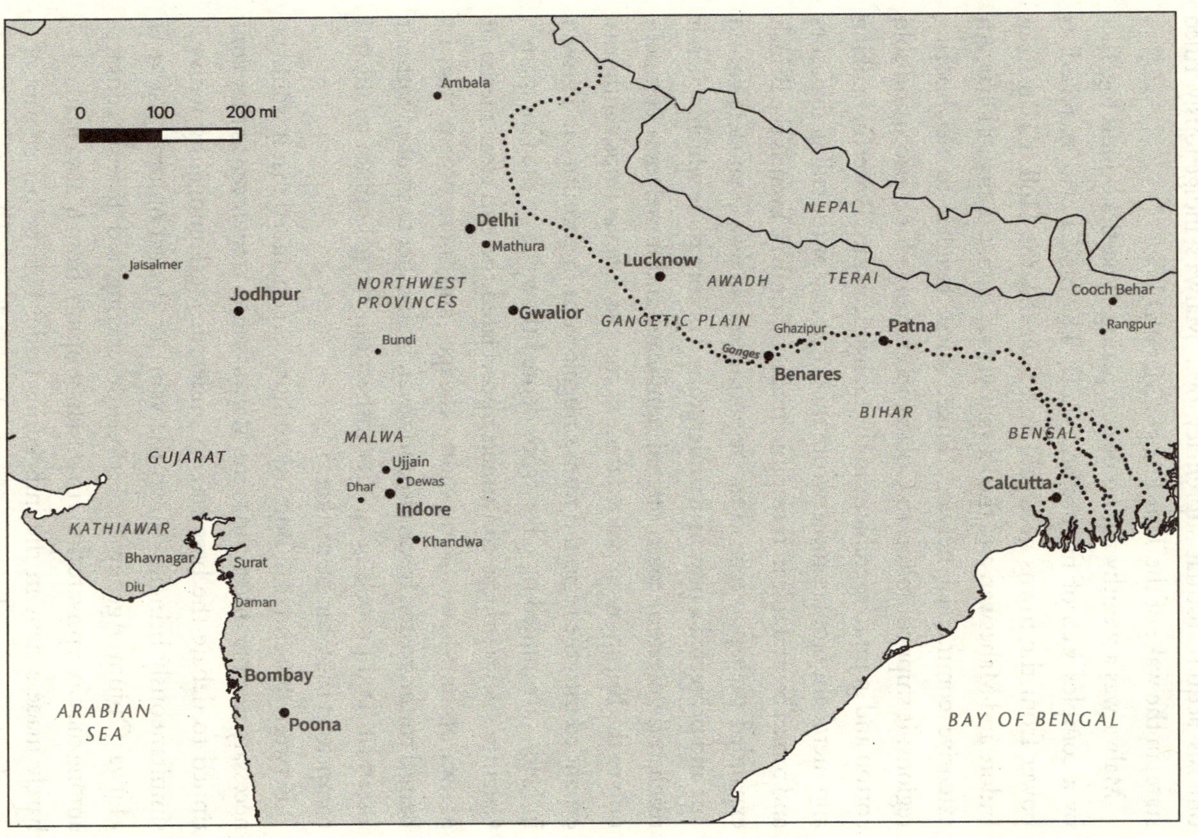

Figure 1.2 Opium production in nineteenth-century British India.

under Bombay's jurisdiction. The export ban was a turning point in the colonial administration of western India: not until 1818 did Company officials acquire formal supremacy over Malwa's indigenously ruled states in the wake of the Third Anglo-Maratha War.

Malwa was a wealthy region of competing dynasties bound together by a complex web of finance and trade. The Sindia clan exercised its power from the towns of Ujjain and Gwalior, the Holkar clan from Indore and Maheswar, and the Pawar dynasty from the city of Dhar. An extensive commercial network linked these families to neighboring regions: it shipped opium to Gujarat in exchange for tobacco and sold cotton and grain to merchants in the Gangetic plains. Powerful banking and merchant families underwrote the authority of the ruling dynasties and took a central role in the opium trade to Bombay. Even as the British expanded their power into the region, these Malwa financiers carved out and protected a powerful underground opium trade which, when it reached the western coast, offered significant and unwelcome competition to the British-monopolized trade in the east. Even as British authority expanded into the region, opium smuggled out in coconuts and grown in fields surrounded by taller crops dented the value of the Company's Calcutta sales. Chinese consumers appreciated the two clear merits of Malwa opium: it was significantly cheaper and more potent than its Bengal counterparts. It was also, however, far harsher to smoke. Without a standardized process or quality inspection, Bengal opium could still compete in the Chinese market.[20]

Between 1819 and 1821, Bombay authorities concluded that it would be necessary to enter directly into the Malwa opium trade, even as they continued to debate the best way to undercut local smuggling without simultaneously bringing down the value of Bengal opium. The new Malwa Opium Agency's solution—leveraging old British contacts among the city's private firms to purchase opium from Malwa markets—barely made a dent in the indigenous trade. For the better part of a decade, Bombay authorities wasted substantial capital trying to staunch an industry that eluded all such efforts. Indigenous traders avoided Bombay but brought Malwa opium to Portuguese ports at Daman and

Diu to ship to Macau. With Gujarat's ports closed to them, they made use of longer trade routes to bring opium via trading hubs like Jaisalmer and Sind to Karachi. Early nineteenth-century British power in the east of India was robust enough to enforce a real monopoly, but in the country's west, it was never formidable enough to extirpate indigenous smuggling networks.

The enduring debate over the nature of the smuggling of opium from Malwa to China and elsewhere cuts to the core of how power and capitalism functioned on the colonial Indian subcontinent. One influential view is that smuggling from Malwa, a project largely engineered by Marwari, Parsi, and Bohra Muslim traders, represented a powerful assertion of indigenous agency and resilience in the face of imperial expansion.[21] The capital that these groups accumulated through opium was crucial to the emergence of an Indian capitalist class. This subversion of imperial authority, in this view, was essential to creating a later generation of family-led industrial firms that would underwrite India's nationalist movement. A more restrained interpretation holds that opium's role in the creation of that class and those firms has been profoundly overstated. Opium smuggling profits, this view contends, provided seed capital for later ventures like Bombay's indigenous-run cotton mills. But those ventures relied equally, if not in greater measure, on the financing of British military expeditions and other speculative projects. Malwa opium, in this view, was far more central to British imperial expansion than to indigenous capitalism, and local merchants and financiers were highly aware of this.[22]

In either case, in 1830, British authorities conceded that their efforts to quash the Malwa opium trade had been in vain and announced that from then on, it could be imported from Bombay for a transit duty of a few hundred rupees per chest. The price was calculated carefully, set just a bit lower than what it would cost to transport to farther-off ports like Karachi.[23] The legalization of the western Indian opium trade—described as Malwa or Bombay opium in most accounts—turned mercantile families into dynasties. Chettiar and Marwari traders, Gujarati Khoja clans, and Parsi and Sindhi investors all made fortunes.[24] The Sassoon family, relocating from Baghdad to Bombay in the 1820s, capitalized on direct relationships with merchants in India's interior to dominate western Indian exports to China.[25] Others fared less well, such as Lakshmi Chand of Mathura, whose staggering loss of seventeen lakh rupees reminded speculators of the business's immense risk.[26] But the legalization and regulation of the western Indian opium industry had profound and immediate impact upon the Bengal opium trade farther east and Britain's Asian opium trade as a whole. Save for a short interregnum during the First Opium War, when the Chinese Viceroy Lin Zexu, a fervent anti-opium crusader, arrested Canton's opium dealers and burned their stock, India's cultivated area of opium and its exports expanded consistently through the middle of the 1860s. Until the end of the nineteenth century, India's opium exports ranged from forty thousand to sixty-five thousand chests, sold at relatively stable prices, even after China legalized opium imports in 1858 and allowed for domestic production in 1886.[27]

That stability was the bedrock of imperial finances in British India. Opium was second only to land taxes in terms of overall revenue to the British Raj. While generous estimates have placed its value to the imperial treasury as close to a third, an average of 14.5 percent of total British India revenues seems a better estimate. Opium's growth was accelerated by other colonial infrastructure: the improved Indian postal system, overseas shipping, and railways all helped facilitate the smuggling of opium within India and overseas.[28] At century's end, the industry would be put in the crosshairs of an international network of reformers and prohibitionists who saw in it an indefensible web of vice and exploitation. But opium had become indispensable to the work of imperial rule and no less to the economic life of Indian peasants themselves. The number of peasant households cultivating opium in the Malwa market is nearly impossible to estimate, since British agents there purchased opium but did not intervene in its cultivation and seem to have made no efforts to count. Bengal opium, however, offered better statistical potential. It seems reasonable that around 1.5 million peasant families, or around 10 million people, were involved growing, tending to, and scraping the sap of opium poppies. The preponderance of these people belonged to three castes: *Koeris*, *Kurmis*, and *Kacchias*, whose names became synonymous with opium cultivation itself.

It is possible to analyze what the relative costs and benefits of growing opium were for these peasants, no less than indigo, cotton, or the other important commodities of the day. What seems clear, however, is that poppy cultivation generally entailed a loss to the cultivator, as the price paid for crude poppy was generally too low to cover even the costs of cultivation.[29] There are competing and overlapping explanations: coercion, the coexistence of other cash crops and food crops alongside poppy, and wage labor that supplemented opium production, perhaps even in the factories at Patna or Ghazipur. But the meanings of this crop, and a heady set of debates over what it might mean for India's peasantry, India's future economic prospects, and its relationships with the wider world became more prominent in Indian political life as a new and contentious era dawned.

◁O▷

In the second half of the nineteenth century, the rise of a new global ideology of prohibition would bring to the fore a set of interlinked and long-delayed questions on the opium trade in India. One had been implicit in the violence of the opium wars, the enforcement of British India's opium monopoly, and China's eventual acquiescence to both the import and cultivation of opium: was opium a commodity like any other, subject to the regular order of the global market, or something whose narcotic qualities rendered it somehow different and bound by different rules? If, as global sentiment increasingly held, the latter were the case, what could India's opium do for its people—either as a crude medicament or as a source of revenue and power for India's indigenous potentates? In most recent accounts of India's engagement with opium in the late nineteenth century, the voices of those who held no place for opium in India are the loudest. Yet an equally vociferous faction defended Indian opium as either an essential component of India's indigenous apothecary or an economic resource to be harnessed in the service of free Indian states.

Opium's high-water mark had come in the 1860s. The Treaty of Tianjin and the Peking Convention that year had lifted all controls over the Asian drug trade, rendering the industry a wholly legitimate government enterprise for European empires. Within a decade, anti-opium activists began putting the industry in their crosshairs. An earlier generation of historians located the roots of this global prohibitionist turn in the work of Anglo-American Protestant missionaries, anti-Chinese "Yellow Peril" sentiments roiling the United States, and the reemergence of a domestic anti-opium push within China.[30] Missionaries from Britain and America cited opium addiction in China as one of the foremost impediments to the work of conversion.[31] Women reformers in South, East, and Southeast Asia cast prohibition of opium, alongside alcohol, as the keystone of social progress.[32] These alliances bore first fruit among European trading houses—which by the 1870s had begun to cede the Asian market to Indian Parsis, Jews, Armenians, and Muslims, and China's indigenous merchants and traders—and then among receptive American diplomats, often socially close to the missionaries who had helped forge them. In 1887, the United States forbade its ships from carrying opium to China, and a decade later, it quashed the Spanish government's opium monopoly in the Philippines after acquiring the islands in the Spanish-American War.[33]

The work of missionaries and marginally more secular-minded Anglo-American reformers was exhaustive, enterprising, and often remarkably aware of India's late nineteenth-century agricultural distress. The Aborigines' Protection Society in 1870 lambasted the diversion of land for food crops to opium, intertwining China's devastation with Indian hunger.[34] The Anglo-Oriental Society for the Suppression of the Opium Trade doubled down on these arguments and added to them the notion that a precarious revenue dependent so wholly on opium was equally indefensible.[35] Anti-opium crusader Joseph Gundry Alexander, writing for the Society for the Suppression of the Opium Trade, suggested that India's administrators make up for that loss by skinflint economizing; James L. Maxwell, a celebrated China missionary who had recently returned to London, offered a more generous subsidy of ten million pounds paid to India over five years, "by which time the deficit would be entirely met, and India would be free to go on as if she had never known an Opium revenue."[36]

Indian reformers—primarily though not exclusively Christian, and primarily but not exclusively in western India—were instrumental in advancing the cause of prohibition on the subcontinent. The most prominent of these Indian reformers was undoubtedly Soonderbai Hannah Powar. Powar had cut her teeth preaching to Kunbi caste workers in Bombay factories, where she drew an early connection between industrial exploitation and the abuse of opium. The real impact of these men's vice, as she saw it, was borne by their wives and daughters, destined to live with the specter of penury and violence. Powar's speaking tour in Britain, undertaken between 1889 and 1890, presaged a widely circulated pamphlet, *Opium Crime of the British Government: An Indian Woman's Impeachment*, which profiled Bombay men, women, and children all wrecked by their encounter with opium.[37] Work like hers marked a shift in prohibitionist sentiments in India. It was not simply that an innocuous Indian habit had ravaged China, but also that India's moral and physical well-being had been spoiled by opium. That analysis dovetailed neatly with the emerging critique of India's economic nationalists. Radical in their critique of political economy, though less so in their political prescriptions, figures like Romesh Chunder Dutt braided opium into their accounts of imperial drain and exploitation.[38]

Powar, Dutt, and others were articulating an increasingly dominant view among India's Anglophone class. Powar could cite showy anti-opium rallies like that held in Lucknow's stately Qaiserbagh complex to call for the eradication of opium poppy cultivation altogether. But her account of a venue "over-flowing with Mohammedans, Hindus, and others" as testament to India's anti-opium fervor stood in stark contrast to other reports, which claimed the event largely represented missionary sentiment. It also clashed with the arguments of those who defended opium's continuance on economic and medical grounds.[39] Throughout the 1880s and 1890s, Indian observers of the opium "problem" warned against a hasty decimation of such a major source of Indian revenue.

That caution was most evident in the Central Indian opium heartland. The Marathi-language *Vrit Dhara* called for a reduction in the Bombay opium tax to support the well-being of India's "agricultural classes [and] native states."[40] The *Suhodh Sindhu*, a Khandwa-based journal, urged Britain's "Christian Government" to contribute an equal amount to the Indian treasury if it were truly considering an end to opium revenues.[41] The opprobrium was no less fierce in western India. Bombay's *Native Opinion* warned administrators that a British attack on Indian opium would presage similar assaults on its indigo and cotton trade.[42] The popular *Indu Prakash*, also based in Bombay, declared opium to have no plausible financial alternative, decrying "English public opinion, which is so easily generous at poor India's expense."[43] The editors of the Parsi *Jam-e-Jamshed* lambasted the "religious zeal" of activists in London's Exeter Hall, which barely acknowledged the financial ruin that would beset India should the trade be extinguished.[44] In a stately Poona theater, an anti-opium meeting was interrupted by a heckler who insisted that the drive for prohibition was a ruse to further tax Indians and to increase the sales of European liquors.[45] While "Anglo-Indian dailies," *Poona Vaibhav* reporters declared, were eager to announce that the meeting had been a great success, the Marathi newspaper instead decried the presence of "our [Indian] social reformers" who had joined the call for prohibition "to deceive our simple people."

If revenue was one concern, opium's boon to Indian health was another. The world of medical knowledge and practice was being radically remade in late nineteenth-century India. Western medical practices, rooted in institutions like hospitals and dispensaries, reached few Indians beyond the most elite, but, as one influential account held, had "broken out of its earlier enclavism to become one of the most confident expressions of British political and cultural hegemony in India."[46] Hindu Ayurveda medicine, Muslim *unani* healing, and hybrid forms of care like Bengali *daktari* and homeopathic medicine faced increased pressure from encroaching Western medicine but did not capitulate. Rather, care in this period was a site for increasingly complex negotiation over the kinds of knowledge suited to the treatment of Indian bodies and Indian maladies.

Opium was not a medicine per se, but it had long become an indispensable informal palliative for Indian laborers and was the most widely used household remedy on the subcontinent.[47] Excise opium, the product sold domestically to Indians through the state-run system, was routinely used to treat a wide range of conditions. It was used for bowel problems and dysentery, chronic cough and indigestion, bodily pains, and sexual dysfunction. Perhaps its most common use—and the one that gave greatest pause to foreign observers—was as a pacifier for infants and young children. For at least one of its intended uses—preventing crying—it was undoubtedly useful, though its prophylactic qualities against bronchitis and diarrhea were less certain. By the late nineteenth century, a great number of claims had emerged about opium's ability to stave off illness: fever, usually, but the alkaloid narcotine was also touted as a treatment for malaria. The phrase "quasi-medical use," which entered the British Indian lexicon in the last decade of the nineteenth century, neatly captured the useful nature of the substance for many Indians outside the purview of formal treatment.[48] When the colonial government piloted a new general primer for schoolchildren in the 1880s, it cautioned against the use of opium, which "ruins both body and mind."[49] But beyond the Anglophone circles in which that textbook was to be deployed, there was no doubt that opium remained an indispensable, all-purpose palliative.

In the summer of 1893, all these questions—the moral sustainability of Britain's Indian opium trade, its profitability to Indian cultivators, and the uses that Indians themselves had for opium—came to the fore with the establishment of the Royal Commission on Opium, Victorian England's most significant parliamentary inquiry.[50] The Commission itself was a response by the British Parliament to the rising crescendo of calls for prohibition. Nine members, roughly split between the pro-opium and anti-opium camps, traveled for two and a half months through India and Burma, questioning over seven hundred witnesses

Figure 1.3 Stereoview photograph of Indian opium smokers in Ahmedabad, Gujarat, 1908. University of Minnesota Libraries.

from a wide range of social classes. The report—an immense, 2,500-page document spanning seven volumes—frequently painted the Indian opium trade in unflattering terms. India's opium revenues were, its members calculated, on a slow decline. Cultivators within the system, they saw, were frequently coerced by the Opium Department's agents to grow poppy, even at a loss to their own households. Decades later, bureaucrats would use this information to bring the opium trade to heel. But for the time being, the Commission's report affirmed that the Indian opium trade was an acceptable, legitimate one. It was broadly innocuous to Indians and damaged Chinese commercial interests but did no undue bodily harm.

Prohibitionists were dismayed by the Commission's conclusion that opium was an anodyne commodity. The state monopoly continued its exports to China and moved opium to smaller Asian and African ports, reserving smaller amounts for excise shops that proffered "quasi-medicinal" opium to Indian consumers. Smugglers, perhaps with some official complaisance, ferried it to Nepal across the submontane Terai region. But opium's future was by then uncertain. The Commission's report bought British India time as it considered the future of its imperial industry, but it also stoked new conversations about how that industry might be reconstituted.

◁O▷

Even as they have preferred divergent interpretations of the Asian opium trade, historians of the industry have offered uniformly declensionist accounts of the years between the Commission's report and the conventions and revolutions that led to the rise of international prohibition. But even as India's opium industry was headed toward rupture, an observer at the Sudder factories or in India's poppy fields might not have known it. In those two compounds, and on those tens of thousands of plots, Indian opium evinced a distinct pluripotency. If its Chinese market was slowly evaporating, there were other real if uncertain possibilities for opium as a useful material for both Indian domestic use and overseas markets.

Much had changed at the two opium factories since the middle of the century. The Ghazipur factory had been fortified intensely during the rebellion of 1857, and the 200-yard entrenchment cleared around the factory had been converted into a permanent line of defense protecting exportable opium from opportunistic theft.[51] By the 1870s, it and its counterpart in Patna resembled bustling, fortified villages.[52] Four of the five gates inside the entrenchment remained closed, and the one that opened each day was manned at all times by a male and a female guard, charged with frisking the dozens of workers who streamed in and out of the compound. Within its walls were wells, warehouses for storing opium, a small printing press, and a stately bungalow for the factory's manager. An oversized coal-stoked boiler hummed around the clock, powering the processing facility and drying trays, and a team of thirty coolies grouped into a makeshift fire brigade stood guard against the occasional blaze. Yet the agent in charge of the factory bemoaned the constant leak of opium from the factory. The underpaid guards, he charged, did little to prevent the stream of coolies leaving the compound on the pretext of getting drinking water from the well outside, only to sneak out small balls of opium in their *mussucks*, canteens made of goat-skin. The situation was similar in Patna, where immense fortifications were still confounded by regular theft. The well-compensated managers of the two factories corresponded regularly about whether to standardize security and operations between the two facilities, though they ultimately agreed that they were separate operations bound to different schemes.[53] The imposing walls surrounding each factory concealed real changes in what India's opium might one day do. As prohibitionists and apologists argued over opium's future, it continued to be dried and standardized, rolled into balls for export to China and a number of other destinations in Southeast Asia. A smaller volume of Indian opium was being reserved for domestic, "excise" consumption. But by the 1860s and 1870s, the managers of each factory were trained physicians. These men, and other administrators, were then imagining an additional possibility for India's opium: the supply of painkilling drugs to India and other markets.[54]

Figure 1.4 Indian workers mixing and balling opium, c. 1900. Wellcome Collection.

This shift was first evident in the reanimation of earlier ideas about the improvability of Indian opium—whether poppy was merely subject to the caprices of labor and soil, or whether its commercial worth and use value might be augmented through breeding and cultivation. Since the late 1700s, ideas of "improvement" had tied together ideas of political economy, aesthetic taste, and moral judgment, and individual crops' potential economic value were central to those ideas.[55] In the late 1780s, Colonel Robert Kyd, a Scottish member of the Bengal Engineers, had offered his botanical knowledge to the East India Company and had transformed his private garden in Calcutta into the Indian Botanic Garden, dedicated to the notion of finding useful food crops and plants that might have unknown commercial use.[56] Kyd's initial plantings were focused on crops like indigo, cotton, coffee, clove, and nutmeg, all cast as beneficial to both Indian agriculture and British trade. Within a year of the Garden's founding, Kyd had begun experiments on opium poppies, "to enable hereafter this Government," he wrote, "to furnish wherewith to provide the future China Cargoes, for stead of impoverishing the Company's Treasury of Hindoostan by successive species of Bullion."[57] Kyd believed, erroneously, that poppy was cultivated with only limited success "beyond the limits of the Bahar Province" and sought to breed a variety of poppy that would thrive under a wider range of climates. He had found, among the workers in the botanical garden, a number of Bihari cultivators who claimed to have extensive experience with poppy cultivation and had dedicated a small plot to breeding improved poppies under their supervision.

Nothing appears to have come from this early experimentation in Calcutta. But nearly a century later, as the China trade was under siege, John Scott, the current curator of the Indian Botanic Garden, was asked to resume the long-abandoned poppy improvement project.[58] Scott, a thoughtful and skilled plant breeder (and regular correspondent of Charles Darwin), transferred the poppy project to two plots in the Deegah and Meetapore experimental gardens in Bankipore, closer to the opium heartland. From 1876 to 1878, Scott oversaw the planting of local Bihari poppies, Malwa poppies, and imported strains from Europe, experimenting with different furrowing, irrigating, and manuring techniques. The oblong-capsuled Teyleah poppy was the clear winner to Scott—but more important in an era of surer breeding techniques was the notion that poppy crops, like other crops, could be inured to some degree by breeding against the caprices of weather and blight.

Improved poppies would require a new approach in the factories as well. In 1859, W.J. Palmer, Assistant Surgeon and First Assistant and Opium Examiner in the Benares Opium Agency, began experimenting with the production of morphine and narcotine in the Ghazipur factory, first using "good opium" and then switching to confiscated opium of lesser quality. The work was successful, but the production was expensive and inefficient. His successor, Surgeon Major T.W. Sheppard, resumed the experiments in 1870 after a five-year hiatus, using a new extraction method that produced modest amounts of the two alkaloids for India's three presidencies and a small surplus that was sent to London. The amount was quantitatively small, but the *Indian Medical Gazette* trumpeted the production of domestic alkaloids as a major development in "the question of how far India can supply itself with drugs and serious medicinal preparations" in place of indigenous medicines.[59] "The drug now produced in the Ghazeepore Factory," its correspondent wrote, was "a much purer and more reliable article than that formerly manufactured," certain to replace the "colored, inert, and unequal article formerly supplied."

The *Indian Medical Gazette*'s plaudits spoke to a question that was growing more urgent as the future of Chinese exports grew uncertain: to what degree could Indian alkaloids be used in the preparation for Western pharmaceuticals? E.M. Holmes, one of Britain's leading pharmacists, asked that question explicitly in the *Pharmaceutical Journal and Transactions* in 1891. Turkish opium, Holmes explained, was the source of most American and European morphine and heroin. But if China's increased domestic production obviated the need for Indian imports, the subcontinent's supply would prove a ready source for medicinal opium. The technical challenges were real: the morphine content and composition of Indian opium differed significantly from the regular Turkish supply. If Turkish production methods and the strictures of the *British Pharmacopoeia*, the official compendium of standards for UK medicinal substances, were effected in India, its dwindling industry might be given new life.

The Royal Commission on Opium had come to the conclusion—following the advice of pharmacists at Merck, the German medicinal powerhouse—that Indian opium was not generally appropriate for Western medical use.[60] By the turn of the century, sixty pounds of codeine and three hundred pounds of morphine "equal in purity to any manufactured in Europe," were being shipped from Ghazipur to government medical stores, civil surgeons, and Indian chemists, and a small supply was also being sent to London for auction.[61] But British India's highest administrators generally hewed tightly to the notion that, were it possible to use Indian opium for Western medicine, the market would have already seen to it.

Scientific and medical minds were more bullish than Indian administrators. Sir George Walt, a Scottish proponent of the idea of "economic botany," spent the last two decades of the nineteenth century as "Reporter on Economic Products" for India's Department of Revenue and Agriculture, compiling a massive reference work, *The Dictionary of Economic Products of India*, which laid out Indian crops' potential commercial value. In 1894, skeptical of the Royal Commission's dismissal of opium's value as a medicinal resource, he proposed a study on Indian opium that would attend to the variables that made it less suitable than its Turkish or Egyptian counterparts.[62] Two years later, Professor Wyndham Dunstan, Director of London's Imperial Institute, made a similar proposal to the Government of India. Granted permission to take on this investigation on "scientific rather than upon commercial lines," Wyndham professed "little doubt that Indian opium, of some varieties at any rate, could be produced of the same, if not better, quality than the Turkey opium which is now almost exclusively used both directly in medicine and indirectly for the manufacture of the alkaloids morphine and codeine."

The impending closure of the China trade forced Indian administrators to listen. In 1907, J.S. Meston and H.F. Howard, Secretary and Under Secretary, respectively, to the Government of India's Finance

Department, convened a group of Indian administrators to take stock of "the possibility of Indian opium capturing the market of opium for medical purposes in other countries." The five countries that they highlighted—the United States, the United Kingdom, France, Germany, and Canada—were, in descending order, the world's most enthusiastic importers of opium for medicinal purposes, with the United States in the undisputed lead.

Two years earlier, the superintendent of the Patna Opium Factory had expressed some hesitation that Indian poppy cultivation could be reorganized so as to produce "medicinal opium of a uniform morphine strength." J. Christian confessed that, while occasionally he had encountered opium of a truly global caliber, it was impossible to predict where that opium would come from. "One such parcel," he had written, "may contain the product of a village in Hazaribagh, while another may come from a district in the extreme west of the United Provinces." His reluctant conclusion was that a shift to medicinal purposes, even with Turkish poppy seed, could not come without a total revolution in India's poppy cultivation techniques. But the Secretary and Under Secretary deputized H. St. Clare Carruthers, the Madras Government's Inspecting Medical Storekeeper, to go to Patna and Ghazipur to investigate the question again. Carruthers, a "skilled enthusiast in all matters pertaining to the treatment of drugs and the production of efficient pharmaceutical preparation," had gained a reputation in India and abroad for his invention of "Camphoradine," a potent anesthetic made of camphor, peppermint, cannabis, capsicum, and morphine.[63] He spent a week investigating the two factories and the opium fields that supported them, concluding that, with systematization, new expertise, and a greater attentiveness to process, Indian opium could indeed be improved to the standards of European medicine. J.S. Meston, Secretary of Finance, concurred. "There is no possible reason," he wrote, "why we should not lay ourselves out, if we can, to capture part of a trade which is presumably remunerative and to which no discredit attaches. We must still continue to cultivate opium in India for Excise purposes, and it is also probable that the Malwa opium industry, which is now seriously threatened, might advantageously be guided to some extent into the path of this possible new development."

The question of reorganizing India's opium industry was a thorny one. Even the administrators who had been enthusiastic about a pivot to medical markets were unsure which department was the right one to assume responsibility for such a project. But the opium industry's overall organization and structure continued to attract new interest beyond India. In 1900, the Indian government responded to two inquiries from Japanese colonial officials from Formosa seeking to visit the Opium Agency's factories and its Calcutta facilities, perhaps eager to transform its newly acquired island's consumers into industrious producers as well.[64] Five years later, the Chinese government made inquiries for a similar mission to study both opium and tea cultivation in India.[65] These visits were furtive ones, at odds with the prohibitionist sentiments of the day. But they hinted at the potential for India's poppies to do something more than simply wither under the glare of global condemnation.

❈

Opium, at the turn of the twentieth century, had become many things for different Indian constituencies. For social reformers and certain nationalists aligned with an international prohibitionist movement, it was material evidence of the exploitation wrought of colonial rule. For imperial administrators, it was a source of revenue whose structure would need to be remade to meet the changed exigencies of a new era. But for a certain strain of Indian elites—largely princes and merchant families—it remained a resource that could be funneled to regional development and profit. And for some Indians looking to an independent future, opium remained one cheap quasi-medical resource that might serve a useful purpose in a state where formal medical care remained drastically limited.

Agents of the British imperial state had structured the subcontinent's opium markets, but opium interests in the country's west had forced new accommodations. Throughout the century, opium interests continued to move state resources toward their own ends. In the wake of the

Figure 1.5 Workers in the Ghazipur opium factory, c. 1920. *Scientific American.*

uprisings of 1857, Bombay opium merchants had successfully petitioned for protection and compensation for shipments attacked en route to the port.[66] By the 1870s, opium taxes were being used to underwrite infrastructure in the opium tracts of central and western India. The most important "opium road" in Malwa, stretching twenty-three miles between the towns of Dewas and Ujjain, was cleared and paved with funds from a levy on opium sales.[67] The money that flowed to princely states had pumped up the coffers of Malwa *sahukars* (creditor-moneylenders) and royal families alike.[68] The potentates of states where opium had not been permitted chafed at the opportunity to grow their own.[69] Regional powers across India's Bombay Presidency were particularly vocal in their demands that cultivation be permitted in their own territories. *Talukdars*, or hereditary landowners, in the hilly, commercially rich Kathiawar peninsula in Gujarat, alongside the princely rulers of Bhavnagar, also in Gujarat, petitioned for the right to cultivate opium in place of cotton, whose price was plummeting. Opium revenue engendered a certain feeling of entitlement from traders, particularly as

China revenues sank. Toward the end of the nineteenth century, the Sassoon family firm rallied other Bombay opium merchants to petition for a reduction in the "pass duty" on Malwa opium.[70] The economic centrality of opium to regional actors as well as merchants and traders, in addition to the imperial state itself, made the potential end of the trade a fiscally ruinous proposal.

This economic reality stood alongside the concomitant indispensability of opium to India's uneven medical landscape. The limited ingresses of Western medicine into India in practical and not merely symbolic terms meant that Indian actors frequently made the case for its continued use in the absence of better palliative treatments. The Royal Commission on Opium had charted opium's extensive use in Indian practices of care from childhood to death, and Indian advocates for opium continued to offer full-throated arguments for its continued use in informal medical care. In a report prepared for the princely Kingdom of Marwar, state officials testified that three-quarters of its children were given small daily doses of opium to calm them and "counteract the effects of unhealthy milk," while 125,000 adult users gained protection from overexertion and a purported immunity to alcohol.[71] Lucknow's *Oudh Akbar* cited the physical prowess of India's Rajputs, Marathas, and Muslims—its "warrior-like races"—as evidence that opium was more balm than poison.[72] Doctors in Bombay protested when city officials proposed new regulations limiting the amount of opium they were allowed to keep or prescribe.[73] When, in 1894, the Secretary of State solicited provincial reports on the use of opium for children, he received reams of paper testifying to the drug's importance in soothing "fretful children" and warding off fever.[74] Whatever sympathy prohibitionists had cultivated for their claims over opium's ultimate malignancy among metropolitan reformers and Indian social reformers, it was up against major bulwarks of support among other Indian constituencies.

On the eve of the First World War, India's opium industry stood at a precipitous crossroads. Its once-formidable imperial administration was undoubtedly in crisis, but its predicament was far from the encompassing and terminal decline that historians of prohibition, international advocacy, and imperial trade have generally posited. There were pressures against opium on multiple fronts, from the assaults of global prohibitionists and the declamations of Indian nationalists and social reformers to the shifting dynamics of the global drug trade itself. But opium had become so deeply entangled with the economic, social, and medical fabric of colonial India that its wholesale dissolution was an unrealistic prospect. Opium was economically indispensable to a range of Indian constituencies, including princely rulers and merchant families; the potential end of the opium trade would be financially ruinous for these groups who had come to rely on opium revenue. Opium interests, particularly those in western and central India, had come to wield significant political and economic influence on the colonial state, successfully lobbying authorities for concessions, protections, and infrastructure investments. This lobby complicated any plans for radical prohibition in India.

Opium's use as a medical resource—either as an informal palliative domestically or as a raw material for Western pharmaceuticals—similarly confounded the thought of total extirpation. In the absence of widespread access to modern medical facilities, opium continued to serve as a crucial palliative and household remedy for a significant portion of the Indian population. Its purported medical benefits were trumpeted forcefully by Indian commentators who saw it as an essential resource in a landscape of uneven medical care. Bureaucrats who were largely uninterested in questions of health were nonetheless interested in exploring ways to repurpose India's opium industry toward the production of medicinal opiates and alkaloids. The possibility of pivoting to medicine posed formidable challenges but also represented a lifeline for an industry facing an uncertain future.

India's opium industry, in the first decade of the twentieth century, stood poised between the legacy of its colonial structures and the uncertainties of a new era. There were similar transformations taking place in another late imperial administration. In Ottoman Turkey, opium, too, had grown bound up in radical shifts in its political economy and role in global trade. Both these contexts would be transformed by the profound impact of two global wars, which would fundamentally alter the global political economy of the drug's production and consumption. Indian thinkers, administrators, and bureaucrats would revisit these questions as an incipient nation navigating a changed world.

2

No Crop in Anatolia Is as Important as Opium

The father and son worked together, side by side—in that, they were no different than the countless other pharmacists whose shops lined the Grand Avenue of Pera, Constantinople's regal central artery, and who passed on the trade through the generations.[1] Like those other pharmacists—the proprietors of the Pasteur Pharmacy, the Pharmacie d'Angleterre, the Hungarian Pharmacy, and a dozen others, all licensed by the chief physician of Topkapı Palace and possessing a *gedik*, the permit issued to druggists and spice merchants—Francesco and Giorgio Della Sudda were non-Muslims and foreigners. They were, however, foreigners who had been wholly shaped by and incorporated into the social fabric of the nineteenth-century Ottoman Empire. Giorgio's integration into Ottoman life had earned him a name to suit: Fayk Bey, a regal-sounding sobriquet under which he worked and wrote.

Francesco, the father, had been born into an Italian family on the island of Syros. Orphaned at twelve, he had been raised in a convent in Constantinople, before apprenticing with a pharmacist at that city's Maltepe hospital. His rise was meteoric: appointed Chief Pharmacist at that institution, he had been selected by Abdülhak Effendi, Chief Physician of the Ottoman Empire, to head the Central Pharmacy of the Armies in 1837. The pharmacy he opened a decade later earned him international repute, and by 1858, had been given the title of Pasha—a title that had been previously reserved for Muslims alone. Giorgio, the son, had been born in the shadow of Galata Tower but had been educated at Paris's leading pharmaceutical institutions. Working together, the two men had transformed their central pharmacy into the Empire's leading store of modern formulations, its shelves filled with the imported compounds that were the mainstays of French medicine. The styrax, turpentines, scammony, and other compounds were brought in from France—only the water and the labor, they joked, were local. But some ingredients, in fact, did come from Ottoman soil—sticky Chios mastic, as well as opium, of which the father and son had no fewer than ninety-two varieties, and which they packed and brought to the Paris Exhibition in the summer of 1867.

For months prior to the exhibition, the pair had written to the governors of the Ottoman Empire's opium-growing provinces, asking them to catalog the extent of cultivation under their purview and to offer up samples of their best exportable opium.[2] The governors had obliged, and the Suddas had packed their trunks full of opium from Bursa and Smyrna, Angora, Konya, and Kastamonu. In Paris, the two men touted Ottoman opium to a parade of pavilion visitors. The cultivation of opium, the two men explained, did not vary significantly from region to region. The seeds were sown in the fall, and the plants hardened throughout the winter and spring. When the capsule itself emerged and turned from a bluish-green to green with a tinge of gold, farmers would score it horizontally at dawn before collecting the sap a little before noon. Regardless of region, those farmers used a similar set of instruments, a little knife and a small collecting spoon, before a chain of three or four brokers or middlemen brought their product to Smyrna and Constantinople.

Ottoman opium, Sudda *père et fils* averred, deserved its world-class pharmaceutical reputation. The pair had always titrated the opium they supplied to the Central Pharmacy to an even 10 percent of morphine content, in line with the best European standards. But the opium they received, which they displayed in Paris, could contain anywhere from 3 to 15 percent morphine. The rich varieties from İzmit, Bursa, and Kütahya were far removed from the weak stuff produced near Angora, Konya, and Malatya. So-called experts, they added, trumpeted their ability to discern the best product at a glance. But a product of international quality deserved better care from production to marketing. Those informal assessments, so easily fooled by mashed-up raisins, wax, and pine resin, would need to be replaced with proper chemical testing. The Ottoman Empire's peasants would need new knowledge, better credit, and better raw materials to produce a product that was consistently of the highest caliber.

And yet, the two were optimistic about the commodity's pharmaceutical future, and the seriousness with which the Ottoman government was treating the quality of its exports more generally. In a general sense, the Tanzimat, the Ottoman program of rapid reform and modernization, had seen a major streamlining and centralization of the Empire's organizational structure and new efficiency in tax collection and administration. More specifically, aware of the need to educate Ottoman cultivators about the value of their crops, the Ottoman government had been promulgating agricultural offices in each *vilayet*, or subdistrict, staffing them when possible with "native graduates of the Grignon school," France's pioneering institution of agricultural modernization.[3] The Suddas' pitch in Paris, therefore, was twofold. Druggists in Europe should indeed prioritize the use of Ottoman opium, the best available anywhere in the world and a product that was rapidly improving. And the Ottoman Empire, they were implicitly adding, should concentrate the promises of modern agriculture and marketing upon opium, rendering it a modern product suited to the dynamism of modern markets.

☾☉☽

The Suddas' trip to Paris to tout the promise of Ottoman opium came as the Empire's push for reform was putting agriculture at the center of its modernizing agenda. Opium, a commodity long braided to commercial life in the Eastern Mediterranean, was at the foreground of these changes.

Prior to the late eighteenth century, poppy had been a notable but not preeminent crop in Ottoman society and commercial life.[4] Its productive value was high: across Anatolia, poppy was grown as much for seed as for its sap. That seed could be pressed into oil, used in baking, or fed to

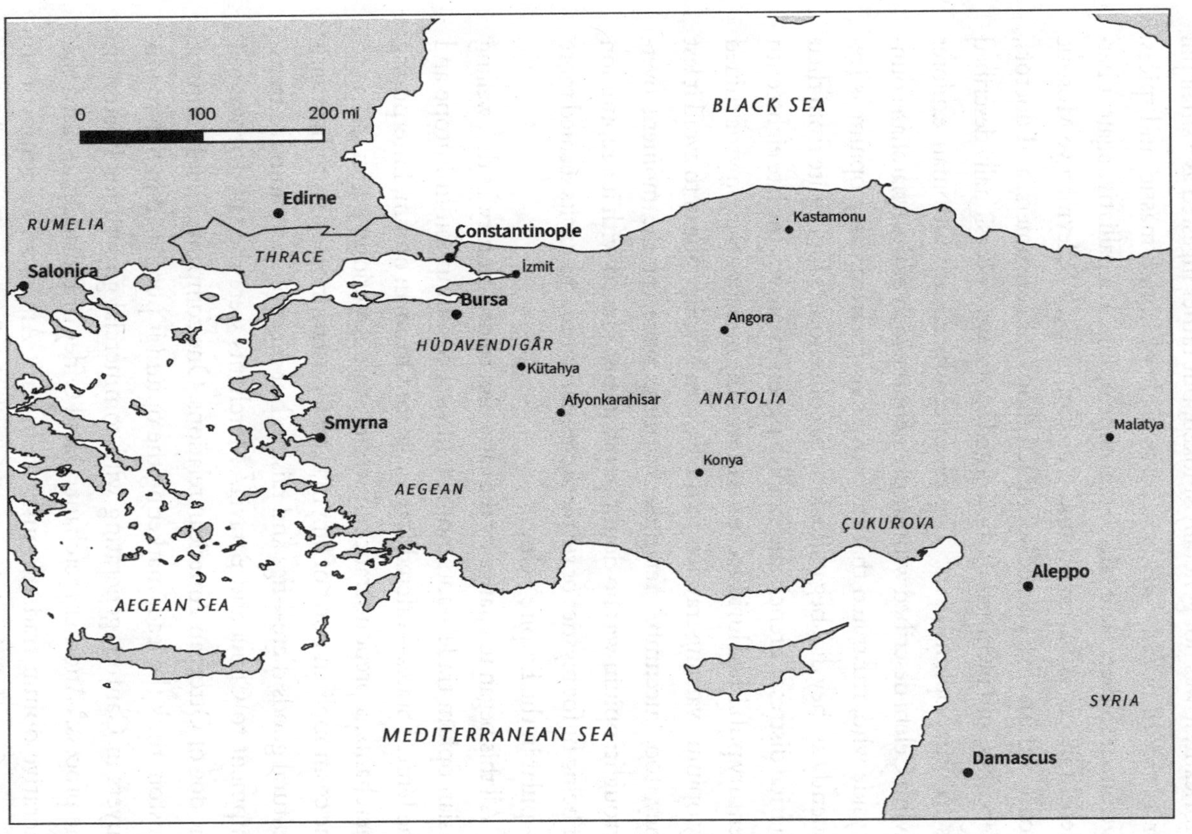

Figure 2.1 Opium production in the nineteenth-century Ottoman Empire.

animals; poppy stalk could likewise be burned and used as fertilizer or dried to make roof thatching. When opium was consumed as a social lubricant, it was not generally smoked, but rather ingested as a small pill or as *macun* or *bers-i-afyon*, a paste made of honey, mastic, and spices. Ottoman soldiers were said to consume opium as a palliative against battlefield jitters. A bazaar around Constantinople's Süleymaniye Mosque boasted thirty-five packed sofa-lined shops for consumers, and doctors, dervishes, and members of the learned *ulema* were occasionally described as habitual opium users. The seventeenth-century Ottoman explorer Evliya Çelebi described with amusement the men of the Anatolian countryside who, frustrated that their wives had started using opium as frequently as they did, began flocking to coffeehouses for respite from their marital distress.[5] French and English papers as early as the late eighteenth century published lurid accounts of wealthy merchants in Smyrna ruined by opium, warning travelers to the Eastern Mediterranean to avoid it lest they, too, succumb.[6] Yet these warnings were for the moment overwrought: opium was no doubt popular, but carried with it a reputation of being fit for mystics or rustic parvenues; wine and spirits seemed more popular in the Empire's cities.

All this began to change by the early nineteenth century, as the swelling Asian opium trade—and more incidental consumption in Europe and the United States—offered a new role for Ottoman opium. Enterprising merchants, a preponderance of whom were American, began sailing to the cosmopolitan ports of Smyrna and Constantinople to purchase agricultural goods there—figs and raisins, but most of all, opium for transshipment to China and Batavia.[7] Merchants were the tail that wagged the dog of Ottoman-American relations. One company, T.H. Perkins of Boston, took the lead, marketing the opium it purchased in Smyrna to buyers in Canton, generating wild commercial growth for Boston in the process.[8] Another merchant, David Offley of Philadelphia, used the lucrative opium trade to push a reluctant American government to pursue formal diplomatic relations with the Ottoman Empire.[9] In the process, these American merchants created a second "triangle trade" linking the Eastern Mediterranean, the northeastern United States, and southern China.[10]

In fiscal conceit, this triangle model was not terribly different from Britain's own trade from India to China: American sales of opium in Canton took the place of specie, primarily Spanish dollars, in the purchasing of tea and silk. Whereas British ships did not directly participate in the China trade, American merchants were under no such restraint. Initially, American vessels from Boston, Philadelphia, and Baltimore—and then, increasingly, smaller New England ports like Salem, Duxbury, and Gloucester—ferried Ottoman opium directly to China. By the 1810s, opium was generally shipped back to American ports to siphon off a small amount for the domestic market there before being forwarded to China, or it was repacked in other Mediterranean ports like Malta, Gibraltar, or Livorno to ships fitted for the China trade. American efforts to establish their own consulate in Smyrna yielded little, and so, barring a brief interregnum during the War of 1812, American merchants worked largely under the protection of the British consuls as they developed a formidable rival trade to Britain's Indian opium industry. Dutch buyers competed for the trade as well, and trading families like the Van Lenneps and the Keuns built vast fortunes from their control of the trade to Southeast Asia.[11] But by the early 1820s, most exported Ottoman opium was being purchased by American merchants. Even as they were mounting an early critique of the deleterious effects of opium in China, Protestant missionaries who followed those merchants to Smyrna turned a blind eye to its production and export there.[12]

The merchants who purchased opium from the cosmopolitan port of Smyrna—and after 1828, from Constantinople as well—were seeing only the ends of a complex set of networks that stretched deep into the Ottoman interior. The beginning of that chain was the work of the poppy cultivation itself, largely the same from the earliest records of cultivation until the time that the Suddas were touting its economic and pharmaceutical potential. Cultivators sowed and tended plants on a staggered schedule and then harvested, months later, on alternating days. On the first day the cultivators, largely women, would walk in one direction while scoring the capsules, and on the second, they would walk backward while scraping the thickened gum on long knives. The collected opium, still sticky to the touch, would be dried in clay drums for two days.

Afterwards, the women would roll the gum into two-pound cakes and dust them in chicory or sorrel leaves to ready them for the market. The process was similar across the Empire, from the ancient Nile city of Thebes, whose name was conjured up in the alkaloid thebaine, to the Greece and Macedonian fields that brimmed with scarlet and ivory flowers. But the industry's epicenter was undoubtedly Anatolia, inland from the Aegean, where fertile soil grew sturdy poppies alongside potatoes, beets, barley, and sour cherries. Afyonkarahisar, a town in Western Anatolia where bustling storage depots stockpiled opium in the shadow of an imposing black crag, often laid claim to being the industry's epicenter. But in truth, the trade was far more diffuse.

Equally integral to that trade were the networks of creditors, brokers, and intermediary merchants who helped bring cash advances to those peasants and brought the product to the market at season's end. Few of these creditors were themselves Turks—it was primarily, though not exclusively, Armenian, Kurdish, and Sephardic Jewish clans based in Smyrna and Constantinople who brought *para*, *kuruş*, and *lira* coins in copper, silver, and gold to the countryside to finance the crop, alongside reports of worldwide demand and mandates to leverage peasants' indebtedness to get the lowest prices for their gum.[13] Turks tended to view the trade, if not the cultivation, as too speculative. "The opium plant is low," a common aphorism held, "but those who fall from it are shattered."[14]

As the June harvests that these intermediaries brought back to Smyrna grew larger, buoyed by the rise in the China trade, opium was increasingly differentiated by its grade and intended destination: *yerli*, or "local" opium containing less than 10 percent morphine, *roba* opium with more than 10 percent, and *konakli* opium, theoretically from the town of Konya but in fact simply representing any opium with a negligible morphine content. Adulteration was, from the very beginning of the trade, an overweening concern for foreign merchants and very often ascribed by Christian traders to the Jews with whom they negotiated. "Ingenious modes have been discovered of adulterating that very expensive article," Scottish writer Charles Macfarlane wrote after returning from a year in the Ottoman Empire in 1829, "and only a limited number of appointed brokers or *conoscitori*, all Jews, whose honesty is scarcely to be depended upon are said to be in possession of the secret."[15]

The encroachment of American, British, and Dutch merchants and a significant uptick in opium exports—from a few thousand pounds annually in 1800 to over 100,000 pounds by 1830—was concurrent with a major crisis of the Ottoman state.[16] Mahmud II, the Empire's reigning sultan, had been weathering a series of political crises: war with Russia in 1828, uprisings in Greece and Serbia, and Muhammad Ali Pasha's insurrection in Egypt, which would culminate in outright rebellion in 1831. Against the backdrop of financial precarity, the sultan's push for reform included strengthening the sultanate, building a modern army and bureaucracy, and increasing state revenues—a project that included the creation of an opium monopoly to take control of an increasingly pivotal crop. In 1828, the Ottoman government established the Yed'i Vahit—a monopoly system that attempted to take control of the free-wheeling opium industry, with other divisions for commodities like olive oil and silk.

The Yed'i Vahit attempted to do away with the free internal trade in opium. Under the authority of the Superintendent of Customs in Smyrna, Ömer Lütfi Efendi, the monopoly stipulated that only author-ized agents of the state could purchase opium directly from the cultiva-tors at a fixed price—a system vaguely akin to the British monopoly being reworked on the Indian subcontinent. In theory, opium would stay wholly under state control until merchants in Smyrna and Constan-tinople would purchase it for sale to foreign traders. The reality was thornier. In a context of strained finances, monopoly lacked permanent operating capital, relying on advances from state treasuries that had to be paid back as the opium was sold: the Yed'i Vahit's ensuing cash shortages made it difficult to purchase future harvests on time. The monopoly was understaffed and had little of its own infrastructure, and its officials fre-quently had to enlist the help of the same intermediaries it had been designed to eliminate. Perhaps most importantly, the monopoly faced substantial opposition from both provincial elites and merchants who resented the encroachment upon their trade and British representatives who saw it as an impediment to the ends of free trade. Despite generating substantial revenues for the Ottoman state—perhaps three or four times the amount that its earlier taxation schemes might have garnered—the monopoly barely lasted a decade. Under pressure from the British Foreign Secretary, the Ottoman government was compelled to agree to the abolition of all monopolies, including opium, in the Anglo-Turkish Commercial Convention signed in 1838, and the Ottoman opium market was reopened to British and other foreign merchants the year after.

By the end of the monopoly, the Ottoman sultan had concluded that opium was no longer worth the trouble. The trade, in the Porte's view, implicated the Empire in smuggling, diverted land away from food crops, and, as British-Chinese tensions heated in the lead-up to the First Opium War, it seemed from Constantinople that the trade's future was limited. In 1839, he issued a *firman* that banned opium production in a number of Anatolian regions, ordering them to grow wheat, barley, and other grains in its place.[17] The effort was risible. Late that year, a British merchant in Smyrna took note of the *firman* and others that had followed. No local newspaper had dared to publish his damning report, so he instead sent it to *Echo de l'Orient*, a French commercial journal in Constantinople.[18] If the emperor were concerned, he wrote, "that the [opium] cultivators will no longer find an outlet for this product, and will be disappointed in the hopes they have conceived following the abolition of the monopoly," he need not have worried. The entire export enterprise had been predicated upon smuggling, and there was little doubt that it would continue. He laughed at the thought that cultivators could not, as per the sultan's logic, cultivate opium and cereals at the same time. And he knew that the "benefits that [Anatolian peasants] derive from the oil that this plant provides them make its cultivation for them indispensable." More importantly, the anonymous merchant added, "consumption of this drug in the United States and Europe has doubled in recent years," and cultivators in Anatolia would continue to have growing markets in the West, in addition to the extant Chinese one.

The British merchant's report was prescient. Opium—a crop that, as in India, had moved to the fore of international commerce in only a few decades—would be remade anew in the decades to come, marketed to and destined for a new set of purposes.

In the second half of the nineteenth century, Ottoman opium exports were subject once more to the forces of the free market, its price and production tied to previous years' harvests, foreign demand, and the dynamics of overseas cultivation and exports, largely from India.[19] In 1857 and 1858, Ottoman production spiked, as Anatolian produce was called upon to make up for the shortages wrought of the Indian uprising. But even before the opium monopoly was shattered, European pharmaceutical manufacturers had come to perceive Ottoman opium as a product of uniquely high quality. The earliest accounts, like many later ones, were tinged with anti-Semitism. In the middle of the 1830s, before the opium monopoly had ended, Jacob van Lennep, the Smyrna opium merchant and Consul General for the Netherlands, regularly complained about Jewish merchants who sent "bad opium" to Europe for processing into laudanum and other opiates.[20] Until his death, he would regularly report on new methods that Jews were purportedly using to adulterate otherwise good opium and trick European importers into purchasing it. What was apparent, beyond the bigotry, was that, as the China trade had withered, there were new pharmaceutical markets in Europe for the Ottoman product. By the 1840s, the demand for Ottoman opium was largely coming from druggists in Europe. Its morphine content was inconsistent, but the best samples were unequaled by any other supply. By the time the Suddas were touting the product in Paris, Ottoman opium exports to Britain, the United States, and other European markets were nearing 10 percent of the Empire's total agricultural exports.[21]

German, French, and British physicians, chemists, and druggists had come to see Ottoman opium as a prized pharmaceutical commodity by the 1850s. The first substantive report on the product in Europe was published in 1852. Xaver Landerer, an expatriate German physician who served as pharmacist to the first king of Greece, sent a small but influential report on the Smyrna opium trade to a German pharmaceutical review, next to a report on Black Sea caviar.[22] He described the arrival of camels laden with cargo from the opium "plantations" of Afyon district and the meticulous probing of the port's Jewish and Armenian opium examiners, which preceded the export of opium in wooden boxes lined with tin. A more substantive report came three years later, when Sidney Maltass, scion of a large British trading family in Smyrna, made a longer report on the production of opium in the Anatolian hinterlands.[23] Maltass's ethnographic report, published in London, followed opium from cultivation to the meetings between buyers and sellers that took place in front of district administrators and the processes by which good opium was mixed with sand, pounded poppy capsules, "half-dried apricots," turpentine, and figs. Like van Lennep, he blamed Smyrna's Jews for adulterating what good opium they did receive from the provinces, though suggested that the usual adulterant was tragacanth, and not *salep*, as Xaver Landerer had suggested.

The continental reports on Turkish production took on a more analytical quality by mid-decade. Constantin Descharmes, a professor at the Lycée Impérial in Amiens, had made a minor pharmaceutical stir in 1855 through the case he published for domestic French opium production.[24] The nation's seven thousand pharmacies, he established, used an average of two or three kilograms of the commodity each year, before counting morphine or codeine salts, and the millions of francs spent on imports would be better spent supporting agricultural societies and horticultural associations in the promotion of the *oeillette* variety at home. Druggists in France and Germany proffered new analyses of the Turkish product to determine whether such a proposal would be economically or pharmacologically desirable. Mohamed Effendy Charkauy, an assistant to the head of the Central Pharmacy Laboratory in Cairo, had come to Paris to pursue a doctorate in pharmacy, which he defended in 1856.[25] Charkauy, who dedicated his thesis to Sa'id Pasha, the Wali of Egypt and Ottoman Viceroy, defended Egyptian opium with nationalist zeal—its poor reputation, he averred, owed mostly to the ways in which it was formed and packed, which facilitated adulteration. But he conceded that Ottoman opium, from either Constantinople or Smyrna, was the superior product. French pharmacist Nicolas Guibourt shared Charkauy's rosy assessment of Anatolian opium after comparing samples that the Suddas had sent with those from Egypt, Persia, India, and France.[26] A team of German druggists writing one of the country's leading pharmaceutical almanacs drew upon Maltass's report and the favorable assessments of Merck's importers in coming to a similar conclusion.[27] German botanist Eduard Winkler offered a comparative account of the Smyrna and Constantinople "varieties" of opium found in the German trade, alongside samples from Malwa and Bengal, and agreed with Merck's assessment that the Smyrna variety was unequalled for pharmaceutical preparations.[28]

Germanic medicine was particularly appreciative of Ottoman opium's pharmaceutical value. Hermann Hager, Germany's preeminent pharmaceutical writer, extolled Smyrna opium as the only variety suitable for modern pharmacies, describing the rich range of nineteen alkaloids found in good concentrations within it.[29] The University of Vienna's first lecturer on medical chemistry, Franz von Schneider, compared Smyrna opium with its Indian counterpart, "of which none reaches Europe," and drew similar conclusions.[30] Austrian natural scientist Karl Scherzer, traveling through Smyrna, traced the footsteps of Xaver Landerer and Sidney Maltass to see the production of opium in the Anatolian inlands.[31] His only critique of the product was that its price fluctuated wildly, subject to speculation by local buyers as well as the whims of the market in Europe and the United States—the latter, he declared, "less for medicinal purposes than for the Chinese who have immigrated since the construction of the railroad in California."

French, German, and American opium purchasers were all vexed by the specter of adulteration and uncertain morphine content. Wholly dependent on local inspectors, mostly Jewish or Armenian, these merchants were at turns impressed and frustrated at their own inability to discern good product from bad. Occasionally they put their faith in the system: a Parisian pharmacist wrote of his encounter with a Smyrna opium merchant, who had convinced him that the city's opium inspectors were, through their meticulous visual and tactile inspection, the indispensable guarantors of pharmaceutical opium's quality.[32] "This procedure," he wrote to *France médicale*, "indeed a bit barbaric, offers, you will agree, a very serious guarantee, especially practiced by men who have a very great habit of it. I would even add, and this always between us, that I would place more faith in the words of these experts than in all the scholars who have studied the question." An American buyer in Smyrna wrote in 1868 of being similarly impressed by the inspectors' precision.[33] "There is no rule," he wrote, "by which one can become a judge of Opium, however moderate his aspirations; this ability can only be acquired through many years practice. In examining this article nearly all the use of the faculties is required: color, appearance, weight, scent, etc., serve as a guide, for often one light, or dark colored cake is as good as another; soft, hard, etc., may be both good or bad; one scent may be as good as another, etc." But a later account published in the *Revue commerciale du Levant* suggested that even the best inspectors could struggle to detect fresh earth, plum paste, egg yolk, shoemakers' glue, or other substances, noting that chemical analysis was usually too costly and time-consuming to take on.[34]

By the time, then, that the Suddas were in Paris with their ninety-two samples of Ottoman opium, it is fair to say that the product was already in high repute, if dogged by concerns over purity. German and French druggists were prioritizing the use of Smyrna opium above all other varieties, as were a wider network of European-connected pharmacists stretching into the Eastern Mediterranean.[35] Since the decline of the China trade, American merchants had been increasingly invested in the Ottoman supply for domestic use in the United States. The Suddas' pitch, then, might be read as having two less obvious motives. The first, as the wide reception of Constantin Descharmes's treatise might suggest, would have been an implicit case against the domestic cultivation of poppies in France—a move that would have dramatically undercut the capital that opium exports were bringing into the Ottoman economy. The second, however, would have been directed more obliquely at the administrators of the Ottoman state itself: a call, in the context of a changing imperial landscape, to put the idioms and instruments of scientific agriculture in the service of increased productivity and state revenue.

The Suddas had gone to Paris at the end of the Tanzimat—a period of profound transformation and modernization, when a series of sweeping reforms were implemented by forward-thinking sultans and statesmen, aiming to revitalize the Empire and align it with a strain of progressive values in Europe. Beyond the centralization of the Empire's bureaucracy, its tax collection, and its legal and educational systems, the Tanzimat had fostered a new sense of Ottoman citizenship and belonging, extending equal rights to non-Muslim citizens. But the Tanzimat era had also effected similarly large changes on the Empire's agriculture and ecology. A centralizing state had worked to make its internal and external provincial hinterlands from coastal Çukurova and Cyrenaica to marshy Iraq more legible to the state itself, seeking to integrate these spaces into imperial administrative structures by settling nomadic populations and developing agriculture. These efforts were ambitious in their scope and uneven in their implementation, pegged to very real and thorny political ecological constraints.[36]

The question of how agricultural development in the Empire might be advanced emerged with new primacy in this moment. Centralization and increased extraction had been two increasingly urgent imperatives ever since the Ottoman Empire had grown indebted to European creditors in the middle of the nineteenth century, falling into a pattern of recurrent loan refinancing. The language of reform in agriculture—in all the essential export commodities of tobacco, wheat, barley, raisins, figs, and raw silk—could justify state intervention and buttress both state power and revenue collection across the Empire's hinterlands. But the nature of agricultural development was the site of pitched debate. Increasingly connected to European idioms and institutions of scientific agriculture, Ottoman technocrats enthusiastically promoted the application of "modern" technologies and expertise to agriculture as a means of increasing the value extracted from its land.[37] Different actors held varied and conflictual ideas about which types of technologies, infrastructures, and practices would be best suited to these ends, but came to share a set of relatively stable beliefs about the value of expertise, the application of new technologies, and the supremacy of modern agricultural knowledge over the rustic practices of Ottoman cultivators. Within this context, the expansion of poppy cultivation—so integral to state power during the monopoly era, and no less so against the backdrop of rising pharmaceutical demand—became newly sutured to the instruments of modern agricultural development.

The Suddas had spoken of the new steps that had been taken in agriculture: the establishment of regional agricultural offices, staffed, when possible, by returning graduates from France's premiere agricultural institutions. In the years that followed, they had evidence of a deepening commitment to poppy cultivation along modern lines. Within three years of the Suddas' presentation in Paris, at least one enterprising agricultural official had taken up their call. Hagop Amasyan Efendi was one of the modernizing officials whom the two pharmacists had referenced. He had studied agriculture and silkworm cultivation at Grignon and specialized at the Institut Agronomique in Versailles, and the year that the Suddas had gone to Paris, he had been appointed as Director of Agriculture and Public Works for Hüdavendigâr Province, among the most productive of Anatolia's opium-producing regions.[38] Amasyan Efendi would in time be named Agriculture Director for the Ottoman Empire. But in 1870, responding to Sultan Abdülaziz's *firman*, or royal decree, to expand the cultivation of opium in Anatolia, Amasyan Efendi traveled throughout his *vilayet* to chronicle the optimal conditions for the cultivation and dissemination of opium there and elsewhere in the Empire.[39] Amasyan Efendi's account was steeped deeply in the modernizing imperatives of the day and a concomitant paternalism toward his provinces' peasant cultivators. Those peasants, he insisted, too often ignored proper cultivation schedules that would optimize the collection of morphine-rich sap, preferring to remain bewildered when their poppies produced poor yields rather than listening to expert advice.[40] Amasyan Efendi's successor in Hüdavendigâr, Ali Haydar, published a meticulous account of the value of poppy to his province, alongside the best way of fertilizing and tilling soil, and the very many pests—cockchafers, cutworms, and field mice—that could fell an otherwise promising crop.[41]

He detailed, for cultivators' benefit, a pesticide made of strychnine mixed with melon or pumpkin and stuffed inside small grapes. Mostly, he encouraged farmers to be encouraged by the profits that opium cultivation could yield. "Poppy cultivation in the Ottoman lands," he insisted, "is spreading, and farmers are smiling by virtue of their full pockets."[42]

Ottoman opium production reached a quantitative high in the 1880s and would remain near that high until the end of the century.[43] There is considerable doubt and debate concerning how effective the Ottoman state's inducements were. Its public proclamations about the value of opium and its dispatch of French-trained experts were at odds with what it concretely did with the commodity, namely exempting it from the tithe after 1881.[44] What is less debatable is that in that same period, opium appeared to enjoy a new public centrality in Anatolia. *Hazîne-i Evrak*, a prominent Constantinople-based modern literary journal, offered its urban readers an account of poppy cultivation in the Anatolian country-side, situating it as a commodity at once steeped in rural tradition and suited to the forward-looking economic program of the day.[45] Students at the Bursa Ziraat Mektebi, the hilly northwestern town's agricultural college, were taught alongside students of the local teachers' college to sow poppy seeds with a new motorized drill, putting the crop at the fore-front of new agricultural techniques.[46] A new railway was built near the end of the century to connect the opium heartland of Afyonkarahisar to the port of Smyrna.[47] "No crop in Anatolia," a French commercial report from the 1880s noted, "is as important as opium."[48] Another on Smyrna's commercial prospects echoed the sentiment: "Among the products of Anatolia, none has taken on the commercial importance of opium, the most precious of exported substances."[49] A hagiography of Sultan Abdul Hamid II lauded his reign's efforts to support the expansion of opium cultivation. "France," the Sultan's biographer boasted, "now consumes the whole of Smyrna's opium."[50] A French-language primer for Turkish language learners offered the following evocative passage to translate:

Monsieur Ali Effendi, Your Excellency: I had written to you some time
ago, requesting that you send me three baskets of opium, and as of yet,
I have not received a response from you. Sir, upon receipt of this letter,
I beseech you, if you have not already done so, to purchase these three
baskets and send them to me without fail—pray do not neglect this—for
I have entered into a contract with Monsieur K, and have received from
him thirty thousand piastres, having committed myself in writing to
deliver to him within twenty days the aforementioned three baskets of
opium, Sir.[51]

The rising production of opium for export stoked occasional concern
among the Empire's urban physicians, attuned to similar concerns in
continental Europe.[52] Zambaco Pacha, a prominent Constantinople
physician working in France, offered a concerned account of *morphéomanie* among the city's erstwhile smokers or eaters. While rural
Turks, he wrote, continued to take opium in pill form and certain urban
elites continued to buy annual supplies of opium in bulk for regular
consumption, Constantinople was seeing the scourge of morphine
injections.

It was not merely physicians disquieted by the opium boom of the last
two decades of the nineteenth century. The revenues made by private
traders in opium were increasingly tempting to the progressively more
insolvent Ottoman state. In 1881, right as the Porte was calling for the
expansion of opium cultivation, a new organization, the Ottoman
Public Debt Administration, had been founded to consolidate the
Empire's growing public debt to European companies.[53] Three years
later, tobacco, one of the Empire's other prestige commodities, was
handed over to the *Regie co-intéressée des tabacs de l'Empire ottoman*, a
semi-state agency that enjoyed monopoly control. By the 1890s, opium
was floated as the next logical monopoly.[54] In 1892, a syndicate of bankers
in Constantinople advanced a scheme to remake the monopoly system
of the 1830s—presumably with plans for greater enforcement than had
been possible half a century earlier, and likely in exchange for a massive
cash payment that would help ease the Porte's significant debt burden.
The British consul of Salonica objected strenuously—British merchants
and, much more importantly, American merchants would not have been

able to countenance a return to monopoly control of a product that had grown increasingly central to their trade. Those merchants, too, had come to rely on the expansion of Turkish cultivation as a bulwark against greater price fluctuations.[55] "We should not like to say," one American trade journal opined at the end of the century, "that the time will never return when opium may quadruple in price in a month, or even that it is impossible that we may stand upon the threshold of such an event at this moment; but the opportunities for such excessive fluctuations are growing less and less every year."

In the years before the First World War, two foreign travelers arrived in Smyrna, each determined to understand an industry that appeared to be on the precipice of great change.

Richard Millant, a French physician with a swashbuckling streak, had left Paris by rail, traveling down the length of the Vardar River and eastward toward the Ottoman Empire.[56] Millant traveled with a camera in tow, eager to capture on gelatin dry plates the way that poppies were scored, scraped, and transformed into the world's most valuable medical substance. The closer he got to the Sea of Marmara and the Gulf of Smyrna, the more curious and complicated this industry seemed: a mix of modern science and medieval labor, desire and aversion, people, movement, and land. It drew up in its orbit rustic cultivators, savvy urban merchants, and men of science and industry. What Millant knew for sure was that opium was the substance that linked French pharmacies to Ottoman fields, even if those linkages were rapidly changing.

One of those changes was taking place in the realm of labor. The First Balkan War had cleaved the Ottoman Empire of some of its more productive opium-cultivating lands in Macedonia and Thrace; many Greek cultivators who had once tended poppies had also left, in recent years, for the United States. In their place, Bulgarians had come to cultivate European fields and Turks had come to tend Asian ones. But the French physician was more concerned with the way in which the Ottoman opium industry was adapting to the idioms of science and commerce that had changed so head-spinningly fast in the last decade.

French pharmacies were still brimming with preparations made from Smyrna opium. But on a relative scale, Millant noted, French merchants purchased little from the Ottoman Empire's bustling markets. So did the British, who of late seemed to be acquiring more from their Persian dominions. The Germans were continuing to buy from the markets of Constantinople and Smyrna, and the agents of Merck were ensuring that Darmstadt was still "the morphine supplier for almost all of Europe." Millant found it hard to ignore the Americans who were doing such a brisk trade in Smyrna. If their scientific acumen was duller than their German counterparts, they bested them in sheer moxie, working easily with the Armenian and Jewish merchants who plied the profitable export trade. Their prowess felt similar to the American dominance of the Ottoman trade a century earlier. But if those earlier Yankee merchants had been packing Anatolian opium for China, the Americans were now scooping up half of the Ottoman Empire's production to use for domestic morphine manufacture in the United States. The Americans could pick out the subtle adulterants that Parisian merchants struggled with: gum arabic and apricot gum were the hardest to spot. They also were quickly catching up with their German counterparts in the scientific analysis of opium gum, ready to partner with the merchants transforming their trading houses into makeshift laboratories more fit for the modern trade.

The shift was underway in the Empire's major trading house. The Gulbenkians had opened up a new opium testing laboratory in their Constantinople warehouse, as had the Scialoms of Salonica. But for Millant, there was no more impressive modernization than that which had taken place in the trading house of Nissim Taranto. The Taranto family had been titans of the opium business in Smyrna and Constantinople for much of the century. Longtime fez-maker, the family's patriarch, Bochor Taranto, had become the chief opium inspector during the monopoly years, and Bochor's descendants, in both cities, had come to dominate much of the trade through the trading houses of J. Taranto

Figure 2.2 "Opium Experts in Constantinople," from Richard Millant's *La culture du pavot et le commerce de l'opium en Turquie*, 1913.

and Nissim Taranto.[57] Nissim's warehouse, Millant wrote, was in its own league: his two sons had been educated in chemistry in Europe, and his recently upgraded factory "leaves nothing to be desired: ovens, crystallizers, vacuum devices, and all else are arranged to ensure the most expert precision." The Tarantos' output could meet even the most exigent German or American laboratory standards, to say nothing of the less demanding French or English ones.[58]

The Americans' ascent as primary consumers, not mere merchants, of Ottoman opium, had been decades in the making. American demands had dictated pricing in Smyrna from at least the 1870s, and beginning in this period, American importers, later assisted by consular officials, had tracked Smyrna weather patterns with great interest, buying up existing supplies when poppy fields were damaged.[59] A persistent rumor among British merchants held that an American syndicate was trying to drive out their European competitors. "The American agents in Smyrna," a British importer declared, "are buying up practically everything they can lay their hands on, and seem to have carte blanche from their principals."[60] US druggists' journals had tracked the changing systems of opium measurement in Anatolia, trying to equip pharmacists with greater insight into the opium they were receiving.[61] By 1881, American pharmacists were suggesting that the quantity of Ottoman opium they were using—though only a quarter of which was used for morphine—would grow from half the available supply to far more.[62] Even after several years of middling harvests, by the time the American Chamber of Commerce for Turkey was established in March 1911, the Chamber could identify more than a dozen opium dealers of excellent repute in Smyrna, Constantinople, and Salonica (alongside a single trading house in Baghdad).[63]

Shortly before Millant traveled through the Anatolian opium heartland, another traveler had made a similar pilgrimage. John Uri Lloyd, an American pharmacist with a particular honed interest in ethnobotany, had arrived in Smyrna in the winter of 1905, armed with letters of introduction from the US Agricultural Department and the Smithsonian Institution.[64] Like many springtime visitors to Smyrna, Lloyd was taken by the "beautiful, scarlet, single poppy" blossoming around the city. Unlike those visitors, he knew that this poppy was not the opium poppy, which was not "cultivated in less than five hours by rail from Smyrna." In those fields, Lloyd saw peasant families working the poppy crop with intense precision. "No other people," he wondered as he watched peasants score and scrape, "can be more frugal, more patient, more resigned to adversity or more ready, when failure occurs, to begin over than are the Turks of today, and the preceding generations of Turks."

Like Millant, Lloyd could also report back to his patrons in Washington that the world of Anatolian opium was changing. If its manner of cultivation seemed dutifully rustic, scarcely changed in centuries, its production had become ever more modern as it reached the point of sale. The camel trains of a century earlier had been replaced by a sleek railway into the Anatolian interior. More importantly, there were changes afoot in the trading houses themselves. The American Consul in Smyrna introduced Lloyd to Alfred Keun, scion of the formidable Dutch trading house, which had come to trade more with the Americans as the Dutch *regie* had declined. In the Keun warehouse, Anatolian opium merchants bearing linen-lined bales of opium from the interior were met with a

Figure 2.3 "Inspecting Opium, Smyrna," from John Uri Lloyd's *A Treatise on Opium and Its Compounds*, 1908.

rustic figure. Jacob Gabbaï, a third-generation Sephardic Jewish opium inspector who checked each purchase with a knife belonging to his grandfather, was paid half a percent of the opium he inspected. Gabbaï, Lloyd wrote,

> Sits cross-legged on a mat on the floor. The purchaser and the seller having agreed to abide by his decision, the opium baskets are successively dumped before him. Rapidly he cuts a deep circular cone from each ball, inspecting the interior by both sight and smell, rejecting those he considers inferior or adulterated. From some baskets most of the opium is condemned; from others, only a few balls are rejected. During the time I witnessed one of the inspections, the seller protested but once against the decision. But the inspector refused to reconsider, stating that the ball was adulterated with prunes.

The major European importing houses, a slightly later account held, "would not take delivery of any shipment of opium unless it was accompanied by a declaration signed by Gabbaï."[65] More important to American importers was what happened after Gabbaï had accepted the seller's opium. From a hundred balls of opium, a hundred small pieces the size of a walnut were scooped out and kneaded together in mechanical mixer. From there, a hundred grams of the blended opium was taken out and chemically assayed to determine the percentage of "crystalline white morphine" in the homogenized purchase itself. Overseeing the Keuns' process was Agop Alpiar, an adroit Armenian chemist who had for fifteen years been working to bring the world's leading "opium and alkaloidal assay methods" to his laboratory, equipped with "the most modern apparatus, including stills, vacuum apparatus, machinery, and delicate glassware and reagents." At one end of the Keuns' operation stood the subjective assessment of a hereditary inspector. That inspector, another French observer noted with some creative embellishment, possessed "a privilege recognized by the Ottoman government and which the members of a sworn Israelite family have passed down from father to son for more than three centuries."[66] At the other stood all the best instruments of modern pharmaceutical science: the assaying, the precision measuring, and standardization that rendered raw agricultural product legible as an appropriate commodity to a modernizing pharmaceutical market in the West. If, half a century earlier, the Suddas had called for agricultural reform that would turn Ottoman opium into a choice commodity, at the precipice of the First World War, that commodity was being channeled with great precision into a new set of pharmaceutical networks.

Ottoman opium, like Indian opium, had called together a web of actors whose work at turns underwrote and confounded the economic life of empires. An important but never dominant crop, once merely a notable feature of the Empire's agrarian landscape, had been brought into the ascendant transnational opium trade, with illicit Chinese markets offering the promise of extraordinary riches. A thriving but anarchic commercial trade from Smyrna, primarily American, had been brought to heel by an imperial monopoly, which tried but failed to bring opium's economic potential under state control.

The similarities between Indian and Ottoman opium, however, largely ended here. After the sultan's abortive attempt to limit opium production, the commodity grew increasingly valuable for European and then American pharmaceutical markets. As the Ottoman state tried to reform its agricultural production and revenue collection in the face of a deepening fiscal crisis in the latter half of the nineteenth century, opium became the subject of efforts to improve its cultivation and potential for pharmaceutical use. Indian opium had no real place in the European and American pharmaceutical industries of the late nineteenth century, but Ottoman opium had become central to their functioning. At the precipice of the First World War, the Americans had begun to edge out their European and British competitors in Anatolia's bustling opium markets. The industry's traditional intermediaries—the largely non-Turkish inspectors and merchants so long integral to the trade—were looking to the future of an industry that was increasingly governed by scientific idioms. But the Ottoman Empire, like India, was on the cusp of epochal political change, and opium's traditional networks would need a radical reworking in its incipient republican era.

When Ottoman opium has appeared in accounts of the nineteenth-century opium trade, it has broadly been peripheral to the more evident dynamics of the trade in Asia Minor. Where opium from Anatolia does appear, it is as a supplement to the weightier supply from British India, ferried by American merchants, sometimes alongside or with the connivance of their British counterparts, to ports in southern China and Southeast Asia. Even accounts of the Ottoman trade itself focus largely on this subsidiary role for Anatolian opium.[67] What is lost in these accounts is how, over the course of the nineteenth century, opium became bound up in a set of changing relationships and political economies within the Ottoman Empire, as well as a set of global networks moving successively from east to west. As these political economies and the destinations of Ottoman opium shifted, different arrangements were called into being between cultivators, intermediary traders, merchants, and the state.

As opium entered the twentieth century, the intermediary actors who had produced opium as a desirable, world-class export commodity were increasingly cast as vestigial relics of pre-modern commerce.

The pharmacists rooted in European learning who had cast Ottoman opium as central to a modern apothecary, the French-trained experts who had proffered improvement as a central idiom in the development of Ottoman agriculture, and the Jewish and Armenian inspectors, traders, and merchants who had helped ferry Anatolian opium to foreign traders had each been integral to the creation of a dynamic export economy. Yet assaying, standardization, and the language of scientific pharmacy was ascendant by the turn of the twentieth century. Within a few decades, those intermediary figures who failed to adapt would be pushed out of the trade entirely. In Anatolia, as in India, two world wars and new national politics would radically reshape the life of a commodity that had for a century been in the midst of radical change.

PART II

Building the
Twentieth-Century
Opium Order

3

The Problem of Distance

For fifteen years, while he had been teased and ignored, Emanuel Weiss had worked assiduously on his plan to remake the world of medicine and trade.[1]

The Bohemian botanist and physician had traveled far from his erstwhile Austrian home, animated by the bold notion that the world's living things could be rearranged across the world in the service of new industry. On a first trip to Arizona and California in the 1840s, Weiss had stood on the banks of the Colorado River, scheming to import camels, date palms, figs, olives, and sesame to the Palo Verde Valley, where, in the shadow of Fort Yuma and the wake of native dispossession, he would render these crops the centerpieces of a lucrative new Mediterranean. The plan had gone nowhere. Humiliated, Weiss had traveled east by land and sea, arriving in the port of Alexandria in search of new opportunities in a booming cosmopolitan port. It was there, among the long shadows of the Great Minaret and Pompey's Pillar, that Weiss happened upon opium.

It wasn't as if opium had been easy to miss. The city's markets teemed with gum, and merchants in this Ottoman port packed Thebes opium carefully in wooden crates lined with straw. If the use of opium there was in low repute, Egyptian opium vendors nonetheless distinguished between four different types of *barsha*, or confections, which had putatively different effects on the user.[2] Weiss had arrived in Egypt in a moment of change. The Ottoman opium monopoly, brittle and understaffed, was on its last legs. As some American and European merchants were arranging for the transshipment of heavy crates on camelback toward Suez, and from there on to Canton or Hong Kong, others were shipping those crates west, to Europe or new markets in the United States. Weiss, sensing a plan electric with possibility, began mapping the flows of opium around a world that railways, steamships, and canals were making ever smaller.

Weiss thought back to the Colorado River. A friend assured the doctor, by post, that there was no climatological impediment to his plan: poppy had been grown in places as dismal as England and Germany, and even once in Pennsylvania. What then prevented enterprising American farmers, Weiss wondered, "assisted by all the modern improvements in the tillage of the soil and the ginning of the cotton," from growing opium of their own? Weiss wrote to papers in Boston, St. Louis, and Arizona to announce what he was sure to be an irresistible proposal: five thousand dollars, the whole of his life's savings, for an initial investment in an opium plantation deep in the heart of the Palo Verde Valley. But where he expected plaudits, there were crickets. Weiss's correspondents in the land he had made his home were silent on the possibility of home-grown opium. Determined, he returned to North America to make the case himself.

As the clipper headed west past Gibraltar, Weiss had time to formulate just how global trade and medicine would be radically remade through his plan of growing opium in the United States. His first argument was economic, rooted in the lopsided balance of trade between China and the United States that had disturbed even the most casual commercial observer.[3] Americans who might, a generation back, have aspired over the course of a lifetime to own a longcase clock, a silver spoon, or a Wedgwood vase had become insatiable consumers, unable to slake their thirst for cheap Chinese goods. They yearned for Fujianese tea, bales of silk, and a host of consumer goods from porcelain to coarse nankeen cloth.[4] Chinese consumers, by contrast, wanted little from the United States—a modest amount of rice, copper, ginseng, and cotton—and the latter would soon be made economically unviable after the Civil War and the emancipation of three and a half million enslaved people. Opium stood to bring American and Chinese trade to an even keel.

The global world of opium in the 1840s was a tessellation of intersecting triangles. Britain's Bengal monopoly and its eventual sanction of the Malwa trade connected the subcontinent's opium to Chinese ports. The silk, tea, and porcelain those merchants bought in Canton were the same products that Americans had come to covet and crave, making for ready profits in the United States. American merchants, for their part, were buying Anatolian opium in Smyrna and, to a lesser degree, in Constantinople and Alexandria. Masters of the Eastern Mediterranean trade, they ferried that opium on sleek clippers to China alongside cotton and rice, underwriting their own fledgling Asian enterprises. Weiss's plan of obviating Ottoman purchases and undercutting the British maritime trade was doubly genius. In a single swoop, the United States could push cheap, American-grown narcotics into Chinese ports, even the score with China, and undercut British power across Asia.

Weiss was scarcely troubled by the questionable ethics of his plan, bound up in the erroneous notion that opium's habitual use was a distinctly Chinese vice. "If the Orientals abuse opium," Weiss wrote, "they will not do so the less because we refrain from cultivating it." But it was not merely Chinese opium smokers who would clamor for the American product. American physicians and pharmacists, he calculated, were doling out more than half a million pounds of opium each year. In the absence of more effective cures and palliatives, American men and women consumed opium in salts and tinctures, as well as in preparations like Dover's powder and laudanum. Within a few years, they would be pumping it into their veins with the hypodermic needle as well. If opium were an Asian vice, Weiss reasoned, it was also the most useful ingredient in the American apothecary, and it was utter folly that it was not produced on American soil.

Back in his adopted homeland, Weiss surveyed the mission town of San Diego, increasingly doubtful that its "Pueblo Indians" would take to poppy cultivation. Once again, he looked to the Palo Verde Valley, which, during his long sojourn away, had been violently depopulated and incorporated into the new territory of Arizona and was teeming with opportunities for the ambitious homesteader.[5] There, Weiss envisioned, he would build his 100,000-acre joint venture in American opium—a crop that would remake empires and underwrite the growth of American medicine. To work his plantation, Weiss proposed sponsoring the immigration of ethnic Greeks fleeing from Smyrna. If they did not come, the "lately Freedmen of the South" could no doubt be persuaded to resettle there and work opium with the same assiduity they had tended to cotton under bondage. Weiss sent his proposal to Congress in 1866. Four years later, when he died of a self-inflicted gunshot wound on a ship in Singapore, he had still not heard back.[6]

◖◗

If Weiss had teetered into madness in his last years of life, he had nonetheless identified a conundrum at the heart of American medicine and commerce. So much of the young nation's pharmaceutical materials were imported from distant shores. American fevers were brought down with cinchona bark from South America, and Asian camphor disinfected American wounds and decongested American sinuses. Sandalwood from India was used to treat American bladders and kidneys, Central American sarsaparilla alleviated American syphilis, and African castor beans, pressed into oil, became the essential laxative and purgative for American digestive tracts. All of these plants required particular ecologies minimally present in the United States—tropical mountain forests, subtropical heat, and tropical rainforests—and it was obvious that they needed to be imported. But opium poppies could grow in a range of climates, from the farmland of the Northeast to the arid borderlands of the Southwest. With no geographic or climactic impediment to its domestic cultivation, why was it that the United States' most useful medicine was not grown at home?

Weiss's question was many decades in the making. Nineteenth-century fantasies cast opium as the avarice of China or, as the century progressed, Chinese migrants to the United States.[7] But opium was a ubiquitous curative and occasional vice for a great many Americans, and the problem of distance was attached to opium from the very beginning.

American medicine in the late eighteenth and early nineteenth centuries was not known for its great restraint. In the absence of meaningful therapeutics and antiseptic surgery, American doctors practiced "heroic medicine." Rarely content to let an illness run its course or to cure by tincture of time, physicians depleted their patients with bloodletting and purging. They poisoned them with mercury and lead, burnt their flesh with mugwort leaves and wool, and ran small threads and cloths under their skin to drain a constant stream of pus. Alongside these treatments, these doctors had an extensive domestic and global *materia medica* by which they could putatively cure. American tobacco could be used for pain or as an emetic, Mexican jalap was deployed as a cathartic, and mercury from the Spanish mining town of Almadén or the Idrija mine in Habsburg Slovenia was called upon to cure skin and venereal ailments.[8]

Opium was part of this emerging global trade in medical substances, and American druggists used it as liberally as they cut veins. It was the first-line treatment for cough, pain, insomnia, diarrhea, malaria, smallpox, syphilis, and tuberculosis—as well as the scourge of "general insanity."[9] Doctors and druggists debated the exact nature of the drug, disagreeing over whether it was a stimulant or a sedative. But they universally cast it as the most useful substance in their quiver, whether administered as a tincture, as a gum, or—after 1817, when German chemist Friedrich Wilhelm Sertürner isolated the substance he called an "alkaloid"—as morphine crystals.[10] Opium use in the United States, or at least the perception of that use, was also beginning to change.[11] Over the course of the nineteenth century, opium shifted—gradually and then with greater velocity—from an indispensable and widely acceptable curative into a substance that intertwined both medical concern and racial enmity.

By the 1830s, opium had emerged as a notable if not overwhelming public health concern in the United States. Physicians began to write in this decade about the habitual opium users whom they described as a characteristic feature of American cities.[12] There were plausible reasons for the uptick. With American sanitation lackluster, outbreaks of cholera and dysentery surged in these decades, and many of the afflicted may have availed themselves of the usual treatment long beyond the course of their illnesses. Thomas De Quincey's lurid *Confessions of an English Opium Eater* (1821) encouraged American physicians to take a second look at their prescribing patterns. Within a decade, the *Boston Medical and Surgical Journal* published an evocative early assessment of opium's deleterious effects on American users, noting that physicians were less likely to discern habitual opium use than alcohol use in their patients, making it difficult for them to assess its harms.[13] John McNeil Stewart, a Texas physician, chronicled through his meticulous record-keeping the quickness with which American doctors recommended opium to their patients.[14]

This incipient concern was transformed into a full-scale crisis by the American Civil War. Both Union and Confederate armies used opium and morphine liberally as they treated soldiers' wounds, pain, and enduring illness. Union troops alone received nearly 10 million opium pills and over 2,841,000 ounces of other opium powders and tinctures from military physicians. Connecticut physician Nathan Mayer doled out opium on horseback, offering wounded soldiers an "exact quantity" to lick from his hand.[15] Pills, powders, and other formulations were less worrisome, however, than the improved hypodermic needle, perfected in the 1850s. Its glass tube and screw syringe, engineered to deliver a more precise dose than its cruder early iterations, ushered in a new way of delivering morphine to the bloodstream and from there to the brain. Hundreds of thousands of American Civil War veterans returned home from Bull Run, Antietam, and Gettysburg bearing signs of "the soldiers' disease"—morphine addiction whose scale confounded American families, cities, and underprepared public health institutions.[16]

As American physicians and families grappled with the aftermath of the Civil War, a new front opened in the American West. While a small number of Chinese migrants had arrived in American cities prior to the California Gold Rush of 1849, their opium smoking became a focal point of white American concern after well over twenty thousand migrants came to "Gold Mountain" from China's southern coastal regions of Guangdong, Fujian, and Guangxi within a few years.[17] If white Americans no doubt exaggerated the extent to which Chinese migrants smoked opium—Harry Hubbell Kane, a physician and proponent of Chinese exclusion estimated that 35 percent of the Chinese community in the United States were users—their anxieties over what an "Asiatic Vice" would do to "degenerate the white race" led to a spate of laws restricting opium use and the establishment of opium dens in American Chinatowns.[18] By the time the Chinese Exclusion Act of 1882 was passed, restricting Chinese migration for a period of ten years, opium had been transformed from a wholly medical problem into a racial one.

In the late nineteenth century, the anxieties around Chinese use helped to deepen the notion among physicians that white use was a medical problem as well as a social ill. In an unregulated market, opium and its derivatives like morphine and laudanum were "all-purpose anodynes," as useful as they had been a century earlier for concerns as varied as coughs and cramps.[19] Self-medication through over-the-counter patent medicines, freely dispensed at American pharmacies, stoked new concerns in this period among physicians and reformers, who would soon coin a new term—"iatrogenic" addiction—to describe habitual use that stemmed from medical treatments.[20] As physicians tightened their prescribing at the turn of the century, they first targeted women, limiting their use of opium for menstrual cramps and other ailments. Those who remained, among white users, were predominantly working-class men who used these drugs—or sniffed and snorted heroin—as a palliative or as a prophylactic for their demanding industrial jobs. The men whose habitual use precluded regular work in this period were rechristened "junkies" for their alleged propensity to hound junkyards in search of scrap metal to barter for narcotics.

At the beginning of the nineteenth century, opium had been the essential American medicine, with scant thought given to abuse or addiction. By its end, there was a rich American vocabulary to describe an altered and varied landscape of use and abuse.[21] Physicians offered the terms *morphinism* and *heroinism* to describe Americans' predilection for each chemical substance. The *Journal of the American Medical*

Association offered *opiokapnism* to describe the habitual smoking of opium that it cast as the sole purview of Chinese migrants. But the richness of language and the ready categorization of American use belied a global market that was not a given but had been just as much in flux.

◖O◗

Where did American opium come from and where should it have come from in the heady nineteenth century? In the late eighteenth century, with American medicine in its infancy, the supply of opium to the United States had been regular and abundant. Inasmuch as anyone in this period demonstrated a propensity for misuse, it was physicians who, flush with gum and tincture, were among the first groups to evince dependence on their own wares.[22]

But there was a sense, too, that opium's ready supply could be easily disrupted. Connecticut physician Thaddeus Betts warned in 1778 that "opium is an article, which no Physician ought ever to want; it is so extensively useful, and in cases so perilous and urgent where no substitute will supply its defect, that physicians (as one observes) would be lame and deficient without it."[23] But the Revolutionary War, he lamented, had torn apart the gossamer webs linking American medicine to its global pharmacy. The war had rendered prices high and supplies scant. Dr. Betts embarked upon an experiment to cultivate his own opium on his Norwalk estate, producing a pound of opium on a mere fifteen square feet of Connecticut soil. If less potent than imported opium, Betts nonetheless commended the domestic production to other physicians and druggists who might be similarly deprived of their regular supply.

Betts and other physicians had a fuzzy sense of where, exactly, their opium came from. Betts had described the United States as reliant "on Turkey and the East Indies ('tho vastly distant) for a supply of that drug." His contemporary John Leigh was one of the young country's most celebrated medical researchers. He had won the Harveian Prize, then medicine's highest honor, for his extensive testing of opium on puppies, rabbits, and children.[24] But he could only venture that opium likely came to his native Virginia from far-off eastern India.

Slowly, however, American physicians and druggists began to distinguish between the various forms of opium that merchants brought to the East Coast on clippers. George Washington Carpenter, one of Philadelphia's most prominent druggists and scientists, lamented in the 1820s "the common black drop of our shops," which was different from shop to shop and was often adulterated with yeast, nutmeg, or saffron to mimic a characteristic pungency.[25] There were, he wrote, three types of opium found in American shops. English opium was the most exquisite product: rare and expensive, but "as smooth and uniform [as] liquorice," and potent beyond measure.[26] The cheapest opium, by contrast, came wrapped in "enormous quantity of leaves" and was unusably weak—this he described as Indian opium, though it is implausible that this was indeed its source. Most prominent, however, was Turkish opium: reddish-brown, with a "strong narcotic odor," and the mainstay of pharmaceutical preparations. But Carpenter, perhaps aware of the disruption that the War of 1812 had caused as well, saw the risk in relying on such a distant supply of this mainstay. Opium was inconsistent in its quality, and its import was subject to sudden disruption. Carpenter made the recommendation that the United States support the cultivation of opium domestically. If England's climatic conditions produced such exquisite opium, American lawmakers should no doubt consider allocating land in Georgia and the Carolinas for an even finer product.

By the time Carpenter made this suggestion, enterprising American cultivators had been experimenting fairly extensively with the cultivation of opium. Shadrach Ricketson, an intrepid Quaker physician from the Hudson Valley, had spent the spring of 1788 planting poppy on his farm, tapping the opium capsules in "the Asiatic method" and producing opium which he had assessed as equally potent as the imported stuff.[27] In the first decade of the nineteenth century, a Dr. Wilkins of Baltimore harvested a small batch of usable opium from his garden plot; shortly thereafter, Dr. Milton Anthony of Petersburgh, Georgia, inspired by the high prices opium was commanding during the War of 1812, produced half a pound of his own, which, when analyzed twenty-one years later, was found to contain good amounts of morphine and narcotine.[28]

These early experiments had stoked strong interest in the possibilities of growing American opium on a larger scale. A Cape Cod physician, James Thatcher, surveyed the "abundantly successful" efforts to grow opium throughout the United States.[29] But "even in our northern climate," he wrote from chilly Barnstable Harbor, where poppies bloomed in his garden plot, opium could still grow and yield a profit "greatly exceeding that of the ordinary crops of Indian corn or other grain." Thatcher voiced an argument that would echo in many later cases for American opium: the notion that such a project would both meet medical needs and shore up tidy profits. "The citizens of the United States have not in general been apprized," he wrote, "that this exotic may be cultivated on our own soil to an extent adequate to every exigency, and with a profit exceeding that of many other productions of husbandry." His vision was grand and stretched down the coast to the American South:

> It is a subject of grateful reflection that in every exigency we may resort to that all bountiful source of national and individual wealth, our native soil, which with the labour of our hands, may administer to our necessities, and supersede the importation of expensive and frequently adulterated foreign productions. To the cultivators of rice in our southern states enjoying a climate and soil, supposed to be peculiarly adapted to the growth of the poppy, it must be a very interesting inquiry, whether the culture of this plant might not be an excellent substitute for that of rice.

The South's climactic advantages grew more alluring in the decades ahead. The *New England Farmer* urged cultivators to follow the lead of a New Hampshire farmer who had eked out a good opium crop in the state's Marlow soil and also pointed out the excellent results that farmers in Georgia had achieved.[30] A South Carolina planter grew another potent crop, and similarly superlative opium was produced in the early 1830s from wild poppies growing in Virginia.[31] But between the 1830s and the end of the Civil War, these experiments lost steam. There are three plausible reasons for this decline. The first wave of concern over opium use may have dampened enthusiasm for domestic experiments in opium cultivation. So, too, might the increasingly reliable supply of opium from Anatolia, as American merchants shifted their exports from southern China to the eastern United States, have rendered these efforts less enticing. And the deepening entrenchment of cotton, cultivated by enslaved people in the American South, might also have made opium a less immediately desirable possibility.

While American experimentation faltered, Europeans undertook their own efforts. In 1866, Professor Hans Karsten of Berlin planted a large plot of "gigantic poppies" on the *Akklimatisationsfeld*, or experimental farm, which he tended outside of Charlottenburg.[32] His results were as fine as the Smyrna opium that German merchants regularly imported. "Rational cultivation techniques," he suggested, might well lead to a fine domestic morphine for German pharmaceutical use, leaving the country free to import only a very small amount of crude opium still in favor with certain traditional physicians there. Karsten appealed to German apothecaries and agricultural schools to support these modernizing pharmaceutical efforts.

French researchers had been involved in this effort for even longer. Constantin Descharmes's efforts to produce a French opium crop to compete with the prodigious amounts it imported from Smyrna presaged a flurry of similar experiments.[33] H. Aubergier had zeroed in on a purple poppy variety with high quantities of morphine, while Louis Renard, a particularly industrious French farmer, had continued to trumpet the value of the *oilette*.[34] By the end of the 1850s, a comprehensive survey conducted by a pharmacist at the Faculty of Medicine in Paris offered the notion that France could easily produce enough morphine for its own needs while offering the basis of a good export economy.[35] The French government gazette, in 1873, spoke favorably of French production alongside many similar efforts to produce opium in the industrialized world, as well as in certain French colonies.[36] American, English, German, Australian, Greek, Italian, Swiss, and even Swedish cultivators had all produced respectable trial opium plots. There was even one in Algeria, where poppies from Bengal had been recently introduced.

When Emanuel Weiss made his pitch for an American opium concession at the end of the American Civil War, he was reanimating a proposal that had remained largely dormant for the previous three decades. In the context of an agricultural economy decimated by the abolition of slavery and wartime destruction, proposals for opium's domestic cultivation seemed to have new traction. Just south of the Mason-Dixon Line, a Baltimore druggist dug up his sandy asparagus patch to plant a crop of poppies a year after the war's end, harvesting a crop that rivaled the best imported product.[37] Virginia druggists looked to see whether poppies grown there could be processed effectively into laudanum.[38] After growing it in his garden, a South Carolina farmer described opium to his fellow Carolinians as a promising crop for the South's rural reconstruction.[39] In 1875 the United States Department of Agriculture sent trial packages of white poppy seeds to farmers in the country's warmer climates, lauding a crop raised in Germantown, Tennessee, as the champion of American opium, "equal to good Egyptian and East Indian products."[40]

At the turn of the century, American opium seemed on the precipice of change. For an increasing number of American physicians and druggists, the case that opium should be grown domestically seemed too clear to ignore. A Chicago physician, inspired by Weiss's proposal, outlined in 1901 the trial harvests he had documented in California, Pennsylvania, Vermont, and Connecticut: the question of cheap labor was as yet unanswerable, but he contended that such a shift would confer immeasurable benefits to American medicine.[41] The American Consul in Smyrna himself weighed in on the question, contending that the United States could easily reduce its dependency on Turkish opium—reflected in over a million dollars in imports each year—if it cultivated opium in the foothills of the Appalachian range and upland regions near the Rocky Mountains, which reminded him of Turkey's most productive opium-cultivating regions.[42] At the turn of the twentieth century, Emil Weschcke, Professor of Material Medica at the College of Physicians and Surgeons in San Francisco, studied the wide range of poppy cultivation experiments being undertaken in the United States, commending as a new location

Washington State, "where soil and temperature, and in certain localities cheap Oriental labor would favor cultivation of the poppy."[43]

And yet, no such transformation was in fact imminent. The long supply chains bringing Turkish opium to American shores was about to grow further entrenched, as American pharmaceutical companies began to claim a global preeminence that German firms once held. Pharmaceutical manufacturers continued to mull over the question of whether or not one day, they might grow opium domestically.

◖◗◖◗

Weiss and others could make a rousing case for the domestic cultivation of opium. But in the nineteenth century, global commerce hinged on both the control of far-off commodities and the management of commodities transported far from their ecologies of origin. The world had been shrinking rapidly since the eighteenth century, but in the nineteenth, the telegraph, telephone, transatlantic cable, and typewriter, alongside steam engines, brought the world's commodities ever closer.[44] The tinned foods that had once made for unpleasant military provisions were becoming as commonplace in Arizona as in London. The sweet and pungent condiments that had powered trade and war in a bygone moment were as mundane as salt. The corpses of cows slaughtered in Chicago could be transformed into porterhouse steaks in New York in a few days' time. The Suez Canal was bringing Asian goods closer to Europe and the United States. And the garments that had once been so precious were rendered ever less so by the power loom and the sewing machine. In this world, transformed by new technologies, the question of which commodities moved, and how, took on new vitality.

Many staples had spread far from their origins. Corn had long since moved from its Mesoamerican origins to Africa and Asia, its calories padding stomachs and powering an explosive global population boom. Life without a Peruvian tuber was unimaginable in places as far-flung as Ireland and India. A wild grass from the Fertile Crescent had been bred into the foundations of a global wheat granary linking Ukraine, the American Midwest, Canada, Germany, and Argentina. And rice had long since become a crop dispersed across the world, from Asian terraces to African wetlands to the coastal lowlands of the Southern United States.[45]

But other crops did not move or did so unevenly. Coffee's global purview had expanded from its Ethiopian and Yemeni origins, but only to cover some of the Arabian Peninsula and the uplands of Colombia and Brazil.[46] Tea had migrated from southern Anhui and northwest Fujian only as far as Upper Assam.[47] Jute's long, strong fibers had been conscripted into the service of global trade via mills in Scotland, but the plant had barely left the wet Bengal Delta.[48] The bark of the cinchona tree, taken as quinine, proved too fickle to cultivate well in India or Taiwan.[49] Despite fantasies of working it through plantation labor, it remained largely confined to its Peruvian origins. So, too, did many other New World substances remain locked in place, from curare, ipecac, and jalap, to lobelia, Peruvian balsam, sarsaparilla, and cocaine. And if all these crops were embedded within particular forms of labor and law, some were bound up in particularly violent ways. Even as European chemists learned how to produce sugar from knobby, hard beets, this discovery did not fully obviate the work of enslaved, indentured, and bonded people who harvested and pressed sugar torturously from cane. When emancipation and the US Civil War undercut the South's violent dominance over global cotton production, other ugly arrangements of labor in Egypt and India came to take its place. These questions of geography, ecology, climate, and labor were of renewed importance in all domains, from staple foods to rare ones, from textiles to stimulants. But they were of distinct urgency in the domain of pharmaceutical knowledge, where the management of familiar and novel substances was becoming a central concern.

Pharmacy had come of age in Germany.[50] An early tradition of alchemy had given rise to a rich experimental tradition by the nineteenth century. In its first decade, Friedrich Serturner, a German apothecary from Hannover, isolated opium's key narcotic substance, naming it morphium after the Greek god of dreams. A decade and a half later, Carl Meissner, a German pharmacist, coined *alkaloid* to describe an active botanical compound. German chemists, isolating substances like codeine, quinine, cocaine, and ephedrine, transformed pharmacy from a speculative field reliant on herbs to an empirical science capable of producing powerfully effective pharmaceuticals.

German scientific advances, driven by massive state investment in research and teaching, were bolstered by a savvy industrial shift. Leading dye companies like Bayer and Hoechst leveraged their chemical synthesis expertise to enter the pharmaceutical market, whose mid-nineteenth-century profitability was outpacing dye production. A competitive business environment pushed German firms to innovate and expand their pharmaceutical offerings, focusing on lab-synthesized substances. Bayer's introduction of aspirin in 1899, a triumph of organic chemistry, heralded a future where drugs might originate in laboratories, not plants. But for the time being, plant compounds were still integral to pharmacy, and the command of these substances was essential to the industry's development. Even as they focused on laboratory synthesis, German firms sought a ready supply of exotic substances: Brazilian ipecacuanha for ipecac, and Peruvian cinchona bark and coca for quinine and cocaine, respectively. Opium, of course, remained integral for an expanding range of narcotics, including those which German chemists could transform in new ways: a year before introducing aspirin, Bayer's scientists had discovered how to extract morphine from opium, convert it into a more soluble form, and transform that new substance with acetic anhydride into a new compound. Diacetylmorphine, marketed as heroin, was marketed as a non-addictive substitute for morphine, particularly useful for coughs, and was a discovery no less precipitous than that of aspirin.

Even as it lagged behind the precision of its German counterpart, the American pharmaceutical industry underwent profound transformation after the Civil War. The emergence of a national market for medicines dismantled a long tradition of pharmaceutical secrecy. As drug store preparations became more standardized, American druggists initially sourced their products from Europe, with American manufacturers playing catch-up. German migrants, unsurprisingly, played a crucial role in the nascent American chemical and pharmaceutical industries, which were nearly indistinguishable at the time. German businessman Charles Rosengarten amassed a fortune in Philadelphia by producing quinine for the Union Army.[51] The Pfizer cousins, migrants from Ludwigsburg, established a successful medical business in a Brooklyn warehouse. In St. Louis, the three Mallinckrodt brothers founded their own chemical works, later amassing wealth from their development of barium for X-rays. George Merck, heir to the Darmstadt-based pharmaceutical behemoth, had migrated to New York to build his own American empire.[52] It wasn't only German migrants who transformed the industry. Edward Squibb, a Navy physician disillusioned with the poor quality of ship medicines, founded a forward-thinking pharmaceutical company in Brooklyn. Civil War veteran Colonel Eli Lilly figured out how to encapsulate medicines in gelatin in his Indianapolis laboratory. Parke, Davis and Company, based in Detroit, used profits from an herbal laxative to fund the world's first modern clinical trials. Gradually, American firms adopted the German model of scientific research, marketing investment, and legal protection while aggressively seeking new botanical compounds from around the world.

Pharmaceutical industries in other rapidly industrializing nations were advancing their own, alternative models of modernization. The Japanese industry leaned on government patronage, subsidies, and protectionist policies to fuel its own growth, sourcing morphine from its colony of Taiwan and quinine from plantations in which it had invested in Peru.[53] American pharmaceutical genius was, in part, the grafting of modern marketing onto particularly bold global prospecting. Nowhere was this more evident than in the American industry's capture of cocaine, a new Andean wonder drug.[54] Cocaine, in the latter half of the nineteenth century, was touted as a panacea. Doctors, dentists, chemists, and pharmacists mooted it as a cure for labor pains, toothaches, sexually transmitted infections, and digestive ailments. Its stimulating properties were posited time and again as an effective treatment for alcoholism and

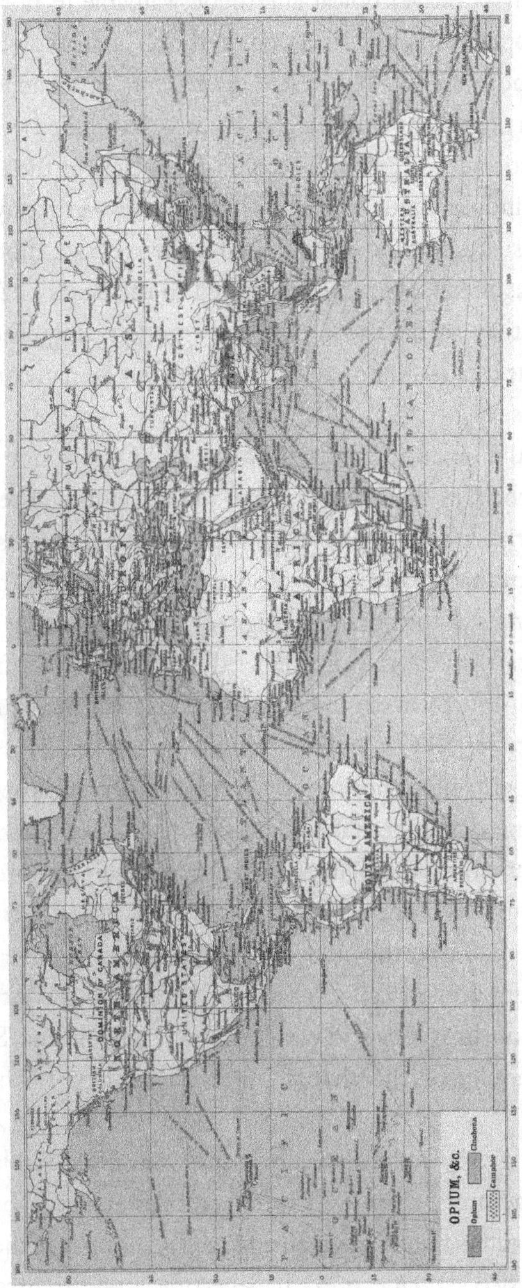

Figure 3.1 Global sources of the world's opium, cinchona, and camphor, from *Atlas of the World's Commerce*, 1907. David Rumsey Historical Map Collection.

morphine abuse. It had, in all likelihood, only a few true medical effects: it was an entirely effective topical anesthetic, valuable in nose, throat, dental, and eye operations, and its action on the respiratory system made it useful for conditions like hay fever and asthma. From inauspicious beginnings as an ingredient in tonics like Coca-Cola—billed as a cure for morphine addiction—cocaine had become a mainstay of the American pharmaceutical industry. Buyers in the United States were convinced by Peru's nationalist leaders and scientists that theirs was a modernizing industry that was predictable and well-suited to the needs of American medicine. And they worked to convey that modernizing ethos in the new products they sold—not merely in cocaine, but in many other alkaloid preparations.

New York Quinine and Chemical Works (NYQ) was not a wholly new company when, in the 1880s, it began to market itself assertively as the most "modern" American pharmaceutical manufacturer. Its cocaine, quinine, ergot, cannabis, and other products were packaged tastefully. Subtle visuals hinted at the botanical origin of the products, all of which came in clean kraft paper wrapping labeled in an elegant vermillion. It was the first company to advertise opium products with a similar sense of purity and certitude. NYQ's "cube morphine" was a standard preparation sold to druggists in authoritatively clear glass jars, and the product signaled morphine as a modern medicine worthy of a new pharmaceutical era.[55] This marketing confidence belied the continuing improvisation around opium imports in the same period. Pharmaceutical manufacturers continued to mull over the question of whether or not one day they might grow opium domestically. For the time being, they continued to rely on the relationships they had with purchasers in Smyrna, Salonica, and Constantinople, or merchants in Persia or Egypt when they ran short.[56]

Even if growing opium domestically at scale was not a viable option for these manufacturers, there were other supplies available, both near and far, that importers might have considered. By the turn of the twentieth century, Mexico's Pacific ports had become opium entrepôts—a

Figure 3.2 An advertisement for New York Quinine and Chemical Works' different preparations of opium, 1897. *The Pharmaceutical Era.*

southern counterpart to those on the American West Coast.[57] Opium smoking in Mexico's booming Chinatowns was the pretext for a fervently xenophobic backlash. But even as they heaped opprobrium on Chinese users, Mexican consumers were just as fond of opium-based patent medicines as their US counterparts. Chinese laborers may have been the first to plant opium fields in Sinaloa, Sonora, Durango, and Nayarit, but Mexican cultivators quickly followed their lead. Baja California's governor helped turn the state into an easy transshipment point for opium going north. American importers did not look south. Nor did they look to the many other places around the world where opium was being transplanted into new ecologies and state projects—in Afghanistan, for example, where the new emir, Abdur Rahman Khan, was ordering the planting of poppies around Jalalabad to smuggle or export into India for consumption there.[58] American importers remained reliant on the import networks they had been cultivating since the early nineteenth century, rooted in the Eastern Mediterranean.

The ascendant American pharmaceutical industry was linked, like so many other domains of commerce, to the control of commodities in far corners of the world.[59] In the absence of domestic production, preparations like NYQ's cube morphine and Mrs. Winslow's Soothing Syrup—a pediatric formulation meant to, and which undoubtedly did, calm fussy infants—all required the import of the same distant product. But opium was a strange commodity. It was neither dispersed widely like the world's staple crops, nor was it wholly linked, like quinine, qat, or coca, to a particular ecology. Opium's lumpy global distribution was not a product of ecology in any significant manner. Instead, it was the legacy of empires on the precipice of decentralization. That legacy was remarkably difficult to change. And as opium itself became the object of new scrutiny worldwide, it was easier for some to imagine a world where opium was replaced altogether, rather than a world where opium's networks were fundamentally remade.

Figure 3.3 Mrs. Winslow's Soothing Syrup, an opium- and alcohol-based "patent medicine" which was meant to calm fussy infants, with occasionally fatal consequences. National Library of Medicine.

Beginning around the time that Emanuel Weiss offered up his proposal for an American opium industry, the global opium regime was being broken down wholesale by an emerging transnational network of reformers.[60] Over the course of several decades, these reformers—missionaries, diplomats, women's activists, and public health reformers—transformed opium from a wholly acceptable item of global trade into an object of intense global scrutiny and regulation. The impetus of this reform was Asian, but soon called into being a wider network of collaborators in Europe and the United States. In 1869, Prince Gong, a high-ranking Qing official, issued a scathing critique of the opium trade, accusing Britain of deliberately poisoning China for profit. Gong's demarche resonated widely in Europe and the United States, and the trope of China's ruin through opium served as a new and potent rallying cry for anti-opium sentiments worldwide. Soon, other voices were taking up the cudgel against opium. Soonderbai Powar, from India, cast opium as an insidious form of Asian slavery. In Singapore, the brilliant physician Lim Boon Keng lobbied his elite colleagues against the anti-modern practices of Chinese queue-wearing and opium alike. Public sentiment against opium rose up precipitously in Burma, where, its British commissioner wrote in 1880, "native opinion is unanimous in favour of stopping the supply altogether, and no measure we could adopt would be so popular with all the respectable and law-abiding classes of the population."[61] In 1906, after nearly a century of conflict, British and Chinese representatives signed the "Ten Year Agreement," a pact that stipulated a quick end for British exports of Indian opium to China, and China's elimination of opium cultivation and use.[62]

American diplomats had watched anti-opium fervor mount for decades, as the ambitions of its merchants in China clashed with the moral implications of a dubious trade.[63] They were thrust into the debate more directly when the United States acquired the Philippines, and William Howard Taft, its newly appointed governor, faced the question of how to manage the opium trade in the new territory.[64] Taft's lieutenant in this campaign, Charles Brandt, was a Canadian-born Episcopalian bishop who worked with fervor to combat opium use in the Philippines before organizing an international conference that he hoped would deliver a knockout blow to the opium trade. "It is at Shanghai," the *New York Times* effused, "that the nations of earth are drawing back to deliver what is hoped will prove to be the knockout blow" to the opium trade.[65] But the European powers who participated in the International Opium Commission in Shanghai in 1909 fiercely defended their opium monopolies, making self-serving cases for the "quasi-medical" use of opium in their possessions which scarcely concealed their financial imperatives.[66] Two years later, a follow-up convention in The Hague offered a stricter set of international drug controls, albeit riddled with countless loopholes and exceptions.

For their flaws, the Shanghai and Hague conferences represented a new assertiveness in American approaches to the Asian and global opium trade. If Asian reform had transformed opium from a legitimate commodity to a mendacious vice, ascendant American power would consign it to unequivocal illegality. Hamilton Wright, an Ohio-born physician who had inveighed against opium's ravages during a long career in China, Japan, India, and Malaya, had been appointed the United States' first Opium Commissioner and served as its delegate to Shanghai. His reputation as a zealot notwithstanding, Wright was able to whip up support in the House of Representatives for a new piece of legislation that restricted the ways in which American druggists could sell opium-based products domestically. The Harrison Narcotics Act, passed in 1914, was also a tool that diplomats could use as they promoted an increasingly fervent prohibitionist agenda overseas.[67] Over the next decade, US representatives underwrote the passage of increasingly ambitious international legislation, from the provisions for the ratification of the Hague Opium Convention in the Treaty of Versailles to the League of Nations' assumption of responsibility for overseeing drug control efforts, rendering the issue a staple of international relations.

Within this prohibitionist turn was a set of unresolved contradictions: The substances that proponents of this incipient international order sought to regulate remained among the most important raw materials of modern pharmaceutical practice. The reconfiguration of one of those substances, however, offered a roadmap for what might be done to another. Cocaine, the wonder drug of the late nineteenth century, had become the object of great scrutiny in the United States in the century's last decade. A new ideology of "anticocainism," fueled by racial anxieties over Black use and progressive concerns over corporate power and greed, had dramatically reined in its medical use.[68] Cocaine's space for legitimate medical use had been drastically curtailed by the turn of the century, but in 1896, the Frankfurt-based firm Schering & Glatz introduced the first equivalently priced synthetic replacement for cocaine, eucaine, to the United States, billing it as a "substitute for cocaine that is free of its disadvantages."[69] Several years later, Farbwerke Hoechst brought procaine on the market as Novocain, touting it explicitly as a non-addicting substitute for cocaine in topical anesthesia. Though cocaine was already marginal in medicine before these substitutes, the rise of Novocain, amid a new era of global prohibition, posed an urgent question: could a synthetic replacement for opium provoke a similar revolution?

As the First World War scrambled opium networks worldwide, one man was particularly keen to help answer that question. New York's Herman Metz had made his name and his riches as a manufacturer and importer of chemicals and dyes.[70] His specialty was coal tar, and all the colors that could be produced from its derivatives, from bright scarlets for lipstick and blush to deep blues for working clothes. Metz was a titan of a fundamentally disruptive industry. A century earlier, India's deep indigo had made fortunes for British merchants when Napoleonic blue became the go-to shade of global fashion, before sturdy new synthetic blues entered the market at the turn of the twentieth century and those fortunes crumbled.

As Metz traded industry for politics, serving briefly as a Democratic House Representative, he found himself caught up in the prohibitionist impulses of the era. In 1916, he had been called upon by a group of judges to help envision "remedial legislation for the drug evil."[71] He was inspired by the introduction of Novocain, which had proven a harmless substitute

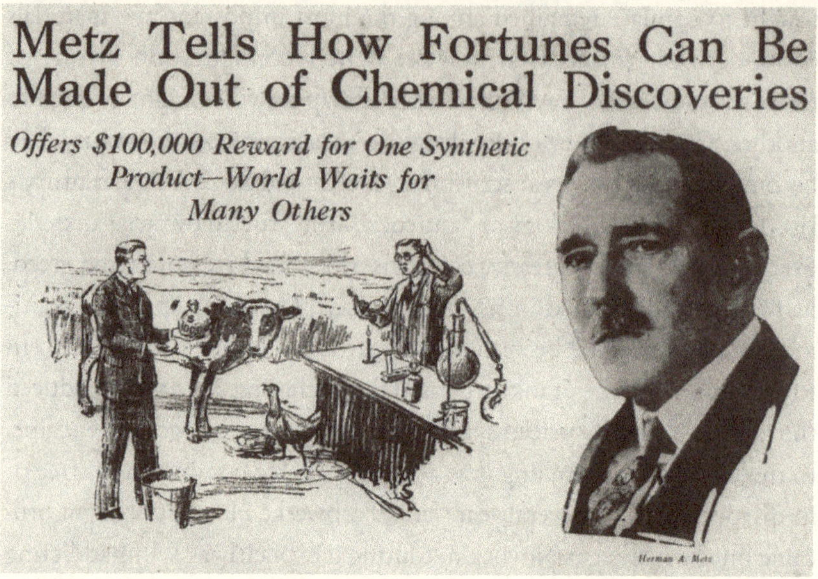

Metz Tells How Fortunes Can Be Made Out of Chemical Discoveries

Offers $100,000 Reward for One Synthetic Product—World Waits for Many Others

Figure 3.4 Herman Metz's $100,000 prize for the first scientist to develop a commercially viable formula for "synthetic morphine" crystalized the fantasy of a painkiller that did not require opium to produce. *The Brooklyn Daily Eagle.*

for cocaine in many analgesic applications.[72] Opium, Metz thought, was not so dissimilar from the world of dyes he knew so well, where raw agricultural commodities had been rendered useless by the advent of good synthetic substitutes. There was work underway, he saw, but proceeding too slowly. Heroin offered a blueprint for drugs that modified opium's action, but what was needed was a product that would wholly replace the poppy. In 1925, Metz advertised a staggering $100,000 prize—the equivalent of around two million dollars—to the first chemist to produce a commercially viable formula for synthetic morphine. That chemist would need to be civic-minded; the compound's commercial value, Metz admitted, was far greater than that hefty award. But, he ventured, there were "many chemists in this country who would gladly turn over such a formula as a safeguard for the public health to the Government."

Metz's proposal was less warmly received than he had hoped. Critics were quick to point out the obvious flaw: narcotic drugs' dependence on a limited supply of raw materials was an important check on their overall supply. "If the habit-forming drugs may be made anywhere by anybody who knows how," *Scientific Monthly* contended, "the question ceases to be an international issue and becomes a matter of local police powers."[73] The rise of "moonshine morphine" would be an even harder problem to solve than that of opium. Others were plainer in their critique. Leading New York journalist John Palmer Gavit could envision no worse plan than the easy manufacture of a morphine-like compound anywhere in the world.[74] The amount of opium-based drugs in circulation, Gavit calculated, was already four times larger than the world's two billion people required. Synthetic morphine, he warned, would represent a "new and dangerous factor in a problem already sufficiently baffling."

The project was as technically challenging as it was politically unpalatable, and American researchers were also particularly underprepared to take it on. As a leading Harvard pharmacologist wrote at the time, the "field of medical research in which the United States is most conspicuously backward is that concerned with the discovery of drugs."[75] After setbacks during the First World War, German pharmaceutical researchers had rapidly leapfrogged their American counterparts, making quick strides developing opiates that either modified the chemical structure of opium alkaloids significantly or sometimes obviated the need for opium altogether. Three years after Metz's proposal, the US National Research Council's Committee on Drug Addiction sponsored a similar effort to develop a compound with all of morphine's palliative properties, but none of its addictive potential.[76] But during a decade's research, the Americans only managed to synthesize a compound they named desomorphine, around the same time that Swiss and German chemists did the same. It was ten times more powerful by weight than morphine, but just as addictive, and was removed from the market shortly after its introduction.[77] Each successive compound that reputable American, German, and Swiss researchers discovered, whether confined to the laboratory or released onto the market, seemed to have a greater propensity for addiction than the older opiates. (Perhaps equally damningly was the realization that Metz's critics had been correct: the promise of synthetic opiates was as attractive to the underworld as it was to legitimate researchers.

Federal agents kept tabs on gangsters in Hong Kong and southern China rumored to be employing German chemists to produce a black-market substitute.[78]) Each such failure deepened researchers' conviction that, for scientific and political reasons alike, poppy, unlike coca leaf or cinchona, was indispensable in the production of modern pharmaceuticals.

☽☉☾

Before and after the ravages of the Civil War, Emanuel Weiss had dreamed of an American opium empire. In Arizona, he could see American enterprise remaking the world of medicine and trade by planting the world's most useful substance in American soil. If his vision was most radical and concrete, Weiss was far from alone in asking why a crop that could be grown productively in many climates needed to be imported. Early American physicians and druggists had asked similar questions, planting experimental fields across the country with poppies that thrived in the country's northeast, south, and west. The idea had grown even more compelling in the years after the Civil War, when the dismantling of a violent cotton industry begged the question of what might productively replace it. The idea was no less compelling in Europe, where French and German experimentation yielded equally acceptable products and stoked equally bold visions.

As that question lingered, the world of pharmacy itself was also remade. German researchers applied the lessons they had learned in crafting a dye and chemical industry to the related world of pharmaceuticals, producing a field characterized by heavy state investment and focused, diligent research. Americans lagged behind their German counterparts, but made up for it in marketing acumen and a keen awareness of how to transform and sell the products that they imported from distant shores. The question of opium refracted a larger set of questions in nineteenth-century capitalism—how best to command and leverage faraway commodities in the service of expanding use—but was inflected by the notion, advanced in its closing decades, that opium was no longer the purview of legitimate commerce. As the prohibitionist agenda turned into a new regime of global governance, the fantasy of domestic cultivation—at least in the United States—gave way to the hope that opium might be replaced by a synthetic substitute entirely. No such replacement, however, was forthcoming. New opium-like compounds were more potent than morphine, but more addictive as well.

Herman Metz's proposal, separated by a half century from Emanuel Weiss's, represented a similar hunger for new arrangements and a sense that the world of pharmaceutical opiates needed radical transformation. The failure of both proposals hinted that opium's future would remain rooted in politics more than climate, ecology, or science and that for those nations which required opium for their modernizing pharmaceutical industries, the management of distant agrarian production would represent a preeminent imperative of geopolitics. War would soon remake this management again, as the United States' growing political prowess drew up more of the world's opium-growing peasantry into its expanding orbit, remaking cultivators' lives and livelihoods in turn.

4

Bureaucratizing Opium

Mümtaz Ziya and his revolutionary comrades never shied away from the biggest issues of the day.[1] As writers for *Kadro*, a radical socialist magazine published in Ankara in the 1930s, they spilled endless vats of ink describing just how the Turkish Republic's new *devletçilik*, or statist, economy should function. Liberal capitalism and Soviet-style communism, they knew, had both failed, and if the Kemalist revolution in Turkey were to serve as a blueprint for a "third way," it was essential that they tackle even the thorniest questions of national development. For Ziya, it was simple: was opium not the biggest question of all?

Opium concretized the challenges facing the Turkish economy. A quintessential agricultural product and lifeline for the country's peasantry, it also embodied their crisis. Its price had fallen precipitously since the Great Depression, but more critically, the crop itself had become anathema in global trade, rendering the whole of Turkey's national economic project suspect. The new national monopoly in opium had borne little fruit. The opium issue had, in essence, alarmed "all those interested in maintaining the disorganized state of affairs that works against our national economy."

The world, Ziya reported, had become saturated with opium, and it was no wonder that the prices paid for the Turkish crop had plummeted. The countries of the Far East that had traditionally bought Turkey's opium were abandoning those old habits. Turkey remained the major supplier to the European and American pharmaceutical houses, but the twenty or so buyers were, he knew, a "cartel" conspiring to fix prices and keep opium sellers poor. Other countries provided useful points of comparison. Russia's command economy had allowed it to expand its own domestic production, and the thought that it might export its opium one day was a daunting one. Iran had made efforts to render its own production more attractive. Mostly, Ziya looked at India. Though it had been forced to shut off the spigot in response to League of Nations agreements, India had long run its opium exports as a state monopoly, offering long-term contracts to consuming countries and giving what he imagined were favorable terms to producers as well.

Ankara, Ziya wrote, could readily help the Turkish peasant and the national economy by nationalizing the purchase and sale of the country's opium, control the amount that reached the world market, and most of all, it could help Turkey develop "new markets, beyond the ones we have been tied to until now." Turkey could reasonably hope to double its historic highs in opium revenue to 20 million liras—a sum that, at close to 10 percent of the national budget, could pay for no end of infrastructure for the new and ambitious republic.

Ziya's proposal was foresighted in certain ways and off base in others. Within a year's time, Turkey's republican government would indeed nationalize the country's opium industry. Its producers would be organized into a corporatist union, and the country would accede to the international regulations it had spent a decade eschewing in exchange for a privileged role in global trade. His thoughts of developing new opium markets in Asia were less prescient: Southeast and East Asian countries, too, would come to accept the terms of global prohibition and put an effective end to their own domestic recreational use. Yet Ziya's scheme to harness opium's economic might in the service of national development was representative of a wider vision in this period, one that animated great hope in the two historic producing countries of Turkey and India. In the face of growing international prohibitionist pressure, voices like Ziya's made strident and cogent cases for opium's continuance, arguing that it was an important, even indispensable resource that could be put in the service of national development.

From the closing decades of the nineteenth century, European and American prohibitionists had cast opium as an increasingly unviable object of global trade. Morally suspect and economically untenable, opium seemed destined, from this vantage, for total extirpation. Even if opium were, for the moment, still required for an expanding modern pharmaceutical market, it, too, could be replaced by synthetics like so many other once-valuable commodities. Synthetic aniline dyes had undercut indigo, cochineal, and madder. New fertilizers had rendered guano just so many bird droppings. Opium, from Geneva or Washington, or from certain circles in Bombay, Saigon, or Hong Kong, seemed destined for a similar end.

This posture of terminal decline was far from apparent in the sites where opium was consumed, traded, and, most of all, produced. In the opening decades of the twentieth century, a disparate set of actors, motivated by divergent and often contradictory rationales, made fervent cases for opium's continuance.[2] These actors made for strange, even impossible bedfellows: the merchants and traders who continued to ply Indian opium overseas; the colonial banks that financed opium purchases and became entangled in its storage; the Asian entrepreneurs with investments in opium farms; the dock workers, rickshaw pullers, and coolies who used opium as a palliative; and the tax farmers, physicians, and labor contractors who all saw useful economic, medical, and social ends for the drug.

In Southeast Asia, the many different groups involved with the opium trade—financiers, shippers and brokers, and local buyers and sellers, no less than colonial bureaucrats themselves—advanced distinct, self-serving, and often contradictory ideas about the value of continuing it.[3] Yet pro-opium forces were more coherent in the context of India and Turkey, where, in a contemporary moment, both forward-looking economic modernizers and more reactionary forces were imagining what role opium might play in national and regional political economies, respectively. For economic nationalists in Turkey, optimistic about the modernizing schemes of the Kemalist state, opium was a resource that could be transformed into essential infrastructure. Wrenched from the control of smugglers and the mafia—and, in a context of rising xenopho-bia, the Jews and Christians so long associated with the trade—Ankara could transform an essential staple of the Anatolian landscape into the capital needed for its infrastructural designs. In India, where sovereignty and administration were divided between direct British administration and the indirect, regional rule of its princely states, opium was differen-tially though no less acutely seen as a potent resource for economic futures. The rulers of "native states," generally hostile toward the designs of global prohibition, foot-dragged and complied fitfully with British India's efforts to bring the trade to heel, aware of the licit and illicit excise revenue that opium brought to their territories. For India's mainstream nationalists, opium in its unreformed state was inappropriate to the modernizing imperatives of the incipient state—but the bureaucracy that controlled its cultivation, processing, and export was anticipating and planning for an industry attuned to opium's legitimate uses in pharmaceuticals.

Increasingly—as Ziya had suggested—both states would bureaucra-tize the problem of opium. In Turkey, after other models had failed, opium would become the purview of a new state monopoly designed to regulate opium's commercial life within the country and control its export to manufacturers overseas. In India, British administrators would compel reluctant princely rulers to comply with the new imperatives of international regulation, before engulfing much of opium's institutional machinery within the state's Central Board of Revenue. As these bureau-cracies tightened their respective controls over opium's cultivation, mar-keting, and sales, their administrators were increasingly bound to a small number of useful end markets. The European pharmaceutical market had long commanded a major share of the Turkish product. But the United States would soon come to make outsized claims on the opium that both the Turkish and Indian monopolies produced. As German pharmaceutical prowess yielded to its expanding American counterpart after the former's decimation in the Second World War, India's and Turkey's opium grew destined, increasingly, to the needs of American drug-making.

That the United States could and did make these claims through economic might and legislative fiat is unsurprising: the expansive American narcotics bureaucracy has long been seen as being central to the remaking of the postwar drug order. But zealous bureaucrats, in deciding which producers could indeed produce the United States'—and to a lesser extent, much of Europe's—opium did not simply look to places where it grew in abundance. Rather, they could turn to the increasingly legible bureaucracies in Turkey and India that had grown out of new projects of state consolidating and building: the republican revolution in Turkey and the nationalist movement in India, each advancing claims about how powerful new economies might operate at home and in the wider world.

◁◐▷

Opium posed a dilemma for Ottoman Muslim nationalists as they envisioned a new republic and debated the role that opium might play within it.[4] The Young Turk Revolution of 1908, led by the Committee of Union and Progress, ushered in a new sense of Turkish identity, distinct from a wider imperial Ottoman identity. Opium's associations with so many nonmodern, non-Turkish aspects of the Empire's economic life rendered it increasingly suspect. Opium was a lucrative Anatolian household and agricultural staple, and in port cities it was rendered wholly modern by chemical assays and industrial standardization. But the industry was still heavily governed by hereditary inspectors, and the significant involvement of Jews and Armenian Christians in the trade, as in many other industries, fueled the Young Turk notion that non-Muslims were complicit in the West's plans to subjugate the Ottoman state and economy.

Ottoman opium consolidated its position in global pharmaceuticals after the outbreak of the Great War. In spite of an initial decline in exports early in the war, Anatolian opium saw increased demand from pharmaceutical producers in Europe and the United States. But opium's management was a problem for the government formed by the Committee of Union and Progress in 1913. A year after a coup brought the Young Turks to power, its government abolished the long-standing system of "capitulations," commercial privileges given to foreign powers, which they correctly perceived as undercutting Ottoman sovereignty. Internationally, opium was subject to new international restrictions after The Hague Conference of 1912; at home, it was under new scrutiny on account of the outsized role that Jews and Christians played in managing its trade.[5]

Nissim Taranto, who had built one of the Empire's most impressive modern trading houses and who enjoyed a close relationship with many CUP members, felt the shift acutely. Writing to a French correspondent in the midst of the Balkan conflicts that shortly preceded the Great War, he lamented that, in spite of high global demand, traders could not export. "Despite the progressive increase in opium prices," he wrote, "native traders have little or no benefit from this movement, and the Government has indirectly contributed to this state of affairs."[6] Seven years later, writing in the wake of the Paris Peace Conference, Taranto wondered whether Turkey's days as an exporter were numbered. "This product is losing a large part of its commercial importance," he wrote. The global sentiment against opium was formidable, and the increased quality of India's opium, he added, had made it a "new competing producer."[7] Taranto's concern was both prescient and premature. Trading houses managed, for some years after the Great War, to sell effectively to both black-market and pharmaceutical purchasers.[8] Fils de Jacob Scialom, the Salonica-based trading firm, relocated from Salonica to Belgrade shortly after the war, where it sold Balkan opium to Mallinckrodt in St. Louis.[9] Taranto sold his wares to Merck and heroin makers alike.[10] G.B.E. Keun, scion of the legendary Smyrna trading firm, sold to European manufacturers from a sophisticated building on the Alsancak seafront.

Nonetheless, when the Grand National Assembly declared Mustafa Kemal president of the new Turkish Republic in 1923, there was no certainty about what would happen to these venerable trade networks. The ruling elites of the new states were split as to how opium might be managed.[11] Those in the Ministry of Economy were keenly aware of the wealth generated by a vital export crop and the value that it might have in meeting the republic's vast fiscal needs. Bureaucrats in the Ministry of Health, perhaps expectedly, saw opium as a "poison" increasingly at odds with the emerging international laws of the day. Overseas, Turkish officials uniformly bristled at the charges that its opium industry was a wholly illegitimate one. Mazhar Bey, Turkey's representative to the League of Nations, lambasted any proposed "restriction on her economic growth," likening international regulations on opium to the capitulation system that had so long stymied Turkish sovereignty and growth.[12]

The young Turkish Republic, eschewing the new restrictions of the 1925 Geneva Convention that limited opium production beyond medical needs, became a magnet for investors in a trade increasingly scorned elsewhere. Izmir's once-formidable infrastructure for opium exports had been decimated by the fire in 1922 that had marked the nadir of the Turkish campaign against its Armenian and Greek populations. Constantinople quickly became the center of a free-wheeling gray-market opium business. Japanese capital was the first to arrive in the city.[13] While Japan's growing pharmaceutical industry had long purchased alkaloids from European firms, the Turkish Chamber of Commerce was quick to suggest that they cut out the middlemen. The Oriental Products Company, established by Japanese entrepreneurs in a dilapidated building in the Mecidiye Barracks, quickly grew to employ a large team of Japanese-trained workers and exported substantial quantities of morphine and heroin to Asia.[14] The Taranto family, with patronage from important republican politicians and investment from a French pharmaceutical firm, founded their own larger factory, Etkim, in Istanbul's Eyüp neighborhood.[15] And the Turkish Pharmaceutical and Chemical Company, the largest of the three, opened on the Asian side of the Bosphorus with investments from Belgian and Mexican businessmen, producing codeine and papaverine for pharmaceutical buyers. While some of these factories' products were used for pharmaceuticals, the overwhelming majority found its way into the illicit trade: morphine and heroin circulated easily in suitcases and olive oil tins to Europe and the United States, and turned up in Egypt, Hong Kong, Shanghai, Tianjin, and Saigon.

Turkish politicians were full of bluster. The republic's silver-tongued ambassador deflected calls in Geneva for Ankara to abandon the trade.[16] But it was the direct threat of losing its largest legitimate pharmaceutical market that forced its hand. Since slightly before the crisis of 1929, American manufacturers, loath to touch the Turkish product, had substituted it with Yugoslav opium.[17] In late 1930, a bill in the US Congress introduced legislation banning the purchase of opium derivatives from countries that had not complied with The Hague Convention. A month later, authorities shuttered the three Istanbul factories.[18] The decision upset many of Mustafa Kamal's confidants, who joined Leon Taranto, Nissim's son, in protesting a capitulation to international pressure.[19] The other factory managers saw the writing on the wall. The Japanese factory owners burned it to the ground to collect its insurance policy, while the Belgian-Mexican venture was sold off immediately for parts.[20]

Turkey's political leadership played for time. In the summer of 1932, the Turkish Grand National Assembly passed a law establishing a new Turkish Opium Producers' Union.[21] The Assembly's formation of a corporatist union had lofty goals. It would call together the country's 150,000 opium cultivators, pool and manage their excess stocks of opium to protect against price crashes, and organize the country's opium production within a single institutional framework. Every opium producer would be required to join the union, report his crops to the board of directors governing his respective opium zone, and sell the whole of his crop on predetermined dates. Mostly, however, the union was a strategy meant to convince international bodies that Ankara was taking the problem of opium smuggling seriously without enacting real change.

The gambit was a losing one. Turkish merchants, by the 1930s, were already anxious about the stigma that the country's association with illicit wares would have on its other areas of trade.[22] At the end of 1932, pessimistic about the economic consequences that resisting international legislation might portend, Mustafa Kemal made the case to the Council of Ministers that Turkey had no choice but to accede to the terms of The Hague and Geneva Conventions.[23] The Istanbul factories would remained shuttered, the country would police smuggling, and all raw opium sold would go through the union and the state. Little changed on the ground. Quickly, small morphine and heroin workshops replaced the large factories. But in short order, Turkey's representatives signed on to the international agreements they had so thoroughly repudiated just years before. "As a Republican regime," Celal Bayar, Turkey's Minister of Economics, wrote shortly thereafter, "we are obliged to prove that we act with integrity, first to ourselves and then to the entire world."[24]

Several months later, the Grand National Assembly passed another piece of ambitious legislation, establishing the Narcotic Substances Monopoly as a well-funded new division of the Ministry of National Economy.[25] The Monopoly would limit the provinces in which opium could be traded, surveil the movement of opium within the country, and coordinate its export to pharmaceutical buyers overseas. It would, via an official agreement, collaborate with its counterpart in Yugoslavia to synchronize the export of the region's opium.[26] In the broadest terms, as one longtime student of the Turkish trade noted, the Monopoly would "clean up the managed economy of opium while safeguarding the legitimate interests of the growers," rendering it a wholly salubrious national industry.

The national strategy that Mümtaz Ziya had described a year earlier had come into being, and the entire apparatus seemed designed to show the modernizing imperatives of the Turkish Republic. "If you want to see a very modern office," the state mouthpiece *Cumhuriyet* trumpeted, "visit the General Directorate of the Narcotic Substances Monopoly."[27] There, on the fourth floor of an Ankara office building, a smartly dressed team worked away in a wood and glass office, files kept in "state-of-the-art metal cabinets," all open plan and visible to the manager so that no one could be absent, come late, or ignore the work of processing opium cultivators' applications and arranging for export permits. Ali Sami Bey and Sefik Feyzi Bey, the office managers, had created an extraordinarily sleek office, "rare even in Europe." The office set to work permitting cultivators, asking for declarations of stock, and arranging for auctions.[28] In well-placed features overseas and in a glossy publicity book with a foreword

Figure 4.1 Publicity photographs of Turkish opium monopoly workers preparing cakes of opium, 1934. *The Illustrated London News.*

by Celal Bayar, the Monopoly lauded its smooth operations, which brought opium from the country's interior to pharmaceutical firms overseas.[29]

The Monopoly's pride was somewhat aspirational. For the first several years of its operations, large European and American firms appear to have engaged in a de facto boycott of the Monopoly, unwilling to patronize a national industry still tainted by its illicit predecessor. But Turkish diplomats worked to tout the Monopoly's efforts at home and overseas. Shortly after the Monopoly was moved from the Ministry of National Economy to the Office of Agricultural Products, the Monopoly's director, Hamza Osman Erkan, spoke in Geneva of the "sincere and great sacrifices" the nation had made on the opium issue.[30] He lamented that, since nationalizing and legitimizing its trade, Turkey had exported a piddling amount of opium at "very low prices that have never been recorded in the country's opium history." Its opium producers, already poor, were growing more precarious. If countries in Europe and the United States wished Turkey "to go even further," he suggested, it would need them to take seriously the plight of the Turkish opium cultivator. There were hints at the carrots and sticks that Turkey's representatives would offer foreign partners in the decades to come.[31]

For the time being, there was some subdued optimism about what the future might portend.[32] Ihno Bensussan had grown up with the Ottoman opium industry, before watching the world he knew collapse before his eyes.[33] A Greek Jew from Salonika, Bensussan had learned the trade under the supervision of Albert Scialom, heir to the storied Fils de Jacob Scialom trading house. His work took him to the poppy fields of Macedonia, and not infrequently to Anatolia as well. During the Great War, he had helped leverage connections in Italy and France to try to help the firm evade an Entente blacklist of Salonican firms that also traded with the Central Powers. At the war's end, he had followed Scialom to Belgrade but eventually fled Serbia for Paris. His luck grew worse and worse. As he watched the deportation of Jews from Paris in terror, narrowly avoiding the same fate, Bensussan distracted himself by poring through the endless stacks of clippings on opium he had kept as remnants of a commercial world now gone. At turns maudlin and boastful—Bensussan described himself as once the "principal supplier of opium" to Europe's pharmaceutical industry—the aging trader paid particular attention to what was taking place in the young Turkish Republic.

Bensussan claimed to know the Turkish peasant well. "Rustic but thoughtful," he recalled, "tenacious, industrious, intelligent in certain respects, and full of common sense, Turkish farmers generally lived isolated, uninformed and without sustained contact with the rest of the world and almost the rest of the country. The price of the opium they harvested rarely aligned with the labor the crop cost them." The years since he had last been in Turkey had been filled with tragedy for these peasants and for the Jews and Christians who had been pushed out of the trade. But he allowed himself a bit of muted optimism about the future of the Turkish trade. The "sensible men, full of calm and composure," who staffed the new Turkish Narcotics Monopoly had given themselves an ambitious set of charges. They were to align Turkey with the norms of international law, stabilize the prices paid to Turkey's poppy farmers, train those cultivators in modern methods, and improve the quality of the country's poppy itself. These were tall orders, not entirely free of contradiction. But with other sources of poppy available to European manufacturers—not least the possibility of growing their own—"it is almost certain that Turkey will feel compelled, in order to escape the ruin of its opium farming, to play the card of creating a national narcotics industry," one keenly attuned to the needs of modern pharmacy.

◖○◗

As the British Indian opium monopoly and the regimes it had managed in the country's west had yielded to the transnational imperatives of prohibition, imperial administrators were faced with a mounting set of challenges that transcended mere economics. Despite decades of declining revenue, British bureaucrats clung to the notion that their vast opium apparatus, which managed the economic lives of millions of peasants, could be put into the service of something productive and remunerative. Increasingly, this view was at odds not only with prohibitionists, but with incipient nationalist voices in India that saw the vestigial opium industry as an affront to the nation's moral and material well-being. Yet opium remained integral to the social fabric of much of the country— and more importantly, it was a potent economic force in India's princely states, where authorities relied on direct revenue and levies to fund their own governance and consumption.

Even as the Royal Commission on Opium had staved off the industry's complete collapse, the value of the Indian opium trade had declined precipitously since the 1870s. The China trade was given a fatal blow in 1906, when an imperial edict from Beijing had commanded "that within a period of ten years the evils arriving from foreign and native opium be equally and completely eradicated."[34] A year later, an Anglo-Chinese agreement outlined the terms of opium export reductions from India over a three-year trial period. The *New York Times* was succinct in its assessment of the agreement: "Opium Trade Doomed."[35] In 1911, the agreement was renewed, with British officials successfully arguing for a gradual end to the trade by 1917. But as Chinese provinces banned imports unilaterally and prices for Indian opium stayed high, Britain reversed course. Its agents ended the auctioning of opium in late 1912, and the last case of Indian opium was shipped to China a few months later. What remained was a small flow of opium exported to Nepal, East Africa, Burma, and Aden, and the substantive domestic "excise" product sold to Indians for "quasi-medical" use.[36]

The cessation of the opium trade in British India itself was implemented with relative ease. Since the turn of the century, bureaucrats in Calcutta and then New Delhi had crafted ever more stringent regulations on how opium was to be traded. They had grown ever more precise in how poppy products were labeled, had prohibited poppy cultivation altogether in some states, and had endeavored to replace excise opium grown in "native states" with opium grown within British India itself.[37] When the Anglo-Chinese agreement was signed, the bureaucracy in the Bengal Opium Agency set to work rapidly reducing the area whose cultivation its agents were overseeing.[38] Yet their work was made vastly simpler by the fact that many cultivators had already abandoned the crop: staples like rice, barley, wheat, chili peppers, potatoes, mustard, and sugarcane had seen their prices soar, while opium's prices had remained fixed for over a decade. "The future diminution and ultimate cessation of opium revenue," Indian economist Pramathanath Banerjea wrote in 1911 with an eye toward the country's future revenues, "is a matter of grave concern to the finances of India."[39] But India's British administrators had already come to dismiss its economic centrality to their own operations.

The notion of ending the opium trade was far more fraught in India's opium-growing "native states," semi-autonomous regions whose economies heavily relied on opium revenues. If the British administration might have wished to allow some autonomy to what they described, regardless of its actual region of cultivation, as the "Malwa" opium trade, their hands were forced by the 1912 International Opium Convention in The Hague. As a signatory to the Convention, Britain's Indian administration was obligated to implement the convention's provisions throughout its territories, including the princely states.[40] It did so in the way it had done so much proxy administration: by appointing one of its political agents to "guide" the states in modifying a template to fit the particulars of each state. After an initial conference in Lahore in 1922, where representatives were asked to help develop new regulations on opium's cultivation, manufacture, and possession, the states set to work enacting them with varying degrees of enthusiasm.[41] If abolition were a goal on paper, it proceeded in fits and starts, with princely state officials generally loath to participate too enthusiastically in the erosion of a generally lucrative commodity.[42] (Until the end of the 1910s, state governments were supporting the publication of pamphlets and tracts on the expansion and improvement of opium cultivation.[43])

British India had a limited number of carrots to offer opium-producing states. In the years following The Hague Convention, it made arrangements to purchase opium from states for excise sale in India, gradually reducing the quantity throughout the 1920s.[44] Its agents built a warehouse in Indore specifically to buy up the old stocks of opium that princely states were no longer sending to China.[45] As these stocks and British inducements dried up, and the prices of opium in British India increased, smugglers were quick to ferry in cheap opium from princely states.[46] Mewar State was a particular bane for British officials: its opium prices were rock-bottom, and its craggy hills offered easy cover for smugglers to move cheap contraband opium into directly administered territory.[47]

In 1926, the Viceroy of India, Lord Irwin, made an appeal to India's princes. "The Rulers of India," he wrote, "took their place beside us in the Great World War. I appeal to them to come forward and take their place beside us in another Great War: the war against drugs, which inflict damage so baneful and insidious upon the character and physique of the human race." India's poppy, he offered, "must not be allowed to stain the fair name of her sister-flower in Flanders." The Viceroy's purple appeal, made after the Geneva Conference on opium, was followed by a conference held in Shimla to discuss the possibility of ending the cultivation of opium in princely states altogether.[48] But India's princes showed scant interest in that conference and in the joint investigation committee established in its wake. For bulwarks of the old colonial regime, there was little to commend a policy of prohibition that would upend social orders and livelihoods with little apparent return.

In the wake of the Non-Cooperation Movement, India's first mass civil disobedience campaign, the mainstream Indian National Congress had hitched its wagon to the promise of prohibition. Mohandas Gandhi had pushed the Congress toward this stance. After an initial campaign to stamp out opium consumption in Assam, the Mahatma had lobbied the party in public and private to adopt a policy of prohibition in independent India.[49] For mainstream nationalists, opium's persistent cultivation and use in India was portrayed as a tangible example of the corruption of colonial rule, no less than its recurrent famines and its rapacious taxation: Jawaharlal Nehru, leader of the Indian National Congress, urged party members to raise the opium issue "continually both in the assembly and in outside agitations," linking the cause of Indian independence to the cause of prohibition itself.[50] Before the Geneva Convention, Gandhi and Rabindranath Tagore jointly called for a "total extirpation of the plants from which [opiate] drugs originate, except as found necessary for medicine."[51]

India's princes and their conservative allies had little patience for the Congress's moralizing stance. In international venues, they grew increasingly vocal in their defense of opium's merits. V.S. Srinivasa Sastri, a moderate liberal from Madras who preferred greater Indian autonomy to outright independence, declared the effort to limit opium's use to medical purposes an affront to Indian vernacular knowledge. "You do not know how opium is produced and is used in India," he told a League of Nations committee in 1923.[52] The Maharaja of Nawanagar urged the same body to consider opium "the Indian parallel to wine and beer in Europe and America."[53]

With India's future uncertain, and the tension over opium unresolved, its colonial administrators bureaucratized the problem. In 1935, the Government of India Act reorganized the working of the British administration in India, expanding some elements of Indian self-governance through new provincial autonomy. All this raised new questions about how opium was to be taxed or regulated in a new federal structure.[54] Increasingly, questions about opium were delegated to a new division within the Central Board of Revenue, India's tax office, where thornier political problems could largely be avoided.[55]

One particularly important question fell within the purview of this reorganized bureaucracy: whether or not Indian opium could be used, as a recent generation of administrators had hoped, to produce modern medical alkaloids. The Bengal government had, in the early 1900s, asked for the appointment of an English chemist to the Ghazipur opium factory laboratory with this very goal in mind.[56] Scientists in the laboratory conducted new experiments to see if usable alkaloids could be extracted from otherwise unusable opium with coal tar solvents.[57] Administrators in the United Provinces worked to import Persian opium seeds from Meshed and Isfahan to see if they could produce the levels of morphine required to supply to the London market.[58] After the Great War, the Indian government hired a number of British chemists to recommend improvements to the Ghazipur factory in the interests of modernizing its output for medical production.[59] The payoff was slow in coming. A plan to sell Indian opium to the United States was abandoned in the 1920s, and it was not until the Second World War that British importers would even contemplate the commodity.[60]

By the late 1930s, Asia's prepotent imperial industry had been reduced in meaningful terms to a modest wing of British India's tax collection service. Its physical infrastructure remained immense. Workers in the compound in Ghazipur streamed through open-air processing facilities, outsized storage warehouses, and countless administrative bungalows.

The Patna factory had been converted into a government press in 1912, but in 1933, a new factory had been opened in the dusty town of Neemuch, in the Malwa opium heartland, to produce alkaloids for military use.[61] Clerks, peons, and petty bureaucrats staffed a network of sub-agencies and *kothis*, which tendered licenses to perhaps two million cultivating families. The Government Opium Sale Room in Calcutta had been turned into a warehouse, like the newer one in Indore, and smaller facilities all across India's north held vast quantities of opium.[62] That opium, which had once flowed in great volumes to China, was nearly all destined for a dwindling domestic excise industry. A trickle flowed to buyers in other British territories and the French and Portuguese Indian colonies of Pondicherry and Goa.[63] The reluctance of princes to give up their own opium revenue and a sprawling administrative machine dedicated to opium production all begged the question of where—if it were not to simply disappear from the earth—Indian opium might eventually go.

One Indian civil servant felt this problem acutely. Bazlur Rahman was a consummate colonial bureaucrat.[64] He had done what many ambitious young Indian men did in the early twentieth century, joining the United Provinces Civil Services for an opportunity to excel in the prestigious bureaucracy. With no obvious background in poppy cultivation, Rahman had nonetheless climbed the ranks of the Opium Agency, impressing his superiors as he worked to improve the poppy crop in his jurisdiction. By the 1940s, with Indian independence a question of when, and not if, Rahman had been named Benares Opium Agent, working alongside his departing English counterpart who staffed the Bengal Agency. Despite the future's uncertainties, Rahman, as independence dawned, allowed himself some optimism. The Ghazipur facilities were slated for a big upgrade. Beyond the morphine that could be eked out there, it now seemed possible to extract thebaine as well. If that alkaloid was not yet in major demand, there was a growing interest in it from overseas pharmaceutical markets. India, Rahman concluded, had everything going for it. But its "future policy of production of alkaloids will depend on the possibility of the sale of the alkaloids in foreign markets."[65]

Throughout the 1920s and 1930s, dock workers in Philadelphia awaited the arrival of plodding ships stocked with Asian opium.[66] A stream of Persian opium arrived from Bushehr, the bustling port on Iran's Gulf coast. In the years when Yugoslav opium was playing an outsized role in American pharmaceuticals, that product went by rail from Belgrade to Trieste or Hamburg before heading across the Atlantic. Mostly, it was Turkish opium that arrived in American ports, whether purchased directly from Greek, Armenian, Dutch, and Jewish brokers or, in the years when direct purchases from Turkey were fraught, from traders at the Deutsche Bank und Disconto Gesellschaft.

Most of that opium looked similar: sticky brown balls of gum, wrapped in wax paper and sealed in wooden chests lined with tin. After the establishment of the Turkish monopoly, those chests bore the emblem of the Narcotic Substances Monopoly, a grid of intersecting shapes surrounded by the flares of the Turkish republican crescent.

Figure 4.2 Standardized Turkish opium being prepared for export in metal-lined wooden crates, 1950. United Nations.

Each shipment was accompanied by triplicated import permits, stamped by the American consulates that had issued them. When it arrived in Philadelphia, and the accompanying import permits were checked, stevedores unloaded the cases of opium, sending it by rail to its purchaser. Merck, the pharmaceutical giant in Rahway, New Jersey, took the major part of the imported opium. Mallinckrodt, in St. Louis, vied for freight space and a second share of the imports. In distant third was the New York Quinine and Chemical Works. Its titular drug and the cocaine it had once processed notwithstanding, NYQ imported only a small amount of opium, primarily for processing into codeine.

In opium's arrival in American ports in the 1930s, it was possible to imagine a world set to offer up its useful commodities to the United States' expanding regulatory authority and economic might—a sense that would grow more concrete after the transformations of the Second World War. For decades, Americans had been making ever larger claims about the resources which they were entitled to use and regulate. Missionaries, doctors, and social reformers had done this in their campaigns against opium at the turn of the century; by the 1920s, their capture of American diplomatic power was complete. Opium was far from the only commodity through and on which Americans were making new claim. In an era when European empires were faintly beginning to envision the ends of their own extractive economies, American diplomats and industrialists were coming to see the command of foreign markets, Asian ones most of all, as integral to the expansion of US power in the world.[67]

American empire resembled its European antecedents. It, too, was commodifying: it brought new goods into its orbit, and its proponents framed the accumulation of those goods as essential to the proper arrangement of global power and order. Unlike the French and British Empires, and the Spanish and Portuguese Empires before them, the US empire was less distinctly territorial. The United States' acquisition of territory—from the Midway Islands to Hawaii, the Philippines, Guam, Puerto Rico, and Samoa—ran less on bureaucracy and more on trade pacts and military leases. It midwifed goods and capital without much of a claim to direct rule and framed goods and not people as central to its expansion. And in this expanding empire, drugs were a particular form of commodity. Beef and coffee and rubber and tin were all goods that could be marshaled together in new ways. But narcotics like coca and opium had unique constructive powers in the creation of American empire: they were instruments for shaping human behavior, regulating populations, and segmenting the world into places that could legitimately or only illegitimately participate in the global market of drugs.[68]

The unique role that narcotics played in American power had been evident by the time American missionaries and reformers arrived in the Philippines. This role expanded radically through the relentless crusading of Harry Anslinger. Paranoid, xenophobic, and utterly uncompromising in his approach to the question of narcotics, Anslinger saw the globe through the lens of those substances and imagined an outsized role for the United States' expanding power in managing them.[69] There were few hints in his early career of the ways in which Anslinger would remake the world of global narcotics regulation. The son of Swiss and German immigrants had cut his teeth investigating insurance fraud for railroad companies before taking on a range of diplomatic and quasi-diplomatic roles in Europe, Japan, the Caribbean, and South America. Anslinger's singular obsession with narcotics and alcohol earned him a new position when he was, in 1930, recruited to serve as Commissioner of the Treasury Department's newly formed Federal Bureau of Narcotics, flush with a healthy budget and ambitious staff.

In the decade before the Second World War, Anslinger advanced a putative, prohibitive approach to narcotics control domestically, crusading against drug use, working to criminalize marijuana, and confronting physicians who prescribed narcotics. Overseas, he leveraged the Bureau's connections to advocate for stricter international controls on opium and coca, particularly in shaping the terms of the 1931 Geneva Convention. As Anslinger deployed the might of American diplomacy to dictate new restrictions on raw narcotic materials, he faced a corollary concern: how to ensure their abundant and ready supply for the needs of American pharmaceuticals. As the global landscape of opium procurement changed in the wake of successive agreements, Anslinger collaborated regularly with pharmaceutical executives—primarily at Merck and Mallinckrodt—to ensure their continued supply.

Anslinger was building on a preexisting legislative and commercial framework. During the First World War, shut off from finished German alkaloids, American importing firms had struggled to find the raw materials needed to produce opiate medicines, relying primarily upon older stockpiles. A decade later, the US Surgeon General had been granted authority to stockpile seized opium in case of a national emergency; over the next decade and a half, a reasonable cache was built up for this contingency, mostly stored next to gold bars in Fort Knox. The Second World War raised the question of whether this supply would indeed be enough to underwrite American pharmaceutical production in conflict, and prompted a new assertiveness in how the American procurement apparatus was to relate to the world's supply.

Two days after the Japanese bombing of Pearl Harbor, a group of pharmaceutical executives assembled in the Mayflower Hotel in Washington, DC. The head of the Federal Security Agency gave his assurances that the United States had stockpiled enough opium and quinine to last even a very long war.[70] Its scientists, he added, were close to making substitutes for each of these raw materials. But for Anslinger, the war was a justification to expand the power of the FBN over the procurement over raw materials, opium in particular. It was not merely the US stockpile the Commissioner was concerned about. The "preclusive purchasing" of opium could also keep the global glut of opium out of Axis hands and the black market alike.[71] Anslinger rebuffed manufacturers' requests to import opium on their own accord. Merck, Mallinckrodt, and NYQ agreed to let Anslinger manage the import of opium on their behalf.[72]

Turkey's Narcotic Substances Monopoly, attuned since 1933 to the needs of foreign pharmaceutical manufacturers, was a ready source for Anslinger's procurement operation—though, to the Commissioner's frustration, the Monopoly sold just as readily to the Axis Powers.[73] Anslinger was quick to co-opt the commercial networks of private industry into the service of governmental purchasing. Well after the

Monopoly's establishment, Merck had kept Leon Taranto on its payroll to inform the company about local conditions; the Commissioner fed this information to the American ambassador to Ankara to help advance his negotiations.[74] Turkish opium was difficult to ship in the midst of a war. Prices were high, and most traveled through the port of Basra, in British Iraq. But Anslinger, assisted closely by a Merck vice president, brokered creative agreements with Ankara, occasionally offering wheat in addition to cash.

India was a more ambivalent source for Anslinger's Bureau. The Commissioner had taken a particular interest in Indian opium from his earliest days in the role. He dog-eared copies of reports on India's excise opium and held frequent meetings with his counterparts in the Indian police.[75] Of particular concern to Anslinger had been the large excess stock of opium stored in countless Indian warehouses. In the absence of any substantive overseas purchasing for pharmaceuticals, this store seemed to Anslinger a dangerous supply for illicit use elsewhere in Asia.[76] The evidence of that oversupply grew even more apparent during the early years of the war, when American and Chinese sailors, having purchased opium legally from excise shops in India, were caught with opium in American cities with alarming frequency.[77] The Commissioner's series of purchases of Indian opium for American pharmaceutical use, beginning in 1941, represented another form of "preclusive purchasing": building up American stocks while reducing a possible source of illicit Asian opium.[78]

Preclusive purchasing was broadly unsuccessful in its aim of preventing opium from reaching the Axis Powers. Though German and Italian supplies were diminished, Turkey sold opium to Germany throughout the war, and German anxieties over raw material shortages had the unintended consequence of stoking research into new synthetic opiates.[79] The goal of acquiring an opium stockpile to weather even a much longer conflict was a clearer success. By the middle of 1943, even the most conservative estimates suggested that American stores were well above what was needed for pharmaceutical needs.[80] Before the war, American manufacturers and federal stockpilers had around 120 tons of morphine equivalent opiates; by the middle of the war, it had more than 400. Small amounts of that wartime stockpile, held in government medical depots in New York and Denver and the federal depository at Fort Knox, came from Iran, Bulgaria, and Afghanistan. Relatively scant amounts came from two experimental opium plots in Vermont and Washington State.[81] The overwhelming majority of the stockpile, doled out in amounts proportionate to prewar market share to the three major opium drug producers, came from Turkey and India, to the tunes of three-fourths and a fourth, respectively.

The United States' wartime procurement strategy had many knock-on effects. It helped the US pharmaceutical industry, once a capable but secondary competitor to its German counterpart, emerge from the war as its undisputed better. In short order, American firms would seize German pharmaceutical and chemical assets, co-opt German know-how, and craft a postwar strategy that deepened its own power in domestic and international contexts.[82] The three large importers who had lent expertise and authority to the Federal Bureau of Narcotics chafed at the terms under which their importing power had been subsumed to federal authority, but ultimately accepted the terms of the compromise in the interest of a closer relationship with the federal bureaucracy.[83] From the perspective of the world's opium-producing places, this ascendant American power had offered a place of privilege to both Turkey and India—the two producing nations whose modernizing bureaucracies had already put forward their opium as a legitimate, staple commodity of their new economic orders. The exact terms of that privilege were as yet indeterminate. In quantitative terms, Turkey offered far more to American producers than India did, and neither place was as free as its bureaucrats might have wished to use opium as a source of revenue for infrastructure and state-building. But if American might had divided the world's opium-producing places into more and less legitimate ones, Turkey and India were now squarely among the former.

❂

Opium, for a particular group of Indian and Turkish thinkers in the interwar years, had held out the promise of a lucrative commodity—but one that had national value beyond mere economic terms. A crop that had been the staple of imperial trade and power appeared, briefly, as something that new national or regional economies could harness on their own terms, underwriting projects of infrastructure and development. For India's princely leaders like the Maharaja of Nawanagar or the Diwan of Sitamau—who fought British officials for the right to retain control over excise opium in their own territories—opium was too bankable a crop to cede fully to the designs of international regulation.[84] Mümtaz Ziya, whose writers' collective would ultimately fall out of favor with Turkey's political elite as its business classes objected to its socialist fervor, imagined a world where new opium markets, perhaps in Asia, would underwrite a constructive program of infrastructural modernization. These visions, like many of the pro-opium arguments advanced in countries that largely consumed and did not produce the commodity, were fractured and contradictory. But they broadly held out that opium might be remade as a powerful staple in economies that did not quite accede to the rising global order.

By the middle of the 1930s, both Turkey and India had committed themselves—or had been committed—to new international restrictions on their opium output. Quickly, opium became managed within new and expanded state bureaucracies that rendered opium legible and legitimate to purchasers. The opium question, as Turkey consolidated its new republican regime and India's administrators prepared for eventual independence, increasingly became the purview of men like Hamza Osman Erkan, director of Turkey's Narcotic Substances Monopoly, or Bazlur Rahman, head of the Benares Opium Agency, technocrats ready to shepherd a useful product to new foreign markets in exchange for revenue and legitimacy.

In a similar period, the United States' new narcotics regime had come to formalize the increasingly important role that drugs were playing in notions of American power. Harry Anslinger's Federal Bureau of Narcotics had been making claims about drug production and consumption long before the Second World War, but the outbreak of conflict and questions over the adequacy of America's procurement efforts allowed the Commissioner to advance a bolder program of acquiring, not merely controlling, the world's opium. Yet this program was rendered possible only for Turkey and India's thick opium bureaucracies—new state machinery that had, in a matter of years, transformed opium into a managed, legible commodity purportedly under full state control.

In thirty years' time, Turkey and India's opium regimes had been wholly reengineered. The merchants and traders who had plied Turkish opium had been shut out of the trade, and the country's Monopoly was selling opium through a single channel to pharmaceutical buyers, primarily in the United States. A tiny amount of Indian opium flowed to other British territories, largely fulfilling other contracts, but where none had before gone to medical use, it subsequently flowed west, increasingly to the United States as well. In the aftermath of the Second World War, Turkey and India's strong opium bureaucracies were poised to play a critical role in the United States' pharmaceutical industry, their carefully managed opium becoming a key resource in the exercise of American economic and political power. Yet nothing was fixed about this arrangement. The new global opium order, bristling with contradiction, remained ripe for remaking.

5

Mr. Nargolwala Goes
to Mallinckrodt

In 1956, Dinshaw Nargolwala stepped off a plane at St. Louis's Lambert International Airport, anxious but brimming with optimism.[1] Just over forty, Nargolwala had never shied from a big challenge.[2] Like all members of the Indian Civil Service, he went where the job took him. He had begun his career managing a state-owned coal mine; diligence and hard work had found him appointed independent India's second Narcotics Commissioner, managing the country's export of opium abroad.

Since his appointment, Nargolwala had corresponded regularly with all the big pharmaceutical firms that used India's opium. There were Canadian purchasers and Japanese ones—and Nargolwala had made stops in both countries—but most of all, he wrote to American firms, which gobbled up the lion's share of the world's opium. There was Merck and Penick, the firm that had purchased New York Quinine and its alkaloid production business. Then there was Mallinckrodt, the most eclectic of the American firms. A chemical business as well as a pharmaceutical one, it made chemicals for film developing and barium for X-rays. But it also coordinated closely with Harry Anslinger and the Federal Bureau of Narcotics to decide upon the best sources of opium for the United States' massive pharmaceutical production.

Nargolwala made his best case in St. Louis. India's opium, he told the Missouri executives, was pricey but potent. Its high morphine content was the first draw, but much of India's export opium had a good amount of free codeine in it as well. India was reliable: its factories, warehouses, and ports could deliver opium to the United States quickly, efficiently, and on the exact terms Americans might request. He was crestfallen when, several months later, Harry Ansligner told the Indian Commissioner that the United States would not be accepting the Indian offer. Nargolwala protested. The United States, he felt, had not given Indian opium a fair chance. Anslinger cited the adequacy of the twenty-five tons of opium it had purchased from "another country," at a price that was "distinctly advantageous." Nargolwala did not need to guess which country had made the successful sale. Turkish opium was India's only real competitor. If Nargolwala had one challenge in his work managing one of India's uniquely lucrative exports, it was in convincing American buyers that theirs was the superior buy.

In the 1950s and 1960s, the bureaucrats who managed Indian and Turkish opium production and marketing, drawn into the orbit of American governmental purchasing since the Second World War, grew increasingly attuned to the demands of the US pharmaceutical procurement and production regime. Other countries vied for and purchased Indian and Turkish opium. European manufacturers in Italy, France, and the United Kingdom, and a number of smaller Asian purchasers, all purchased Indian opium; the Turkish monopoly sold to West Germany, France, Italy, and Japan, as well as a number of other European producers. But the United States' postwar dominance over global pharmaceutical production, and its increasing command of the international regulatory framework that governed it, drew Indian and Turkish planners into Washington's orbit.

In the same period, Indian and Turkish bureaucrats, like Dinshaw Nargolwala, found themselves implicitly competing with one another for greater access to the American market. India's politicians at the dawn of independence found a policy of total prohibition less fiscally tenable than many of its mainstream nationalist leaders had once hoped. It needed the revenues from excise opium sold domestically for its infrastructural, military, and social planning and could not wind down that source of revenue without developing a more robust policy of exports abroad.[3] India in this period sought to modernize its opium production, improve its supervision of cultivation itself, and tout Indian opium as a first-choice source for American production. Turkey, however, found itself increasingly the object of American scrutiny and suspicion. Turkish peacocking aside, observers found little to commend in the republic's opium monopoly. Producers sold their wares freely to middlemen within the country, heroin laboratories mushroomed, and opium remained a staple of Turkish rural life and economics. Whereas India broadly acceded to the terms of international agreements, Turkey largely delayed. By 1961, the year that a Single Convention on opium gave international regulation new weight, India had become the world's largest licit opium producer, while American diplomats came to believe that the only reasonable future for Turkish opium was its wholesale eradication.

Seen from Washington, the transformation of Indian and Turkish opium in this period was an extension of earlier imbrications of narcotics and American power, tied to the modernizing imperatives of the postwar years. American regulators and diplomats had long used machinations over the legal drug trade to extend US influence overseas.[4] In a slightly earlier period, Federal Bureau of Narcotics and State Department officials had worked with pharmaceutical manufacturers and private industry—including the Coca-Cola Company—to manage the flow of coca leaf worldwide, funneling an ever-greater share to the United States. In the early Cold War era, similar actors could tie the issue of opium to another strategic imperative: modernization theory. American social scientists and policymakers were increasingly animated by the notion that "traditional" societies could be transformed into modern ones through developmental projects, technical assistance, and attempts to reshape social and cultural norms, transforming them into societies characterized by industrialization, urbanization, secularization, and democratic institutions.[5] India and Turkey were paradigmatic examples of traditional societies with outsized potential for modernization, and their control of opium could serve as a key benchmark of whether state institutions and social norms could be properly modernized.[6]

Historians have long cast modernization as primarily a practice of development rooted in specific ideas and institutions. But it was inseparable from its material concerns. In the postwar years, American diplomatic power was used to extract and redirect new mineral and agricultural resources from "territories, foreign nations, and earthly and extraterrestrial expanses" far from its borders: mineral resources like mica and beryl, and agricultural ones like coca and opium as well.[7] The expansion of American bureaucratic power and commercial prowess under the guise of development and modernization offers one way of understanding the ways in which opium grew tied to American markets, beyond merely representing an extreme form of customer-specific investment. Americans had an outsized role in the shaping of pharmaceutical opium's global geography and the spaces where poppy could and could not be cultivated.

Yet the view from Washington obscures how integral the question of opium was to questions of state-making, international legitimacy, and national development—and how critical the role of the Indian and Turkish intermediaries were in rendering legible and then marketing a product that was increasingly bounded by international regulation. In an era of tightening prohibition, Turkish and Indian bureaucrats and politicians had reasons to move slowly. India's revenue from excise opium, sold domestically, represented up to a tenth of the new state's budget, and replacing it with opium exported for pharmaceutical purposes was an uncertain and slow prospect. In Turkey, opium played an outsized role in the rural imagination, and politicians had every reason to turn a blind eye to opium sold beyond the state monopoly, constituted under duress in the 1930s. If India and Turkey were to sacrifice the economic and political capital, respectively, that opium represented, the trade would need to be a worthwhile one. For both, in different ways, the promise of regularizing opium production and redirecting it to the legitimate pharmaceutical trade offered a rare opportunity to leverage resources for more favorable terms in an international arena. Neither were passive recipients of ideas about modern governance—rather, representatives of both countries engaged strategically with those ideas in an effort to gain credibility and in turn access a vital market.[8]

Ultimately, even as Washington's relationship with New Delhi was frostier than its relationship with Ankara, Indian bureaucrats were successful where Turkish ones were not. Indian civil servants like Dinshaw Nargolwala were savvy marketers, and they could offer Washington the promise of stable institutions. The Indian Administrative Service and the new Narcotics Bureau were stable, strong bureaucracies and drew upon colonial paradigms of extraction that dated back more than a hundred years. They could foster and tap into the new technical knowledge that India's ascendant research network was producing about opium as a crop.[9] India could present its opium industry as forward-looking and scientifically managed, in consort with the needs of American manufacturing. Turkish bureaucrats, by contrast, could not boast of their much weaker bureaucracy. The opium monopoly, poorly run, was a new and far weaker institution, likely incentivized to ignore the cultivation and sale of opium outside of its purview.

Opium, in India and in Turkey, played into starkly different visions of national development. For India, that vision was tied to the transformation of colonial bureaucratic and agricultural infrastructure into forward-looking production that was suited for the modern age. In one move, India could replace the capital it garnered from opium smoking and eating, a vestigial sign of colonial misrule, with high-value commercial agricultural exports. Its bureaucrats could twin developmental and technocratic logic to make modernization work on their own terms. In Turkey, by contrast, rural traditions and the black-market allowances historically afforded to cultivators made for a far more difficult accordance with the tenets of modernization and regulation. For all the revolutionary designs of the republican state, it was difficult for a weak bureaucracy to overcome rural inertia. By the middle of the 1960s, these divergent developmental trajectories would render Turkey and India radically unequal participants in the global opium trade.

A month after India's independence, two men who could barely countenance one another came together in rare agreement.[10] They concurred: if independence had brought so much promise alongside so much suffering, the promise of self-rule remained incomplete so long as India remained in the thrall of its opium revenues. Bijoy Chandra Bhagavati was the Indian National Congress's leading organizer in Assam, the lush northeastern province where Gandhi had pushed the party toward a policy of prohibition two decades earlier. He reminded his colleagues in the provincial legislature that the Assamese people, throughout the nationalist struggle, had picketed opium shops as reminders of British malevolence. But the province's work crafting legislation to ban opium in all nonmedical forms in the state had been undercut by the central government, which was, he declared, "not in consort."[11] Even the United States, he noted, had had to ask for "international measures" to help it prevent the smuggling of opium. And "the situation," he added, "demands an All India measure to uproot the opium evil." For once, Syed Muhammad Saadulla, the leader of the Assamese opposition with whom Bhagavati had fought bitterly, agreed. The central government, Saadulla added, should "stop Ghazipur Factory entirely" or at least limit its production to India's "barest possible medical need and nothing else."

In the waning days of colonial rule, it indeed seemed as if the Indian nationalists poised to take control of its ministries and, soon, the state itself did not fully countenance the complexity of the opium problem. Most bureaucrats at the highest level seemed to agree that opium smoking would, in independent India, be banned by all "except those addicts in possession of medical certificates."[12] This posture belied real tension. V. Narahari Rao, India's top auditor and a veteran civil servant, insisted that India's inadequate medical facilities would continue to necessitate the informal palliative use of opium. "The people of India," Rao averred, "have by long experience acquired an empirical skill in the use of opium for medical and semi-medical purposes, and until proper medical aid becomes generally available throughout the country it would be neither practicable nor humane to prohibit the use of opium altogether." Others were bolder still. Raghubir Sinh, the scion of the princely state of Sitamau, proposed a draft constitution for its incorporation into the future republic that would reserve all rights to opium cultivation, manufacture, sale, and export.[13]

The partition of British India into two new nations in August 1947 stoked pogroms and mass migration across a new border. In the chaos of partition, the Indian opium smokers who had been buying their "quasi-medical" supplies from the state bureaucracy turned briefly to black marketers hawking a pilfered supply.[14] But as in many other domains of public life, India's civil servants restored order quickly. Within a year and a half, an All-India Narcotics Board had been convened to discuss the question of drugs in India in its entirety.[15] Its chair, A.N. Sattanathan, embodied many of the modernizing hopes of the new state. A low-caste southern Indian from Tamil Nadu, Sattanathan had made a name for himself as an enterprising member of the Indian Civil Service.[16] Under his leadership, the Board vowed to make good on the nationalist promise to end the country's "quasi-medical" opium sector, limiting its use to medical or scientific use alone. At a subsequent meeting, the Board outlined new steps to control the use of opium and wean addicts, setting a ten-year window for full domestic prohibition of opium. But, its members added, "there should be no objection to growing raw opium for export." B.K. Mukhupadhyay, the Opium Agent at Ghazipur, was keenly aware of the export market's growing significance.[17] "A market has to be found abroad," he wrote, "for our surplus stocks of opium alkaloids." He was certain India could increase its share of the world's alkaloids and was obligated to do so if, as he was certain, the sale of excise opium was about to be ended. The country, he felt, needed to "organize sale of Indian opium alkaloids in overseas markets as early as possible so that increased production of these drugs could be synchronized with the decrease in the production of excise opium."

The Board's pat recommendations and the enthusiasm of civil servants like B.K. Mukhupadhyay belied a great deal of conflict among Indian planners, politicians, and bureaucrats.[18] The legacy of Mohandas Gandhi's campaign for prohibition and the cudgel that India's nationalists had raised against opium loomed large in politicians' imagination. At the same time, others within the Congress doubted whether the economic sacrifice that prohibition would entail was worth the effort. These questions came to the fore during the meetings of the Constituent Assembly, the assembly that debated the future of India's governmental structure. "Nothing," a member from Orissa said in late 1948, "can be gained by appealing to sentiments in the name of Mahatma Gandhi," whose assassination in January had largely exorcised his constructive program from formal politics. A math professor from Uttar Pradesh warned that prohibition would mean "voluntarily forgoing" 250 million rupees—a number somewhere between 5 and 10 percent of the annual budget, which some members tied directly to India's military needs in the restive provinces of Kashmir and Hyderabad. Most importantly, B.R. Ambedkar, the anti-caste activist put in charge of the Constitution Drafting Committee, rejected the notion of outright prohibition on financial grounds—and, likely, posthumous antipathy for Gandhi, his longtime political foe.

Ultimately, India could not afford to dismiss the revenue—pounds and dollars from exports and rupees from excise—that opium represented. The Constituent Assembly rejected the stricter interpretations of prohibition, adopting an approach that left a great deal of discretion to Indian states. The result was a tripartite prohibition system across states: some implemented total bans, others partial restrictions, and some had no prohibitions at all.

In November 1950, the Government of India took the ad hoc board it had convened to discuss the question of narcotics at a central level and transformed it into a new bureaucracy. The Central Bureau of Narcotics was housed in the Department of Revenue, and A.N. Sattanathan was made India's first Narcotics Commissioner.[19] Alongside questions of smuggling, the bureau was charged with administering the opium production that the colonial agencies had once managed.[20] Sattanathan was a consummate civil servant, dedicated to efficiency and standardization regardless of the sector. He updated a process that had remained largely unchanged for more than a century.[21] Each year, the Commissioner was to take stock of export requirements, then charge district officers with surveying lands and interviewing potential cultivators. Most of the collection was to be done collectively, under the supervision of a village *lambardar*, or foreman, paid on commission. After the harvest, cultivators were to present their gum for weighing and grading by the district officer, before the product was sent to Ghazipur for processing into morphine, codeine, and narcotine. In the interests of supervision and streamlining, the CBN consolidated and reduced the number of licensed opium-growing districts in the country.[22] Sattanathan was an equally capable marketer, aware that the future of India's opium industry relied in large measure on the ability of the country to convey its willingness to play according to the terms of the legitimate international trade.

Increasingly, this meant strictures dictated by the United States. Since the Second World War had forced Harry Anslinger and his colleagues in the pharmaceutical industry to look to India for a supply of opium, both to rebuild the American stockpile and to forestall the threatening possibility of an International Opium Monopoly, an idea that the Director of the United Nations' Division of Narcotic Drugs had proposed in the late 1940s.[23] The particular role that India would play in this rebuilding, however, had been unclear. Immediately after the war's end, Harry Anslinger had tried unsuccessfully to station a full-time opium investigator in India.[24] When the United States established its first diplomatic mission to India shortly before independence, the subject of India's opium was among its first investigations.[25] In the State Department, two camps formed: those who saw India as incapable of being brought into the legitimate narcotics order and those who cast India as a promising source of opium for the United States' postwar pharmaceutical industry. The foremost proponent of the former view was Helen Howell Moorhead, the head of the Opium Committee of the Foreign Policy Association. A campaigner against the Indian opium trade for nearly thirty years, Moorhead showed up regularly at the State Department to urge it not to dismiss India's lax opium enforcement.[26] The US Congress, on the whole, agreed. A House bill called for the marking of all ships returning to the United States from countries where opium was sold freely; India was essentially the only country to which this law would apply.[27]

American pharmaceutical manufacturers were by contrast more bullish. Some of the opium they had purchased during the war had been mixed with flaxseed and was difficult to process.[28] There were questions about its economic viability.[29] Broadly, the Indian product had worked well to produce codeine, morphine, and other alkaloids.[30] In a letter to Anslinger, the head of the State Department's Division of Far Eastern Affairs summarized the opium conundrum. "India," he wrote succinctly, "is at the crossroads."[31]

It would reach that crossroads quickly. Sattanathan had the rare ability to put Harry Anslinger at ease.[32] He collaborated readily with his American counterpart, helped him ferret out the source of smugglers who brought Indian opium to the United States, and built collaborations between the two bureaucracies. In 1953, in an effort to prevent plans for that international opium monopoly to come to fruition, Harry Anslinger strong-armed the passage of a new opium agreement, putting new limitations on production of opium in exchange for the right to produce it legally for the international market. Its signatories agreed to buy opium only from a list of seven producing countries. Sattanathan wasted no time in accepting the terms of the protocol and subsequently helped India become one of two countries (the other being Iran) to ratify it in parliament.[33]

By the time that Sattanathan's successor, Dinshaw Nargolwala, was flying to the United States to tout India's opium to manufacturers there, the industry was enjoying a new buoyancy. In spite of the failure to make the sale to Washington that year, India's clout was rising among pharmaceutical purchasers, its exports were rising, and American manufacturers were expressing new confidence about the Indian product even when they did not purchase it on account of price.[34] The upgrades to the Ghazipur factory meant that it was producing finished alkaloids as well as raw opium.[35] In 1955, the country's Revenue Department described India as being in a battle to "recapture" the world's licit opium market.[36] The effort was of scant interest to most politicians and lawmakers, who remained largely unaware of the distinction between licit and illicit imports.[37] Those lawmakers did sign off on more funding for the Ghazipur factory when the Narcotics Commissioner asked for new processing equipment to help India "overcome competition from Turkey and Iran."

India, by the middle of the decade, appeared to be squarely on board with international narcotics standards.[38] In a context of broader geopolitical suspicion, American executives cheered the quickness of the Indian civil servants who fielded short-order requests.[39] Those civil servants trumpeted a rare success overseas. S.N. Asthana, who worked in the District Opium Office in Bareilly, beamed with pride at the accolades of overseas purchasers who had "nothing but good words to say both for the quality of the drug supplied, the method of packing and dispatching and the promptness in executing all the orders."[40]

Figure 5.1 An Indian cultivator scoring an opium poppy, mid-1960s. Government of Madhya Pradesh.

Leon Taranto, the scion of Turkey's most storied opium families, still traveled elegantly. On the steamboat plying the waters from Izmir to Istanbul, the sixty-something businessman cut a distinguished figure in a neat three-piece suit and a white beard. Taranto's career had been predicated upon his good instincts. His knowledge of commercial dynamics across the Mediterranean and Europe had helped him consolidate his family's business in its most turbulent years. While aboard the ship, his powers of observation had not failed him. The tall American sitting next to him with a Mississippi drawl was assuredly a government agent.[41]

Taranto was not wrong. Garland Williams was one of Harry Anslinger's most trusted lieutenants. First the Federal Bureau of Narcotics' regional director in New York, Williams had been sent in the late 1940s on a long mission to the Eastern Mediterranean to chase down the source of the cannabis and heroin that kept appearing on East Coast streets. Lebanon and Iran had been his main ports of call before a stop in Turkey. Taranto, in his mellifluous, crisp English, could not resist a diatribe. For hours, he showered Williams with thoughts on the industry from which he had been forced out by Turkey's nationalization of the opium trade. Taranto described an industry in free fall. The Turkish opium monopoly, he declared, was incompetent. Its bureaucrats knew nothing of the global trade, priced opium on a whim, and made it even more attractive for peasants to sell their crop to smugglers. It would never happen, but Taranto knew one thing: If opium were given back to private traders, they and only they could work with global pharmaceutical producers to ensure good medicine around the world and end the rising scourge of heroin. If Williams had been feeling more puckish, he might have asked Taranto about the years in which his Istanbul factory had been selling heroin to all and sundry. But Williams was too gobsmacked by Taranto's knowledge of a staggeringly complex industry. "I have never seen a man," he later wrote, "who could talk so comprehensively about the world narcotic traffic from the commercial viewpoint."

Taranto was describing the global ramifications of a dynamic that Williams had seen at work throughout his stay in Turkey and which Americans in the private and public sector had lamented since the end of the war. In the wake of the Second World War, American importing firms had been registering their discontent with the Turkish monopoly.[42] The bureaucrats who staffed the office were, executives alleged, slow to communicate and unclear and clumsy in their contracts. American buyers wrote privately about their desire that opium be returned to the private trade in Turkey, and they kept local fixers like Taranto in place to help them understand an opaque production landscape. The State Department and the Federal Bureau of Narcotics had regularly sent field officers to the Turkish countryside since 1946, double-checking any production numbers they considered suspect.[43] The country's enforcement, they concluded, was exceptionally weak, and most opium left Turkey without ever passing through a monopoly warehouse. By the end of the decade, the American embassy tried to hire a well-connected Turkish journalist to monitor monopoly operations and smuggling directly.[44]

Turkish officials in the 1950s trumpeted the success of their nationalized opium industry. The monopoly's head touted the ways in which opium had been putatively limited to certain regions and tightly coordinated with a commercial attaché in Washington.[45] Turkey's top security official vowed to sponsor a maximum increase in sentences for opium traffickers and invited Anslinger to come to Ankara as a guest of honor—though seemed most interested in American gifts of cars, Jeeps, and helicopters.[46] Politicians in Ankara politely considered ratifying the 1953 Opium Protocol while making no specific commitments.[47] Turkish administrators at home were more willing to say that a certain domestic laxity around narcotic substances like opium needed to be brought into line with international standards.[48]

Williams's stay in Turkey, even before his chance meeting with Taranto, confirmed much of what the Americans had suspected.[49] In Ankara, Necati Topcuoglu, the bureaucrat from the opium heartland who had been placed in charge of the opium monopoly, spouted platitudes about international cooperation, proffered samples of Anatolian opium for analysis, and mimeographed flowcharts showing how peasants' products moved through a disciplined bureaucracy. But in Afyonkarahisar, where he declared to be an American seaman, Williams found himself deluged with offers of black-market opium and tips for how to best smuggle it in his suitcase.[50] A second agent confirmed that opium was indeed readily available for purchase. More ambitious smugglers, he learned, could sneak it out in modified olive oil barrels.[51] By the end of the decade, even casual newspaper readers in Europe and the United States knew about the "French Connection," the well-trodden route by which Sicilian and Corsican mobsters were smuggling Turkish opium to American ports.[52]

Taranto seemed to have been right about one thing: the existence of eighty thousand opium cultivators and an uncountable number of middlemen who participated freely and legally in the domestic opium trade in Turkey undercut whatever pretenses Ankara had to state control.[53] The system was a sieve. Until the mid-1950s, cultivators had no bookkeeping requirements, and opium could change hands endlessly as long as its final destination was listed as a monopoly warehouse. Turkish officials half-heartedly floated a plan to build their own alkaloid factory on the grounds that finished alkaloids had far less value than raw opium to the illicit trade.[54] But foreign observers increasingly concluded that Turkey's efforts were largely for show and that there was significant political advantage in a system that allowed so much leakage.[55] A cultivator had little incentive to sell to the monopoly directly, given the costs of transporting, and every incentive to sell to brokers instead. Brokers had more than three months after the start of the harvest in June to buy from farmers at or below the official rate—but there was little monitoring to prevent them from offering a bit more and selling at a much higher price to laboratories, and sentencing was light in any case.

Turkish opium's underworld connotations had a chilling effect on pharmaceutical purchases.[56] American purchasers were not in a rush to resume their purchasing from Turkey. The stockpile the United States had assembled during the war would last some years before degrading, and even as Turkey's monopoly reported record-high crops, manufacturers showed little interest. When the United States began purchasing, it did so slowly and was motivated heavily by price—as was evident when India lost out on the opportunity to sell in 1953. The United States was, in the 1950s, the largest importer of Turkish opium, with Spain, West Germany, Hungary, and Japan vying for a distant second.[57] But American firms were not thrilled with the inconsistent product they received, which was just as likely to show up as unwrapped loaves in wooden cases as in the metal-banded and wax-sealed containers, protected by a tamper-proof nail, which the monopoly had promised.[58] In most years, American firms spent thirty times the amount on Turkish tobacco that they did on Turkish opium.

Was opium worth growing at all? The question seemed more important as Turkey's erstwhile prestige crop grew more and more fraught. Fethi İncekara, a professor of agricultural sciences, had studied many of Turkey's important cash crops, from sunflowers and flax to tea and tobacco. But opium, he knew, held a particular place of importance in the Turkish rural imagination. He and his colleague Celal Tarman were part of a forward-looking cadre of Turkish agronomists trained in West Germany and animated, like some of their Ottoman predecessors, by European idioms of improvement.[59] İncekara and Tarman asked the question in a 1954 treatise.[60] For them, it was a contextual question: given that poppy's legal prices were low, it was better for cultivators to focus on all the other things that could be done with the crop. Poppy oil could be used for all sorts of industrial processes, they averred, from paints to soaps.

Others seemed far gloomier. In 1955, an anonymous opinion piece appeared in the popular daily newspaper *Cumhuriyet*—though officials at the American embassy were certain that it was penned by Osman Sulhi Dönmezer, Dean of the Faculty of Law at Istanbul University and Turkey's leading criminologist.[61] It opened with the many indignities that Turks knew well from regular headlines: the arrests of smugglers and raids on heroin factories that were the mainstay of the press. Opium was a staple of Turkish agriculture, but the "white poison" of heroin had become "a blot on the country's international reputation." The moral case against Turkey's cultivating poppy was clear. "The shortest path," he wrote, "to preserving the integrity of our society and the lives of our citizens is to implement a complete ban on poppy cultivation. The social and moral benefits of such a decision far outweigh any potential economic drawbacks." He issued a challenge to Turkish lawmakers: could they incentivize Turkish villagers to give up opium? That Turkish peasants, long accustomed to the black-market worth of opium, would give up opium in favor of tobacco, cotton, sesame, wheat, and sugar beets seemed unlikely. But it was a proposal that would carry more weight as Turkish pharmaceutical exports seemed outweighed by Turkey's dubious contributions to the illicit trade.

◖◯◗

L.D. Kapoor put it succinctly in the pages of *Indian Farming*.[62] "Poppy cultivation," he wrote, "is paying." Kapoor was a rising scientist at the Regional Research Laboratory in Jammu-Tawi, a branch of the wider Indian agricultural research network. Having worked extensively on India's indigenous drugs, he felt confident in declaring that poppy was a safe bet. A surge of demand from overseas buyers, primarily the United States and the United Kingdom, meant that there was good money to be made from the crop. Not every Indian could avail himself of the opportunity. A farmer needed to live in one of the licensed districts in Madhya Pradesh, Rajasthan, and Uttar Pradesh, and the total acreage of land available for cultivation to farmers was less than a tenth of what it had been forty years prior. But for those who were legally able and who were willing to work with the enterprising opium officers experimenting with techniques for higher yield—everything from new breeding trials to the use of polythene-lined canvas bags to reduce alkaloid loss—the yield of ten to sixteen pounds of opium per acre could be sold to state Opium Agents at a very decent price.[63] Once officials in New Delhi had agreed to the terms of the new Single Convention on opium earlier that year, it was clear that Indian opium would have a promising place in global trade.

By the end of the 1950s, Indian opium had turned a corner. In the waning years of the decade, Indian states had enacted a series of increasingly stringent policies, and some, including Madras and Maharashtra, had opted for complete prohibition and an end to the excise industry altogether. Legal opium smoking had been nearly entirely stamped out.[64] In Rajasthan, India's opium-smuggling heartland, a new set of rules were put on the books, allowing the state government to confiscate illegal opium and control its movement out of the state. In 1959, in the wake of a third All-India Narcotics Conference, New Delhi trumpeted the formal end to the country's "quasi-medical market," declaring it the culmination of fifty years' progress since the Shanghai convention.[65] This success, the Revenue Minister asserted, was the result of ten years' progressive reduction in the excise opium allotted to states, and their weaning from that opium as a source of income. (Ending legal use at home did not, of course, end consumption altogether. Opium addiction, Indian economists and health writers knew, was "prevalent" in the 1950s and 1960s.[66]) Finally, in 1961, India's representatives agreed to the terms of the 1961 convention that superseded the 1953 agreement and offered toothier provisions for narcotics control.

Indian officials' willingness to play by the new rules of international narcotics regulation earned them a privileged role in the American market. When floods hit Uttar Pradesh in 1959, Merck executives personally persuaded Harry Anslinger to send assistants to India to investigate their impact upon American pharmaceutical production.[67] That company's executives were particularly appreciative of Indian opium. Within a few years, they were sending their own representatives to examine the facilities at the Ghazipur factory.[68] American narcotics officials were similarly satisfied by India's turn to the legitimate trade. In 1961, the FBN's top brass arrived in New Delhi for a congratulatory meeting and dinner with their Indian counterparts.[69] After hearing the new Indian Narcotics Commissioner promise a continued reduction in the legal cultivating area, Anslinger's top aide declared India's control regime to be "vastly superior to the Turkish." When Anslinger finally retired, his successor, Henry Giordano, made India his first overseas stop, and he declared India's narcotics bureaucracy to be decidedly "pro-American."[70] Indian narcotics officials were soon regular participants in American police training courses, a rare point of cooperation in a relationship that was in many other ways frosty.[71]

The material dimensions of this cooperation were clear. In 1961, India became the world's largest producer of opium for the global market, with its 763 tons of exported crop making up more than two-thirds of the global total.[72] Turkey was a distant second. Indian parliamentarians generally understood little of the particulars of licensing cultivators, collecting opium, or selling it overseas. But they did apprehend the dollar and sterling income coming in from these sales—and the political value of votes from licensed opium-growing districts.[73] Two hundred thousand opium growers and their families represented a large number of possible votes. The question of whether or not enforcement was deliberately lax in some areas to incentivize favorable voting was a live one in a similar period.

Indian opium was undoubtedly more controlled in this period than Turkish opium. But in a period of deepening cooperation, it was more likely to circulate in domestic or regional markets. In the early 1960s, India's Narcotics Department was overwhelmed by increased and increasingly sophisticated opium smuggling from the country's licensed districts.[74] In the year after the 1961 agreement, there were more than two hundred opium seizures undertaken by intelligence officers. Cars, Jeeps, and trains were frequent conveyances in smugglers' schemes. Opium was often found in secret chambers in car doors and back seats, or in battery boxes fitted under train compartments. The smuggling rings grew more organized. Many coordinated across multiple states, and one particularly large one, run out of Mandsaur district, in the dusty Central Provinces, took years of the Narcotics Department's efforts to smoke out. An increasing amount of opium seemed to be traveling across India's borders into Pakistan, Nepal, and Burma, and new forces—the Special Armed Constabulary on the Punjab border and the Anti-Smuggling Force in Rajasthan—were deployed to combat these new routes. Smugglers used new coding systems and more complex financial transactions, often tied to a legitimate business's work, to evade detection. Yet India's largest customer, the United States, was willing to ignore a great deal of this smuggling since little reached American shores. In July 1961, an Indian sailor in Alameda, California, was arrested after showing balls of opium marked with government deals and promising to sell a steady supply to American purchasers.[75] But the case, and the other small instances of Indian opium seized in the United States, were quickly written off as aberrations.

In 1968, Indian novelist Srilal Sukla published *Raag Darbari*, a comic account of rustic village life being remade by India's ambitious but flawed modernization schemes; the following year, the bestseller won the Sahitya Academy Award, India's highest literary honor. One of its main characters, Ramadhin Bhikhmakhervi, was an opium dealer, cast, like many of the other villagers, as a rustic buffoon.[76] The book's narrator described Ramadhin's easy entry into a backward trade, where his lack of literacy was an asset. "There was good money in the opium business," the narrator recalled, "and the rivalry between traders was not too great. There was just one small problem with the trade, and that was that it was against the law." On trial for selling opium, Ramadhin patronizingly lectures the British judge about the unfairness of the prohibition against selling opium. Only during his two-year prison sentence does Ramadhin realize that it would be better to break the laws of the colonial salt monopoly than the laws against opium selling, in the interests of impressing his nationalist friends. Srilal Sukla imagined the informal opium trade as many Indians did in the late 1960s—rough, cloddish, and a vestigial remain of the colonial order. Opium's future, it seemed possible to believe, was in its usefulness to Western pharmaceuticals.

◖O◗

In 1957, a serialized novel ran in the pages of *Cumhuriyet*.[77] *Despot* was written by Reşat Enis Aygen, a prominent journalist turned novelist who penned patriotic rural dramas set in the Turkish countryside. *Despot*, set during the Turkish War of Independence, told the story of a venal landlord who collaborated with the Greeks to protect his own class interests. The story was not subtle, and the controversy it stoked resulted in his termination from the nationalist mouthpiece. Among its characters was Fikret, an opium dealer touring the villages of Isparta district, and Cumaali Aga, a shrewd opium farmer.

Fikret and Cumaali see the world through poppy. As they make plans to siphon off thirty-five kilos of opium to the black market, paying off village headmen and monopoly officials, Aga waxes obscenely about his mistress, Suzan, in Istanbul, who has breasts shaped like poppy capsules. They give lascivious glances at the women working in Cumaali's field, carrying bouquets of poppy pods on their heads which make them look like Assyrian goddesses. As Cumaali hawks his sap, swearing that there is not a drop of plum, pine resin, egg white, raisin, date, or fruit leather adulterating it, a boy in the field nibbles on poppy seeds. Cumaali reminds the dealer that he is well aware of the massive profit he will make selling his product to heroin manufacturers. But the two men allow themselves to continue their reverie:

> The poppy pods, swaying in the breeze, nodded like opium addicts in a stupor. You should see them twenty days before harvest: adorned with flowers of crimson, ivory, gold, and azure, they stand like vibrant maidens in their prime. But once their petals fall and they yield their precious sap, they wither, their beauty fading, like young women losing the bloom of youth. As dusk approached, the same women returned to the poppy field, armed with scoring knives. With practiced hands, they harvested the dark, viscous sap—raw opium—that had oozed from the scored pods, carefully collecting it in the earthen pots at their feet.

Fikret stays at Cumaali Aga's house for several days, watching workers knead opium into small, uniform lumps. He remembers reading that it wasn't the hemlock that killed Socrates, but rather opium admixed with it. Yet he remembers a more important figure, Haci Efendi of Urfa, whose opium consumption had kept him alive until the age of 134.

Three decades into the republican experiment, and two since the establishment of the monopoly that was to tame an unwieldy industry, opium had lost none of its luster. Reşat Enis Aygen saw opium as an integral, vivid, even erotic feature of the Turkish landscape. If the crop perhaps did harm abroad, it seemed to offer potency and pleasure at home. This fact was aggravating to the international observers—Americans chief among them—who had held high hopes for Turkey's accession to the hegemonic legal norms of much of the rest of the world.

Americans had staked a great deal on Turkey's modernization. The Turkish Republic was not merely a laboratory for American-led modernization theory—the Cold War–era strategy positing that that developing nations could rapidly advance through targeted economic aid and agricultural modernization—but a central site where its strictures and premises were themselves developed.[78] American foreign policy experts had seen in Turkey the promise of a modern Muslim state keen to embrace market-based notions of development and a potential model for neighbors in the Middle East. Some of this was in fact easy to actualize. Turks' eagerness to build highways and hotels telegraphed to Americans that they shared the values of mobility, hospitality, and empathy that were the hallmarks of modern subjectivities.

But peasants had been harder to bring into the fold than middle-class city-dwellers. Atatürk had declared in 1922 that "the peasant is the master of the country." The postwar Democratic Party under Prime Minister Adnan Menderes had made great capital among peasants during his long rule between 1950 and 1960, promising them better markets for their wares and tractors sold cheaply on Marshall Plan credit.[79] The state had promoted the economic worth of tobacco, beets, hazelnuts, apricots, and wheat. But black-market opium—far more lucrative than any of these options—had remained a predictably desirable crop to produce.[80]

By the turn of the 1960s, diplomats from the United States—still the largest purchaser of Turkish opium, but an increasingly reluctant and frustrated customer—had had enough. For years, internecine fighting between Turkey's Ministry of Economy and Commerce and its Ministry of Agriculture had prevented Ankara from accepting Washington's offer of American narcotics control assistance.[81] Eventually, a skeleton crew of two Narcotics Agents had been sent to work from the American embassy.[82] By 1963, when bureaucrats in Ankara agreed to sign the 1951 Opium Protocol as a last-ditch effort to please Washington—a dozen years after its drafting and after the newer Single Convention on opium had superseded it—American officials grew vocal. Turkey, they insisted, should not be encouraged to grow any more opium.

By 1963, staffers at the American embassy in Ankara were taking stock of what it might mean for Turkey to abandon opium.[83] Their most conservative estimates held that 11 percent of Turkey's opium crop was being diverted, but it was likely that far more was simply being converted to morphine base in the country. Turkey, those staffers felt, was the ultimate source of more than three-fourths of the world's heroin. A far greater number of Turkish peasants, well over 100,000, were being permitted to grow opium legally than even the most generous estimate of global pharmaceutical needs would require. It seemed likely that the monopoly itself was being run at a loss as some kind of rural subsidy. In 1965, an American narcotics officer based in Rome was tasked with assembling a proposal for a technical assistance program to "help" Turkey give up opium cultivation. "The Turks produce opium poorly," the officer wrote, "and market it even more inefficiently. They could not possibly compete with the present manufacturing countries in alkaloid production. Also, the world [sic] needs for alkaloids is decreasing with the synthetics and if codeine is ever synthesized, the market for opium would be ended."[84]

Within a year, the Americans had outlined the basic contours of that proposal.[85] Turkey would be asked to issue a decree prohibiting all opium poppy cultivation. Over a four-year period, the country would be issued compensation payments equivalent to its old sales, decreasing each year, while being given technical assistance to transition to "alternative, high-value crops." The government would be given new resources for narcotics enforcement and compensation for lost foreign exchange earnings, and it in turn would destroy or liquidate all existing stockpiles of opium. By the end of the year, the proposal had been communicated to the White House, where a National Security Council staffer presented it to President Lyndon Johnson.[86]

It was one thing to calculate the economic value of opium to Turkish farmers, even if the calculations that American staffers made did not account for the black-market value that so much opium was actually fetching. It was another, however, to contemplate the eradication of a crop that was part of the Turkish rural imagination itself. Fikret and

Cumaali might have only been characters in a serialized socialist realist novel, but their connection to the poppy—abiding, alive, imbued with desire and meaning—was something that many of Reşat Enis Aygen's readers, and many Turks beyond them, could feel deeply themselves.

◖◗

Throughout the 1950s and 1960s, international drug control treaties had offered up shifting visions of what regulatory frameworks would govern narcotics in the postwar order.[87] The regulation of opium was central to these visions. The 1953 Opium Protocol had proposed a limitation of opium production and trade to medical and scientific purposes. It had proposed that only seven countries worldwide be authorized to produce opium: Bulgaria, Greece, Iran, Yugoslavia, the USSR, and of course, the largest two producers, Turkey and India. But three of the producing states had been required to ratify the terms of that agreement for it to come into force. India did so within a year of its passage, and Iran did so under American pressure in 1959. After a decade of noncommittal responses, Turkey's diplomats suggested that it would do so in 1963—by which point an entirely different proposal for international control was on the table.

The 1961 Single Convention on Narcotic Drugs was a somewhat more moderate vehicle than its failed predecessor. While it aimed to regulate all narcotic drugs, not only opium, it did away with the proposal that only certain countries would be authorized to produce it. Any country, theoretically, could produce opium, so long as it had a government-operated agency that would license producers; buy, warehouse, and sell the product; and report the entire process to the newly formed International Narcotics Control Board. Producing states generally found the Single Convention an easier pill to swallow. It was ratified by 1964, and the International Narcotics Control Board began its functioning four years later.

By this point, India had rendered itself indispensable in the global pharmaceutical market and, most significantly, to the production needs of the United States, the world's largest customer of raw opium. It was, for the time being, the quintessential legal producer for the world. India's value was evident in the composition of the new International Narcotics Control Board itself. Among its eight inaugural members were its president, Harry Greenfield, the last colonial Chairman of India's Central Board of Revenue and its former representative to the UN's Commission on Narcotic Drugs, and E.S. Krishnamoorthy, also a former chairman and representative.[88] Turkey, too, had a member on the board, but Sükrü Kaymakçalan had no connection to the Turkish monopoly or to opium at all; he was a professor of pharmacology at Ankara who had largely devoted his career to the deleterious effects of cannabis.

India's star had risen where Turkey's had crashed. India's bureaucrats had operated savvily, suppressing the quasi-medical use of opium domestically. By playing nice in international venues, they had captured a steadily increasing share of the world's opium market. Turkish bureaucrats, obstinate and defiant, had done little to convince international

Figure 5.2 Dr. Olav Brænden, head of the United Nations' drug laboratory in Geneva, with Jane Beck, a laboratory member, marking opium-producing regions in India in 1965. United Nations.

buyers or regulators that their commitment to a dominant model of control represented much more than lip service. In the years that followed, those bureaucrats and the politicians who built capital through the domestic opium trade would find themselves at the center of a new geopolitical maelstrom.

PART III

Opium Disassembled

6

Import Substitution Pharmaceuticals

Lüfti Yıldız turned off the radio in indignation.[1] How could it be, the forty-year-old farmer wondered, that the Americans had bought off the Turkish government so easily? It had taken a mere $20 million for Ankara's politicians to agree to end the livelihoods of seventy-five thousand farming families. The American president had been quoted on the TRT morning broadcast describing the prime minister's decision as "statesmanlike and courageous." But there was nothing courageous, Yıldız knew, in ending the industry that sustained him. "If the government tells me not to plant poppies," he lamented, "it would be like saying that I can't eat bread. I could not obey such an order and live."

The Turkish state's decision to put an end to the country's poppy trade, announced in June 1971, had in many ways been decades in the making. In 1948, Garland Williams, the FBN agent who had been investigating the heroin routes of the Eastern Mediterranean, had suggested to uninterested Turkish bureaucrats that peasants be induced to substitute opium with "an edible agricultural crop," most likely sugar, given its similar legal prices and the country's shortages at the time.[2] Osman Sulhi Dönmezer, Dean of the Faculty of Law at Istanbul University and Turkey's leading criminologist, had also made the suggestion that Turkey abandon the trade altogether in an anonymous opinion piece in *Cumhuriyet*. American narcotics staffers had come up with a vague plan in 1963, developed it into a formal proposal in 1965, and had presented it to Lyndon Johnson at the end of that year. Turkey's then prime minister, Süleyman Demirel, had floated the idea in parliament but stumbled on the question of farmer compensation.[3]

Yet suddenly, the seemingly impossible became reality. On March 12, 1971, the Turkish military leadership issued a memorandum skewering the current government's inability to implement reforms, the country's economic instability, and its descent into "anarchy." Forced to resign, Prime Minister Demirel gave way to Nihat Erim, an unassuming law professor tasked with forming a new cabinet. Rumors circulated that the "poppy issue" had been one of the main reasons for the military's soft coup. Demirel's government had agreed to limit the areas of legal cultivation but resisted anything more drastic. This speculation hardened into certainty when the poppy solution featured in the Erim government's new parliamentary platform.[4] Erim, claiming that he himself had written this section of the platform, assured parliamentarians that nothing would be done without first seeing to the well-being of the poppy cultivators.

A long-simmering issue in relations with the United States suddenly boiled over. Immediately after taking office, Nihat Erim heard a proposal from the US ambassador for the eradication of poppy cultivation in Turkey. The American Secretary of State soon echoed this demand, portraying Turkey as negligent when compared to India and its watertight regime. "To convince farmers to accept the ban on opium cultivation," Erim countered, "it would be necessary to offer them an opportunity that will provide a better standard of living."

The nature of that "path" sparked fierce debate throughout late spring. While Nihat Erim took a conciliatory stance with the Americans, one of his deputy prime ministers, Attila Karaosmanoğlu, presented bolder claims in his more contentious meetings with officials from the United States Agency for International Development (USAID). The $6 million USAID had calculated to offset Turkey's opium exports, Karaosmanoğlu argued, vastly underestimated the crop's economic impact. The United States, he suggested, would need to help transition the country's opium-growing regions to relatively higher-value industries like cotton, flax, and animal husbandry. More ambitiously, he proposed a $300 million US contribution to Turkey's industrial development.

By May, US diplomats had laid their cards on the table. In exchange for banning poppy cultivation in Turkey outright, Washington would offer $10–15 million to compensate farmers, paying them 110 percent of their expected sales of opium to the Turkish opium monopoly. They further proposed a World Bank–partnered grant to finance new industrial and agricultural projects in the region. The offer came with a stark ultimatum: if Ankara did not agree to the terms by the end of June, the US Congress would be asked to end all aid, including military aid, to Turkey. Erim protested, deeming the terms unfit to present to the Turkish public. But the American Secretary of State's offer to increase the compensation to $35 million—$15 million to the farmers, and $20 million for a development program—led to an agreement by mid-June.

The broadcast that Lufti Yıldız and millions of others heard on Turkish radio laid out Ankara's position starkly.[5] "It is certain," Erim declared, "that an internationally organized smuggling network constitutes a political and economic issue for Turkey. They will not be allowed to play with our country's reputation any further." Casting the eradication of heroin in the world as "a great humanitarian duty," the prime minister outlined the terms of the compensation payments and the economic investment that the deal with the United States had secured. Few Turks outside of the military brass, however, seemed convinced. "The Americans," one village *mukhtar* from the opium heartland scowled, "are putting us in a bad position because they take away our good crop. The Americans use it and they die: they must not use it like that. We produce it and don't use it. Don't they have brains?"[6]

Elite voices joined the dissent. Şevket Süreyya Aydemir was perhaps uniquely qualified to weigh in on the decision. The septuagenarian writer and Marxist economist had once been the leading thinker behind the collective that published *Kadro*, the socialist magazine that, forty years earlier, had published Mümtaz Ziya's account of how opium should be used to underwrite Turkish infrastructure and development. As an elder intellectual, he did not mince words in the pages of *Cumhuriyet*.

"Astonished" by the decision to end poppy cultivation, he described it as a "death sentence for a world-class asset and a treasure trove whose doors we have never managed to unlock."[7] Conservative nationalist writer Ahmet Kabaklı agreed. "I fear," he wrote, "that we'll deeply miss the opium poppy, against which we've spoken so much and which has actually done us no harm—and which, in fact, might have made us wealthy if we had wanted. I'm afraid we've given up one of God's blessings for the sake of friendship and to put on airs of 'humanitarianism.'"[8]

Turkish politicians across the spectrum lambasted the decision. A representative from Malatya, in Eastern Anatolia, wondered why Turkey and not other opium-producing countries had been singled out. Increase criminal sanctions for smuggling, he insisted, but reject the ban on poppy cultivation, the lifeblood of the Anatolian villager. His colleague from Adıyaman agreed. "We have given the ultimate punishment," he declared, "to the Turkish villager." Deputy Prime Minister Attila Karaosmanoğlu told the American ambassador that Afyon province would have to be renamed "Little America" in light of who was calling the shots there.[9]

By the fall, a team of American agronomists had touched down in Afyon, as well as in Kütahya, Uşak, Denizli, Isparta, and Burdur, six provinces that comprised the Anatolian opium heartland.[10] The Turkish component of the joint Turkish-American team tasked with planning an economic future for the region was drawn from the upper echelons of different ministries, while the American delegation was a mix of Department of Agriculture and USAID workers. The de facto head of the American team was Quentin Jones, an Agricultural Research Service scientist who led the group's investigation into the region's chalky soil. There were evidently profitable crops that could be grown on former opium land: cherries, grapes, apricots, nuts, tomatoes, and peppers. With enough investment, farmers could plan on raising Denizli chickens and Dagliç sheep and could one day look forward to a large dairy and beef industry. With good surface and groundwater irrigation, it would be possible to increase wheat yields, and where agriculture was limited by local agronomic conditions, Turkish villagers could be trained in public works or cottage industries or could simply be induced to relocate.

Those villagers, unsurprisingly, could barely contain their contempt. Many hid opium in unassuming sheds and barns, saving up to pay for dowries and other major expenses.[11] The Turkish-American team was proposing crops that would sustain an annual family income of around $500—an amount that they could easily match by selling a small amount of opium on the black market, to say nothing of more prosaic domestic use: cattle feed, oil, or a rustic bread that many embossed artfully with the cap of a seed pod before baking.[12] By the time the American Secretary of Agriculture came to Turkey to finalize a compensation deal in November, it was clear that the plan was underdeveloped and that American experts would only be available to help in small numbers on a contract basis.

There was, in the domestic Turkish discussion of the opium ban, a vestigial hint of the promise of what opium had once offered to Turkish bureaucrats, planners, and thinkers in the years after the founding of the republic. The prime minister asserted that it was not US pressure alone that had called the ban into being. Rather, he claimed, it was the backward state of the four provinces where opium was still legally cultivated that had motivated his thinking. Afyon province, the historic center of Turkey's opium production, was ranked fifty-first out of sixty-seven provinces in economic development. Erim had seen firsthand what US investment could do to Turkey when, decades earlier, he had worked closely with American planners in creating a modern interstate highway system. For Erim, "Little America" was not an epithet; in 1949 he himself had declared that "barring some unforeseen catastrophe…in the near future Turkey will become a 'little America.'"[13] When his other deputy prime minister, Sadi Koçaş, objected that there were few other lucrative crops that could indeed be grown in the four remaining provinces, Erim made his position clear. "When I was Minister of Public Works," he recalled with some embellishment, "I had the Americans establish the highway system. I'll apply the same strategy here. I'll leverage this advantage effectively. I'll have industrial facilities established in poppy-growing areas.…And the villagers' standard of living will be exponentially higher than it is now."

But the plans that had been hashed out by the end of 1971 belied this optimism. If opium had once animated visions of development and had fueled fantasies of new infrastructure schemes wrought from its income, this was a diminished, late-in-the-day effort to sell off the remains of a suspect crop in the hopes of garnering a one-time investment. Opium's days as a lucrative legal crop were indeed, finally, numbered—and there were new visions at work that had reshaped the game entirely.

◖◯◗

In June 1971, the same month that the Turkish poppy ban was announced, Richard Nixon stood at a podium in the White House and declared a war on drugs. "America's public enemy number one in the United States," the president snarled, "is drug abuse." Heroin, more than any other drug, was the object of this war. In the weeks leading up to the war, Nixon's staffers had been asked to drum up dramatic statistics on the number of heroin users in the United States. Their estimate of 300,000 American addicts was five times greater than the best professional estimates.[14] Yet heroin abuse, these bloated figures aside, was indeed a real and resurgent concern. Long a staple of the postwar American city, heroin use appeared to be increasing with the return of servicemen from Vietnam. Different factions in the federal administration engaged in a pitched debate over whether heroin imported from Southeast Asia was eroding the formidable French Connection that linked Turkish opium to American cities. But heroin was clearly the chief villain in the newly framed war on drugs.

The bureaucratic dimensions of this war and its longer antecedents have long been central to accounts of American power at home and abroad, sutured to the nation's control over drugs' procurement, production, and use since well before the Second World War.[15] In the years prior to the president's announcement, a robust bureaucracy had grown even thicker. In 1968, the Federal Bureau of Narcotics was subsumed by the Bureau of Narcotics and Dangerous Drugs (BNDD), and under Nixon's watch, the BNDD had expanded its roster of agents from four hundred to two thousand, with an increasing number stationed abroad.[16]

When the president spoke to Congress later that afternoon, he outlined his plan for a new, $371 million "comprehensive drug control program"; soon, he would create a new White House agency, the Special Action Office for Drug Abuse Prevention, giving the United States its first "drug czar."[17]

But these accounts elide an equally substantive and material transformation that was taking place in a similar period, one which in fact underwrote the United States' new assertiveness in assaulting poppy directly. By the late 1960s, the most optimistic voices in pharmacological research had come to believe that the development of fully synthetic opioids that could wholly replace poppy-based ones was both inevitable and near. Nixon made this vision plain in his more technical address to Congress after his declaration of a war on drugs. While morphine and codeine were at present indispensable, and a "legitimate" source of income for some countries, the United States' goal would be to end opium production and poppy cultivation globally. The president announced that he would be "directing that Federal research efforts in the United States be intensified with the aim of developing at the earliest possible date synthetic substitutes for all opium derivatives." He had also asked the Director General of the World Health Organization to work with the United States to assess the potential of synthetic substitutes to replace opioid drugs and to implement them globally at the earliest possible date.[18]

Nixon and many others would soon discover that this goal, more than half a century old, well outpaced the technical realities of opioid research and development. As a stopgap, and informed by new discoveries about opium alkaloids themselves, the US federal bureaucracy would attempt a project that had been essentially dismissed for more than a hundred years: the growing of poppies domestically. When this project, too, was deemed unfeasible, that same American bureaucracy would be forced to confront an old reality anew: the management of opioid painkillers was inextricable from the management of global agricultural and developmental politics in the two nations where licit opium was largely grown.

The $100,000 prize that Herman Metz had dangled out in 1925 as a reward for the discovery of a synthetic substitute for morphine had foreshadowed a major transatlantic research agenda. From the late 1920s, scientists in the United States and in Europe worked toward two goals that were broadly seen as inseparable: the discovery of that synthetic substitute and of a painkilling drug that did not have the addictive potential of opium-based drugs.[19]

Much of this early research was undertaken by the US National Research Council's Committee on Drug Addiction. The committee brought together chemists, pharmacologists, and government agencies in a coordinated research effort. Despite initial resistance from organized medicine and industry to what was seen as government interference in commercial drug development, the Committee was able to get buy-in for its promise to take on the practical challenges and expenses of testing new drugs for addictiveness.[20] Lyndon Small's chemistry lab at the University of Virginia synthesized new opiate compounds, while Nathan Eddy's pharmacology lab at the University of Michigan tested them in animals before experimenting on inmates at the US Narcotic Farm in Lexington, Kentucky.[21] A small number of compounds emerged from this research. But desomorphine, fully synthetic, was found to be highly addictive. Metopon, a semisynthetic opiate analog billed as less addictive, was brought to the market as something of a clinical trial, but the compound made little dent in wider prescribing patterns.

A concurrent strain of research in Germany led to the synthesis of pethidine, marketed as Demerol, and methodone.[22] Both of these substances were requisitioned and expropriated by the Allies during the Second World War; by the 1960s, methadone would become an important, though controversial, substance used as a "substitute" for heroin in the new strategy of maintenance therapy for addiction.[23] In 1959, a Belgian chemist screening chemicals similar to pethidine synthesized fentanyl. A hundred times more potent than morphine, it was used cautiously for general anesthesia in surgery after its market introduction in 1968.[24]

The most promising lead in this work came through a renewed focus on opioid "antagonists." Drug researchers had understood, since the interwar years, that certain compounds could block or reverse the effects of opioid. Pharmacologists hypothesized that these compounds were competing with opioids for some kind of binding site in the body, and the search for that "receptor" would become its own major area of research by the late 1960s. Beginning in the late 1940s and well into the early 1960s, newly discovered synthetic antagonists like nalorphine and naloxone moved to the center of pharmacological investigations, particularly after the discovery that the former had its own analgesic properties. Most of these antagonists came with severe side effects, including hallucinations.

A watershed moment came in the early 1960s, however, when researchers at Sterling-Winthrop, which manufactured Demerol, identified a new compound with a painkilling strength similar to morphine, and which did not appear to prevent withdrawal symptoms in opioid-dependent monkeys.[25] WN 20,228 wowed the Committee on Drug Addiction's most prominent and skeptical member, who declared that the drug "need not be subject to narcotics control." The new drug, pentazocine, was brought onto the market as Talwin in 1967, and it was touted by many authorities as the compound that, after thirty years, was wholly synthesized in the laboratory and had no addictive potential. Within a year, the American Medical Association and the Food and Drug Administration were expressing new reservations, and Sterling-Winthrop was forced to rein in their claims. Not until the late 1970s would Talwin become a clear substance of abuse when Chicago heroin users found that, mixed with a common antihistamine and injected, it mimicked heroin's high and addictive properties.

Surveying the state of research and drug development at the beginning of the 1970s, it seemed to optimistic observers that the end of addictive and poppy-based opioid painkillers was near. A meeting of physicians and pharmacologists meeting under the auspices of the World Health Organization contended that, with non-poppy drugs for pain, cough, and diarrhea under development, "the natural and semi-synthetic opiates may be considered not indispensable in the practice of modern medicine."[26] For the time being, as something of a stopgap, there also appeared to be new ways of using opium itself. The first was a new valuation of the alkaloids contained within opium, and the second was the reanimation of an older idea of how poppy itself might be processed more directly into these alkaloids.

Since its identification as an opium alkaloid in the 1830s, thebaine had been something of a curiosity. The two French chemists who had discovered it called it paramorphine, but the name that another chemist gave it a decade later had stuck. Thebaine was an homage to the ancient Egyptian city of Thebes, later Luxor, where some of the earliest opium crops were alleged to have been grown. Pharmacologists had not seen in thebaine any great medical use. In the 1940s, India's opium bureaucrats had worked to equip the factory at Ghazipur to produce it, but they had abandoned the project shortly thereafter.[27] Thebaine, unusable in its own right and only theoretically possible to transform into codeine, was commercially unviable.

By the postwar years, pharmacologists were developing new chemical extraction and conversion processes.[28] In the late 1940s, French pharmacologist André Barbier came up with a number of interlinked techniques for modifying opium alkaloids. Most importantly, thebaine could be treated as a "mother liquor" from which to distill codeine.[29] If not yet commercially viable, the process would soon let pharmacologists transform thebaine into other compounds like hydrocodone and oxycodone, both semisynthetic opiates at the forefront of pharmaceutical research. In the 1950s, Endo Pharmaceuticals combined a thebaine-based semisynthetic drug, oxycodone, with aspirin, marketing it as Percodan. It also sponsored research at Columbia University on the possibility of extracting thebaine from *Papaver orientale*, a brilliant-hued poppy cultivar from the Caucuses.[30] The transformation of thebaine into powerful semisynthetic drugs was, by the late 1960s, animating new pharmacological agendas, largely rooted in the idea that opium could be made more efficiently into useful products.

Finally, there was the new hope that pharmacologists had come to place in poppy straw. For many centuries, the laborious process of scraping mature poppy capsules for sap had been the sole means of extracting usable painkillers from the plant. But since Sertürner's discovery of morphine itself, scientists had imagined means of using poppy directly without the need for such immense human input. French chemists, within years of that discovery, had experimented with ways of processing cut capsules directly. A chemist from Dijon had used pure magnesia to produce morphine as an expensive proof of concept.[31] Heinrich Emanuel Merck and two other apothecaries worked to develop a similar process in the 1830s.[32] It was not until the late 1920s that a Hungarian chemist developed a method to extract morphine from the dried capsules and upper part of the stalk, collectively referred to as poppy straw, which would otherwise have been fed to cattle.[33] This breakthrough allowed year-round production and reduced the labor costs involved in producing alkaloids. The "Kabay method" was improved over the following decades, and several countries—Hungary, Czechoslovakia, East Germany, the Netherlands, Norway, and Poland—eliminated their need for opium imports altogether.[34] By the early 1960s, it was apparent that the Kabay method had other, positive knock-on effects. Using poppy straw not only saved labor—all that was needed was to pass a combine through a field—but also avoided the production of opium altogether.

The political implications of this technological possibility were plain to the bureaucrats who had been planning the end of Turkish poppy cultivation and, in turn, the eradication of opium production worldwide. By 1970, John T. Cusack had been dealing with the poppy problem for a decade. He had gone to India on behalf of the Federal Bureau of Narcotics in the early 1960s to negotiate terms there, and in 1965, he had been the official who had sketched out the initial drafts of the plan for Turkish eradication.[35] As Turkish and American officials negotiated, and as the Nixon administration prepared its opening moves in the "war on drugs," Cusack outlined his own plan for the future of US pharmaceutical production.[36]

The United States, he noted, was in a place of particular vulnerability. The countries of Eastern and Central Europe had been able to build domestic alkaloid capacities through the cultivation of poppy straw. Western Europe was heading in this direction, and the Soviet Union was rumored to be converting to poppy straw production, too. Only the United States was relying on opium gum to such a large degree. With Turkey's exit from the market, and synthetic opioid production moving slower than was being stated publicly, American pharmaceutical production was to become uniquely dependent on India. "Should India," Cusack wrote, "once she becomes the sole producer of opium, begin to arbitrarily raise crude opium prices the U.S. would probably be forced to import crude morphine or produce its own poppy extract. In the view of this writer, the latter alternative is by far the more preferable." The United States, he estimated, could use the poppy straw method in creating its own domestic industry, finally doing what so many American schemers had imagined and what other countries appeared to be doing themselves. The amount of land required, Cusack estimated, would be between 25,000 and 150,000 acres, equivalent at the high end to around 350 average-sized American farms.

American officials spent the better part of two years wrestling with the proposal.[37] They debated the feasibility and costs associated, the likelihood that synthetic opioid would or would not replace poppy-derived ones. Ultimately, the narcotics bureaucracy largely demurred.[38] If members saw the practical advantages of autarky, they balked at the outlay that would be needed for land and extraction prices. The pharmaceutical companies consulted would not undertake the costs in light of an uncertain future market, and State Department employees wondered what the diplomatic and legal ramifications of producing alkaloids at home would be.

The Nixon administration officials who had envisioned the impending end of opium production were far outpacing the state of pharmacological research. But the world of opioid production had changed dramatically since the postwar years. If a synthetic substitute for opium was still more the stuff of conjecture, the category itself had come to encompass a range of synthetic, semisynthetic, and fully opium-derived products and products that were derived from poppy straw, as well as from the once-useless alkaloid thebaine. This material diversity seemed to invite a certain openness to novel political and agro-economic arrangements as well. Although Cusack's proposal for domestic cultivation seemed to be a non-starter, it presaged new openness to another one, which came in the form of a wholly different kind of poppy altogether.

ꙮ

On a summer morning in 1966, two Iranian chemists climbed into a boxy Paykan sedan and drove from Tehran to the Alborz mountains, the snow-capped peaks looming dramatically over the capital.[39] Armed with pocketknives, the two returned carrying glass jars of latex, scraped carefully from the poppies that dotted the mountainside. The poppies in question were not *Papaver somniferum*, the standard opium poppy, but *Papaver bracteatum*, a botanical cousin known for its distinctly large scarlet blossoms. Back in the laboratory, the chemists pulverized ten grams of dried latex, extracting its compounds in a bath of warm benzene. To their surprise, there was no morphine. But the powder did contain more than two and a half grams of pure thebaine—five times more than what was usually found in the standard opium poppy itself. The poppy straw method that had been coming into vogue in much of Europe had the advantage of allowing manufacturers to create pharmaceutical alkaloids without producing opium itself. But *bracteatum* had its own advantage: it was full of thebaine, which could be converted into codeine and from there into many other semisynthetic opioids. But it had no morphine and, as such, could not ever be converted into heroin. Processed by the poppy straw method, it offered the possibility of pharmaceutical production with no incentive or means for diversion.

The assault on Turkey's poppy production in 1971 brought *bracteatum* from the realm of botanical research into the domain of practical experimentation.[40] In the fall of 1972, a team of English scientists harvested a trial crop from a plot outside of London. Its thebaine yield was fifteen times greater than the equivalent alkaloid production expected of

Turkish poppy, and five times greater than Indian poppy. That same fall—a year after shelving the idea of growing *Papaver somniferum* domestically—a team at the US Department of Agriculture began planning its own large-scale trial with *bracteatum*. The project was headed by Quentin Jones, the scientist who had overseen the joint Turkish-American opium replacement project the previous year. If the British yields were generalizable, Jones estimated, the whole of the United States' pharmaceutical non-synthetic opioid needs could be met from a plot of twenty square miles—around half the lowest estimate of the land needed if the standard opium poppy were grown.[41]

Two of the three authorized importers and manufacturers of opium were brought into the project, tasked with growing *bracteatum* and assessing its commercial viability. The USDA planted initial trial crops in Beltsville, Maryland; Flagstaff, Arizona; and Pullman, Washington, before authorizing the private firms to undertake their own experiments. Mallinckrodt planted one hundred acres in Nebraska with the Iranian Arya II cultivar it had received from the USDA and outlined plans for a more permanent installation that would be located at the end of a five-mile-long country road and surrounded by armed guards. Merck arranged for its trials to be undertaken at the Western Agricultural Research Station in Corvallis, Montana. A few newcomers were brought in as well. General Electric ran a trial of a fully indoor *bracteatum* farm in Syracuse, New York, while Endo Laboratories, the manufacturers of Percocet, planted their seeds on a Wilmington, Delaware, farm while offering their services to the USDA in developing manufacturing protocols.

The *bracteatum* trial came at a time when the stakes of determining the future of alkaloid procurement could not have been higher. It had not taken long after the Turkish opium ban went into effect in early 1972 for American physicians to feel the consequences. The idea that opium was nearing obsolescence had always been an optimistic one, but the degree to which it had been overstated surprised even the most cynical observers. In 1973, the United States' authorized opium importers warned that they were facing a fourteen-thousand-kilogram shortfall of medicinal opium.[42] Soon, physicians' groups were sounding the alarm, too.[43] The White House debated the particulars of the shortage, but it could not debate the shortage out of existence.[44] In the summer of 1973, the United States released a massive cache of opium—around 141,600 pounds wrapped in plastic bags, equivalent to 634 tons of usable alkaloids—from its strategic reserve in Fort Knox for sale to manufacturers.

This stopgap was not enough to ease mounting concerns that the US move to end Turkish production had left its medical practitioners in the lurch. The American Medical Association, an organization that was in the midst of its own major transition in how it institutionally approached the question of pain relief, joined the fray in October 1974.[45] In a petition to the president, its leadership asked that the president "take whatever steps are necessary to assist in the procurement of raw opium from the world." Five months later, a hundred AMA members met in Washington along with the United States "drug czar," the commercial

Figure 6.1 Workers planting *Papaver bracteatum* seedlings for Endo Laboratories, the manufacturers of Percocet, on a farm outside of Wilmington, Delaware. United States National Archives.

attaché of the Indian embassy, and three of the country's most respected pharmacologists to urge the White House to recognize the severity of America's pending opium shortage. The participants in the symposium were agnostic about the particulars of the alkaloids they needed—they could come from Indian imports or Turkish ones or from *bracteatum*— but they soundly rejected the idea that synthetics were soon or ever to fully obviate the need for poppy-derived products.

The *bracteatum* experiments had been promising. Processing the straw was challenging for inexperienced American firms but not over-whelmingly so. These experiments and the apparent opium shortage that the United States was facing brought to the fore a long-suppressed conflict. Once growing poppy and producing useable alkaloids was pos-sible domestically, without any risk of diversion, what was keeping a vital pharmaceutical resource an obligate import? The immediate battle was between those who believed the project of growing poppy domestically was long overdue and those who insisted that the geopolitical impera-tives of managing poppy cultivation worldwide precluded such a radi-cal change.

Proponents of domestic *bracteatum* cultivation employed powerful lobbyists to make their case. The American firms that had undertaken the trials hired one of the United States' most prestigious and well-connected law firms to argue that the uncertainty around synthetic opioids necessitated the United States to buy a small amount of raw opium from India and source the rest of their alkaloids from domestic *bracteatum*.[46] The American Medical Association made nearly identical arguments.[47] The unexpected champion of these efforts was Senator Jesse Helms, the conservative senator whose North Carolina constituents included Burroughs Wellcome, a North Carolina pharmaceutical firm developing novel painkillers using *bracteatum*. These voices were up against the steadfast opposition of the State Department. Sheldon Vance, its Coordinator for International Narcotics Matters, spoke for the Department when he contended that approving any kind of domestic production would make a mockery of the efforts the United States had made to stamp out Turkish cultivation. Turkish newspapers had already begun printing their own bombastic accounts of the *bracteatum* project after an article on the "startling proposal" had appeared in the *Washington Post*.[48] The geopolitical implications of American cultivation, the Department felt, were simply too dangerous to countenance. By the second half of the 1970s, the question would be delegated to a matter of administrative law. Before that, Turkey would make its own priorities known again.

✺

The poppy ban in Turkey had hit cultivators hard, and they knew who had been responsible.[49] "Why," one farmer in Konya lamented to a reporter, "have the Americans done this to us?" The punishments for illegal cultivation had been trumpeted loudly on the radio and in the newspapers. Rumors swirled that violators would be summarily hanged. But many Turks felt equally confident that the ban would be lifted as swiftly as it had been imposed.

The Erim government had moved quickly to implement the ban and the scheme for compensation. American Vice President Spiro Agnew had come to Ankara in the fall to discuss the Turkish-American team's findings, and the US Secretary of Agriculture had visited shortly thereafter. By early 1972, the Erim government had come up with a compensation plan, with higher amounts given to those who abandoned the crop earlier. Erim had been rewarded with a state visit to the United States, but a month later, he was forced out of office in political crisis. Turkey's interim government continued to implement the ban and the compensation throughout 1973 and 1974. It sold off the remainder of its stockpiled opium to American manufacturers in exchange for finished codeine.[50] The compensation payments came slowly, and the immensely unpopular ban made for good political capital for Turkey's opposition parties. In the run-up to the 1973 general election, both leading candidates vowed to reinstate poppy farming if elected.

By the time Bülent Ecevit came to power in 1974, Turkish politicians and media had brought the opium issue to the forefront of public opinion, well beyond the rural constituencies where the ban's effect was practically felt. Turkey's foreign minister took to the airwaves to decry it as a grave geopolitical injustice.[51] The moderate daily *Milliyet* devoted front-page space to the plight of the poppy farmer, the state mouthpiece *Cumhuriyet* described the ban as the culmination of an American assault on Turkish dignity, and the sensationalist *Günaydın* ran a photograph of defiant Afyon villagers scolding an American visitor. When two New York representatives came to Turkey to see the effects firsthand, they were mocked furiously by irate villagers.[52] The opium issue, the US ambassador declared, had whipped up Turkey's "strident nationalism and anti-Americanism" to a point of no return.[53] Foreign correspondents filed reports for American outlets filled with slightly overwrought tales of poppy farmers forced into destitution on the "bleak Anatolian steppes," where Turkish peasants were said to be moving into shantytowns, while women recalled the taste of *Afyon kaymağı*, a thickened sweet cream made with milk from cows fed on poppy leaves. The *Washington Post* profiled the plight of an impoverished elderly farmer who had assailed the New York representatives, and *New York Times* readers learned of Sabri Selek, a poppy-oil presser from Afyon who choked up describing his slide into destitution after abandoning his livelihood of forty years.[54] All this made for good political capital for Bülent Ecevit, who declared in campaign materials that "no one but the Turks can decide what to grow and where in Turkey," and who would later place poppies and poppy farmers on the cover of a collection of his writing and speeches.

In June 1974, nearly three years to the day after the Turkish poppy ban had been announced, the republic's information minister took to the airwaves to announce the resumption of poppy cultivation.[55] "Turkey's opium," he declared, "will feed the international pharmaceutical industry." In the lead-up to the announcement, Turkish state farms had germinated poppy seeds to send to farmers to restart their crops, and the state monopoly had sent letters to American manufacturers announcing their intentions.[56]

The American response was swift. The US ambassador was recalled, and embassy staffers were sent into the Anatolian hinterlands to try to

Figure 6.2 Campaign materials for Turkish politician Bülent Ecevit declaring that "no one but the Turks can decide what to grow and where in Turkey." Bülent Ecevit.

map the "low-lying mountain ranges, rock formations, and sparsely wooded areas" that were to become easy smuggling routes again.[57] Henry Kissinger wondered whether he could persuade the prime minister, a former student, to change course. The Secretary of State asked World Bank President Robert McNamara to consider offering an "Indus Valley" investment in India. A blank check for any rural development project might be too large a carrot for Ankara to ignore. But Kissinger was wrong. Ankara turned their nose up at the offer. Barring avoiding Turkish purchases altogether, the Americans had only one real option: to pledge they would stop buying Turkish opium and instead purchase Turkish poppy straw exclusively. Quentin Jones, the Department of Agriculture employee who had led the Turkish-American team three years earlier, and who had been working on the *bracteatum* project, was sent to Turkey to gain this concession.

Figure 6.3 A collection of political writings and speeches by Bülent Ecevit decorated with images of poppy cultivation and capsules. Bülent Ecevit.

Ankara had forced the Americans' hand. American officials braced for an influx of Turkish heroin on American streets. A meeting between the Turkish and American heads of state on the sidelines of a Soviet-American summit in Helsinki turned argumentative over the opium question.[58] But if American narcotics officials did not want Turkish production to go rogue, they had little choice but to deepen their collaboration with their Turkish counterparts. In the year after production resumed, the United States sent more than $3 million in technical aid to the Turkish monopoly and eight agents to train its employees.[59] The monopoly did seem eager to comply. They sidelined middlemen in favor of "mobile buying units," surveyed growing areas with helicopters and light planes, and kept meticulous statistics on new Altair microcomputers. Turkey's Director of Internal Security assured his American counterparts that "there is no more smugglers' market for poppy products in Turkey." That claim was premature, since big caches of morphine base were unearthed in cities like Izmir and Denizli.[60] But Turkey had managed to bring some order to a once-chaotic market. Monopoly officials, a group of farmers in an Afyon coffeehouse complained in 1975, had come to their village four times to check on the crop.[61] "We see no way to beat this system," one farmer grumbled. Those inspectors were looking for gashes on the dried pods on the top of the cut straw, the tell-tale sign of illegal lancing and opium production.

The resumption of poppy cultivation might have represented a clear political victory for politicians in Ankara. They had, after all, confronted American diplomatic pressure and had won. But Turkish opium, having left the licit market for several years, was less desirable to European and American purchasers than ever.[62] Prices had cratered: poppy straw was picked up for seventy cents a pound and produced on a third of the land it had been grown on before the ban.[63] Many manufacturers—including the three major American ones—had no interest in switching back from Indian opium. A small amount of poppy straw and concentrate of poppy straw arrived by air at New York's JFK airport, where it would wait in a special vault before armored trucks delivered it to manufacturers.[64] Despite Turkish lobbying trips to American firms, the product sat unexpected in monopoly warehouses. At the end of the decade, the monopoly received a single bid for its poppy straw from a Dutch pharmaceutical firm.[65]

In meetings with American officials in Ankara and Washington, Turkish bureaucrats contended that the decimation of their trade was a historical wrong. They railed against the *bracteatum* cultivation project, "impossible to explain to the Turkish peasants," and the United States' "support" for the Indian opium industry. Throughout 1978 and 1979, the United States continued to offer the services of a solitary USAID worker under the auspices of its Narcotics Control Development Assistance Program—a set of carrots it offered to projects where narcotics cultivation was ended.[66] Mostly, however, monopoly officials assailed the United States' seeming unwillingness to purchase their wares. Mathea Falco, the young Assistant Secretary of State for International Narcotics Matters for the Carter administration, was sent on a long tour through Turkey's opium cultivation regions.[67] Democratic Senator Joe Biden followed shortly thereafter to field Turkish requests for renewed access to American narcotic markets.[68] The DEA's Director of the Office of Compliance and Regulatory Affairs, Kenneth Durrin, put it most succinctly. "The Turks," he wrote in 1979, "seemed to feel that the U.S. government guided American firms more than it really does."[69]

Turkey had one last card to play. Since the 1950s, officials in Ankara had floated the idea of building their own alkaloid factory—a facility that would allow them to produce intermediate goods for domestic use or export overseas.[70] Shortly after the resumption of poppy cultivation, Ankara declared that it would invite foreign technicians to Turkey to build that factory. By the end of 1975, a team of West German engineers and pharmacologists had arrived in the small town of Bolvadin to construct a facility there.[71] The Americans had objected. There were already world-class alkaloid plants processing poppy straw in the Netherlands, France, and Australia. Bolvadin was a backwater, and no savvy American firm would want to deal with "the lack of business acumen characteristic of Turkish state enterprises."[72] Perhaps most importantly, this plant

Figure 6.4 The recently opened Turkish alkaloid factory in Bolvadin pictured in the mid-1980s. General Directorate of Pharmaceuticals, Ministry of Health and Social Assistance, Republic of Turkey.

would not be able to produce thebaine, the alkaloid so integral to most newer opioids.[73] The head of the DEA, after a tour of the construction, noted that "the basic elements for running a factory seem to be missing."[74] A Mallinckrodt executive en route to India detoured to Turkey to meet with factory officials there.[75] The project, he declared, was senseless when "India could supply all the US's narcotic raw material needs indefinitely."

After four years of construction, the plant opened in August 1980. It might have been a triumphant event, and it was trumpeted as such by the prime minister, who said that the plant would "silence those who maliciously and incorrectly claim" that Turkey was a source of illicit narcotics.[76] The two bored German technicians and the skeptical USAID worker who attended the opening could see that the plant was a white elephant. The poppy straw concentrate being produced there was too strong to legally import to Europe or the United States, lacked thebaine, and was more expensive than its Indian opium gum equivalent.[77] The plant, like Turkish poppy itself, had no real market. Turkish diplomats cast the plant as the United States' problem to fix, in the interests of repairing the damage Washington had done in decimating the larger industry. But diplomats were scarcely interested in a problem that the Turks seemed to have made themselves, and American executives were no more invested in its solution.

꧅

Toward the end of the 1970s, Robert Dupont, the United States' second "drug czar," would describe the first years of the decade as a period of "chaotic growth" in narcotics enforcement.[78] The moment was indeed chaotic domestically and in the new claims that Washington was making to regulate narcotics production globally. But this chaos also masked the very real and equal uncertainties around how the changing world of opioid production and consumption did and should work in comfort. There were, in this moment, uniquely open-ended and pressing questions about what was technically feasible and possible and what kind of relationship could exist between opium production, opioid drugs, and the treatment of pain itself.

When the Nixon administration had used the full force of American diplomatic pressure to bring about an end to Turkish poppy cultivation in 1971, the move was animated by a bold claim. Poppy-based opioid drugs, their vision held, were soon to be fully replaced by synthetic ones. This vision was built on a half century of laboratory work toward a similar goal. Few credible practitioners or researchers would have agreed with the contention that poppy-based drugs were no longer needed. A World Health Organization report in 1972 had offered highly muted optimism as to the future of synthetic opioids; a subsequent National Academy of Sciences study was more bearish.

Not even those within the administration were convinced of the promise of synthetic opioids. Nixon's domestic affairs advisor conceded shortly thereafter that poppy cultivation would "be required for the foreseeable future."[79] Jerome Jaffe, the inaugural "drug czar," readily admitted shortly after the ban that there was no "synthetic now on the horizon" that could replace basic drugs like codeine and morphine.[80] A focus on synthetic substitutes, he later wrote, ignored "the inherent conservatism of medical practitioners" and the "hundreds of thousands of individual decisions each day by hundreds of thousands of doctors, dentists, and other medical practitioners" that continued to make opium-based drugs essential.[81] His successor added that synthetic substitutes would only come about by "an orderly scientific process where the Government plays a very active collaborative role in developing truly better substances, [not] in the spirit of replacing natural opioids for some political or policy reasons, but purely in the interest of providing better medication and at a lower cost to patients in need of treatment."[82]

At the same time, opioid use in the United States was at the beginning of a significant upward swing. Heterodox voices in pharmacological research were beginning to assert that opioid drugs were being broadly overused. Georgetown's William Beaver, one of the world's leading painkiller researchers, contended that two tablets of acetaminophen would in most cases be just as effective as codeine.[83] But this view was at odds with standard American medical practice. The United States' per capita codeine use climbed steadily over the course of the 1970s. By the decade's end, it was a "high rate" usage country, on a par with Denmark, Australia, Switzerland, the United Kingdom, and West Germany.

The limitations and risks of the synthetic drugs that did exist had also become plain. One senator in the middle of the decade warned of the specter of drugs small enough to be "sold in microgram quantities [and] smuggled under a postage stamp."[84] Joseph Cochin, a Boston University professor who was the world's leading authority on opioid analgesia, was sounding new alarms about the abuse potential of drugs like etonitazene, a synthetic analgesic "1000 times stronger than morphine." In the late 1970s, a team at the National Institutes of Health achieved a seemingly impossible breakthrough: the total synthesis of morphine from a widely available organic chemical. The laboratory synthesis of morphine was a triumph of chemistry, but also an uneconomic and complicated fourteen-step process that yielded a very small usable amount.

The stakes of synthetic opioids to replace poppy-derived alkaloids grew starker as the decade advanced. The United States weathered the storm of the early 1970s, when the AMA and manufacturers had been spooked by the specter of a codeine shortage. By the decade's end, thebaine, too, seemed to be in short supply.[85] But the *bracteatum* project in which many American firms had placed so much hope was smothered in the federal bureaucracy. The decision was handed over to the Office of Management and Budget, which placed a draft set of rules in the *Federal Register*. They showed how *bracteatum* would be grown behind barbed wire fences and how the fields' perimeters would be protected by CB radio linkups to local police stations.[86] The country's major pharmaceutical manufacturers, and a great number of smaller manufacturers of pills, injectable painkillers, and cough syrup, wrote in to support the proposal. They echoed the hopes of one Colorado executive who hailed the prospect of the United States becoming "totally independent in the production of codeine." The American Medical Association joined several of the country's most prominent pathologists and pharmacologists in urging the same outcome. But the State Department lobbied furiously against the proposal, insisting that its cultivation would eviscerate any remaining leverage the United States had with India and Turkey. The decision as to whether the proposal would go forward was in the hands of an administrative judge who presided over a packed hearing in 1977.[87] The judge sent the matter back to the DEA and the White House for reconsideration. Two months later, under pressure from the State Department, the proposal was withdrawn.[88]

American pharmaceutical production had come full circle. It was not technically feasible to replace poppy-based opioids with synthetic ones, and the notion of growing any form of poppy domestically had been ruled out as too geopolitically disruptive. Yet the question of how exactly this convoluted import scheme might be governed had grown even less certain in the frenzied transformations of the decade. In the wake of Ankara's decision to repeal the ban on poppy cultivation, US pharmaceutical manufacturers and their legislative allies had scrambled to import opium from far-flung corners of the globe.[89] Mallinckrodt dispatched a buyer to Kabul, and a New York representative had floated the idea of buying up raw opium from rebel leaders in Burma.[90] A prominent pharmacologist summed up the predicament neatly.[91] "Forcing Turkey to stop production," he insisted, "was the craziest idea anyone has ever had."

In early 1975, spooked by the prospect of shortage, US Senator Birch Bayh convened a three-day series of hearings to examine the future of opium cultivation. White House officials; DEA, FDA, and State Department bureaucrats; international narcotics experts; agricultural specialists; and pharmaceutical company representatives all spoke about the impact of the Turkish ban and its rescission and held different ideas of what might be done. The witnesses all spoke to a lack of coordination and communication between government agencies, a misjudgment of the impact that the Turkish ban would have had, and ultimately the need for a better strategy moving forward. The eradication and substitution camp had largely been defeated, as had those urging self-sufficiency through *bracteatum*.

The consensus view—articulated by DEA and FDA officials, representatives of the International Narcotics Control Board, and Jerome Jaffe, the former drug czar—seemed to be that the United States would need to move toward a policy of pragmatic control. Turkey might be afforded some role in this future import regime. Shutting it out entirely did not seem feasible. India, all parties seemed to know, would be the central, indispensable partner. But to rely entirely on Indian labor, Indian climate and ecology, and above all, the predictability of the Indian bureaucracy seemed foolish. There were other possible partners whose production seemed suited for American use. Countries like Hungary, Poland, and Czechoslovakia had experience with poppy straw and well-established pharmaceutical industries, making them potentially reliable suppliers with a lower risk of diversion. Yugoslavia could be one, as well, if it could improve its system of controls and overall transparency and accountability. If France were able to up its enforcement against clandestine morphine labs, it too could produce for American markets. Australia had the capability to contribute to a diversified supply, though Tasmanian producers were raising poppy straw for the country's domestic needs. The contours of this arrangement would soon grow clearer, as well as the implications for India.

7

Opium's Last Stand

Even by the standards of Indian politicking, the promise was an outsized one. But Sawai Singh Sisodia was an ambitious Madhya Pradesh politician whose own roots were among the opium cultivators of Mewar. In August 1981, ten thousand opium cultivators had converged upon the Indian city of Indore, a bustling industrial hub in the center of the state, to hear India's finance minister speak. The next year, Sisodia announced to an ebullient crowd that New Delhi would vastly expand the number of *pattas*, or licenses to grow poppy, available to cultivators.[1] He would advocate, too, for all the concessions that were given to India's other high-value crops like tea, coffee, and jute, namely, loans and crop insurance, technical training, help with marketing and crop improvement, and subsidies.

The announcement was a gift to Sisodia's rural constituency. It was also ludicrous: India was not even selling the opium it was already producing. By the most conservative estimate, it was sitting on a 3,000-ton stockpile of opium, largely moldering in the Neemuch factory a few hours away. Later that year, after a bit more than half of that stockpile had been exported at cut-rate prices to the Soviet Union and other Eastern Bloc countries through India's State Trading Corporation, the manager of that factory painted a similarly dismal picture of its operations.[2] Three massive warehouses had been constructed for the long-term storage of the unsold opium, since the polythene bags the factory usually used had cracked and burst. The manager of that factory lamented the "unfair" competition it had from Turkish poppy straw, and the inept workers that the Finance Ministry had assigned to work with him. But the record crops that Indian cultivators had been reaping over the past several years were overwhelming the Ghazipur factory as well.

Throughout the 1970s, Indian cultivators had continued to plant, tend, score, and scrape opium gum from poppies across the country's north and central plains. Save some agronomic improvements and better tools, the process was truly little changed from a century prior. But with each passing year, as poppy straw increasingly came to supplant opium itself, the product had grown progressively less valuable for the pharmaceutical purposes for which it was ostensibly destined. It was not the first Indian product to become so outmoded.[3] The ruddy madder root cultivated in the country's west and the inky blue indigo grown on plantations in the east had been swiftly replaced by synthetic dyes.[4] The jute industry of Bengal, the source of the world's ropes and bags, had been decimated with the rise of synthetic fibers.[5] And lac, collected from insects in the woods of central and eastern India, had largely given way to synthetic resins and plastics.[6] Opium had held on longer than all of these Indian products. But not even the expensive investments made in modernizing the Neemuch factory a few years prior could alter the fact that opium gum was increasingly less desirable for foreign buyers.

Sawai Singh Sisodia, when away from the cheering opium cultivators, readily admitted as much. The minister, on his visit to Neemuch, had learned of the rampant thefts at the factory there. And in New Delhi, he lamented the rotten state of the entire industry, with international purchasing as low as it had ever been.[7] In a decade's time, would the industry exist at all? If not, what was to be gained from the big promises made to opium cultivators during that August conference in Indore?

In the closing years of the 1970s, the Indian opium industry had seemed poised for a renaissance. India had benefited tremendously from the Turkish opium ban: the cessation of poppy cultivation in Turkey had helped India increase its global market share, and India capitalized upon the resulting marketing opportunity to remain the dominant supplier to Western pharmaceutical companies even after the resumption of

Turkish production. Yet the euphoria in India had been exceedingly short-lived. By the time Sisodia was making his big promises, pharmaceutical production had changed dramatically. India was in a crisis of overproduction, with unsold opium stockpiles rotting away in warehouses.

Indian officials were caught in a new bind. On the one hand, poppy licenses represented a valuable political asset in the three states where it was legally grown. The country's increasingly capable research apparatus was focusing on the improvement of Indian poppy, the state was investing in the modernization of its opium processing facilities, and politicians like Sawai Singh Sisodia were accruing political capital with the promise of more poppy licenses and more land on which to grow. India's domestic political economy of opium saw the crop become progressively central to patronage networks and rural development schemes in important tracts of Rajasthan, Uttar Pradesh, and Rajasthan. But India's ability to export any opium was tied to its willingness to cooperate with the increasingly demanding strictures of American-led narcotics control. Initially, American officials had accepted the idea that so long as diverted Indian opium remained a domestic or regional concern, it would not disturb the structure of production for pharmaceutical purposes. But as the decade ended and the extent of India's black market became clear, Indian opium was of increased concern to American narcotics officials.

After a bumper crop of opium in 1978 and the massive glut of unsold opium that ensued, a delicate balance was thrown into crisis. India's new top opium official, Jasjit Singh, worked in consort with Mallinckrodt, India's longtime top buyer, to advance a long-term supply proposal with the United States. The plan was mothballed, but within a year's time, new developments in international arenas and then in Washington led to the development of new federal legislation designed to bring predictability to raw narcotic material imports and to the geopolitical realities they underpinned. The 80-20 rule, which reserved 80 percent of the market for "traditional producers," primarily India and Turkey, was on paper a victory for India. But the changing nature of production itself failed to resolve India's problems of overproduction and black-market diversion.

In the decades to come, it would lead to even more dire consequences for India's opium producers.

The creation of the postwar opium order, which relied upon Indian and Turkish poppy production to fuel American and much of Western European pharmaceutical production, had been predicated on the fantasy that it was possible to neatly delineate licit production from the black-market underworld. Pharmaceutical producers in the United States, and to a lesser degree in Europe, had made ready alliances with the reformed opium bureaucracies of Turkey and the United States. India, once a last-choice producer for these firms, had emerged from this moment as the world's leading producer for pharmaceutical markets. But the fantasy of dividing the world into acceptable and unacceptable spaces for opium production had been greatly diminished by the complex wrangling over the Single Convention on narcotics in 1961, the rise of new smuggling networks from Turkey, and a complex geography of substances and spaces that belied easy categorization. Turkey's whiplash-inducing shift from licit to illicit producer and then back again showed the arbitrariness of these categories. And the fragile logic that underpinned India's continuing status as a legal producer was tested mightily by the glut of the late 1970s.

India was to some degree a supplicant in the negotiations of this era. It could not induce greater demand among pharmaceutical purchasers, nor did it hold major sway in diplomatic circles or in international regulatory bodies, save for its seat on the International Narcotics Control Board, the United Nations body monitoring compliance with international drug control treaties. Yet by dint of its formidable industry, it was able to exert a certain amount of influence over the ways in which policy was crafted. As US officials worked to create a policy to bring order to the import of opium products and the geopolitical order that knit together producing states and consuming ones, India was able to leverage its historic relationships to ensure a continued role for its production in global trade. Even as its illicit production undercut the notion that it was a wholly legitimate producer, India would remain statutorily bound to and privileged within the modern pharmaceutical opium order. India's victory, however, was wholly pyrrhic. Enshrining a privileged spot for Indian opium into American regulation would mean little as the material value of raw opium gum became increasingly marginal in pharmaceutical production. Like jute, madder, indigo, and lac, among other crops, opium's economic value as an export commodity would be vastly diminished by chemical and economic transformations in the wider industry that once used it.

◖◗

At the beginning of the 1970s, the Indian and Turkish poppy industries were starkly different undertakings. India's had been secure and legible, while Turkey's was leaky and suspect. The rewards, for India, had been immense. In 1972, the United States Senate Committee on Foreign Relations estimated that over the previous twenty years India had boosted its share of total world opium exports from less than a third to more than 90 percent.[8] The chief exporter of opium to Western European and American pharmaceutical producers, it concluded, was India, "which is rapidly taking on a near-monopoly position in international trade." Up until 1971, the remainder of the licit supply had come from Turkey. But the ban had dealt Turkish production a near-fatal blow. Even after resuming poppy cultivation in 1974, Turkey's contribution to the global supply was greatly reduced.

American diplomats had a pat answer for the Turkish politicians and diplomats who asked why Turkey was being pressured to shutter its poppy industry, while India was not. "We are not making similar appeals there," the American ambassador told Turkey's frustrated deputy prime minister in Ankara, "because India controls its opium, and Turkey does not."[9] Turkish Prime Minister Bülent Ecevit insisted, shortly before the ban's rescission, that it was "absolutely impossible to explain to the Turkish public that Turkey must not grow opium, while India is being asked to grow more."[10] India, Turkish administrators insisted, was being coddled and offered preferential treatment while Turkey was being punished.

In fact, India had also been targeted for an eradication campaign. In 1972, as the Turkish ban was being implemented, State Department administrators were putting together a plan for the subsequent elimination of Indian opium.[11] India's cultivators, they contended, were already switching to other crops that cost less to produce. Such a decision, therefore, would be less politically fraught than in Turkey. The plan for India differed from Turkey's. While offering similar cash compensation, the United States would support India's pharmaceutical industry in developing synthetic opioids, rather than focusing on rural development. Yet after the Turkish recession, and the blowback from physicians skeptical about the push toward synthetics, the plan was never presented to Indian officials.

Indian bureaucrats instead opted for greater cooperation with the United States' expanding narcotics enforcement overseas. Throughout the 1960s, a tacit bargain had governed India's coordination with the American import regime. So long as smuggling remained regional, sales of opium to the United States could continue unfettered. That indeed had remained the case until the end of the 1960s. It was true that India's illicit opium production was immense—the CIA estimated it at around 200 tons annually in 1969, similar to Pakistan's black-market output.[12] Most of that production was being done by unlicensed producers, rather than being diverted from licensed ones. And nearly all of it stayed within India's borders. Two years later, Turkey's ban seemed to have made India's high-quality opium more attractive to the black market. The CIA's subsequent report on the region placed strong faith in Indian controls but urged greater investment in them.[13]

Indian officials were cautious. In 1971, a delegation from the United States' National Commission on Marijuana and Drug Abuse had arrived in New Delhi in an effort to plan collaborative programs with Indian narcotics officials.[14] Indian officials showed little interest, believing they had the opium situation under control.[15] A year later, two American congressmen arrived in India to survey poppy cultivation firsthand and to meet with what they described as their "apprehensive" Indian counterparts.[16] In the absence of a program like Turkey's, they concluded, it would be essential to bring those Indian officials on board. At first, those officials refused to countenance the idea.[17] One American official lamented the "chilly, although correct" tone of the conversations about opium. Indian bureaucrats, he added, invariably insisted "that there is no problem to discuss."[18] US Ambassador Daniel Patrick Moynihan warned his colleagues that Indian officials would bristle at anything that felt like "interference."[19] These conversations mirrored the overall suspicious tenor of Indo-US relations. Cozy with the Soviet Union and on opposite sides of the 1971 Bangladesh Liberation War, India was a deeply suspect partner.

And yet, in the area of narcotics enforcement, a real collaboration ensued. Indian officials, likely seeing collaboration as key to preserving their opium industry, began involving US counterparts in intelligence gathering and raid planning.[20] In late August 1973, after coordinating with officials in the American consulate in Bombay, Indian police conducted a massive raid at Dhobi Ghat—the city's massive open-air laundry. There, against the flutter of drying clothes, the police recovered 857 kilograms of smuggled opium.[21] It was a policing coup, but more importantly, a sign of deepening cooperation to come.

The "opium issue" burst into wider public consciousness in India in this period. Indian newspapers offered inflated accounts of opium smuggling from India to markets overseas. Bombay's *Blitz* described a massive narcotic ring shipping 200,000 kilograms of opium overseas each year, and the *Times of India* alleged that half the opium produced in Uttar Pradesh was being diverted overseas.[22] Pakistani diplomats were all too happy to play up their own inflated estimates of India's illicit opium industry.[23] At the same time, the amounts that India's officials were offering were implausibly low, like Finance Minister Pranab Mukherjee's estimate of five kilograms annually. Staffers in the American embassy, several years after the Turkish ban, offered a credible estimate of around a quarter of India's annual crop going to the black market, largely to markets in the Gulf.[24]

In 1975, India's prime minister, Indira Gandhi, proclaimed a state of "national emergency." After a year of mounting unrest and political agitation, Gandhi leveraged her allies' idiosyncratic reading of India's constitutional law to bring the country to heel.[25] For twenty-one months, democratic institutions were sidelined, civil liberties curtailed, opposition leaders jailed, and the press muzzled. India's authoritarian crisis nonetheless cheered a great number of India's middle-class urbanites, who were eager to see trains running on time, ramped-up industrial production, and improved public services. The convergence of a yellow press selling papers with tales of Bombay addicts using heroin in the shadow of Victoria Terminus or in glitzy Colaba district stoked new cooperation between Indian and American officials.[26] In the months after the Emergency began, DEA officials fanned out from the New Delhi embassy and the Bombay consulate, occasionally overstepping the mandate that the State Department had given them to participate in direct policing operations.[27] During the Emergency, Indian officials also used American intelligence to track opium smugglers shipping to other Asian ports. They arrested notorious Bangalore-based smuggler Khalidad Khan as he prepared to ship five hundred kilograms of opium from Madras to Sri Lanka, and his associate, Abdul Razek, shortly thereafter.[28] The cooperation on enforcement opened up new space for the Americans and Indians to talk about the future of the licit industry— one in the midst of its own contentious transformation.

◖◗◖

When everything else was stripped away, U.S. Kaicker saw poppies for what they were: flowering plants, every bit as beautiful as the roses with which he had begun his career at the Indian Agricultural Research Institute. As a promising young scientist there, he had put his talents toward the development of new roses. With his colleagues in the Division of Vegetable Crops and Floriculture, he had worked to adapt roses from Florida to Indian conditions, cross-breeding "Orangeade" into "Suryodaya" and Saratoga into "Himangini."[29] By 1973, Kaicker had been asked to apply his horticultural knowledge to opium poppies, and he had done so with obsessive care, cross-breeding not for colors and blossoms but for alkaloid content. Over the following years, on his expansive test plots in Delhi, Kaicker had seen how weather, heat, and variety came together to produce better alkaloid output.[30] He identified cultivators that produced higher concentrations of morphine. Eventually, *Dhola Chhotta Gotia*—the "little white ball"—struck him as the one most suited to North Indian growing conditions.[31] Kaicker had enjoyed his work with roses, but opium poppy was something else. It was useful, lucrative, and representative of a rich genetic heritage that was India's own.[32] And it was something that merited a cultivator's attention. In 1975, on the pages of India's leading journal for forward-looking farmers, he urged them to "try their hand at Black Gold," the opium poppy that offered great returns.[33] Journalists touted the promise of that black gold in many places, not least on the cover of the country's widely read Hindi weekly *Dharmayug*.

Kaicker's work came at a pivotal time. Indian opium itself was changing. As with many other Indian crops in the wake of the Green Revolution, it was growing more productive: *Dhola Chhotta Gotia* and many of the other promising cultivars were dwarf cultivars, like the new varieties of rice and wheat whose low, thick stalks were growing bigger grains without toppling.[34] Opium, of course, was not a food crop, but it squared nicely into the new role that higher-value export crops were being afforded in a moment of lessened scarcity.

The focus on poppies also fit uniquely within the radical changes taking place in India's domestic medical sector. At the beginning of the decade, a new patent law had made the novel case that it was not an infringement of intellectual property rights to produce the same compound via different methods. This was a bold interpretation, but it set the stage for a major global generic drug industry. A few years later, the Hathi Committee on Essential Drugs warned that only a quarter of India's 613 million people had access to fundamental, modern medicines.[35] It called for the rapid development of India's pharmaceutical industry, and real painkillers, scarcely a part of Indian health care at this moment, would be afforded a new role within it.

India's new prominence in international markets after the Turkish ban had attracted international efforts to improve the quality and quantity of its crop. In 1974, Quinten Jones—the USDA scientist who had helped develop the crop substitution program in Turkey and who had

Figure 7.1 A March 1973 cover story from India's popular *Dharmayug* weekly on "India's Black Gold: Opium Cultivation in Malwa." *Dharmayug*.

overseen the *bracteatum* project in the United States—was sent to India on a collaborative mission with Olav Brænden, head of the United Nations' drug laboratory in Geneva.[36] The team met with Indian officials and research scientists in Delhi, seeing if there were ways to improve the quantities of codeine produced in Indian poppy and looking at the feasibility of implementing the poppy straw method in India.

This international effort tapped into what had become, by 1975, a wide though somewhat uncoordinated network of research on opium and alkaloid production.[37] Kaicker and his colleagues were working on opium breeding at the Indian Agricultural Research Institute, while the Jawaharlal Nehru Krishi Vishwa Vidyalaya, Udaipur University, and India's National Botanic Gardens in Lucknow formed new teams for research into improved opium production. At the Rajasthan College of Agriculture, one scientist was experimenting with different plant growth regulators to protect poppy plants from frost damage. In the field, opium officers were being asked to note blossoms' colors to see if they correlated with alkaloid output. Two scientists at the Neemuch and Ghazipur factories worked to extract thebaine and other alkaloids from the "waste" opium that had been previously deemed unusable. Indian administrators described the research as "unorganized" and in need of a coordinated research program. But there was a new and intense sense of purpose in this work.

The Narcotics Department's annual reports throughout the 1970s show efforts to consolidate the land upon which poppy was permitted to be grown. Its policy, by the 1970s, was to permit cultivation in compact, contiguous areas and broadly on flat, easily surveilled lands.[38] In the absence of a thicker historical record, it is still clear that poppy remained more politically and economically significant to cultivators than the other secondary, high-value crops vying for cultivators' lands and attention. In the wake of the Green Revolution, sugarcane was taking on new prominence in Uttar Pradesh, soybeans were doing the same in Madhya Pradesh, and oilseeds like mustard were gaining traction in Rajasthan. Yet opium afforded a status that other crops did not: a license to grow continued to offer economic returns both licit and illicit, and extra-economic benefits, from better marriage potential for sons to the social prestige of opium cultivation itself. These dynamics were not always prominent in public or private discussions of opium. But they were manifest in the types of improvement that Indian officials resisted in their dealings with American diplomats. At the end of the decade, when India's overwhelming glut of opium became known, it was also clear just how much license those cultivators had been afforded.

ꓷOꓷ

Indian opium, in this decade, had a particularly capable champion. In the 1950s, Dinshaw Nargolwala had leveraged the managerial competence built through the civil service to bill India's opium as a world-class commodity. After cutting his teeth in the administration of one resource—coal—he had turned his attention to another, with sterling results. Twenty years later, his successor, Jasjit Singh, had been put in charge of India's opium production, owing to his success in a very different professional domain. As Gold Control Administrator, Singh knew a great deal about smuggling and the ways in which a raw material integral to global commerce was also the lifeblood of underworld transactions. In 1973, Singh seemed like a fitting choice for Chairman of India's Central Board of Excise and Customs.

Singh faced conflicting pressures. The United States wanted India to increase opium supply to American manufacturers after the Turkish ban. However, Singh and others were wary, knowing from Turkey's example that the United States felt little obligation to opium cultivators. It would be foolish to induce more cultivators to grow opium than absolutely necessary, given the prospect of smuggling and the political capital that reducing cultivation might one day cost if India fell out of favor as a supplier or if good synthetic substitutes for opium were commercialized. This tension was equally evident in the United States' insistence that India work to convert its production over to the poppy straw method. This new technique, which had the advantage of being essentially smuggling-proof, would also eliminate the livelihood of many rural cultivators. In an era of changing rural politics in India, this was a destabilizing proposition for Indian political life.

The US ban on Turkish poppy assumed Indian opium would fill the gap in pharmaceutical opioid production. American pharmaceutical companies, warning of shortages, urged US policymakers to clarify their expectations for Indian production.[39] Indian officials, in their interactions with the Americans, were filled with "timidity and reluctance to make mistakes," fearful that producing too much or too little opium would provoke American ire and risk the premature end of their industry altogether, even before commercializable synthetic substitutes had been developed and marketed.

Jasjit Singh felt this pressure acutely. As the ban was implemented, Singh met frequently with representatives from Mallinckrodt. One high-ranking executive, August Homeyer, had made regular trips to India throughout the 1960s, coordinating regular purchasing and bidding at auctions for seized opium.[40] In 1973, Charles Gerfen, a senior scientist at Mallinckrodt, also began visiting India, serving as an intermediary between Singh and embassy officials, trying to explain the importance of Indian production.[41] Soon after, the company's chief executive, Harold Thayer, began making his own trips to India to try to cajole officials directly.[42] India, Mallinckrodt executives insisted, owed American manufacturers a "fair share" of the opium crop, since those manufacturers had in large measure built and sustained the industry over the past twenty years. But India had also promised opium to Eastern Bloc countries like Poland, the USSR, and Bulgaria, which had extensive trade agreements with India, negotiated and executed in rupees.[43]

An early sense of optimism soon darkened. American officials initially trumpeted India's cooperation, appreciative of the thoughtful and affable Jasjit Singh's early promises that he would offer American purchasers favorable consideration. "India," Ambassador Moynihan cabled to Henry Kissinger in late 1973, "is prepared to provide a service for the world, and recognizes a responsibility to do so."[44] But relations quickly cooled. Singh privately declared that he was "flooded" by unreasonable demands from pharmaceutical companies to increase production.[45] In the absence of reasonable assurances that the United States would not abandon Indian opium once synthetic substitutes were available, he could not necessarily ramp up production to meet them.

Singh's reticence reflected domestic savvy—licensing more poppy cultivators would have been folly if India's production went the way of

Turkey's. But this reticence also soured American officials, who wished that India would play a greater role in making up the gap left by Turkish opium's absence.[46] By the summer of 1974, embassy staffers were frustrated by noncommittal answers from Indian narcotics officials. Unwilling to increase the area of poppy cultivation, fearing potential control problems and the consequences of eventually reducing it, those officials sought to placate the Americans by outlining their research programs and the growing potency of the Indian product that was being offered. "India," one frustrated staffer wrote, "is not trying to exploit its position as the sole producer of legal opium."[47]

The three American manufacturers were fiercely competitive with one another, but allied in their belief that India owed them at least double the two hundred tons of opium it was allocating the country as a whole.[48] In 1974, Mallinckrodt's chief executive, visiting India as part of the drive for more opium, invited Jasjit Singh to the United States so he could see American production and the need for Indian opium firsthand. Singh complained to embassy officials that he was exhausted by the constant American entreaties.[49] He had fielded near-constant requests from American manufacturers since assuming his position; Mallinckrodt had also sent representatives to ambush India's ambassador to the United States.[50]

In May 1975, Singh was preparing to fly to St. Louis to meet Mallinckrodt officials at the company's headquarters, following on the trip that his predecessor, Dinshaw Nargolwala, had made twenty years earlier.[51] Nargolwala had faced a very different set of challenges. In the postwar moment, Indian and Turkish bureaucrats were vying for shares of the massive American market, and India was a scrappy contender. But by the mid-1970s, with Turkish production more or less irrelevant, Singh was in a stronger position. As he geared up for his trip, Singh was reminded of just how strong the Indian position was at an auction for the supply of medical codeine to India—the primary way in which India's hospitals received their supply in the absence of domestic processing capabilities. Singh had opened one low sealed bid after another. But Penick, the smallest American producer, had offered to supply all of

India's codeine, alongside shipping and insurance, free of charge. Producers were utterly desperate for preferential access to India's product.[52]

This strength gave India cover as it resisted an unappealing proposal: the conversion of India's poppy cultivation to the poppy straw method that had come into vogue elsewhere in the world and to which Turkey had committed itself as well. Jasjit Singh was unerring in his contention that India would countenance no similar transformation.[53] In 1974, India had already begun harvesting a small amount of poppy straw, with the idea of building a plant that could process it directly into alkaloids for domestic use, obviating the auctions for foreign-produced codeine that had become the country's mainstay by the 1970s.[54] But he was insistent that the majority of India's production would remain rooted in the lancing of poppies. Singh had a number of substantive objections. The Government of India had a good sense of how much opium could be produced on a given field and could take away licenses if that yield was not realized. The poppy straw method, however, would let cultivators lance poppies, sell the gum to the black market, and hide the evidence by breaking the poppy capsule for its seeds. Moreover, India's poppy cultivation was dispersed on "250,000 small and scattered holdings," which would be impossible to mechanize and transport. Most substantively, the reduction of cultivation that this conversion would entail would exact a heavy political toll. If the straw method were to be adopted, it would have to be as a complement to, rather than a replacement for, the more traditional methods of scoring and scraping.

Jasjit Singh worked to placate the Americans, but mostly, he and his colleagues played for time. As American firms jockeyed for Indian opium, Singh was helping manage the construction of a modern factory at Neemuch. In 1974, a Yugoslav firm won the tender to build an upgraded facility there, and two years later, reporters attended a ribbon-cutting ceremony and toured the facility humming with the buzz and thrum of the chemical reactions turning raw opium into finished pharmaceutical products.[55] The factory had been marketed as a means of producing the kind of raw codeine that India would need for its own domestic use, supplementing the very small amount that was being produced at

Ghazipur. American observers saw in it a certain kind of ambition: the possibility, at least, that India would one day become more aggressive in seeking foreign exchange from opium alkaloids, not merely the raw material itself.

For the better part of the decade, Indian caution had frustrated American officials. The efforts of American pharmaceutical companies to secure greater supplies from India had yielded little. Singh and his colleagues, an American embassy staffer wrote in 1976, had "frozen the market shares of a commodity in short world supply in order to not be put in the position of playing favorites among potential customers."[56] None of this soured the relationship with Singh himself—the Americans readily supported his candidacy for membership in the International Narcotics Control Board[57]—but the tension between American desires and Indian reticence played out as the supply dynamic was itself changing. In the second half of the decade, as India very slowly increased its output of licit opium through the expansion of cultivation, the overall global supply of opium had been rising. India's opium remained economically competitive. But by 1977, India's slightly expanded production was in far less demand than it had been only a few years earlier.[58]

Matters only worsened the following year.[59] In 1978, a bumper crop of 1,500 tons of opium exceeded even the highest estimates that the Ministry of Finance had anticipated. What would have been a triumph five years earlier was a crisis in a moment of excess global production. Mallinckrodt had reneged on their purchasing plans for the year, and orders from the United States, the Soviet Union, and France had all been underwhelming. For the first time, India's warehouses were overflowing with unsold stock. At the year's end, nearly three hundred tons were left unsold. The Ministry took the unprecedented step of reducing the licensed acreage for the following crop year from 64,000 to 57,000 hectares—but there was an urgent sense that something needed to be done. Jasjit Singh's subordinates increasingly blamed the United States. Pharmaceutical executives, they suggested, had beat the drum for India to increase its production, only to grow silent when that production exceeded global demands in a moment of excess production.

In March 1979, India's narcotics administrators made a proposal to the Americans. This carrot, one bureaucrat suggested, was intended to "stabilize" the world's opium production system.[60] The plan had been cooked up with Mallinckrodt executives, and Indian bureaucrats and American businessmen had been hammering out the details for the better part of the year. It was intended to be a mutually beneficial arrangement. India would commit to supplying the entirety of the United States' alkaloid needs. It would maintain a buffer stock of opium, somewhere around a quarter of its average annual crop, as insurance against climate, production failures, or other unforeseen disruptions. It would tailor its opium production to meet the specific alkaloid profiles that the United States outlined—more thebaine-rich or codeine-rich crops, depending on what was required. In return, India asked for a firm two-year purchase commitment and contracts from the American producers, as well as letters of intent outlining American purchases up to 1985. In a world awash with opioids, India would subordinate itself fully to American needs in exchange for a guaranteed market.

The initial response from American companies, and the American embassy and State Department, was positive.[61] Mallinckrodt, Merck, and Penick all expressed strong interest in the proposal, and officials continued to meet throughout the summer. By November, with the global oversupply worsening, the plan appeared to be defunct. The licensed cultivation for the following year was slashed again, and the companies proceeded with short-term contracts in place of the longer-term arrangements that had been proposed.

A year after the proposal had been abandoned, Charles Gerfen, the Mallinckrodt scientist who had been visiting India for nearly a decade, returned to the country after a trip to Turkey.[62] There was, Gerfen saw, simply no comparison between the two countries in terms of promise. Indian opium had far more thebaine than Turkish poppy straw and was getting better yields from their crop than ever before; in addition, the country's well-oiled export machinery made it a primary supplier for the United States, as well as Japan and the Soviet Union. Turkey, by contrast, was struggling to set up their new factory, and the poppy straw it was sending overseas represented a costly endeavor for international producers. Unknowingly, Gerfen echoed the words of Julius Jeffreys, who, exactly 150 years earlier, had marveled at the stores of opium at the Patna factory and their potential for world medicine. India, Gerfen was confident, "could supply the United States' narcotic raw material needs indefinitely," if only it were given the chance.

But India's growing opium stockpile was turning into a political liability.[63] In place of the long-term contracts that Indian officials had proposed, the country's opium was languishing. In 1980, Merck bought no Indian opium whatsoever. Beginning in 1979, the cost of maintaining old stock at the warehouses in Ghazipur and Neemuch had begun to exceed the value of India's exports themselves. The "huge quantities" of opium moldering there, officials warned, were also beginning to tax India's security efforts.[64] India's Narcotics Commissioner went to Vienna to petition the UN Commission on Narcotic Drugs for help in formulating a plan to reduce India's surplus, warning that India could emerge as a new trafficking hub.[65]

In April 1981, a team of agents from the Central Bureau of Investigation launched twin raids on two clandestine laboratories on the outskirts of Varanasi and Ghazipur.[66] The haul was modest—two kilograms of high-grade morphine base. But the agents were confident that the six men they had arrested would lead them to a larger network of smugglers and drug manufacturers. These laboratories, they knew, were the "tip of the iceberg," with potentially hundreds of similar operations across India's opium belt. A few months later, a similar raid of a factory in Delhi on the Yamuna River nabbed a former employee of the Ghazipur factory— signs, to the CBI, that they were on the right track.[67]

Since India's failure to sell its full crop in 1979, the stockpile that had ensued had worried both domestic and international observers. That year, the United States had opened an office of the Drug Enforcement Administration in the New Delhi embassy with the express aim of preventing Indian opium from entering the international black market.[68] They had reason to worry. In 1979, opium that bore signs of being from Mandsaur, one of India's more productive licensed districts, began to appear in Gujarat and Rajasthan, and shortly thereafter, Interpol began investigating a "brand" of heroin marked with a crescent and a star that allegedly came from the same region.[69] By the time the CBI had begun its raids in 1981, northern India was awash in smuggled opium and morphine made from it. Arrests nabbed smugglers in Madhya Pradesh, Uttar Pradesh, Delhi, and as far south as Pune, where the city's "Narcotics King" was dramatically arrested.[70] Some of the activity was opportunistic and disorganized. Underemployed young men from Nagaland and Mizoram in the country's restive northeast came to Delhi to work as ferries, moving opium in soap cases, drums, and spare tires.[71] There was also more ambitious smuggling. In Delhi, an increasing number of Europeans and North Americans were caught smuggling out morphine base, and the arrest of two heroin-smuggling Frenchmen at Paris's Orly airport led investigators back to a Varanasi chemist running a large laboratory on the banks of the Ganges.[72]

This increasing flow of Indian opium to the black market should have made Ministry of Finance officials keen to reduce the amount of land dedicated to poppy and the number of licenses available to cultivators. But in 1981, Sawai Singh Sisodia was promising a vast and incongruous expansion of poppy licenses, as well as new subsidies and concessions to cultivators themselves. Opium had simply grown too important a crop to restrict. In Rajasthan's Chittorgarh district, a core opium hub, farmers were seeking out more licenses than ever before, and parliamentarians were eager to oblige—at least one requested a license of his own.[73] Even as American diplomats urged Indian officials to reduce the amount of licensed poppy cultivation, the Ministry of Finance had declined to comply "in order to avoid hardship to the poor poppy cultivators."[74]

After three decades of making itself indispensable to global pharmaceutical production, India found itself in a new bind. If, the Calcutta *Telegraph* wondered, New Delhi did not find a solution to the country's opium problem, "India may soon stop being the largest legal exporter in the world and become instead the transit point for the largest amount of contraband."[75]

From the perspective of someone like Sawai Singh Sisodia—aware of opium's diminishing economic value and its geopolitical risks but invested in the domestic politics of poppy cultivation—the proposal that Mallinckrodt had helped Indian officials develop several years earlier was a broadly attractive one. It offered a way to stabilize India's opium industry in the face of volatile global markets and shifting political priorities. By committing to supply the entirety of the United States' alkaloid needs and maintaining a buffer stock, India could secure a long-term, reliable market for its opium production and, in turn, economic stability for the hundreds of thousands of small-scale farmers who depended on poppy cultivation for their livelihoods. India enjoyed broad comparative advantage: its research and production regimes allowed it to produce high-quality opium with desirable alkaloid profiles, and its well-established export machinery was far more efficient than Turkey's nascent and uncertain poppy straw industry. If this arrangement potentially strained relationships with the Soviet Union or Eastern Bloc countries with long-term purchasing agreements, non-alignment allowed India greater room for maneuver. This arrangement would not protect India from the possibility that better synthetic opioids could one day obviate a historic industry, but making arrangements until the middle of the 1980s gave bureaucrats more runway.

For that planner's American counterpart in the US Department of State, a different set of options presented themselves. The fundamental question surrounding opium had changed radically. After widespread fears of a shortage in the opening years of the 1970s, by decade's end the world was awash in too much opium. The question was how to ensure a steady supply of pharmaceutical alkaloids without encouraging more cultivation in places where it was not desirable. The eradication fantasy of the early 1970s—the Nixon-era hope that it would be possible and desirable to end the global production of opium altogether in favor of synthetic substitutes—had been more or less written off. Synthetic morphine had been discovered by the end of the decade, but the process developed at the National Institutes of Health was inefficient and expensive. It was a moonshot campaign to produce something better that was costly and had no certain timeline. Synthetics would have their place in the pharmaceutical inventory, but it was clear that their role would be a complementary one.

The notion of cultivating *bracteatum* poppy domestically remained a possibility, but an increasingly remote one. On a contract farm in Oregon's Rogue Valley, a small field of Mallinckrodt's *bracteatum* poppies would continue to grow into the 1980s.[76] But broadly, by the end of the 1970s, the project was defunct. After the Carter administration had withdrawn the proposal for domestic cultivation for revision, the Iranian Revolution had severed the pipeline that was bringing *bracteatum* seeds from Tehran to the United States. The DEA had worked with manufacturers to process their remaining stock of alkaloids, while most of the *bracteatum* fields were killed with Roundup.[77] All further proposals from pharmaceutical manufacturers to cultivate and process *bracteatum* were summarily denied.[78] *Chemical Week*, in 1980, suggested that the glut of opium had undercut the project's aims and that fundamentally it was not an economically viable proposition.[79] The miracle poppy that produced thebaine but not heroin was ultimately abandoned.

At least one other country was serving as a counterexample to the United States of how pharmaceutical opium procurement and production could be divorced from broader geopolitics.[80] During the Second World War, occupied France's three authorized alkaloid processors had developed a new process to extract opium from the oilette poppy, used largely for oil production. Those companies had subsequently formed a new company called Francopavot, which in turn merged with an older pharmaceutical firm, Société Francopia. In 1959, Charles de Gaulle had called upon Francopia to begin producing a small amount of opium to reduce the republic's expenditure of dollar reserves, largely from purchases from Iran. After the Turkish ban, France had become more aggressive in its efforts to achieve opium autarky: Francopia had implemented the poppy straw method to harvest poppy in Champagne-Ardenne and Poitou-Charentes, regions largely known for champagne and cognac. By 1977, French officials had declared France to be entirely self-sufficient in alkaloid production.[81]

There are plausible reasons as to why France moved so steadily toward a vision of autarky and self-sufficiency in opioid production, while the United States steadfastly refused the same model. Postwar France's much smaller pharmaceutical industry had primarily purchased from Iran, rather than Turkey and India, and its command of global power was not rooted in the control of narcotics overseas. But between the 1950s and the 1970s, opioid production in the United States grew so entangled with international geopolitics that it progressively precluded domestic production as a real possibility. Since the era of preclusive purchasing during the Second World War, American narcotic control and diplomatic power had been built in tandem. Private industry networks had underwritten government purchasing, and the US bureaucracy had worked with keen awareness of, if not always consideration for, the political economy of opium production overseas. By the late 1970s, even in a moment of excess production, it was vanishingly unlikely that the United States would onshore its opium production.

This left two plausible options. The first—which would have pleased politicians like Sawai Singh Sisodia—was to take the Indian proposal seriously and to commit fully to India as its primary source for pharmaceutical needs. The United States would sign long-term contracts with India, invest in the country's opium infrastructure, and deepen its collaboration to minimize diversion. It would secure a stable supply from a single, controllable source and deepen economic ties with India— though the United States would be reliant on a single supplier and would strain its relationships with other allies, Turkey in particular. If something might have tipped the scales in favor of this plan, it would have been the strong relationship that private industry, particularly Mallinckrodt executives, enjoyed with Indian officials. But a diversity of sources would have comported better with strategic thinking in the United States. A second, more probable plan would involve reengaging with Turkey to revitalize their opium industry, exploring new potential suppliers such as Australia or Eastern European countries, and maintaining Indian supply but at reduced levels. If such a plan would involve greater regulatory oversight and costs, it would reduce dependency on any single country.

But the question was not merely an American one—it was enmeshed with parallel conversations in international bodies. If the United States had an outsized role in them, it was nonetheless bound to some degree by the dynamics of regulation in this arena. Since its formation in 1968, as part of the terms of the 1961 Single Convention on Narcotic Drugs, the International Narcotics Control Board had played a constrained but important role in the management of global narcotics. Tasked with monitoring countries' adherence to international drug control treaties, the INCB largely collected data and statistics on drug production, manufacture, trade, and consumption. It had the authority to impose some sanctions, including embargoes, against noncompliant nations, but largely relied on quiet diplomacy and the threat of publicity to encourage cooperation. The INCB was a crucial instrument in defining and regulating the boundaries of legitimate and illegitimate trade. By the 1970s, it had largely eliminated illicit trafficking by reputable pharmaceutical companies.[82]

It was the INCB board that had first noticed the growing threat of oversupply in 1978.[83] Turkey and India's efforts to stem supply, its members found, had been "praiseworthy," from Turkey's strict limitation of its poppy straw production to that which its new factory could produce, to India's decision to hold its cultivation areas steady after years of increase. But they had projected that, unless there was a large unforeseen increase in demand between 1978 and 1982, morphine manufacturing capacity would be, on average, 50 percent greater than requirements. Late that year, the board invited the governments of twenty key countries to formulate plans to reduce stocks, and four producing countries—India, Turkey, Australia, and France—all announced or implemented reductions in poppy cultivation areas or opium production.[84]

By early 1979, the problem had snaked its way up to the United Nations' Economic and Social Council. In February, its Commission on Narcotics Drugs resolved that importing countries should recognize the "positive response" of those countries "in meeting the world requirements and their contribution to the maintenance of effective control systems."[85] In response, it urged importing countries, "in so far as their constitutions and legal authority permit, to support the traditional supply countries and give all possible practical assistance in preventing the proliferation of producing and manufacturing sources for export." Three months later, in May, the Council itself affirmed the same resolution. The notion of "traditional supply countries" was a vague one, perhaps deliberately so. For Sawai Singh Sisodia, or Jasjit Singh, it would have been obvious that India sat atop this short list of producers—but other countries were similarly eager for a spot on it.

For an Indian diplomat in 1980, an assignment to the Commerce Wing of the Embassy of India in Washington, DC, was a plum posting.[86] A staffer there could pore over statistics about India's modest but steady flow of exports to the United States: cashews and shrimp, tea and coffee, leather and textiles. He could monitor the wind-down of India's once-formidable export of animals and animal parts: rhesus monkeys for vaccine development, live birds for pets, and snakeskins to be stitched into handbags and belts. That work done, he could expect a leisurely walk around the gardens of Dumbarton Oaks and lunch in the tony neighborhood of Kalorama. But in 1980, a team of those staffers were wrenched from their files to mount a full-throated defense of Indian opium as an indispensable component of Indian trade.

By the end of the 1970s, the tangle of questions surrounding opium and poppy products to the United States had grown overwhelmingly complicated.[87] The plurality of American painkillers was semisynthetic and required thebaine to produce, and increasingly that thebaine was being produced with concentrate of poppy straw, a product that had only been allowed into the United States via emergency regulation passed during the opioid shortage of the early 1970s. Basic morphine, too, was being produced with concentrate of poppy straw at increasing rates. India produced opium, not poppy straw or its concentrate in any appreciable amount. Turkey's poppy straw factory was not yet functioning, so the United States was consuming Turkish straw only indirectly, through intermediary processors in France and the Netherlands. When the INCB and the United Nations' Economic and Social Council made their proposal to "support the traditional supply countries," it was undoubtedly hinting at India and Turkey, perhaps other producers as well. But the "traditional" production of opium—sowing, scoring, and scraping poppies—had less to do with pharmaceutical production than it had even ten years prior. Peasants in the Golden Triangle of Burma, Laos, and Thailand scored poppies for heroin, as did those in the Golden Crescent in Afghanistan, Iran, and Pakistan. A small but growing number of peasants in Mexico did so for the US market. But pharmaceutical opioid production was increasingly linked to the semi-industrial process of poppy straw cultivation.

While the international bodies deliberated, the State Department and the DEA tapped an administration bureaucrat to formulate a plan that would govern American imports. Robert Pearson had worked as a DEA investigator in South America, Europe, and Turkey before being designated its UN Regulatory Affairs Coordinator. The question that he and his team tackled was straightforward: with domestic production of *bracteatum* or *somniferum* ruled out, how should the United States govern the import of "raw narcotic material"?[88] Pearson and a small working group considered and then threw out the option of restricting imports to India and Turkey. That plan had one key advantage—it would quash the "disturbing rumors rampant in Ankara and New Delhi" that their opium industries were to be summarily ended. But it would also violate the "most favored nation" principle under the General Agreement on Tariffs and Trade, the 1947 multilateral agreement regulating international trade. That principle held that if a country offered a trade benefit to one nation, it must extend the same to all member countries.

In the summer of 1979, the DEA proposed a more expansive rule that it hoped would avoid such a violation.[89] The United States would restrict imports of opium, poppy straw, and concentrate of poppy straw to countries that had been producing and exporting opium for pharmaceutical markets in the ten years prior to 1961, with exceptions for pre-1979 contracts. Effectively, this proposal would have included India, Turkey, and Yugoslavia—but it would have excluded other countries with significant cultivation, like Hungary, France, Poland, and Australia.[90] The responses to the 1979 proposal highlighted predictable fault lines. India and Turkey trumpeted the proposal as a boon to both American pharmaceuticals and domestic cultivators' best interests.[91] Executives at Mallinckrodt gave the proposal strong support.[92] Nearly every other party involved raised bold objections. The board of the American Medical Association could see no way in which the plan would help maintain a supply of opioid drugs.[93] Representatives of Hungary and Poland's pharmaceutical industries objected vociferously to being left out of the "traditional supplier" designation, given their small but long-established poppy industries.[94] The Australian government sent an aide-mémoire to the DEA that rejected the fundamental principles of the proposal. The proposed rule was still, its representatives contended, an unprecedented violation of international trade policy, and its emphasis on "traditional suppliers" discriminated unfairly against Australian-produced poppy straw, a controlled, reliable, and highly sought-after product.[95]

These geopolitical fissures belied less apparent commercial disputes. McNeil Laboratories, the Johnson & Johnson subsidiary that produced Tylenol with codeine, and was thus the United States' largest importer of that alkaloid, argued that the DEA's interpretation of the UN resolution calling for "support" to traditional producers was too restrictive and that this conservative approach would court supply instability in the event that political or environmental conditions in India and Turkey deteriorated.[96] More importantly, Illinois-based Abbott Laboratories, having invested significantly in the Australian poppy industry, declared itself to be "the only US corporation directly involved in the cultivation and processing of basic narcotic raw materials."[97] Its executives not only objected to the plan but also pressured Illinois's two senators to help advance a different proposal in the DEA: a 70 percent share of the market guaranteed to Turkey and India, fixed at their approximate current market share, and a 30 percent reserve from alternate traditional sources—of which Australia would be the major part.[98]

In early 1980, the DEA proposed a slightly modified version of the plan that Abbott had drafted.[99] The Indian diplomats in the embassy's

Commerce Wing were ready to seize the moment. India, they insisted in a long brief, was the traditional opium supplier par excellence, and no other country save Turkey had a similar claim—particularly after the many sacrifices that the country's peasants had already made in the service of narcotics control.[100] Supporting Indian opium production, they added, was the requisite compensation for that sacrifice. "As a result of drastic reduction in the area under poppy cultivation," they wrote, "around 75,000 families have been deprived of their only source of income, [and] about 1,70,000 families have suffered loss of income from this cash crop for the reasons that their licensed holdings have been drastically reduced. It may be mentioned that the bulk of the opium cultivators come from the weaker sections of the rural population living in the interior and backward regions of the country."

Whether American officials affirmed the logic or not, the proposal won the day. Australian, French, and Turkish diplomats made their own petitions to the DEA. But at the year's end, an administrative judge for the DEA—the same person who had delayed the *brateatum* proposal four years earlier—allowed the new rules to go forward.[101] After August 1981, American opioid manufacturers would be allowed to buy 20 percent of the total amount of opium, poppy straw, and concentrate of poppy straw they imported each year from Yugoslavia, France, Poland, Hungary, and Australia. India and Turkey would be given the remaining 80 percent.[102] It was a coup for India—on paper, at least.

❂

In 1979, when Indian bureaucrats had made their proposal for a long-term supply agreement with the United States, they had envisioned a mutually beneficial exchange. The United States, the world's largest customer of raw narcotic materials, had decided that it was politically impossible to produce them domestically. India, despite its frosty relationship with the United States, was well positioned to capitalize on a thirty-year commercial relationship to offer predictability—even if the one product the country offered, opium gum, was no longer the product that pharmaceutical companies desired most.

What India got in 1981 was a commitment on paper, but no more. Sawai Singh Sisodia made his promise to the opium cultivators of central India the same month that the new American rules were on the books—a hint, perhaps, that India's finance minister was speaking in good faith when he promised a rejuvenated export industry and a slew of new licenses. Three years later, however, there was still a "vast opium mountain" going unused in India's warehouses.[103] When an unusually cold winter destroyed 80 percent of the Indian opium crop in early 1984, Indian officials breathed a discreet sigh of relief.[104] But it was not long before farmers were clamoring for compensation and the promise of an expansion of their cultivatable lands the following year—intimating, not particularly subtly, that they would find black-market buyers if the state would not give its approval. With New Delhi reluctant to face the political consequences of reducing the amount of land given to opium cultivation, international diplomats brainstormed other possibilities.[105] The United Nations Industrial Development Organization deputed an American narcotics researcher to India to examine the possibility of using excess Indian opium to produce alkaloids for other developing world contexts.[106] But six years after the 80-20 rule was put on the books, the DEA's deputy administrator was warning that a different course of action was needed.[107]

The domestic consequences of this failure were apparent across India. Indian officials, the editors of the *Hindu* opined, had grown so used to seeing drug abuse and trafficking as a "malady of the richer economies" that they had ignored the growing problem under their own noses.[108] In the early 1980s, those same officials were forced to come to terms with a renewed opioid crisis at home.[109] "Brown sugar," a crude Indian heroin preparation, found new purchase with "executives, students and idlers alike, along with waiters, rickshaw drivers, and handcart pullers" in Delhi and Bombay.[110] Delhi police officers bemoaned the mushrooming of heroin users in the capital.[111] Pandits and priests in the holy city of Varanasi were said to be involved in ferrying raw opium from Ghazipur to the city's *ghats*.[112] In the northeast, addiction among disenfranchised Manipuris gave law enforcement the opportunity to harass young men.

The state, the head of its insurgent People's Liberation Army declared, was in a "heroin war."[113] Drug use, the *New York Times* reported, had impacted everyone "from the farm workers of Punjab, who have opium in their morning tea, to the literati of Bombay, who have begun taking it in cold milk as a party drink."[114]

Much of this reporting was bombastic and overstated, but Indian heroin was a real problem at home and was moving overseas. Between 30 and 40 percent of India's legal opium crop was said to be smuggled out of the country.[115] From districts like Mandsaur, opium was purchased illegally, then shipped to ports in automobile tires or sometimes by children, who carried it unknowingly in containers that described it as soap base. From Bombay, Madras, and Bhubaneswar, where it joined heroin that had been smuggled to India from Pakistan and Afghanistan, Indian opium reached destinations like Pakistan and Nepal, and as far as Europe and the United States.[116] The most enterprising Indian kingpins had empires that rivaled the French Connection smuggling routes of a generation prior.[117]

The irony of the moment was not lost on Jasjit Singh. The erstwhile chairman of India's Central Board of Excise and Customs had joined the International Narcotics Control Board in 1980. From there, he had watched the implementation of the 80-20 rule with concern.[118] In his earlier role, he had contended regularly with the pressure and entreaties of American pharmaceutical executives who had petitioned him to expand Indian cultivation. But that production turned into a problem. The United States had enshrined into its regulatory regime the idea that India was a "traditional supplier" and thus entitled to the lion's share of American purchasing. But that regulatory stricture could not force and was not inducing the firms that did purchase opium to take a greater amount of it. Those companies increasingly were moving on to other production models, and proof of that shift came in the unsold opium in government warehouses and the black-market opium being unearned with alarming frequency. American executives and their allies in governments, Singh lamented, bore "the moral responsibility for making a country with excellent controls a problem country."

Indian officials continued to deepen their commitment to the strictures of international control. In the middle of the decade, the Parliament passed the Narcotic Drugs and Psychotropic Substances Act, a piece of legislation that mandated new punitive measures for drug use and trafficking.[119] A year later, New Delhi inaugurated India's Narcotics Control Bureau (NCB), charged with enforcing the Act and drug trafficking writ large. Three years later, a second law, the Prevention of Illicit Trafficking in Narcotic Drugs and Psychotropic Substances Act, widened the purview of the NCB. Yet none of this staunched the fundamental derangement of India's opium regime: its producers were tending to a commodity that the world had diminishing use for. In the decades that followed, that gulf would grow wider, with profound consequences for actors on each side of a global chain.

8

The Ghost Ship

India's central hinterlands are dotted with settlements like Budha. A quintessential *"mofassil* town"—a historic administrative and commercial hub—Budha emerges abruptly from a flat and dusty rural landscape in Mandsaur district. The town is surrounded by drip-irrigated fields, a shuttered lead pencil factory, and a wholesale vegetable depot whose wares are nearly entirely deep-purple onions flecked with dirt and aging in the dry air. In Budha itself, two dusty thoroughfares crisscross the village's center, where small shops sell fried snacks, SIM cards, household goods, and cigarettes.

Nearly everyone in Budha shares the same last name of Patidar. The dominant community of the region, the Patidars are a subbranch of the *Kurmis,* one of the three caste groups whose name, in the nineteenth century, was synonymous with opium cultivation itself. Some Patidars are reasonably prosperous, and others are struggling, but to nearly everyone's frustration, and despite increasingly frequent mobilizations, the caste group is not low enough to qualify for reserved seats in government and educational institutions. Though Budha's livelihood is nearly entirely agricultural, the nearest well-stocked farming equipment store is an hour away, and men make regular pilgrimages there to purchase or repair drip irrigation and pesticide sprayers. When not in the field, women often stay inside their joint family homes. Recently, some young women have been heading to colleges in Indore, the nearest substantive city, working toward degrees in commerce and communication. For opportunities like that, leaving is essential. There are few signs of India's vibrant service economy here, and only the proliferation of Common Service Centers, government-sponsored shops that connect citizens to digital services, speak to the ambition of the new Indian economy.

The lifeblood of this town remains farming, and opium remains the pride of every field and home. The price of opium has been cratering in recent years, alongside the region's other cash crops, garlic and onion. Even for its diminished economic merits, an *afeem patta*, or license to grow opium, is still the wispy piece of paper that can transform lives—or crush them.

Suresh Patidar and his family know this well. The fields behind his cool concrete and rebar home are green and wide, arranged in loose quadrants around a cavernous well where swifts and swallows come to drink. In one section are the onion fields; in the other, a tangle of green chickpeas and the long parchment stalks of garlic rise from the dirt. Beyond them and a rusty curl of barbed wire are the poppies. Some are still blossoming, bursts of crepe white around a small orb. In the middle of January, most have yielded to plump green orbs flecked with down, some with telltale lines of sap dripping from neat cuts. On mornings when the gum is harvested, a small group of women and children, along with some hired men who are mostly distant cousins, arrive on the field and walk slowly in the gaps between the rows of poppies, collecting the sap on the blade of their curved knives. The opium—sticky, thick, and brown, with a smell that is sweet but acrid with the scent of ammonia—is patted neatly into round aluminum tins, and the family will cache these containers at home until the time comes to sell them.

As the spring approaches, the district collector will arrive at Suresh Patidar's home to check the patriarch's *patta* and examine the relatively small plot of opium set back from the road. The collector will set an initial estimate for the crop, pegged to the amount that the state agency has set for the year. In the 2019 season, each kilogram fetched $20. It is a modest amount—far less than what smugglers would pay for the same quantity. But the license continues to confer social prestige and standing, a sign of respectability that makes the family's children more marriageable.

Figure 8.1 Suresh Patidar, in white shirt, walking with workers in his poppy fields in Mandsaur district. Author's photograph.

On a cool winter day, over milky tea and roasted poppy seeds, Suresh's father spoke of working in the poppy fields as a young man and of building his home and paying for his daughters' dowries with money from opium. It was the crop that had made his family a respectable one.

Suresh's own feelings were more ambivalent. Around forty, he had spent the whole of his life caring for opium "as a mother cares for a child."[1] But the returns seemed to diminish year by year as government prices continued to fall. The family's license, he confessed, gave them cover if they wanted to sell to a local smuggler. The potential rewards were immense: $2,000 in place of the government's $20.[2] But the district's jail, overcrowded with young men who had smuggled opium or poppy husk in car tires or jute bags, was a reminder of the risks involved. And in any case, each year the family's allotted area was growing smaller as nervous regulators in Delhi tried to reduce the opportunity for black-market sales.

Figure 8.2 Suresh Patidar's father showing his poppy-growing license. Author's photograph.

For Suresh, it was clear that some other opportunity should take the place of poppy. His nephews and nieces were heading to cities like Indore to escape farming altogether; one successful nephew was teaching biotechnology at an upstart private college a few hours away. For several years, Suresh had been working to refashion himself as something of a leader in the local farmers' movement, advocating for new concessions to the agricultural sector that he and his collaborators felt had been left behind. His phone was filled with WhatsApp messages from other farmers, sharing photos of their recent, massive march in New Delhi. The group had gone to protest Prime Minister Narendra Modi's seeming antipathy to farmers, even as Suresh had voted for him several years before. But for the time being, Suresh's poppies still needed tending. Behind the house, they fluttered in the winter wind, crops at once invaluable and somehow out of time.

By the 2010s, Indian opium cultivation had become a nearly entirely vestigial operation, integral to the domestic political economy of central India, but more or less worthless as an export commodity. In India, around sixty thousand farmers, nearly a quarter of whom lived in Mandsaur district, continued to cultivate opium gum, receiving payments that were far smaller than what they might receive on the black market, yet still by all available evidence subsidized by the central government.[3] In spite of the preferential treatment it theoretically received in the US regulatory regime, Indian opium was barely desired by any overseas pharmaceutical manufacturer.

The world's use of opium products had changed massively over the previous forty years. Beginning in the 1980s, in the years after the 80-20 rule locked in place one particular export arrangement, most of the world's licit poppy-growing countries had switched over to the poppy straw method, wherein cut poppies could be transformed into alkaloids without the risk of producing opium gum.[4] Turkey had adopted this method after the recession of its poppy cultivation ban; Australia, the world's most important producer, had never produced anything but poppy straw. The two major European producers, France and Spain, used the same method, as did many smaller Eastern European producers. In 2022, India was the only country producing opium gum from lanced poppies in any meaningful sense. The only other significant producer was North Korea, whose much smaller opium crop was entirely destined for its autarkic production. India had also come to use nearly all of its own crop for domestic pharmaceutical production. Barely any of it, after the 2010s, was exported at all. The network of poppy cultivation and opium production that Suresh Patidar and his family stewarded was a capitalist ghost ship, a relic of another time propelled forward by the inertia of networks forged in the crucible of the postwar years.

That ghost ship might not have looked as strange had the participants within it merely seen and described it as it was: a relatively small-scale and fairly inefficient form of domestic production tied by dint of history to a fairly old-fashioned substance. But there remained, in the late 2010s, a Potemkin quality to India's sprawling opium production industry:

A government-appointed Chief Controller of Factories, with a plum administrative posting in the Department of Revenue, oversaw a busy office in New Delhi and two well-guarded factories in Neemuch and Ghazipur. The once-imposing Patna factory, having been converted to a government press in 1912, lingered on as a leafy and somewhat dilapidated compound on the outskirts of the city. A network of district collectors continued to oversee the annual planting and collection of opium—a process exceedingly similar to the one that powered the global opium trade from India in the middle of the nineteenth century and in a reformed manner in the 1950s and 1960s. In the 2020–21 growing season, the Government of India for the first time allowed the cultivation of poppy straw for domestic pharmaceutical production. But broadly, a massive marketing infrastructure peddled the same wares it had peddled a century earlier, sutured to a crop and a means of cultivating it wholly at odds with the requirements of the day.

In his office in New Delhi, the Chief Controller of Factories—a career bureaucrat with little apparent experience with opium and barely more information about the cultivators whose work he nominally oversaw than the glossy brochure he kept referring back to—offered a frustrated diatribe about his American customers. As of 2017, he kept repeating, they were not purchasing any Indian opium whatsoever. Only Japanese manufacturers were purchasing any of India's very reasonably priced exports. He offered some misplaced optimism. Declaring himself to be the manager of a firm that employed sixty thousand Indian cultivators and a few thousand staffers, the Chief Controller suggested that before long, overseas buyers would clamor for Indian opium again. It was a ludicrous proposition. Indian opium brought a certain degree of economic and political stability in parts of the country that strong economic growth had not touched. But this was a subsidy, and not a business. What was it, then, that had finally brought Indian opium to heel?

◁○▷

A thick fog blankets northern Tasmania during the winter months.[5] It rolls across the low emerald hills that separate the island's small towns and hides the rugged mountains that dot the horizon. So, too, does that fog so often cover the island's massive crop of poppies—lilac purple and pastel pink where India's are ivory white—which have been grown for decades across the region. Somewhere between 450 and 600 farmers, depending on the year, grow poppy on this lush tract. They rotate the crop in between harvests of potatoes, peas, and carrots, and they occasionally use the same land as sheep pasture. Where India's poppy fields are rustic, these are thoroughly modern plots. Combines and tractors ply each field, cordoned off by barbed wire and electric fence, and farmers use everything from zippy motorcycles to black Mercedes to ferry between them. On a small island that feels even smaller, there is an intimate and apparent collaboration between Tasmania's well-to-do farmers, its industrial producers, and the police officers who patrol the plots and check each annual license.

The landscape is bucolic, but the gentility of its emerald hills conceals what is in reality an agro-industrial juggernaut. While the area cultivated has been slashed in half since 2013, these several hundred poppy farmers produce nearly 85 percent of the world's thebaine and a quarter of the world's codeine. Depending on the year, Tasmanian farmers have made $80–200 million in total from their crop. The profit is healthy for each individual farmer, who might make $680–800 per acre. It fuels a much more significant global industry: around $12 billion, at its recent height, of opioid painkillers, disproportionally consumed in the United States.

By the time it began to eclipse its Indian counterpart in the 1990s through an act of creative regulatory arbitrage, the Tasmanian poppy industry was nearly three decades old, and its origins were in the same postwar search for order that animated the birth of the dominant opium regime.[6] In 1934, the United Kingdom's two major morphine producers took note of the recently patented Hungarian method for producing the alkaloid from straw.[7] J.F. Macfarlan and T&H Smith, eager to sidestep the need for imports to the United Kingdom, hired an Oxford botanist in 1948 to lead a project examining the feasibility of cultivating opium poppies in England. The project was a bust. Britain's heavy rains led to anemic poppies with poor alkaloid concentrations, and the project was abandoned in 1957. That botanist, hearing that Australia had grown some trial poppies during the war to compensate for wartime shortages, set his eyes on the antipodes. Two years after ending the British trial, he had established trial plots across Australia and New Zealand. Tasmania was the clear winner. It had loamy red soil, the right proportion of sunlight and darkness, and was separated from any other land mass by difficult waters; smuggling anything across the 150 miles of the Bass Strait would be an incredible feat. The team set to work breeding a poppy suited perfectly to the conditions of the town of Deloraine, a quaint settlement known both for its sawmills and the fertility of its soil.

By the early 1960s, the two companies had been purchased by the British Glaxo Group, a company known largely for its work commercializing the polio vaccine. Glaxo bought an old codeine production facility and built a new straw processing and alkaloid extraction plant. In 1970, the first commercial poppy seed was released to contract farmers by Tasmania's newly established Poppy Advisory and Control Board. Shortly after, the farmers founded a Poppy Growers' Association to negotiate growing conditions and prices for the final product. Glaxo's operation in the early 1970s was exceedingly modest. Meant for domestic Australian consumption and essentially only exporting to New Zealand, it nonetheless provided the infrastructure for bigger schemes. By the middle of the decade, Illinois-based Abbott Laboratories had partnered with Ciech Polfa, a Polish company with extensive experience processing poppy straw, to form Tasmanian Alkaloids, a joint venture in Westbury, Tasmania. With a $5 million initial investment, the firm bought seeds to plant a two-thousand-acre expanse, recruited farmers, and funded a small factory.

Since their first trial harvest, Tasmanian farmers had largely billed their new crop as "oil poppies," touting their application in varnishes and paints. But the fear of shortages in the 1970s sandblasted away this cover. In 1975, Quentin Jones—the USDA official who had helped develop the crop substitution in Turkey, overseen the *brateatum* project in the United States, and examined Indian poppy cultivation at a critical moment in its expansion—welcomed an Abbott official to Washington to speak about Tasmanian poppy.[8] A year later, Jones was in Australia, alongside the Norwegian scientist who had joined him in India, reporting on the operations in Tasmania directly. Despite a few underwhelming harvests, Jones reported, Tasmania was on track to produce twenty-five thousand kilograms of codeine each year, more than three-fourths of the world's medical needs. The factory in Westbury was state of the art. Farmers delivered poppy straw to the factory on drive-on scales, before a polished carbon steel extractor spit out concentrate and spent poppy for farmers to use as straw. This facility was a world apart from the feeble operations in Bolvadin, Turkey, and Neemuch, India, where overworked West German and Yugoslav technicians, respectively, were trying to coax creaky machinery into production.

The Government of Australia had objected vociferously to the 80-20 rule and its privileging of "traditional suppliers." Its representatives had described it as discriminatory against Australian commercial interests, and even the United States' own, given Abbott's investment.[9] All they managed to do was secure a small share of the market for Australia and other "nontraditional" producers. But a year after the introduction of the new rules, Tasmanian Alkaloids was purchased by Johnson & Johnson, the pharmaceutical behemoth eager to move past the debacle of the Chicago Tylenol murders, wherein seven people had died after taking Extra Strength Tylenol laced with cyanide. The purchase deepened American investment in Tasmanian production. In time, this investment would prove critical in transforming American and global purchasing patterns.

At the turn of the 1980s, Australia's productive alkaloid output represented around 17 percent of global alkaloid production. Very shortly after the passage of the 80-20 rule, it was supplying nearly all of the 20 percent of the American market reserved for "nontraditional" producers.[10] But production within the two "traditional" suppliers, India and Turkey, was drastically different. India had become the only country producing raw opium gum, while Turkey's poppy straw was seen as impractically weak compared to what was being produced in Tasmania.[11] This sense of a system locked in place, unable to capitalize on the potential of Tasmanian opium due to the regulatory compromises made in 1981, came to vex American policymakers. Beginning in 1986, a small group of American congressional staffers traveled to India, Turkey, and Australia to examine functioning of the 80-20 rule on the ground.[12] Bearish on its effectiveness, those staffers pointed out the fundamental strangeness of an arrangement that, in seeking to bolster certain geopolitical arrangements, promoted massive inefficiency. In India, nearly 150,000 licensed farmers—their families included, perhaps some million people in total—eked out around sixty tons of morphine equivalent. Given that the United States was, in this period, using more than a third of the global supply of alkaloids, those staffers found it questionable that Australian opium's use should be forever curtailed in such a manner. They recommended a "gradual change" away from the 80-20 rule, but gave no timeframe for such a shift.[13]

In 1988, a small proviso in a sweeping new drug bill in the United States called for a speedy review of the 80-20 rule.[14] Two years later, a hearing convened by a New Jersey Democratic Congressman laid bare the conflict among the United States' three major importers.[15] Johnson & Johnson was predictably eager to bolster its investment in Tasmanian Alkaloids, which it ran through Noramco, its international subsidiary. Arguing for an elimination of the 80-20 rule, its representative played up concerns over leakage from India in its testimony, even as the State Department declared that illicit diversion was not, from their perspective, a major concern, and cast doubt on Turkey's ability to offer stable prices. (The DEA contended there was no such worry.) By contrast, Mallinckrodt—the company with decades of experience working in and purchasing from India—insisted that it had relied on "traditional countries" for more than a century with success. It cited a survey that it had conducted the previous year in India suggesting that leakage, if anything, had been overstated.[16] In the several years that followed, Johnson & Johnson would wage something of a trade war with Mallinckrodt. The former continued to argue for a liberalization of the 80-20 rule in the interests of vertically integrating its poppy business, while the latter fiercely defended its advantageous purchasing from India.[17]

Over the course of several decades, while American bureaucrats and executives had wrangled with the question of Turkish and Indian opium production, Australia had nurtured an industry capable of meeting most, if not all, of the world's alkaloid needs. It was something akin to the agro-industrial fantasy Emanuel Weiss had sketched out a century earlier. It was not his autarkic vision, but rather that of a concentrated tract of land where the world's most concentrated production of poppy could take place. It was an economic powerhouse—yet it would take more to unfetter it and to decimate India's remaining production in the process.

⊂⊙⊃

Paul Mahlberg was one of the most trusted names in narcotics. In 1970, the Indiana University botanist had been given one of only two DEA licenses to start a cannabis cultivation program, in the interests of finding out how its active compounds were produced. In 1986, Mahlberg was seconded from his laboratory in Bloomington on a project funded by the United Nations' Industrial Development Organization, charged with finding new destinations for India's increasingly less valuable opium.[18] Five Indian officials met Mahlberg in India to survey the country's production facilities and its best chemical analysis laboratories, before heading to the United Kingdom, Switzerland, and Germany to learn about new processing technologies there. If in some ways much like any other technical development program, there was a feeling of crisis abatement in Mahlberg's work. The most promising market for Indian alkaloids, he and his collaborators felt, was in "developing countries, particularly the countries of Africa." If it had become a last-choice substance for pharmaceutical production in the developed world, perhaps Indian opium might be repurposed as a basic analgesic in the developing one.

Mahlberg's mission—finding a "taker" for Indian opium—was urgent and only grew more so. In the early 1980s, it had still been possible to see something vestigial and rustic in India's illicit opium trade. Some showy city raids beginning in the 1970s notwithstanding, busts and arrests were mostly village affairs.[19] There were still Indians in the country's west who struggled not with heroin but with opium smoking. This was a vice that in large measure had been exorcised by the end of the 1950s but that lingered on in the country's rural tracts. A charity outside of Jodhpur, the Opium De-addiction Treatment, Training and Research Trust, claimed that the 1,500 patients it had successfully weaned off opium was less than 1 percent of the total population of users in the region.[20] India's heroin factories were barely worth the name, just makeshift clandestine laboratories usually fairly close to poppy fields themselves.

By the time Mahlberg arrived in India, that rustic fantasy was hard to sustain.[21] What had begun as relatively isolated incidents in the 1980s had become now a widespread cottage industry, with smuggling hotspots in Mandsaur district, Rajasthan's Chittorgarh district, and sparsely populated areas all along the border between Madhya Pradesh and Rajasthan. There were incontrovertible signs that the makeshift laboratories of an earlier moment had been replaced with something more organized. Acetic anhydride, the pungent, vinegary compound that serves as an essential precursor for producing heroin, was found in large quantities in markets along the Pakistan border, in Bombay and India's west, and across the southern Coromandel Coast. It was possible to piece together two major smuggling routes out of the country. The smaller was a southern route, wherein opium flowed south to Bangalore and coastal cities like Mangalore, Thiruvananthapuram, and Thoothukudi before being processed into heroin and shipped to the Gulf and other destinations. The larger route went mainly through the marshlands of Gujarat, through the watery Kori and Sir "creeks"—tidal estuaries—where small boats plied heroin to larger vessels for transshipment to Europe or North America. After the Soviet invasion of Afghanistan, India was also serving as a "staging area" for heroin being produced in the Khyber Pass area of Pakistan and Afghanistan.[22]

The scale of these routes was not possible without a great deal of complicity from those involved with the licit trade—if not at the highest levels, then certainly at lower rungs within it. In 1985, a Lucknow University research group was caught using its laboratory to produce heroin. A former Narcotics Control Bureau inspector, Ashwini Bhardwaj, ran a heroin factory in Mandsaur for the better part of a decade. The leaders of India's new "cartels" came from India's cities and rarely from the poppy belt itself. They hid their ventures behind brassware exports, real estate, and hospitality ventures.[23] One, from Shahjahanpur in Uttar Pradesh, became a member of parliament himself. A cynical if plausible speculative political analysis held that the Hindu nationalist BJP was making electoral gains in the three official opium-producing states by refraining from enforcing the strictures of the new 1988 drug law.[24]

In 1991, two Mandsaur district farmers lamented the collusion between narcotics officials and the black market. "I don't care if I have to go to jail for saying this," the first snarled, before explaining the narcotics officials who allegedly monitored his crop worked in consort with village headmen to set bribe levels, buy inputs for the extra crop, and help get it to black-market smugglers.[25] The second lamented that it was impossible to turn a profit without selling to those smugglers. Fertilizers, pesticides, and labor ate up whatever price the government was offering.

As early as 1984, American officials, Mallinckrodt executives, and administrators at the UN Commission on Narcotic Drugs were conceding that the 80-20 rule had done nothing to reduce the significant stockpile of opium still held in Indian warehouses.[26] This "enormous opium gum stockpile," guarded and secure, was not the source of the opium being processed into heroin and sent overseas. But it spoke to the rule's absolute failure to find a legitimate outlet for the product. In 1986, the United States House Committee on Foreign Affairs estimated that stockpile at over two thousand metric tons.[27] By the following year, Indian media outlets reported that the United States was prepared to "make good the losses suffered by the farmers if the latter do away with opium cultivation altogether."[28] In 1990, as India's economic liberalization neared, US representatives warned India that failure to rein in smuggling and sell off its stockpile would negatively impact any support Washington would give in supporting India through the World Bank. The United Nations, for its part, called upon consuming countries to help purchase down the stockpile in the name of international drug control efforts.[29]

Indian officials managed to solve the short-term stockpile problem.[30] The price of the country's already inexpensive opium was further reduced at the turn of the 1990s: Indian officials discounted what they sold, offered rebates to purchasers, and, via dumping, turned what was a losing concern into an absurd financial arrangement. Indian officials unloaded their opium primarily to Mallinckrodt, Penick, Boots, and Macfarlan Smith in the United Kingdom.[31] Mallickrodt and Penick processed their Indian imports directly, and Normco—Johnson & Johnson's international concern—processed the Indian opium that had been stockpiled at Fort Knox in a slightly earlier period.[32] India's predatory pricing, combined with two bad harvests in 1993 and 1994, finally eliminated the country's opium reserve. But the spectral quality of this industry, and the production of a zombie commodity—a "stranded asset" with no organic buyer—was readily apparent in the money that New Delhi spent merely running the diminished infrastructure. At the time of liberalization, nearly 1,400 workers were employed in the factories at Ghazipur and Neemuch and in the central bureaucracy, and the whole of the revenue made through exports did not even cover their salaries. "The illicit lines" of opium, one contemporary analysis surmised, had little sanctioned benefit but "sprinkled largesse through rural and urban areas, on lower levels of officialdom, and into campaign coffers. It strengthened buying power and political quiescence."[33] This distortion would grow even more profound as the decade advanced.

❈

Tony Fist, understated as most Tasmanians, seemed an unlikely figure to usher in a revolution.[34] After his graduate work in plant nutrition, Fist had returned home to Tasmania to take a job at Tasmanian Alkaloids, the joint Polish-American venture in Westbury taken over by Johnson & Johnson. He arrived back on the island at a precipitous moment. Tasmanian poppy production had been doing well, within the constraints that the US rule imposed upon it. As Indian officials were busy disbursing the country's opium stockpile, Tasmanian farmers had continued to increase their production—the island produced ten metric tons in 1981 and ninety-five by 1995. Sometime in the middle of that period, around 1991, Tasmania was producing around 30 percent of the world's morphine and codeine, though its contribution to the United States was limited by the 80-20 rule.[35] The 80-20 rule was characterized by a certain ambiguity. Nowhere in the original rule was it specified how those percentages were to be calculated. In practice, the rule was largely determined by "AMA equivalent"—the morphine equivalent of an alkaloid, measured by weight. Tasmanian poppy straw and concentrate of poppy straw was, therefore, limited by the same restrictions that governed any nontraditional producer.

When Fist came back to Tasmania, the farmers growing poppy for Tasmanian Alkaloids and Glaxo were wondering whether, given the slowing pace of growth, they might be forced to return to the sheep-raising for merino wool that had once been their most lucrative export.[36] But Fist, enterprising and determined, set to work seeing what possibilities there were to improve the quality of the island's poppy crop. Poppy mutagenesis—inducing mutations in poppy plants—was not an entirely new technique. But screening individual plants was slow and costly. Fist developed a new analytical method: taking a tiny droplet of poppy sap, extracting its alkaloids via a buffer, and using chromatography to visualize the profile of each sample. In 1994, using this method, Fist identified two useful adaptations in the "top1" poppy he had bred.[37] This variety was missing the ten genes—on a genome that carried seventeen thousand—responsible for morphine production. Like the *bracteatum* poppy discovered in Iran decades earlier, top1 could not be processed into heroin. Just as importantly, this variety produced an enormous quantity of thebaine, the precursor alkaloid that could be transformed into codeine and semisynthetic compounds like hydrocodone and oxycodone.

Since the 1940s, thebaine had been growing ever more important as a pharmaceutical alkaloid. Early attempts to produce it in the Ghazipur factory had been abandoned, but by the 1940s, after André Barbier's discovery that it could be used as a "mother liquor" for the distillation of codeine, it had become progressively more central in North American and European pharmaceutical manufacturing. Endo Pharmaceuticals had used thebaine-based oxycodone to create Percodan in the 1950s; by the late 1960s, the ready transformation of semisynthetic drugs was driving new pharmacological agendas. The high thebaine content of Indian opium gave that commodity an edge over Turkish poppy straw, which had little or none; in 1979, Indian officials, proposing a long-term supply arrangement, had marketed that ready supply of thebaine as perfectly suited to the alkaloid profiles that US manufacturing required.

Several currents had come together to make thebaine more central to pharmacological practice in the United States. In the 1970s, pain reformers like John Bonica and Ronald Melzack had moved pain to the center of mainstream medical thought and practice.[38] Toward the decade's end, Johns Hopkins University's Candace Pert and Solomon Snyder had identified the long hypothesized but elusive endogenous opioid receptor in the body.[39] All this had inspired a new breed of activist-researchers. These physicians imagined a new palliative imperative of bringing opioid drugs from the hospital to the home and using them in a wider variety of contexts than previously imagined.[40] One of the most important of these activists, Kathleen Foley of the Memorial Sloan Kettering Cancer Center in New York, worked alongside her collaborator, Russell Portenoy, to argue that "opiophobia" had precluded the better management of pain. In 1990, when the House Subcommittee on Crime met to discuss the functioning of the 80-20 rule, one of the witnesses that Mallinckrodt called upon was Kathleen Foley. Foley made the case that, in an era characterized by a "better understanding of the neuropharmacology of pain," her colleagues were more convinced than ever of the superiority of basic alkaloids like morphine and codeine and thebaine-based semisynthetic opioids.[41]

Bracteatum, that earlier thebaine-rich, morphine-free poppy, had perhaps been ahead of its time, contemplated at a moment when the political economy of opioid production looked very different. Tony Fisk's "top1" poppy enjoyed a very different reception. It was given a cheeky new name—"Norman," as a nod to its "no morphine" content"—and it set, as one Canadian researcher remarked, "a land speed record for commercialization."[42] Two years after its development, farmers contracted to Tasmanian Alkaloids began planting, harvesting, and delivering the first crops of Norman poppy, six years after Johnson & Johnson had begun lobbying for an end to the 80-20 rule. In the same year, a new painkiller, OxyContin, was brought on the market. There were signs that their strategy was paying dividends: a Clinton administration official came to Tasmania to ride on tractors through the new fields of Norman poppy.[43]

All this agronomic ingenuity would mean little unless it were possible to export Tasmania's thebaine-rich poppy straw to the United States in a significant enough quantity. Since the 80-20 rule's congressional review in 1990, Johnson & Johnson had been calling for an amendment of, or an end to, limits on its ability to import Tasmanian opium. It had initially asked for a 40 percent allocation to "nontraditional" producers and moved over time to calling for an end to this framework altogether.[44] Tasmanian politicians and their mainland Australian counterparts began lobbying for a similar shift, eager to prop up a lucrative but hamstrung industry.[45] In early 2000, shortly before it was purchased by Tyco, a large medical conglomerate, Mallinckrodt changed its tune. With Indian opium an increasingly arcane product for modern pharmaceutical manufacturing, its long legacy of purchasing meant little when a fundamentally better product was readily available elsewhere.[46] Together, Mallinckrodt and Noramco made the case that the DEA should either alter the ratio of the 80-20 rule to 60-40 or exempt thebaine from the rule altogether.

In a surprising bout of regulatory capture, the DEA—which had not so much as mentioned thebaine in the initial rule—agreed to this interpretation shortly thereafter. "There is no doubt whatsoever that demand for thebaine will increase," Tasmania's Attorney General told an Australian radio program, celebrating the new rule, "and the Americans particularly will take all we can provide."[47] Johnson & Johnson, via Noramco, was able to do what no other manufacturer had been able to do: vertically integrate an industry that had been thoroughly constrained by geopolitics. Beyond controlling a supply chain from seed to alkaloid, purchasing from Tasmania meant there was no need to consider agrarian production in anything but its most streamlined, industrial form. And it meant sidestepping entirely the Indian and Turkish state bureaucracies, both of which were inefficient, difficult to work with, and more or less entirely in the business of subsidizing their respective countries' opium production.

The consequences on the consumption side were evident in short order. After the DEA explicitly allowed thebaine to enter the United States beyond the strictures of the 80-20 rule, it also pushed upward the import and production quotas that served as a ceiling for imports. Raw narcotic materials, long held out as products too fraught to be subject to the simple laws of supplies and demand, were quickly given over to those laws. Noramco, in its facility in Delaware, processed increasingly large quantities of Tasmanian concentrate of poppy straw into oxycodone, hydrocodone, and other opioids. The quantitative increase in oxycodone spoke to the dramatic climb. Between 1993 and 2015, the DEA raised its aggregate production quotas threefold, and the quota for oxycodone production was raised from 3.5 to over 150 tons.[48] Equally dramatic but harder to immediately discern would be the effect that these regulatory revolutions would have on the Indian landscape, where a ghost ship of production kept sailing with no apparent destination in sight.

◖○◗

Until its unceremonious shuttering a few years ago, the *Sarkari Afeem ki Dukaan*—the Government Opium Shop—was discreetly located behind a *pan-wallah* on Desh Bandhu Gupta Road.[49] Surrounded by small shops selling packets of chips and *pan masala*, the shop's inconspicuous exterior gave almost no clue as to what was inside. A few days each week, the rust-red door was unbolted to welcome a small number of elderly patients for their monthly quota of opium: somewhere between eighteen and thirty-five grams each, sold at a laughably modest twenty rupees per gram. Around the time that Narendra Modi, India's fourteenth prime minister, came to power in 2014, the slow closure of this shop—and a few others like it across the country's north—offered a strangely poignant reminder of opium's persistent footprint on the

Indian subcontinent. The specter of elderly opium-eaters and smokers was indeed incongruous against the backdrop of a country blanketed by mobile internet and crisscrossed by ride-hailing services and digital payment systems. It was equally striking at a moment when opioid abuse in India more readily called to mind heroin and the misuse of pharmaceutical opioids. By the end of the decade and the outbreak of the COVID-19 pandemic, it was possible to speak of an opioid epidemic in northern India with parallels to its American counterpart, even if its origins were not pharmaceutical.

By the time Tasmanian farmers were planting their first crop of Norman poppy, Indian officials had managed to eradicate the country's large stockpile of opium through low-cost dumping on the global alkaloid market. Subsequent production was an entirely spectral affair. The poppy research network that scientists like U.S. Kaicker had built in the 1970s was reanimated in the 1990s. Scientists in Lucknow patented a new poppy variety in 2000.[50] "Sujata" was a variety that did not produce morphine—but it also lacked the genes to produce any other alkaloid, and scientists could only predict that one day they would be able to produce a poppy like Tasmania's Norman variety. Another team in Gujarat, connected to the Lucknow team via the All India Co-ordinated Research Project on Medicinal and Aromatic Plants, developed six "high-yielding" varieties of poppy with improved latex production and disease resistance.[51] Managers of the Ghazipur factory began to make good on their often-repeated promise to modernize the facility, importing new mechanical mixer-dryers to replace sun-drying opium in wooden trays and perhaps boost the recovery of morphine and codeine above its present, "uneconomical level."[52] None of these modest technical advances, however, could obviate the fundamental problem. If Indian scientists were able to develop a poppy like Tasmania's and convert their production to poppy straw, it would obviate the political benefits that were gained by offering opium licenses to seventy-five thousand poppy farmers and, by proxy, to their extended families.[53]

Absent a real market, the politicking over opium licenses grew deeply contentious in this period. Members of parliament assured farmers that, even in the face of challenges from overseas, opium cultivation would continue to enjoy state support.[54] Nowhere was the political value of opium clearer than in three adjoining districts: Chittorgarh in Rajasthan and Mandsaur and Ratlam in Madhya Pradesh. In these districts, administrative successors to the kingdoms of Mewar and Malwa, opium enjoyed preeminence well beyond the wheat, soybean, mustard, and pulses grown beside it—more than 80 percent of the country's opium was grown in Mewar-Malwa by 1997.[55] In an agricultural tract with limited infrastructure and high rural unemployment, outside the boom towns of liberalization-era India, that preeminence afforded opium an even greater cachet.

In 1996—the same year that Norman poppies were first planted en masse in Tasmania—the Government of India announced a new, liberalized poppy policy.[56] The "trust-based" approach of this policy gave far greater leeway to cultivators. In prior years, farmers who did not meet the "minimum yield" of opium in a given year would have their license permanently canceled, on the assumption that they had sold part of their crop to the black market. The new opium policy gave farmers a year's grace period to return to their expected yield. The government temporarily stopped issuing new licenses but increased the plot sizes that opium farmers could cultivate. It was not merely a consolidation of opium planting but a consolidation of the political value that opium itself represented. The new opium policy was touted as helping India meet the concerns of the International Narcotics Control Board over production from India and Turkey. But the INCB's note had been far more hesitant than officials in New Delhi had suggested.[57] New Delhi's declaration, in 1997, that its cultivators had produced over 1,300 tons of opium for the licit market was worrisome for what it meant for black-market sales. The Ghazipur and Neemuch factories were producing for a slowly growing domestic alkaloid market, but the increased yields were far higher than what that small market could absorb.

With no new poppy licenses being granted under the new policy, the politics of licensing grew more contentious.[58] In Rajasthan's Chittorgarh district, farmers without licenses protested against the limitation of new ones, while licensed farmers protested against the government's low prices and the ingresses of middlemen whom they had needed to bribe to get those licenses. India's right-wing Bharatiya Janata Party, which had huge gains in Rajasthan in the 1993 elections, were worried that the poppy issue would fell them in the 1998 ones. They were right to worry. A politician named Uday Lal Anjana defeated the BJP candidate on the promise of supporting an increase in licenses. Upon his victory, he was rumored to give away 150 Hindustan Ambassador automobiles to pay off underlings.

The more dramatic dynamic, however, was in Mandsaur district, across the border in Madhya Pradesh.[59] On a field in Mandsaur, a forty-eight-year-old farmer named Ajay smiled in a shiny Maruti 800, his newly purchased automobile a sign of sudden new wealth. "Opium is like gold dust," he swore. "It has brought us riches." The increase in licensed land area for poppy—by 1999, the amount had doubled—had brought new opportunities to Mandsaur. Few of them were sanctioned. Smuggling rings moved quickly into the region, and heroin labs mushroomed. A great deal of wealth was created, both on family farms and for the local politicians who lobbied for the trade in exchange for healthy cuts. The matriarch of the Ghansu Patidar family warned her three children to stay away from the "greasy" pails of opium the adults gathered, but confessed that the February harvest had become something of a "festival." Farther away from the center of Mandsaur, residents of Acheri village near the Rajasthan border frustrated efforts to police their sprawling opium tract by moving back and forth across the muddy Shivana rivulet that separated the two states. But the influx of cash was fraught. Heroin was making new inroads into Mandsaur. A *pudiya*, or tiny packet of locally made heroin, could be purchased for less than forty rupees, or barely a dollar. Field laborers were increasingly using it to get through a day's work, much like the cultivators of nineteenth-century Malwa had come to use opium to dull the pain of their own labor producing it.

There were other crops being grown in Mandsaur: wheat and onions, and some higher-value products to rotate in like cumin, ginger, and soy. But opium's cash value, nearly all of it illicit, was the source of any real local prosperity, and the engine of a distorted local economy. After the pause on new licenses was lifted, cultivators were grudgingly offering under-the-table payments of 5,000 rupees (around $120) to local officials to secure their license. That amount was higher than the legal amount a farmer could earn from a single growing season, estimated at around 4,000 rupees. But it was easy to make many times the bribe amount from selling to smugglers—either those who turned it into heroin or those who sold spent capsules, called *doda*, for tea or tinctures in a more gray-market economy.[60] A local circle of patronage and smuggling was the only thing propping up an utterly vestigial market.

That circle began to break at the turn of the millennium. In 2000, a "quantum jump" in the area under opium cultivation represented one of the largest expansions of licenses since independence.[61] Narcotics officials again appealed to the "new opium policy" in place since 1996. By 2002, India was spending as much to staff its narcotics operation as it gained in foreign exchange.[62] When officials also took into account the value of the codeine India had to import for its own modest palliative care system, the system was an entirely losing proposition for the country. As the United States' DEA mulled changes to the 80-20 rule, it offered India help in running a Joint Licit Opium Poppy Survey to understand just how widespread smuggling was in the opium heartland.[63] But with the United States set to import essentially unlimited quantities of thebaine-rich Tasmanian concentrate of poppy straw, the only substantive potential outlet for India's product outside of the black market seemed to exist in growing the domestic market. A series of successive reforms failed to turn much around. New Delhi offered major domestic pharmaceutical manufacturers like Ranbaxy, Dr. Reddy's, and Cipla opportunities to invest privately into the opium sector, but all declined to invest in a "sick company with no profits" and no commercially viable future.[64]

⊂○⊃

In poppy's other graveyard, central Anatolia, the rise of Tasmanian thebaine had been scarcely as devastating. A great number of Turkish poppy farmers, given the opportunity to grow poppy straw for a tightly controlled legal market, but largely unable to sell it to the underworld, abandoned cultivation altogether.[65] Turkey's once feared morphine and heroin runners largely moved west, setting up shop in Bulgaria and the Balkans and moving narcotics from elsewhere.[66] The factory established at Bolvadin, once opened, operated at a modest scale, generally producing alkaloids for domestic consumption rather than for export, since Turkish poppy contained none of the thebaine that would be more valuable for US or European consumption.[67] Several years after Turkey's role as a "traditional producer" was enshrined in American rulemaking, US officials assessed the country's production as woefully inefficient, with 120,000 farmers producing a mere forty metric tons of opium.[68] Ankara was selling alkaloids at lower than production costs and was spending more than $15 million a year in security—more than double the revenue it was gaining from CPS exports. "In essence," they concluded, "the poppy industry is a subsidy for Turkish farmers." It was, however, one subsidy among many. Over the 1990s, Anatolian farmers gradually came to see their sales to the state monopoly as a minor supplement to other income, usually as a by-product of or complement to poppy seed production.[69] Nothing similar could be said about Mandsaur district, where Suresh Patidar lived, the center of the Indian opium heartland and perhaps its last stronghold after a long unraveling close to a century in the making.

In the early 2010s, pockets of great prosperity were still to be found throughout Mandsaur. The greatest example of that prosperity— beyond the flashy new iPhones and beige SUVs spotted around the district—was to be found at the Sanwaliya Seth temple.[70] Just across the Rajasthan border in Chittorgarh district, the tall stone Hindu temple housed a small avatar of Shree Sanwalia Seth, an avatar of Lord Krishna said to have a special reverence for opium growers and traders. A visit and an offering to the temple, pleasing to the deity, was said to inure a grower against the loss of his opium license for the following season and to protect a dealer against arrest or prosecution. It was little wonder, then, that both made regular trips to the temple to make offerings in rupees and dollars en route to consignments or appointments, often promising a share of the year's profits should the crop or the haul be a good one. The 25 million rupees—half a million dollars—that the temple's caretaker was said to collect each month spoke to the sheer volume of black-market wealth moving through the region. Well-connected farmers with licenses continued to lobby for greater concessions at election time.[71] A thick network of smugglers continued to move opium through various cover businesses—most notably the creaky pencil factory in Mandsaur town, which shipped the gum under packets of school supplies.[72]

Yet most farmers were far away from the blessings of Shree Sanwalia Seth.[73] The vast majority of cultivating families in this wholly agricultural region were producing garlic, onions, and soybeans. The prices for those crops fluctuated but were generally very low. The costs of inputs like seeds and fertilizers were increasing well beyond inflation, and much of the countryside was locked in debt. In 2016, the sudden introduction of "demonetization"—the overnight invalidation of high-denomination rupee notes in the interests of rooting out India's shadow economy—plunged the district, like many others, into temporary chaos.

In June of 2017, farmers from across the district, organizing on WhatsApp, marched to the district headquarters in Mandsaur town for a large protest. Carrying placards and taking selfies, they refused to sell their produce in markets until their demands were heard. Their grievances echoed those of farmers across India, from the cratering price of cash crops to the central government's decision to rescind a popular agricultural loan waiver. The peaceful protest soon turned violent. After farmers burnt trucks on the road leading to the opium factory, policemen opened fire, killing six young men. In the days that followed, police raids into villagers' homes allegedly unearthed hordes of opium. The protests grew heated and spread across the opium heartland.

As the conservative Bharatiya Janata Party–led state government downplayed the protests, Rahul Gandhi—leader of the Indian National Congress and Jawaharlal Nehru's great-grandson—arrived in Mandsaur. Marching to town, the opposition leader was first detained by the local police. Upon his release, Gandhi, an awkward and halting politician, gave an unusual stump speech promising a better future to the district's farmers. "If we come to power," he declared in Hindi, "soon Beijing will be eating Mandsaur's garlic."

The line was ridiculed on social media. Gandhi showed little understanding of how far away this dusty district remained from the booming industry of Bangalore or Hyderabad. No amount of subsidies would ever get central Indian garlic to lucrative export markets. And opium farmers knew that the legal price of their crop was unlikely to ever recover. Cultivators spoke instead of folk heroes like Abdul of Billod, a local said to be hiding in Rajasthan while making a fortune on the black market by turning Mandsauri opium into Punjabi heroin. The price paid for black-market opium continued to increase, as the government's purchasing price fell ever lower. For those without the cash and connections to get or keep a license, the opportunities in this rural corner of India, far away from the glitz of the country's big cities or even nearby Indore, were scant. Outside of Mandsaur, the district was dotted with truck stop settlements of *Banchhada*-caste sex workers, whose high HIV rates were stoking anxiety across the region. Even for those farmers with an opium license, the future was uncertain. Suresh Patidar spoke frequently about a future for his children away from Mandsaur district, the temptations of the black market, and life wedded to a crop that had long outlived its commercial usefulness.

In September 2020, tens of thousands of farmers from around the country would converge on New Delhi in a massive protest against three new proposed agricultural laws. Their protests would cripple India's capital for more than a year, as farmers—mostly from the country's more privileged agricultural regions—agitated against these structural reforms. But their defense of productive agriculture, boosted up by subsidies, modern inputs, and the promise of greater returns, was far removed from Mandsaur's bleak reality. In Suresh Patidar's arid corner of India, once so central to the world's apothecary, the ghost ship of opium drifted on.

Epilogue
Opium Crises

Norman poppies were first commercially planted in Tasmania in 1996, the year that New Delhi announced its new, liberalized poppy policy and the year that a small, Connecticut-based pharmaceutical company introduced a new semisynthetic opioid painkiller it called OxyContin. It was also the year when a team of physicians and medical workers from Calicut Medical College in Kerala drove in a small donated van into the lush South Indian countryside.[1] The small group was embarking upon a radical experiment: bringing pain relief to the many people living within a fifteen-mile radius from the hospital who were too poor or debilitated to receive the treatment they needed. In a year's time, the Pain and Palliative Care Clinic workers visited 340 villagers suffering from advanced cancers, most often leaving their car where the paved or gravel road yielded to rougher trails and continuing on foot. Often, upon arrival, they discovered that the patient they had come to see had already died.

When the team did meet a living patient, they had little to offer. Together, they drained urine and intubated patients to feed them. They dressed wounds and offered fluids, leaving equipment behind for families to use. Perhaps most importantly, they spoke with patients and their families, assuring them that the cancers claiming their family members were not contagious and that, to some degree, their suffering could be alleviated. Most of these patients died not long after the team's visit, but they died with access to a certain degree of care and compassion in their final weeks and months. What the team could not offer was morphine. Six patients had pain so debilitating that the group used some of their very limited supply to bring it under control. But morphine, like other opioids, was scarce on the ground.

In the 1980s, Indian physicians, attuned to parallel conversations overseas, began to posit what India would need to develop a meaningful pain relief program.[2] Their planning was fraught. In 1984, advocates at India's National Cancer Control Program had named cancer pain relief as one of the core services that should be provided at any Indian primary care center. The following year, the Narcotic Drugs and Psychotropic Substance Act, passed as a reward of sorts for the benefits that India's opium regime would theoretically receive through the 80-20 rule, made it nearly impossible for Indian physicians to prescribe opioids. Indian doctors struggled to understand and then acquire the six separate licenses needed to receive morphine shipments, nor were they keen to risk twenty-year prison terms for possessing opiates after one of those licenses had expired. In 1985, India's 780 million people used 716 kilograms of morphine. By 1997, that already small volume had dwindled to a paltry eighteen kilograms. The irony was hard to miss: the terms of India's export of raw materials precluded their meaningful use at home. If the system was not fully colonial, it at least echoed the exploitative economics of an earlier century.

The Calicut Medical College team was deeply clued in to the global movement for pain relief. The College's Head of Anesthesiology, M.R. Rajagopal, had been born a month after India's independence. Working in an important medical center in South India, he had been chilled by the suicide of a patient suffering from tongue cancer. In 1989, Rajagopal attended a seminar by Gilly Burn, a British nurse who had been sent to India by the WHO to assess the country's palliative needs. Shortly thereafter, he went to Oxford to study under one of the founders of Britain's hospice movement, learning how British physicians had used morphine, diamorphine, and methadone to treat cancer pain. Back in India, Rajagopal used a modest amount of WHO funding to start the Pain and Palliative Care Clinic, India's first such undertaking.

By the end of the 1990s, advocates in India and the United States—and the Global South and Global North more generally—were advancing very different approaches to the question of pain relief. American pain physicians, aided by unscrupulous pharmaceutical firms, found new ways to sidestep the question of opioids' addictiveness as they advocated for their movement from the hospital to the home as first-line treatments for chronic pain. The pain relief movement in India was far more modest. Rajagopal and his colleagues worked to dispel the idea that morphine could not be given in end-of-life care. They taught physicians to open morphine consignments in front of police officers and were scrupulous in monitoring their own morphine supplies. In two years, not even a thousandth of a percent of their supply went missing.[3] Rajagopal and his colleagues chafed at the discrepancy between the vast quantity of opium that India was producing and the difficulties that physicians had in acquiring it. India's very few morphine marketers had difficulty procuring opium from the Government Opium and Alkaloid Works, quixotically trying to convince overseas purchasers to look to their offerings again. "To communicate the intensity of the dread felt by staff and patients when a morphine shipment was delayed," Rajagopal wrote, "and the joy when the morphine finally arrived, is not possible."

In 2014, after decades of lobbying, India's laws were revised to drastically simplify the procedure of prescription opioids for end-of-life care. But the ten million people in need of palliative care in India each year continued to have access to less than three hundred kilograms of morphine each year, all produced from opium harvested in the country's north and processed in the government factories in Ghazipur and Neemuch.[4] The domestic market barely registered—a low priority for Indian producers and the bureaucracy that had once bent over backward to serve American demand. But growing consumption in the United States, drawn from other sources of alkaloids, did nothing to absorb Indian overproduction. And that overproduction still offered only a little to the many sick and dying Indians whose pain went largely untreated.

In much of the Global North, the word *opioid* has come to signify crisis. The surge of opioid use disorder in the United States since the 1990s has been chronicled as a cautionary tale of pharmaceutical capitalism. Purdue Pharma's release of OxyContin in 1996 marked its beginning, as the Sackler family's aggressive marketing and misleading claims about addiction risk expanded prescribing far beyond acute or palliative care into the management of chronic pain. The US crisis unfolded in successive waves.[5] As dependence on pharmaceutical opioids grew and prescribing was curtailed, users who could no longer obtain pills turned to heroin, largely supplied by enterprising cartels south of the Mexican border.[6] By the mid-2010s, the rise of fentanyl and other synthetic opioids had transformed the market again, amplifying the lethality of the crisis.

The demographics of the crisis also shifted. In its early years, white Americans were disproportionately affected, in part due to differences in access to health insurance and patterns of prescribing, with rural areas experiencing especially high mortality rates. Later waves brought opioid deaths into urban centers and minority communities. In recent years, African Americans have faced the fastest-growing rates of fatal overdose. The numbers, both contested and regularly revised, remain staggering. By 2008, the United States—home to less than 5 percent of the world's population—consumed over 80 percent of global opioid alkaloids and nearly all of its morphine.[7] In 2017, the Centers for Disease Control and Prevention estimated the cost of the crisis at $1 trillion annually, or roughly 5 percent of US GDP.[8] At the onset of the COVID-19 pandemic, opioid-related deaths surpassed one million, far exceeding the annual toll of deaths from HIV/AIDS or gun violence.[9] In 2024, overdose deaths fell sharply for the first time in years, dropping nearly thirty thousand to the lowest level since 2019.[10]

The US opioid crisis—more accurately, a North American crisis, due to smaller-scale trends in Canada—cannot be understood in isolation.[11] Similar patterns of rising opioid prescribing emerged in the Netherlands, England, and Australia. As restrictions tightened in the

United States, pharmaceutical companies increasingly turned to lower- and middle-income markets, deploying the same aggressive tactics that had fueled the American epidemic. By the 2010s, countries such as Brazil, China, Colombia, Egypt, Mexico, the Philippines, and—most ironically—India became targets for industry expansion. The result echoed the contradictions of global food systems: surpluses for a few, scarcity for others.[12] In 2018, the *Lancet*'s Commission on Palliative Care and Pain Relief described this stark imbalance, highlighting ventures like India's fledgling palliative care system and more durable efforts in Uganda, Argentina, and Costa Rica as rare bright spots amid a global failure to meet basic needs. At the time, half the world's population received less than 1 percent of global morphine supply—a disparity the *Lancet* called "a heinous injustice that has been largely ignored in global health."[13] Yet within just four years, a second *Lancet* commission warned that many of these same countries faced the opposite risk: the rapid spread of opioid overuse as rising incomes, weak regulations, and aggressive marketing recreated the conditions that had fueled North America's crisis.

The global opioid crisis is often framed as a crisis of demand—that of patients, users, overdose victims, and sometimes, those deprived of vital painkillers. But the global dynamics of opium and opioids have always been rooted in questions of production and supply. Opioids are farmed, produced, synthesized, regulated, and traded within frameworks shaped by decades of colonial extraction, state power, and pharmaceutical development. Even now, those arrangements are unsettled. In 2024, as US overdose deaths finally began to fall, a start-up called Bright Green secured a federal license to cultivate opium poppies and cannabis inside greenhouses in New Mexico, casting its work as part of a national security agenda to reshore critical medical ingredients. The underlying and unresolved conflicts continue to pit abundance and deprivation, national interests and global markets, and medical need and commercial opportunism against one another in new and contingent configurations of power.

For two centuries, the global opioid economy, built on imperial foundations, bound together the management of pain and the exercise of state power. It did so by organizing labor, regulating production, and redrawing the lines of authority over who would grow, control, and consume these drugs. The rise of synthetic opioids and the fracturing of regulatory control in the late twentieth and early twenty-first centuries were not aberrations. They emerged from a system built on shifting foundations: a global economy that fused agricultural labor, pharmaceutical science, state authority, and global commerce into a single machinery for managing pain. That system was rooted in peasant labor, forged through empire, sustained through the aspirations of postcolonial state-building, and ultimately dismantled as new technologies allowed capital to escape the constraints of state control and rural labor altogether.

For much of the modern era, opioid production depended on the labor of peasant cultivators in India and Turkey, whose labor fed pharmaceutical markets that were largely structured by regulatory imperatives in the United States and Europe. This arrangement yoked bodily suffering to a global supply chain that braided together scientific innovation, extractive agricultural labor, and coercive regulatory regimes and that linked distant forms of production and consumption. The global management of pain was inseparable from the management of labor. Rural cultivators scraped poppy gum; state agents set prices, enforced compliance, and justified their interventions in the name of public health and economic modernization; and pharmaceutical companies and powerful nations secured steady supplies of alkaloids while reshaping forms of medical practice.

The boundary between medical necessity and illicit production was always fragile. The many efforts to isolate legitimate pharmaceutical production from black-market diversion produced elaborate regulatory architectures and chemical and botanical efforts that were never fully secure. The same fields that supplied morphine for pain also fed heroin for the streets; the same plants that stabilized national development budgets fueled illicit economies that states were either unable or unwilling to suppress. Synthetic chemistry was often imagined as a solution to these contradictions—as a way to sever the opioid economy from its dependence on agriculture and finally bring it under stable control. But each technological advance instead produced new vulnerabilities: new markets for stronger drugs, new routes for diversion, new forms of addiction, and new inequalities in the global distribution of access to pain relief. The collapse of the imperial opium economy at the turn of the twentieth century and the rise of postcolonial nations whose regional political economies depended on opium did not resolve these contradictions but remade and heightened them.

Understanding the global opioid system and its many interlinked crises means apprehending these connections in their entirety. The modern global opioid economy organized and still organizes labor, science, and state power around the management of pain, distributing relief, suffering, and power unevenly across borders, markets, and bodies.

Notes

INTRODUCTION

1. Most prominent of these accounts is Patrick Radden Keefe, *Empire of Pain: The Secret History of the Sackler Dynasty* (New York: Doubleday, 2021), which traces the rise and fall of the Sackler family's pharmaceutical empire. Since the publication of Barry Meier, *Pain Killer: An Empire of Deceit and the Origin of America's Opioid Epidemic* (New York: Random House, 2003), many books have offered a similar narrative; they include Sam Quinones, *Dreamland: The True Tale of America's Opiate Epidemic* (New York: Bloomsbury, 2015); John Temple, *American Pain: How a Young Felon and His Ring of Doctors Unleashed America's Deadliest Drug Epidemic*, Reprint edition (Guilford, CT: Lyons Press, 2015); Anna Lembke, *Drug Dealer, MD: How Doctors Were Duped, Patients Got Hooked, and Why It's So Hard to Stop* (Baltimore: Johns Hopkins University Press, 2016); Beth Macy, *Dopesick: Dealers, Doctors, and the Drug Company That Addicted America* (New York: Little, Brown and Company, 2018); and Chris McGreal, *American Overdose: The Opioid Tragedy in Three Acts* (New York: PublicAffairs, 2019).

2. On the politics and periodization of pain, see Isabelle Baszanger, *Inventing Pain Medicine: From the Laboratory to the Clinic* (New Brunswick, NJ: Rutgers University Press, 1998); Roselyne Rey, *The History of Pain* (Cambridge, MA: Harvard University Press, 1998); Thomas Dormandy, *The Worst of Evils: The Fight Against Pain* (New Haven, CT: Yale University Press, 2006); Keith Wailoo, *Pain: A Political History* (Baltimore: Johns Hopkins University Press, 2014); and Joanna Bourke, *The Story of Pain: From Prayer to Painkillers* (Oxford: Oxford University Press, 2017). "Pain studies" owes its origin to both literary studies and the activism of reformist physicians in the 1970s, discussed briefly in chapter 8. The essential text in the former is Elaine Scarry, *The Body in Pain: The Making and Unmaking of the World* (Oxford: Oxford University Press, 1985); for treatments of pain written by those activist-practitioners, see Ronald Melzack, *The Puzzle of Pain* (Harmondsworth, UK: Penguin Education, 1977); Ronald Melzack and Patrick D. Wall, *The Challenge of Pain* (New York: Penguin, 2008); and William Kenneth Livingston, *Pain and Suffering* (Seattle: IASP Press, 1998).

3. The quintessential narrative is J.D. Vance, *Hillbilly Elegy: A Memoir of a Family and Culture in Crisis* (New York: Harper, 2016).

4. See primarily Ben Westhoff, *Fentanyl, Inc.: How Rogue Chemists Are Creating the Deadliest Wave of the Opioid Epidemic* (New York: Atlantic Monthly Press, 2019).

5. Holly Hedegaard, Arialdi M. Miniño, Merianne Rose Spencer, and Margaret Warner, "Drug Overdose Deaths in the United States, 1999–2020," *NCHS Data Brief*, no. 428 (National Center for Health Statistics, 2021); Anne Case and Angus Deaton, *Deaths of Despair and the Future of Capitalism* (Princeton, NJ: Princeton University Press, 2020).

6. I have been influenced by work on agricultural commodities and their incorporation into global systems of consumption, including John Soluri, *Banana Cultures: Agriculture,*

Consumption, and Environmental Change in Honduras and the United States (Austin: University of Texas Press, 2006); Heidi Tinsman, *Buying into the Regime: Grapes and Consumption in Cold War Chile and the United States* (Durham, NC: Duke University Press, 2014); Sven Beckert, *Empire of Cotton: A New History of Global Capitalism* (New York: Vintage, 2015); Joshua Specht, *Red Meat Republic: A Hoof-to-Table History of How Beef Changed America* (Princeton, NJ: Princeton University Press, 2019); Julie Livingston, "Cattle/Beef," in *Self-Devouring Growth: A Planetary Parable as Told from Southern Africa* (Durham, NC: Duke University Press, 2019), 35–60; Casey Marina Lurtz, *From the Grounds Up: Building an Export Economy in Southern Mexico* (Stanford, CA: Stanford University Press, 2019); Stuart McCook, *Coffee Is Not Forever: A Global History of the Coffee Leaf Rust*, Illustrated edition (Athens: Ohio University Press, 2019); Jonathan E. Robins, *Oil Palm: A Global History* (Chapel Hill: University of North Carolina Press, 2021); and Gregg Mitman, *Empire of Rubber Firestone's Scramble for Land and Power in Liberia* (New York: The New Press, 2023). A salient recent debate in the history of capitalism exists over "commodity frontiers," zones where capital expands by incorporating new land, labor, and natural resources into global markets, producing cycles of extraction, dispossession, ecological degradation, and adaptation; see Sven Beckert et al., "Commodity Frontiers and the Transformation of the Global Countryside: A Research Agenda," *Journal of Global History* 16, no. 3 (November 2021): 435–450; and Maxine Berg, "Commodity Frontiers: Concepts and History," *Journal of Global History* 16, no. 3 (November 2021): 451–455.

7. This approach owes much to research on the forging of "modern" cocaine, most significantly, Paul Gootenberg, *Andean Cocaine: The Making of a Global Drug* (Chapel Hill: University of North Carolina Press, 2008). See also Paul Gootenberg, ed., *Cocaine: Global Histories* (Abingdon-on-Thames: Routledge, 1999).

8. Michael K. Steinberg, Joseph John Hobbs, and Kent Mathewson, eds., *Dangerous Harvest: Drug Plants and the Transformation of Indigenous Landscapes* (Oxford: Oxford University Press, 2004); Gabriela Soto Laveaga, *Jungle Laboratories: Mexican Peasants, National Projects, and the Making of the Pill* (Durham, NC: Duke University Press, 2009); Abena Dove Osseo-Asare, *Bitter Roots: The Search for Healing Plants in Africa* (Chicago: University of Chicago Press, 2014); Gabrielle Hecht, *Being Nuclear: Africans and the Global Uranium Trade* (Cambridge, MA: The MIT Press, 2014); Julie Michelle Klinger, *Rare Earth Frontiers: From Terrestrial Subsoils to Lunar Landscapes* (Ithaca, NY: Cornell University Press, 2018).

9. The historiography of black-market opium and its most important derivative in this context, heroin, is substantive, and most often foregrounds the United States. See, very selectively, Alfred W. McCoy, *The Politics of Heroin: CIA Complicity in the Global Drug Trade* (New York: Harper & Row, 1972); David F. Musto, *The American Disease: Origins of Narcotic Control* (New Haven, CT: Yale University Press, 1973); Catherine Lamour and Michel R. Lamberti, *The International Connection; Opium from Growers to Pushers* (New York: Pantheon Books, 1974); Catherine Lamour and Michel R. Lamberti, *The Second Opium War* (London: Lane, 1974; Edward Jay Epstein, *Agency of Fear: Opiates and Political Power in America* (New York: Verso, 1990); David T. Courtwright, *Dark Paradise: A History of Opiate Addiction in America* (Cambridge, MA: Harvard University Press, 2001); Caroline Jean Acker, *Creating the American Junkie: Addiction Research in the Classic Era of Narcotic Control* (Baltimore: Johns Hopkins University Press, 2002); Eric C. Schneider, *Smack: Heroin and the American City* (Philadelphia: University of

Pennsylvania Press, 2013); Claire D. Clark, *The Recovery Revolution: The Battle over Addiction Treatment in the United States* (New York: Columbia University Press, 2017); Nancy D. Campbell et al., *The Narcotic Farm: The Rise and Fall of America's First Prison for Drug Addicts* (Lexington, KY: South Limestone, 2021); and Jonathan S. Jones, *Opium Slavery: Civil War Veterans and America's First Opioid Crisis* (Chapel Hill: University of North Carolina Press, 2025).

10. On the contested boundaries of medical legitimacy and addiction, see David Herzberg, *White Market Drugs: Big Pharma and the Hidden History of Addiction in America* (Chicago: University of Chicago Press, 2020).

11. The modern study of opium can be said to have started with David Owen, *British Opium Policy in China and India* (New Haven, CT: Yale University Press, 1934); the most important recent intervention is undoubtedly Carl Trocki, *Opium, Empire and the Global Political Economy: A Study of the Asian Opium Trade, 1750–1950* (London: Routledge, 1999). Two landmark studies of the Asian trade are Hans Derks, *History of the Opium Problem: The Assault on the East, ca. 1600–1950* (Leiden, the Netherlands: Brill, 2012); and Rolf Bauer, *The Peasant Production of Opium in Nineteenth-Century India* (Leiden, the Netherlands: Brill, 2019). More recently, two revisionist takes have foregrounded the global convergences of the movement for prohibition and the colonial statecraft of prohibition in Southeast Asia; see Steffen Rimner, *Opium's Long Shadow: From Asian Revolt to Global Drug Control* (Cambridge, MA: Harvard University Press, 2018); Diana Kim, *Empires of Vice: The Rise of Opium Prohibition Across Southeast Asia* (Princeton, NJ: Princeton University Press, 2020). Of note are two important popular treatments, Martin Booth, *Opium: A History* (New York: St. Martin's Griffin, 1999); and Lucy Inglis, *Milk of Paradise: A History of Opium* (New York: Pegasus, 2019). Earlier scholarship has largely framed opium's modern history through the rise of international narcotics control, emphasizing diplomatic negotiations, American drug diplomacy, and the expansion of prohibition regimes. Key works in this tradition include Peter Lowes, *The Genesis of International Narcotics Control* (Geneva: Librairie Droz, 1966); Arnold Taylor, *American Diplomacy and the Narcotics Traffic, 1900–1958: A Study in International Humanitarian Reform* (Durham, NC: Duke University Press, 1969); J.B. Brown, "Politics of the Poppy: The Society for the Suppression of the Opium Trade, 1874–1916," *Journal of Contemporary History* 8, no. 3 (1973): 97–111; Kettil Bruun, Lynn Pan, and Ingemar Rexed, *The Gentlemen's Club: International Control of Drugs and Alcohol* (Chicago: University of Chicago Press, 1975); William O. Walker, *Drug Control in the Americas* (Albuquerque: University of New Mexico Press, 1981); S.D. Stein, *International Diplomacy, State Administrators, and Narcotics Control: The Origins of a Social Problem* (Aldershot, UK: Gower, 1985); David R. Bewley-Taylor, *The United States and International Drug Control, 1909–1997* (London: A&C Black, 2002); Kathryn Meyer and Terry M. Parssinen, *Webs of Smoke: Smugglers, Warlords, Spies, and the History of the International Drug Trade* (Lanham, MD, and Oxford: Rowman & Littlefield, 2002); William B. McAllister, *Drug Diplomacy in the Twentieth Century: An International History* (London and New York: Routledge, 2004); Daniel Weimer, *Seeing Drugs: Modernization, Counterinsurgency, and U.S. Narcotics Control in the Third World, 1969–1976* (Kent, OH: The Kent State University Press, 2011); Kathleen J. Frydl, *The Drug Wars in America, 1940–1973* (Cambridge: Cambridge University Press, 2013); Suzanna Reiss, *We Sell Drugs: The Alchemy of US Empire* (Berkeley: University of California Press, 2014); Matthew R. Pembleton, *Containing

Addiction: The Federal Bureau of Narcotics and the Origins of America's Global Drug War (Amherst: University of Massachusetts Press, 2017); and Helena Barop, *Mohnblumenkriege: Die globale Drogenpolitik der USA 1950–1979* [Poppy wars: the global drug policy of the United States, 1950–1979] (Göttingen, Germany: Wallstein Verlag GmbH, 2021).

12. My approach is inspired by the "third wave" of drug historiography, which emerged in the early 2000s. This work has moved beyond earlier US- and British-centered narratives of prohibition and imperial control to foreground actors, spaces, and markets once treated as peripheral. This work interrogates the shifting geographies of narcotics and power, highlights the agency of producers, traders, and users, and foregrounds the social and political construction of illicit and licit economies. See Paul Gootenberg, "Introduction: A New Global History of Drugs," in *The Oxford Handbook of Global Drug History*, ed. Paul Gootenberg (Oxford: Oxford University Press, 2022). A representative selection of "third wave" work includes María Clemencia Ramírez, *Between the Guerrillas and the State: The Cocalero Movement, Citizenship, and Identity in the Colombian Amazon* (Durham, NC: Duke University Press, 2011); Matthew R. Pembleton, *Containing Addiction: The Federal Bureau of Narcotics and the Origins of America's Global Drug War* (Amherst: University of Massachusetts Press, 2017); John Lindsay-Poland, *Plan Colombia: U.S. Ally Atrocities and Community Activism* (Durham, NC: Duke University Press, 2018); Thomas Grisaffi, *Coca Yes, Cocaine No: How Bolivia's Coca Growers Reshaped Democracy* (Durham, NC: Duke University Press, 2019); Maziyar Ghiabi, *Drugs Politics: Managing Disorder in the Islamic Republic of Iran* (Cambridge: Cambridge University Press, 2019); Kojo Koram, ed., *The War on Drugs and the Global Colour Line* (London: Pluto Press, 2019); Lina Britto, *Marijuana Boom: The Rise and Fall of Colombia's First Drug Paradise* (Berkeley: University of California Press, 2020); Haggai Ram, *Intoxicating Zion: A Social History of Hashish in Mandatory Palestine and Israel* (Stanford, CA: Stanford University Press, 2020); James Tharin Bradford, *Poppies, Politics, and Power: Afghanistan and the Global History of Drugs and Diplomacy* (Ithaca, NY: Cornell University Press, 2020); Maziyar Ghiabi, ed., *Power and Illicit Drugs in the Global South* (London: Routledge, 2020); John Collins, *Legalising the Drug Wars: A Regulatory History of UN Drug Control* (Cambridge: Cambridge University Press, 2021); Enrique Desmond Arias and Thomas Grisaffi, eds., *Cocaine: From Coca Fields to the Streets* (Durham, NC: Duke University Press, 2021); Lucas Richert and James H. Mills, *Cannabis: Global Histories* (Cambridge, MA: The MIT Press, 2021); Stephen Snelders, *Drug Smuggler Nation: Narcotics and the Netherlands, 1920–1995* (Manchester: Manchester University Press, 2021); Benjamin Breen, *The Age of Intoxication: Origins of the Global Drug Trade* (Philadelphia: University of Pennsylvania Press, 2021); Erika Dyck and Chris Elcock, eds., *Expanding Mindscapes: A Global History of Psychedelics* (Cambridge, MA: The MIT Press, 2023). See recent debates in *The Social History of Alcohol and Drugs* over the past decade.

13. Paolo Nencini, "Facts and Factoids in the Early History of the Opium Poppy," *The Social History of Alcohol and Drugs: An Interdisciplinary Journal* 36, no. 1 (Spring 2022): 45–71.

14. Yangwen Zheng, "The Social Life of Opium in China, 1483–1999," *Modern Asian Studies* 37, no. 1 (2003): 1–39.

15. Plinio Prioreschi, "Medieval Anesthesia: The Spongia Somnifera," *Medical Hypotheses* 61, no. 2 (August 2003): 213–219.

16. Hamilton Wright, "The Opium Problem: Its History and Present Condition," in *China and the Far East*, ed. George Hubbard Blakeslee (New York: T.Y. Crowell & Company, 1910), 152.

17. Rudolf Schmitz, "Friedrich Wilhelm Sertürner and the Discovery of Morphine," *Pharmacy in History* 27, no. 2 (1985): 61–74.

18. "The Story of 'Porphyroxine-Meconidine,'" *Bulletin on Narcotics* 4, no. 1 (March 1952): 15–25.

19. Abraham Wikler et al., "Factors Regulating Oral Consumption of an Opioid (Etonitazene) by Morphine-Addicted Rats," *Psychopharmacologia* 5, no. 1 (January 1, 1963): 55–76. The adoption of *opioid* as a preferred term was gradual, but this book uses the term for developments after 1963.

20. The acrimonious debate over who ultimately was responsible for this discovery remains one of the great controversies in modern pharmacological research; see Candace Pert, *Molecules of Emotion: Why You Feel the Way You Feel* (New York: Simon and Schuster, 1999); Solomon Snyder, *Brainstorming: The Science and Politics of Opiate Research* (Cambridge, MA: Harvard University Press, 2013); Candace B. Pert and Solomon H. Snyder, "Opiate Receptor: Demonstration in Nervous Tissue," *Science* 179, no. 4077 (March 9, 1973): 1011–1014. See also Garrett Epps, "Brainstormer: Dr. Candace Pert," *Washington Post*, December 31, 1978; Garrett Epps, "Brains and Ambitions," *Washington Post*, November 11, 1979; Neil A. Campbell, "A Conversation with Candace Pert," *The American Biology Teacher* 54, no. 6 (September 1992): 357–360; Emily Langer, "Candace B. Pert, Neuroscientist Who Discovered Opiate Receptor, Dies at 67," *Washington Post*, September 18, 2013; John Schwartz, "Candace Pert, 67, Explorer of the Brain, Dies," *New York Times*, September 19, 2013; Thomas H. Maugh, "Scientist Discovered Opiate Receptor," *Los Angeles Times*, September 24, 2013; Linda S. Brady and Miles Herkenham, "Candace B. Pert," *Neuropsychopharmacology* 38, no. 13 (December 2013): 2730.

CHAPTER 1

1. This chapter references some of the voluminous literature, recent and older, on the Indian opium industry. The classic formulation of that industry remains J.F. Richards, "The Indian Empire and Peasant Production of Opium in the Nineteenth Century," *Modern Asian Studies* 15 (1981): 59–82, but more recently, Rolf Bauer, *The Peasant Production of Opium in Nineteenth-Century India* (Leiden, the Netherlands: Brill, 2019) has offered a more exhaustive account of the industry's working and economics. Some of the description of the industry's operation in the mid- and late nineteenth century relies on Bauer's rigorous work. In addition to the work and specific debates about opium referenced throughout this chapter, see also Anirudh Deshpande, "An Historical Overview of Opium Cultivation and Changing State Attitudes Towards the Crop in India, 1878–2000 A.D.," *Studies in History* 25, no. 1 (January 2009): 109–143; and Andrew Glen, "What Attitudes About Opium Were Driving the Government of India's Policies Between 1857–1906?" (PhD diss., University of Strathclyde, 2018).

2. This figure is Bauer's. Newer estimates tend to suggest that opium made up a larger proportion of the Indian government's revenue than previously suggested; Chris Bayly suggested that opium, in the middle of the nineteenth century, made up nearly 15 percent of government's income, and accounted for about a third of its total trade. C.A. Bayly,

Indian Society and the Making of the British Empire (Cambridge: Cambridge University Press, 1987), 117.

3. R.K. Newman, "India and the Anglo-Chinese Opium Agreements, 1907–14," *Modern Asian Studies* 23, no. 3 (July 1989): 525–560.

4. *First Report of the Royal Commission on Opium: With Minutes of Evidence and Appendices*, 6 vols. (London: Eyre & Spottiswoode for HM Stationery Office, 1895).

5. Ibid., vol. III, 22–23.

6. Ibid., 42–43.

7. Ibid., 114.

8. Ibid., 260.

9. J.F. Scheltema, "The Opium Trade in the Dutch East Indies," *American Journal of Sociology* 13, no. 1 (1907): 79–112; James R. Rush, "Opium in Java: A Sinister Friend," *The Journal of Asian Studies* 44, no. 3 (1985): 549–560; George Bryan Souza, "Opium and the Company: Maritime Trade and Imperial Finances on Java, 1684–1796," *Modern Asian Studies* 43, no. 1 (January 2009): 113–133.

10. John F. Richards, "The Opium Industry in British India," *The Indian Economic & Social History Review* 39, nos. 2–3 (September 1, 2002): 149–180.

11. H.R.C. Wright, "The Abolition by Cornwallis of the Forced Cultivation of Opium in Bihar," *The Economic History Review* 12, no. 1 (1959): 112– 119.

12. Bauer, *Peasant Production of Opium*, 55.

13. Trocki, *Opium*, 2.

14. Julius Jeffreys, *The British Army in India* (London: Longman, Brown, Green, Longmans & Roberts, 1858), 329–330.

15. Tan Chung, "The Britain-China-India Trade Triangle (1771–1840)," *The Indian Economic & Social History Review* 11, no. 4 (January 1974): 411–431.

16. Gunnel Cederlöf, "Poor Man's Crop: Evading Opium Monopoly," *Modern Asian Studies*, October 3, 2018, 1–27.

17. Amar Farooqui, "Opium as a Household Remedy in Nineteenth-Century Western India," in *The Social History of Health and Medicine in Colonial India*, ed. Biswamoy Pati and Mark Harrison (Routledge, 2008), 229–237.

18. William Crooke, *Materials for a Rural and Agricultural Glossary of the Northwestern Provinces and Oudh* (Allahabad, India: North-western provinces and Oudh government Press, 1879), 76–77.

19. Nandini Chatterjee, *Negotiating Mughal Law: A Family of Landlords Across Three Indian Empires* (Cambridge: Cambridge University Press, 2020), 54. The exhaustive account of Malwa opium remains Amar Farooqui, *Smuggling as Subversion: Colonialism, Indian Merchants, and the Politics of Opium, 1790–1843* (Lanham, MD: Lexington Books, 1998). See also Amar Farooqui, "Opium Enterprise and Colonial Intervention in Malwa and Western India, 1800–1824," *The Indian Economic & Social History Review* 32, no. 4 (December 1, 1995): 447–473; Archana Calangutcar, "Marwaris in Opium Trade: A Journey to Bombay in the 19th Century," *Proceedings of the Indian History Congress* 67 (2006): 745–753; and Muhammad Faisal Abdullah, "Trade and Cultivation of Opium in Malwa and Rajasthan During 1750–1900" (PhD diss., Aligarh Muslim University, 2008).

20. Frank Dikötter, Lars Laamann, and Zhou Xun, *Narcotic Culture: A History of Drugs in China* (Chicago: University of Chicago Press, 2004), 26–27. More generally, on the need to locate opium histories within broader histories of knowledge, transmission of techniques,

modifications of taste, and cultural practices, see Amar Farooqui, "The Global Career of Indian Opium and Local Destinies," *Almanack*, no. 14 (December 2016): 52–73.

21. Farooqui, *Smuggling as Subversion*; see also Bharat Deora, "Opium Smuggling into British India from Rajputana," *Proceedings of the Indian History Congress* 80 (2019): 749–757.

22. Claude Markovits, "The Political Economy of Opium Smuggling in Early Nineteenth Century India: Leakage or Resistance?" *Modern Asian Studies* 43, no. 1 (January 2009): 89–111.

23. Over the next several decades, there would be efforts by Indian states to widen the purview of ports allowed to export. See "Establishment of an Opium Agency at Palee," NAI, Foreign—General A, February 1, 1871.

24. A recent account of these families and their relationship to indigenous capitalism is Medha Kudaisya, "India's Merchant Communities," in *Oxford Research Encyclopedia of Asian History* (online), 2022, https://doi.org/10.1093/acrefore/9780190277727.013.606.

25. On the Sassoon dynasty and its capture of the Bombay trade, see Joseph Sassoon, *The Sassoons: The Great Global Merchants and the Making of an Empire* (New York: Pantheon Books, 2022); and Geoffrey Jones, *Merchants to Multinationals: British Trading Companies in the Nineteenth and Twentieth Centuries* (Oxford: Oxford University Press, 2000), passim.

26. C.A. Bayly, *Rulers, Townsmen, and Bazaars: North Indian Society in the Age of British Expansion, 1770–1870* (Oxford: Oxford University Press, 1988), 399.

27. Man-houng Lin, "Late Qing Perceptions of Native Opium," *Harvard Journal of Asiatic Studies* 64, no. 1 (2004): 117–144.

28. Devyani Gupta, "'Black Mail': Networks of Opium and Postal Exchange in Nineteenth-Century India," *Literature & History* 29, no. 1 (May 2020): 78–96.

29. Bauer suggests opium was, on the main, a losing crop for peasant cultivators; his are the most comprehensive statistics I have found. Dietmar Rothermund, with less available data, reached the same conclusions but suggested that it could be more profitable than indigo or other cash crops in certain circumstances; Dietmar Rothermund, *An Economic History of India: From Pre-Colonial Times to 1991* (London: Routledge, 2003), 26.

30. The work of Anglo-American missionaries and social reformers has long been central in accounts of the anti-opium movement; see Arnold H. Taylor, *American Diplomacy and the Narcotics Traffic, 1900–1958: A Study in International Humanitarian Reform* (Durham, NC: Duke University Press, 1969); David F. Musto, *The American Disease: Origins of Narcotic Control* (New Haven, CT: Yale University Press, 1973); Kathleen L. Lodwick, *Crusaders Against Opium: Protestant Missionaries in China, 1874–1917* (Lexington: University Press of Kentucky, 1996); Ian Tyrrell, "Opium and the Fashioning of the American Moral Empire," in *Reforming the World: The Creation of America's Moral Empire* (Princeton, NJ: Princeton University Press, 2010), 146–165; William O. Walker, *Opium and Foreign Policy: The Anglo-American Search for Order in Asia, 1912–1954* (Chapel Hill: University of North Carolina Press, 1991).

31. Lodwick, *Crusaders Against Opium*; Tyrrell, *Reforming the World*.

32. Steffan Rimner has argued convincingly for an international, networked approach to the prohibition movement, which situates Asian actors as equals with Anglo-American prohibitionists in this period; see Steffen Rimner, *Opium's Long Shadow: From Asian Revolt to Global Drug Control* (Cambridge, MA: Harvard University Press, 2018). Rimner's

work nonetheless echoes a declensionist strain in the literature on prohibition, which casts it as essentially a foregone conclusion by the 1880s or thereabouts; I argue here for a far more robust Indian case for opium than he and others have made. More broadly, on the Indian temperance movement in this period, see Lucy Carroll, "The Temperance Movement in India: Politics and Social Reform," *Modern Asian Studies* 10, no. 3 (1976): 417–447; and Robert Eric Colvard, "A World Without Drink: Temperance in Modern India, 1880–1940" (PhD diss., University of Iowa, 2013). See also M. Emdad-ul Haq, *Drugs in South Asia: From the Opium Trade to the Present Day* (Basingstoke, UK: Palgrave Macmillan, 2000); and Harald Fischer-Tiné and Jana Tschurenev, eds., *A History of Alcohol and Drugs in Modern South Asia: Intoxicating Affairs* (London: Routledge, 2014).

33. Daniel Wertz, "Idealism, Imperialism, and Internationalism: Opium Politics in the Colonial Philippines, 1898–1925," *Modern Asian Studies* 47, no. 2 (March 2013): 467–499. On the Philippines and on American narcotic policies in Asia generally, see Arnold Taylor, *American Diplomacy and the Narcotics Traffic, 1900–1958: A Study in International Humanitarian Reform* (Durham, NC: Duke University Press, 1969) and William Walker, *Opium and Foreign Policy: The Anglo-American Search for Order in Asia, 1912–1954* (Chapel Hill: University of North Carolina Press, 1991).

34. *The Opium Trade Between India and China in Some of Its Present Aspects* (London: William Tweedie, 1870).

35. *The Indian Opium Revenue: Its Nature and Effects* (London: Yates and Alexander, 1874); *The Opium Revenue: Sir William Muir's Minute* (London: Anglo-Oriental Society for the Suppression of the Opium Trade, 1874).

36. Joseph Gundry Alexander, *India's Opium Revenue: What It Is, and How It Should Be Dealt With* (London: P.S. King and Son, 1890); James L. Maxwell, *Questions on Opium Answered* (London, 1892), 2.

37. Soonderbai H. Powar, *Opium Crime of the British Government: An Indian Woman's Impeachment* (London: Dyer Brothers, 1892).

38. Romesh Chunder Dutt, *The Economic History of India in the Victorian Age* (London: K. Paul, Trench, Trübner, 1906), 153–156.

39. "Anti-Opium Meeting at Lucknow (The Hindustani, Lucknow, 7th October)," *Selections from the Vernacular Newspapers Published in the Panjab, North-Western Provinces, Oudh, Central Provinces and Berar*, October 15, 1891, 699.

40. *Vrit Dhara*, cited in *Selections from the Vernacular Newspapers Published in the Panjab, North-Western Provinces, Oudh, Central Provinces and Berar*, July 24, 1881, IOR.

41. *Suhodh Sindhu*, cited in *Selections from the Vernacular Newspapers Published in the Panjab, North-Western Provinces, Oudh, Central Provinces and Berar*, May 7, 1891, IOR.

42. *Native Opinion*, cited in *Report on Native Papers for the Week Ending December 31, 1881*, IOR.

43. *The Indu Prakash or Moonlight*, April 20, 1891.

44. *Jam-e-Jamshed*, cited in *Report on Native Papers for the Week Ending April 18, 1891*, IOR.

45. *Poona Vaibhav*, cited in *Report on Native Papers for the Week Ending March 19, 1892*, IOR.

46. David Arnold, *Colonizing the Body: State Medicine and Epidemic Disease in Nineteenth-Century India* (Berkeley: University of California Press, 1993), 12. See, selectively, Biswamoy Pati and Mark Harrison, *The Social History of Health and Medicine in Colonial India*, Routledge Studies in South Asian History (London: Routledge, 2009);

Rachel Berger, *Ayurveda Made Modern: Political Histories of Indigenous Medicine in North India, 1900–1955* (Basingstoke, UK: Palgrave Macmillan, 2013); Projit Bihari Mukharji, *Doctoring Traditions: Ayurveda, Small Technologies, and Braided Sciences* (Chicago: University of Chicago Press, 2016); and Shinjini Das, *Vernacular Medicine in Colonial India: Family, Market and Homoeopathy* (Cambridge: Cambridge University Press, 2019).

47. Farooqui, "Opium as a Household Remedy."

48. This phrase was coined by Sir Robert Mowbray, a member of the Royal Commission on Opium who came to it first in a January 1894 session in Patna. See *Minutes of Evidence Taken Before the Royal Commission on Opium from 3rd to 27th January 1894*, Volume III (London: Her Majesty's Stationery Office, 1894), 103.

49. "Introduction of the Sanitary Primer Entitled The Way to Health into the Junior Classes in European Schools," NAI, Home—Education, October 1887.

50. The nine volumes were published between 1894 and 1895 by Her Majesty's Stationery Office in London.

51. "Regarding the Entrenchment Round the Opium Factory at Ghazeepore," NAI, Military—Quarter Master General, 1858; "Report on Entrenchment of Ghazeepore Opium Godowns," NAI, Military—Quarter Master General, 1858; "Instructions Have Been Given for the Defences of the Opium Godowns at Ghazeepoor Being Commenced," NAI, Military—Quarter Master General, 1859.

52. "Scheme for the Manufacture of Narcotine and Morphia in Benares Agency and for the More Efficient Working of the Factory," NAI, Finance—Separate Revenue—A, June 1871, 26.

53. "Preparation of Two Separate Manuals for the Behar and Benares Opium Factories," NAI, Finance and Commerce—Separate Revenue, May 1891.

54. "Correspondence on the Subject of the Manufacture and Shipment to London of Morphia and Narcotine," NAI, Finance—Separate Revenue—A, March 1876; "Dr. Sheppard's Further Report on the Progress Made in the Manufacture of Morphia and Narcotine; and the Grant of a Special Allowance to Mr. Francis, the Assay Registrar, Benares Opium Agency," NAI, Financial—Separate Revenue—A, December 1877.

55. David Arnold, "Agriculture and 'Improvement' in Early Colonial India: A Pre-History of Development," *Journal of Agrarian Change* 5, no. 4 (2005): 505–525.

56. *Annals of the Royal Botanic Garden, Calcutta* (Calcutta: Bengal Secretariat Book Depot, 1888), i–iii.

57. "Letter from Lieut.Col.R.Kyd to Mr.E.Hay, Secretary, Reporting on His Experimental Cultivation of Poppy Plants and the New Process of Extracting Opium from the Pericarps, in the Neighbourhood of Calcutta," Home—Public, National Archives of India (henceforth NAI), 1788.

58. *Report on the Experimental Culture of the Opium Poppy for the Season 1876–77* (Calcutta: Bengal Secretariat Press, 1877); *Report on the Experimental Culture of the Opium Poppy for the Season 1877–78* (Calcutta: Bengal Secretariat Press, 1878).

59. "Manufacture of Morphia at Ghazeepore," *The Indian Medical Gazette*, March 1, 1876, 80.

60. "Notes on Opium by Lieutenant Colonel Carruthers I.M.S. Manufacture of Medicinal Opium from the Poppy Grown in India as the Possibility of the Indian Drug Capturing the Market of Opium for Medicinal Purposes in Other Countries," NAI, Finance—Separate Revenue—A, December 1907.

61. H.R. Nevill, *Ghazipur: A Gazetteer, Being Volume XXIX of the District Gazetteers of the United Provinces of Agra and Oudh* (Allahabad, India: Government Press, United Provinces, 1909), 62.

62. *Return of an Article on Opium by Dr. Watt. Reporter on Economic Products with the Government of India, Recently Written by Him, and Intended to Be Published in the Sixth Volume of the Dictionary of Economic Products of India* (London: Her Majesty's Stationery Office, 1892).

63. "Camphoradine," *The Lancet*, December 9, 1899, 1638.

64. "Visit of Mr. N. Akuzawa, Adviser to the Formosa Govt. and Another Gentleman to India, for the Purpose of Studying the Cultivation of Opium"; "Visit to India of Mr. T. Iyenaga, Japanese Commissioner of Formosa, to Study the System of Poppy Cultivation and Opium Industry," NAI, Foreign—External—B, 1900.

65. "Chinese Mission to India to Study Tea and Opium Culture," NAI, Foreign—External—B, June 1905.

66. Tirthankar Roy, "The Mutiny and the Merchants," *The Historical Journal* 59, no. 2 (June 2016): 393–416.

67. "The Issue of Allocating Opium Profits to a Road Between Dewas and Oojein," NAI, Foreign—General—A, February 1, 1871.

68. Subir Rana, "The Metahistory and Afterlife of a Public Institution: Natnagar Shodh Sansthan, Madhya Pradesh," *India International Centre Quarterly* 47, nos. 1/2 (2020): 188–204.

69. "Cultivation of Opium in Bombay Presidency," NAI, Finance—Separate Revenue, May 1871.

70. "Memorial from Messrs D. Sassoon & Co. and Other Opium Merchants of Bombay, Praying for a Reduction of the Pass Duty on Malwa Opium Exported to China and Negative Orders Thereon," NAI, Finance Department—Separate Revenue, August 1892; *Aligarh Institute Gazette*, July 21, 1893.

71. "Opium Mawar," NAI, Rajputana State Agency (Residency)—Royal Commission Opium, 1893, NAI.

72. *Oudh Akhbar*, cited in *Selections from the Vernacular Newspapers Published in the Panjab, North-Western Provinces, Oudh, Central Provinces and Berar*, December 27, 1893, IOR.

73. *Indu Prakash*, cited in *Report on Native Papers for the Week Ending October 31, 1891*, IOR.

74. "Report on the Practice of Administering Opium to Children in India," NAI, Finance and Commerce—Separate Revenue, January 1894.

CHAPTER 2

1. Michèle Nicolas, "La pharmacie d'officine ottomane," in *Histoire économique et sociale de l'Empire Ottoman et de la Turquie: 1326–1960: actes du sixième congrès international tenu à Aix-en-Provence du 1er au 4 juillet 1992*, ed. Daniel Panzac (Paris: Peeters, 1995); Michèle Nicolas, "Deux personnalités du monde pharmaceutique dans l'Empire Ottoman," *Revue d'Histoire de la Pharmacie* 84, no. 312 (1996): 429–432; Michèle Nicolas, "La pharmacie ottomane à Istanbul," *Revue d'Histoire de la Pharmacie* 90, no. 334 (2002): 257–270.

2. Georges della Sudda, *Monographie des opiums de l'empire ottoman envoyés à l'exposition universelle de Paris* (Paris: Imprimerie Poitevin, 1867).

3. "Le Gouvernement a fait un grand pas vers ce but, lors de la création des vilayets, en instituant dans chacun d'eux des directions générales pour l'agriculture; la nomination aux emplois de directeurs généraux d'indigènes, anciens élèves de l'école Grignon, possédant toutes les connaissances requises, est aussi de très-favorable augure."

4. Ibrahim Ihsan Poroy, "Expansion of Opium Production in Turkey and the State Monopoly of 1828–1839," *International Journal of Middle East Studies* 13, no. 2 (1981): 191–211.

5. Abdulkadir Erkal, "Divan Şiirinde Afyon ve Esrar [Opium and cannabis in divan poetry]," *A.Ü. Türkiyat Araştırmaları Enstitüsü Dergisi* 33 (2007): 25–60; see also Abdulkadir Erkal, *Osmanlı toplumunda ve edebiyatında afyon ve esrar* [Opium and cannabis in Ottoman society and literature] (Ankara: Birleşik Yayınevi, 2016).

6. "Note sur l'usage de l'opium chez les Turcs, d'après une observation faite à Smyrne en 1763, par le Docteur Edouard Smith," *Gazette du commerce*, June 13, 1778, 375.

7. A. Üner Turgay, "Ottoman-American Trade during the 19th Century," *Osmanlı Araştırmaları* 3 (1982): 189–246.

8. Michael E. Chapman, "Taking Business to the Tiger's Gate: Thomas Handasyd Perkins and the Boston-Smyrna-Canton Opium Trade of the Early Republic," *Journal of the Royal Asiatic Society Hong Kong Branch* 52 (2012): 7–28.

9. Ayşegül Avci, "Yankee Levantine: David Offley and Ottoman-American Relations in the Early Nineteenth Century" (PhD diss., Ekonomi ve Sosyal Bilimler Enstitüsü, Bilkent University, 2019).

10. The classic formulation of this trade is A. Üner Turgay, "The Nineteenth Century Golden Triangle: Chinese Consumption, Ottoman Production, American Connection, Part I: Opium Trade in International Perspective and Early American Opium Trade," *International Journal of Turkish Studies* 2, no. 2 (Winter 1981–1982): 105–125; A. Üner Turgay, "The Nineteenth Century Golden Triangle: Chinese Consumption, Ottoman Production, American Connection, Part II: Ottoman Opium Production and Government Policies," *International Journal of Turkish Studies* 3, no. 1 (Winter 1984–1985): 65–92.

11. Jan Schmidt, *From Anatolia to Indonesia: Opium Trade and the Dutch Community of Izmir, 1820–1940* (Istanbul: Nederlands Historisch-Archaeologisch Instituut te Istanbul, 1998).

12. Timothy M. Roberts, "Commercial Philanthropy: American Missionaries and the American Opium Trade in Izmir During the First Part of the Nineteenth Century," *Journal of Mediterranean Studies* 19, no. 2 (2010): 371–388.

13. X. Landerer, "Über den Opiumhandel in Smyrna [On the opium trade in Smyrna]," *Neues Repertorium für Pharmacie* I (1852): 473–476. On Ottoman credit networks, see Yavuz Cezar, "The Role of the Sarrafs in Ottoman Finance and Economy in the Eighteenth and Nineteenth Centuries," in *Frontiers of Ottoman Studies*, ed. Colin Imber and Keiko Kiyotaki, Vol. I: State, Province, and the West (London: I.B. Tauris, 2005), 62–76. On the Sephardic Jewish role in the trade, see Devi Mays, "Becoming Illegal: Sephardi Jews in the Opiates Trade," *Jewish Social Studies* 25, no. 3 (Spring/Summer 2020): 1–34.

14. "Afyonun ağacı alçaktır, düşen parçalanır," cited in Charles Issawi, *The Economic History of Turkey 1800–1914* (Chicago: University of Chicago Press, 1980), 262.

15. Charles MacFarlane, *Constantinople in 1828: A Residence of Sixteen Months in the Turkish Capital and Provinces: With an Account of the Present State of the Naval and Military*

Power, and of the Resources of the Ottoman Empire, Vol. 2 (London: Saunders and Otley, 1829), 33.

16. Poroy, "Expansion."

17. Turgay, "Nineteenth Century Golden Triangle Part II," 74.

18. Reprinted as "Culture de l'opium en turquie," *Le Moniteur industriel*, February 9, 1840, 3.

19. Turgay, "Nineteenth Century Golden Triangle Part II," 14.

20. Schmidt, *From Anatolia to Indonesia*, 47.

21. Poroy, "Expansion," 198.

22. Landerer, "Über den Opiumhandel in Smyrna."

23. Sidney H. Maltass, "On the Production of Opium in Asia Minor," *London Pharmaceutical Journal*, March 1855.

24. C. Decharmes, *Memoire Sur l'opium Indigène* (Amiens, France: Duval ed Herments, 1855).

25. Mohamed Effendy Charkauy, *École supérieure de Pharmacie de Paris: Thèse sur l'opium, etc* (Paris: Henri Plon, 1856).

26. Nicolas Jean-Baptiste Gaston Guibourt, *Mémoire Sur Le Dosage de l'opium et Sur La Quantité de Morphine Que l'opium Doit Contenir* (Paris, 1862).

27. *Canstatt's Jahresbericht Über Die Fortschritte Der Gesammten Medicin in Allen Ländern Im Jahre 1855* [Canstatt's annual report on the progress of general medicine in all countries in the year 1855], Vol. 5 (Würzburg: Stahel'schen Buchhandlung, 1856), 40–44.

28. Eduard Winkler, *Pharmazeutische Warenkunde oder Handatlas der Pharmakologie* (Winter 1857).

29. Hermann Hager, *Commentar zur Pharmacopoea germanica* (Berlin: Julius Springer, 1874), 519–520.

30. Franz Coelestin Schneider, "Opium (Laudanum, Meconium, Opium, Mohnsaft)," in *Pharmacognostischer Theil* (Wien: G.J. Manz'schen Buchhandlung, 1874), 410–414.

31. Karl Scherzer, ed., *Smyrna: Mit besonderer Rücksicht auf die geographischen, Wirthschaftlichen und Intellectuellen verhältnisse von Vorder-Kleinasien* (Wien: A. Hölder, 1873), 136–140.

32. *Du Titrage de l'opium, lettre à M. Favrot, rédacteur de la partie pharmaceutique de la France médicale* [On the Tittration of opium, letter to Mr. Favrot, editor of the pharmaceutical section of France médicale] (Paris: Dubuisson, 1859), 4–6.

33. E.R. Heffter, "Notes on the Culture and Commerce in Opium in Asia Minor," *American Journal of Pharmacy* (July 1868).

34. E.G., "Opium," *Revue commerciale du Levant*, September 30, 1900, 478–488.

35. On the influence of French pharmacy in the Ottoman Empire, see Nicolas, "La pharmacie ottomane à Istanbul."

36. See, from an increasingly vibrant literature, Sam White, *The Climate of Rebellion in the Early Modern Ottoman Empire*, Studies in Environment and History (New York: Cambridge University Press, 2011); Alan Mikhail, *Nature and Empire in Ottoman Egypt: An Environmental History* (Cambridge: Cambridge University Press, 2013); Faisal Husain, "In the Bellies of the Marshes: Water and Power in the Countryside of Ottoman Baghdad," *Environmental History* 19, no. 4 (2014): 638–664; Fredrick Walter Lorenz, "The 'Second Egypt': Cretan Refugees, Agricultural Development, and Frontier Expansion in Ottoman Cyrenaica, 1897–1904," *International Journal of*

Middle East Studies 53, no. 1 (February 2021): 89–105; Faisal H. Husain, *Rivers of the Sultan: The Tigris and Euphrates in the Ottoman Empire* (New York: Oxford University Press, 2021); Chris Gratien, *The Unsettled Plain: An Environmental History of the Late Ottoman Frontier* (Stanford, CA: Stanford University Press, 2022); Nora Barakat, *Bedouin Bureaucrats: Mobility and Property in the Ottoman Empire* (Stanford, CA: Stanford University Press, 2023); and Samuel Dolbee, *Locusts of Power: Borders, Empire, and Environment in the Modern Middle East* (Cambridge: Cambridge University Press, 2023).

37. Elizabeth R. Williams, *States of Cultivation: Imperial Transition and Scientific Agriculture in the Eastern Mediterranean* (Stanford, CA: Stanford University Press, 2023). Williams locates these ideologies within the context of Syria and Lebanon, contrasting Ottoman ideologies with their French mandate successors, which foregrounded "intensified extraction, less protection from the inroads of foreign capital, increased tensions between technocratic officials, and decreased attention to ecological constraints" (7).

38. Mehmet Ali Yildirim, "Osmanlı'da Modern Ziraatın Gelişimine Katkı Sunan İki Ermeni Mütehassis [Two Armenian experts who contributed to the development of modern agriculture in the Ottoman Empire]," *Kilis 7 Aralık Üniversitesi Sosyal Bilimler Dergisi* 6, no. 12 (December 2016): 126–143.

39. Amasyan Efendi, *Hüdâvendigâr Vilâyeti Celîlesi Ziraat ve Nafia Müdürü Rif'atlû Amasyan Efendi'nin Afyon Tohumu Zir'aine Dâir Kaleme Aldigi Lâyîhadir* [A treatise on opium poppy cultivation, authored by the esteemed former director of agriculture and public works of the sublime province of Hüdavendigar, Amasyan Efendi] (Istanbul: La Turquie Matbaasi/Matbaa-yi Âmîre, 1870).

40. There is a similar dynamic in Ahmet Hilmi's slightly later account of opium production in Kastamonu district; Ahmet Hilmi, *Kastamonu Vilayeti Ziraat Müdürü Ahmet Hilmi* [Report of Kastamonu province agricultural director Ahmet Hilmi] (Afyonculuk: Kastamonu Matbaası, 1913).

41. Ali Haydar, *Haşhaş Ziraatı* (Hudavandekâr: Vilayet Matbaası, 1908).

42. "Işte esbâb dola yasini ile memalik osmanya da haşhaş ziraatı giten ki taammüm itmekte çiftçiler bemizin giyse seni doldurarak bozuleryeni güldür mekkte der."

43. Turgay, "Nineteenth Century Golden Triangle Part II," 75.

44. Issawi, *The Economic History of Turkey*, 262.

45. Sari Pasha, "Afyon [Opium]," *Hazîne-i Evrak*, November 1881.

46. "Bir Vilâyet Daru'l-Mualliminde Mesut Temâşalar: Bursa Daru'l-Muallimini Talebesi Mübezzer Makinasıyla Haşhaş Zira' Ederlerken [Happy scenes in a provincial teacher's school: students of Bursa teacher's school sowing poppy seeds with a seed drill]," April 1330 (1914), İBB Atatürk Kitaplığı.

47. Schmidt, *From Anatolia to Indonesia*, 71.

48. "Report on Agriculture in Smyrna Region," September 30, 1881, CC Smyrne, vol. 54, quoted in Issawi, *The Economic History of Turkey*, 263.

49. Demetrios Georgiadēs, *Smyrne Et L'Asie Mineure: Au Point De Vue économique Et Commercial* (Paris: Impr. Chaix, 1885), 16–17.

50. *Le Siècle de Sa Majesté Impériale Le Sultan Abd-Ul-Hamid II/Par Th. Hassoun* (Constantinople: Imprimerie Zareh, 1892), 90–92.

51. Nassif Mallouf and Clément Huart, *Grammaire élémentaire de la langue turque* (Paris: E. Guilmoto, 1890), 165–166.

52. Démétrius Alexandre Zambaco Pacha, *De la morphéomanie* (Paris: G. Masson, 1883).

53. Murat Birdal, *The Political Economy of Ottoman Public Debt: Insolvency and European Financial Control in the Late Nineteenth Century* (London: Bloomsbury, 2010).

54. Turgay, "Nineteenth Century Golden Triangle Part II," 76–77.

55. "The Opium Boom," *The Chemist and Druggist*, April 1, 1893, 450–451.

56. Richard Millant, *La culture du pavot et le commerce de l'opium en Turquie*, Bibliothèque d'agriculture coloniale (Paris: Augustin Challamel, 1913); Millant's address is discussed in F. Ashford White, "Growing Opium in Turkey," *American Druggist and Pharmaceutical Record*, February 1, 1914, 30.

57. Lolita Nahmias Haleva, "37.439 Parçalık Bir Yapbozun Mimarı: Leon Taranto [Leon Taranto: architect of a 37,439 piece jigsaw puzzle]," *Şalom Dergi*, August 2013.

58. On the changing interplay between the French and German pharmaceutical industry in this era, see Tobias Cramer, "Building the 'World's Pharmacy': The Rise of the German Pharmaceutical Industry, 1871–1914," *Business History Review* 89, no. 1 (April 2015): 43–73; Bruno Bonnemain, "L'industrie pharmaceutique en France: le tournant décisif de 1915," *Revue D'histoire De La Pharmacie* 63, no. 388 (December 2015): 399–422; P.E. Caquet, "France, Germany, and the Origins of Drug Prohibition," *The International History Review*, March 4, 2021.

59. "Pepper, Opium, and Camphor: A Great Change in Values—Prospects of an Opium Famine," *Chicago Daily Tribune*, July 14, 1873; "A Corner in Opium: New York Capitalists Buying Up the World's Stock," *New York Tribune*, July 12, 1880, 2. The question of frost on Ottoman opium fields was regularly tracked in pharmaceutical publications; see Richard Barker, "Opium Report," *Druggists' Circular and Chemical Gazette*, March 1, 1882, 37; or "The Opium Crop of 1889," *American Druggist*, September 1, 1889, 18. See a characteristic report from the Smyrna consulate, "Dealers in Opium at Smyrna Experience Considerable Losses," in *Monthly Consular and Trade Reports, Department of Commerce and Labor, Bureau of Manufactures*, vol. 331 (Washington: Government Printing Office, 1908), 208–209.

60. "The Coming Opium Crop: A Chat with a Smyrna Merchant," *The Chemist and Druggist*, May 6, 1893, 637.

61. "Weighing Opium," *American Journal of Pharmacy*, October 1875, 473–474.

62. "The Consumption of Opium in the United States," *Medical and Surgical Reporter*, April 16, 1881, 438–439.

63. "Opium Dealers," *Levant Trade Review (Published by the American Chamber of Commerce for Turkey)* 1, no. 1 (June 1911): xiv–xv.

64. John Uri Lloyd, *A Treatise on Opium and Its Compounds* (Cincinnati: Lloyd Brothers, 1908).

65. Abraham Galanté, *Les Juifs d'Izmir (Smyrne)*, Histoire des Juifs d'Anatolie (Istanbul: Babok, 1937), 143–144.

66. Georges Thibout, *La question de l'opium à l'époque contemporaine* [The opium question in the present era] (G. Steinheil: Paris, 1912), 27. French-speaking observers were particularly interested in the role of the Jewish intermediary as inspector; see a similar description in Demetrios Georgiadēs, *Smyrne Et L'Asie Mineure: Au Point De Vue économique Et Commercial* [Smyrna and Asia Minor from the economic and commercial perspective] (Paris: Impr. Chaix, 1885), 16–17.

67. This is true of Turgay's two essential accounts of the nineteenth-century trade.

CHAPTER 3

1. Emanuel Weiss and Bayard Clarke, *The Cultivation of Opium in the United States of America: Being a Memorial to Congress, 1866*, private copy in the Boston Athenæum. See also Emanuel Weiss, "Opium: Can We Compete with the East in Its Production?," *DeBow's Review: Agricultural, Commercial, Industrial Progress and Resources* 20, no. 1 (January 1856): 60a–66a; and Emanuel Weiss, "Opium in Arizona," *Arizona Miner*, June 27, 1866.

2. Edward William Lane, *The Manners and Customs of the Modern Egyptians* (London: J.M. Dent, 1836), 96.

3. On American trade with China in this period, see Shannon Brown, "The Partially Opened Door: Limitations on Economic Change in China in the 1860s," *Modern Asian Studies* 12, no. 2 (April 1978): 177–192; David Pletcher, *The Diplomacy of Involvement: American Economic Expansion Across the Pacific, 1784–1900* (Columbia: University of Missouri Press, 2001); James Fichter, *So Great a Proffit* (Cambridge, MA: Harvard University Press, 2012); Eric Jay Dolin, *When America First Met China: An Exotic History of Tea, Drugs, and Money in the Age of Sail* (New York: Liveright, 2013); and Kendall Johnson, *The New Middle Kingdom: China and the Early American Romance of Free Trade* (Baltimore: Johns Hopkins University Press, 2017).

4. Giovanni Federico, *An Economic History of the Silk Industry, 1830–1930* (Cambridge: Cambridge University Press, 1997); Eacott, *Selling Empire*.

5. See Michael Logan, *The Lessening Stream: An Environmental History of the Santa Cruz River* (Tucson: University of Arizona Press, 2006).

6. "Nachrichten Über Dr. Eman Weiss," *Verhandlungen Der Kaiserlich-Königlichen Zoologisch-Botanischen Gesellschaft in Wien* 20 (1870): 626–631.

7. Diana L. Ahmad, *The Opium Debate and Chinese Exclusion Laws in the Nineteenth-Century American West* (Reno: University of Nevada Press, 2011).

8. On the global drug trade in the early modern world, see Benjamin Breen, *The Age of Intoxication: Origins of the Global Drug Trade* (Philadelphia: University of Pennsylvania Press, 2021).

9. John Duffy, *Epidemics in Colonial America* (Baton Rouge: Louisiana State University, 1953).

10. Rudolf Schmitz, "Friedrich Wilhelm Sertürner and the Discovery of Morphine," *Pharmacy in History* 27, no. 2 (1985): 61–74; A.P. Klockgether-Radke, "F. W. Sertürner und die Entdeckung des Morphins [F. W. Sertürner and the discovery of morphine]," *Anasthesiol Intensivmed Notfallmed Schmerzther* 37, no. 5 (May 2002): 244–249.

11. Much, of course, had changed in the American medical profession itself; the classic account remains Paul Starr, *The Social Transformation of American Medicine* (New York: Basic Books, 1982).

12. David T. Courtwright, *Dark Paradise: A History of Opiate Addiction in America* (Cambridge, MA: Harvard University Press, 2001), 45–47 and passim.

13. "Effects of Opium Eating," *Boston Medical and Surgical Journal* 6, no. 8 (April 4, 1832): 128–131.

14. John Stewart McNeill Medical Log, 1836–1837, MS 0452, Woodson Research Center, Fondren Library, Rice University, Houston, TX.

15. Courtwright, *Dark Paradise*, 54–55.

16. The classic formulation is David T. Courtwright, "The Hidden Epidemic: Opiate Addiction and Cocaine Use in the South, 1860–1920," *The Journal of Southern History*

49, no. 1 (February 1983): 57–72. See also Jonathan S. Jones, *Opium Slavery: The Civil War, Veterans, and America's First Opioid Crisis* (Chapel Hill: University of North Carolina Press, 2025).

17. Ahmad, *The Opium Debate and Chinese Exclusion Laws*; and Diana L. Ahmad, "Opium Smoking, Anti-Chinese Attitudes, and the American Medical Community, 1850–1890," *American Nineteenth Century History* 1, no. 2 (June 1, 2000): 53–68. See also the classic account of Chinese migration, Gunther Barth, *Bitter Strength: A History of the Chinese in the United States, 1850–1870* (Cambridge, MA: Harvard University Press, 1964), as well as, more recently, Ronald Takaki, *Strangers from a Different Shore: A History of Asian Americans* (New York: Penguin Books, 1989); Yong Chen, *Chinese San Francisco, 1850–1943: A Trans-Pacific Community* (Stanford, CA: Stanford University Press, 2000), and Gordon H. Chang, *Ghosts of Gold Mountain: The Epic Story of the Chinese Who Built the Transcontinental Railroad* (Boston: Mariner Books, 2019).

18. Harry Hubbell Kane, *Opium-Smoking in America and China: A Study of Its Prevalence, and Effects, Immediate and Remote, on the Individual and the Nation* (New York: G.P. Putnam's Sons, 1882).

19. Caroline Jean Acker, "From All-Purpose Anodyne to Marker of Deviance: Physicians' Attitudes Toward Opiates from 1890 to 1940," in *Drugs and Narcotics in History*, ed. Roy Porter and Mikuláš Teich (Cambridge: Cambridge University Press, 1995), 114–132; Acker, *Creating the American Junkie*.

20. On the pre-regulation period, see Elizabeth Kelly Gray, *Habit Forming: Drug Addiction in America, 1776–1914* (New York: Oxford University Press, 2022).

21. "'Opiokapnism' or Opium Smoking," *Journal of the American Medical Association* XVIII, no. 23 (June 4, 1892): 719–720.

22. Courtwright, *Dark Paradise*, 35–60.

23. Thaddeus Betts, "To the Public" *Connecticut Journal*, April 21, 1778, 1.

24. John Leigh, *An Experimental Inquiry into the Properties of Opium: And Its Effects on Living Subjects* (Edinburgh: C. Elliot, 1786).

25. George W. Carpenter, "Observations and Experiments on Opium," *American Journal of Science and Arts* 13, no. 1 (January 1828): 17.

26. On the domestic use and cultivation of poppy in England, see Virginia Berridge and Griffith Edwards, *Opium and the People: Opiate Use in Nineteenth-Century England* (New Haven, CT: Yale University Press, 1987).

27. Shadrach Ricketson, "On the Cultivation of the Poppy-Plant, and the Method of Procuring Opium, Etc.," in *Transactions of the Society for the Promotion of Agriculture, Arts and Manufactures*, vol. 1 (Albany: Charles R. and George Webster, 1801), 264–266.

28. John Redman Coxe and E. Staples, "Papaver," in *The American Dispensatory, Containing the Natural, Chemical, Pharmaceutical and Medical History of the Different Substances Employed in Medicine*, ed. John Redman Coxe (Carey & Lea, 1831), 510–529.

29. James Thacher, "On the Cultivation of the Papaver Somniferum, or Poppy-Plant, and the Method of Preparing Opium," in *The American New Dispensatory* (Boston: T.B. Wait, 1810), 454–457.

30. "On American Opium," *New England Farmer* V, no. 26 (January 19, 1827): 206.

31. Coxe and Staples, "Papaver."

32. C.O. Harz, "On the Production of Opium Near Berlin," *American Journal of Pharmacy* 41 (July 1869): 311–313.

33. J. Constantin Decharme, *Memoire sur l'opium indigène* (Amiens: Duval ed Herments, 1855).

34. H. Aubergier, *Des Préparations d'opium Indigène de H. Aubergier, Approuvées Par l'Académie Impériale de Médecine* (Clermont: Hubler et Dubos, 1855).

35. Oscar Réveil, *Sur la culture du pavot a oeillette et sur l'extraction de l'opium indigène* (L. Martinet, 1857). Réveil's suggestion would indeed come to pass a century on.

36. *Journal officiel de la République française*, August 19, 1873, 5.

37. Israel Grahame, "On American Opium," *American Journal of Pharmacy* 39 (1866): 50–53; "Report on the Progress of Pharmacy," in *Proceedings of the American Pharmaceutical Association at the Fifteenth Annual Meeting Held at New York City, September 1867* (Philadelphia: Merrihew & Son, 1867), 123–266.

38. "Cultivation of Opium in the United States," *Scientific American* 20, no. 23 (June 1869): 362.

39. M. LaBorde, "The Opium Poppy and Its Culture," *The Rural Carolinian*, February 1872, 241–243.

40. William McMurtrie, "American Opium," in *Monthly Report of the U.S. Department of Agriculture, January and February, 1876* (Washington, DC: Government Printing Office, 1876), 39.

41. Adolfo Luria, "An Essay on Opium and Its Alkaloid Morphine, and Their True Value in Modern Therapeutics," *Merck's Archives of Materia Medica and Drug Therapy: A Monthly Journal for the Practicing Physician* III (April 1901): 129–136.

42. "Opium: Turkey Supplies America with Vast Supplies of the Drug," in *Monthly Consular and Trade Reports, February 1906*, 305 (Washington DC: Government Printing Office, 1906); reprinted as "Says Opium Should Be Raised Here," *New York Tribune*, June 7, 1906.

43. Emil Weschcke, "On Poppy Culture and Opium Production in the United States," *Pacific Medical Journal* 48 (1905): 457–461.

44. A concise account of the question of distance and purity in food is Jeffrey M. Pilcher, *Food in World History* (London: Routledge, 2006), 59–61. On grain, see William Cronon, *Nature's Metropolis: Chicago and the Great West* (New York: W.W. Norton, 1991); on meat, see Joshua Specht, *Red Meat Republic: A Hoof-to-Table History of How Beef Changed America* (Princeton, NJ: Princeton University Press, 2019).

45. Francesca Bray, *The Rice Economies: Technology and Development in Asian Societies* (Berkeley: University of California Press, 1986); Judith A. Carney, *Black Rice: The African Origins of Rice Cultivation in the Americas* (Cambridge, MA: Harvard University Press, 2002).

46. Ralph S. Hattox, *Coffee and Coffeehouses: The Origins of a Social Beverage in the Medieval Near East* (Seattle: University of Washington Press, 1985); Stuart McCook, *Coffee Is Not Forever: A Global History of the Coffee Leaf Rust* (Athens: Ohio University Press, 2019).

47. Andrew B Liu, *Tea War: A History of Capitalism in China and India* (New Haven, CT: Yale University Press, 2020).

48. Tariq Omar Ali, *A Local History of Global Capital: Jute and Peasant Life in the Bengal Delta* (Princeton, NJ: Princeton University Press, 2018).

49. Patricia Barton, "The Great Quinine Fraud: Legality Issues in the 'Non-Narcotic' Drug Trade in British India," *Social History of Alcohol and Drugs* 22, no. 1 (2007): 6–25.

50. A good general account with attention to German innovation is Bob Zebroski, *A Brief History of Pharmacy: Humanity's Search for Wellness* (New York: Routledge, 2016). This account is drawn from Carsten Burhop, "Pharmaceutical Research in Wilhelmine Germany: The Case of E. Merck," *Pharmacy in History* 51, no. 3 (2009): 104–124; Arthur

Daemmrich, "Pharmaceutical Manufacturing in America: A Brief History," *Pharmacy in History* 59, no. 3 (2017): 63–72; Jonathan M. Liebenau, "Scientific Ambitions: The Pharmaceutical Industry, 1900–1920," *Pharmacy in History* 27, no. 1 (1985): 3–11; Betsy McTavish, "What Did Bayer Do Before Aspirin? Early Pharmaceutical Research at Bayer," *History of Pharmacy and Pharmaceuticals* 41, no. 1 (1999): 17–29; and John P. Swann, "The Evolution of the American Pharmaceutical Industry," *Bulletin of the History of Medicine* 69, no. 2 (1995): 254–285.

51. E. Digby Baltzell, *Philadelphia Gentlemen: The Making of a National Upper Class* (Piscataway, NJ: Transaction Publishers, 2011), 98 and passim.

52. On Merck, see Leon Gortler, "Merck in America: The First 70 Years from Fine Chemicals to Pharmaceutical Giant," *Bulletin for the History of Chemistry* 25, no. 1 (2000): 1–9.

53. Timothy M. Yang, *A Medicated Empire: The Pharmaceutical Industry and Modern Japan* (Ithaca, NY: Cornell University Press, 2021).

54. Paul Gootenberg, *Andean Cocaine: The Making of a Global Drug* (Chapel Hill: University of North Carolina Press, 2008).

55. "Morphine and Its Salts," in *American Druggist and Pharmaceutical Record*, vol. 36 (New York: American Druggist Publishing Company, 1900), 356.

56. Charles R.R. Beck, "Novelties in Opium Farming and Commercial Values," *The Pharmaceutical Review* 1, no. 4 (April 1892): 79–80; George B. Wood and Franklin Bache, "Opium," in *The Dispensatory of the United States of America* (Philadelphia: J.B. Lippincott, 1892), 1098–1125; "Pharmaceutical Progress: Greek Opium," *American Druggist and Pharmaceutical Record* 28 (January 25, 1896): 45–46.

57. James Sandos, "Northern Separatism During the Mexican Revolution: An Inquiry into the Role of Drug Trafficking, 1910–1920," *The Americas* 41, no. 2 (1984): 191–214; Gabriela Recio, "Drugs and Alcohol: US Prohibition and the Origins of the Drug Trade in Mexico, 1910–1930," *Journal of Latin American Studies* 34, no. 1 (February 2002): 21–42. The authoritative account is Guillermo Valdés Castellanos, *Historia del narcotráfico en México* (Madrid: Aguilar, 2013); in English, see Benjamin Smith, *The Dope: The Real History of the Mexican Drug Trade* (New York: W. W. Norton & Company, 2021), chapter 3 in particular. See also Eric Perramond, "The Dynamics of the Drug Trade in Northwestern Mexico," in *Dangerous Harvest: Drug Plants and the Transformation of Indigenous Landscapes*, ed. Michael K. Steinberg, Joseph J. Hobbs, and Kent Mathewson (Oxford: Oxford University Press, 2004), 209–217. An extensive account of drug policy and control in Latin America, with particular attentiveness to international conventions and agreements, is William Walker, *Drug Control in the Americas* (Albuquerque: University of New Mexico Press, 1981).

58. James Tharin Bradford, *Poppies, Politics, and Power: Afghanistan and the Global History of Drugs and Diplomacy* (Ithaca, NY: Cornell University Press, 2020), 28–29; Mir Munshi Sultan Mahomed Khan, ed., *The Life of Abdur Rahman: Amir of Afghanistan* (London: John Murray, 1900), 75.

59. On the broader American expansion into global resource frontiers from the late nineteenth to the mid-twentieth centuries, see Paul A. Kramer, "Embedding Capital: Political-Economic History, the United States, and the World," *Journal of the Gilded Age and Progressive Era* 15, no. 3 (2016): 331–362; Emily S. Rosenberg and Shanon Fitzpatrick, eds., *Body and Nation: The Global Realm of U.S. Body Politics in the Twentieth Century* (Durham, NC: Duke University Press, 2014); Courtney Fullilove, *The Profit of the Earth: The Global Seeds of American Agriculture* (Chicago: University of Chicago

Press, 2017); Megan A. Black, *The Global Interior: Mineral Frontiers and American Power* (Cambridge, MA: Harvard University Press, 2018); Kristin L. Hoganson and Jay Sexton, eds., *Crossing Empires: Taking U.S. History into Transimperial Terrain* (Durham, NC: Duke University Press, 2020); and Christopher R.W. Dietrich, ed., *Diplomacy and Capitalism: The Political Economy of U.S. Foreign Relations* (Philadelphia: University of Pennsylvania Press, 2022).

60. Rimner, *Opium's Long Shadow.*

61. Ibid., 135.

62. At first, the agreement enjoyed unexpected success, confounding many international skeptics: British India tapered off its exports to China, exporting its last licit chest of opium in 1913. Chinese nationalists, capitalizing upon a new, nationalist anti-opium sentiment, proved themselves eager to eliminate opium use through an aggressive eradication program. But with the collapse of the Qing dynasty in 1911, China was plunged into turmoil: poppy cultivation boomed again under the aegis of warlords, returning to mid-nineteenth-century highs by the 1920s. For a contemporary account, see Alexander Hosie, *On the Trail of the Opium Poppy: A Narrative of Travel in the Chief Opium-Producing Provinces of China* (Boston: Small Maynard & Co, 1914), reflecting travels in the precipitous years of 1910 and 1911. The literature on Chinese opium is too large to summarize here; see Timothy Brook, ed., *Opium Regimes: China, Britain, and Japan, 1839–1952* (Berkeley: University of California Press, 2000); Edward Slack, *Opium, State, and Society: China's Narco-Economy and the Guomindang, 1924–1937* (Honolulu: University of Hawaii Press, 2000); Alan Baumler, *Modern China and Opium: A Reader* (Ann Arbor: University of Michigan Press, 2001); Frank Dikotter et al., *Narcotic Culture: A History of Drugs in China* (Chicago: University of Chicago Press, 2004); David Bello, *Opium and the Limits of Empire: Drug Prohibition in the Chinese Interior, 1729–1850* (Cambridge, MA: Harvard University Asia Center, 2005); Alan Baumler, *The Chinese and Opium under the Republic: Worse than Floods and Wild Beasts* (Albany: SUNY Press, 2012); and Peter Thilly, *The Opium Business: A History of Crime and Capitalism in Maritime China* (Stanford, CA: Stanford University Press, 2022). See also Hans Derks, *History of the Opium Problem: The Assault on the East, ca. 1600–1950* (Leiden, the Netherlands: Brill, 2012); and the essays in Bob Tadashi Wakabayashi and Timothy Brook, eds., *Opium Regimes: China, Britain, and Japan, 1839–1952* (Berkeley: University of California Press, 2000).

63. On this period, see Musto, *The American Disease*, 24–68; and William B. McAllister, *Drug Diplomacy in the Twentieth Century: An International History* (London: Routledge, 2004).

64. Anne L. Foster, "Prohibition as Superiority: Policing Opium in South-East Asia, 1898–1925," *The International History Review* 22, no. 2 (2000): 253–273; Daniel J.P. Wertz, "Idealism, Imperialism, and Internationalism: Opium Politics in the Colonial Philippines, 1898–1925," *Modern Asian Studies* 47, no. 2 (March 2013): 467–499.

65. Allan Benson, "Nations Join in a War to Stamp Out Opium," *New York Times*, February 7, 1909.

66. On the decline of the British and French monopolies in Southeast Asia, see Diana Kim, *Empires of Vice: The Rise of Opium Prohibition Across Southeast Asia* (Princeton, NJ: Princeton University Press, 2020).

67. It was not the first major piece of anti-opium legislation: the Smoking Opium Exclusion Act of 1909 had banned the importation, possession, and use of "smoking opium," still

primarily seen as a Chinese practice. Later regulation would continue to narrow the purview of acceptable use of opiates, including the Heroin Act of 1924, which prohibited the possession, medical use, or importation of crude opium for the manufacture of heroin.

68. Joseph F. Spillane, *Cocaine: From Medical Marvel to Modern Menace in the United States, 1884–1920* (Baltimore: Johns Hopkins University Press, 2000), 134.

69. *Eucaine Hydrochlorate: A New Local Anaesthetic and a Substitute for Cocaine That Is Free of Its Disadvantages* (New York: Schering & Glatz, 1896).

70. "Herman A. Metz Offers $100,000 Prize for a Harmless Substitute for Opium," *New York Times*, May 15, 1925; Silas Bent, "Metz Explains Reward for Morphine Formula," *New York Times*, June 7, 1925; James E. Homans, "Metz, Herman A.," *The Cyclopædia of American Biography* (New York: The Press Association Compilers Inc., 1918). On Metz and New York public life, see Ryan P. McDonough, Paul J. Miranti Jr., and Michael P. Schoderbek, "The Search for Order in Municipal Administration: Herman A. Metz and the New York City Experience, 1898–1909," *Accounting Historians Journal* 47, no. 1 (February 5, 2020): 55–74.

71. "Charles Opiates Are Shipped Illegally to Canada," *The Pharmaceutical Era* XLIX, no. 12 (December 1916): 493.

72. H.A. Metz, "T.D. 2194 to Be Protested," *The Practical Druggist* XXXIII, no. 9 (September 1915): 18.

73. Edwin E. Slosson, "Moonshine Morphine," *The Scientific Monthly* XXI, no. 1 (July 1, 1925): 107–108.

74. John Palmer Gavit, "The Opium Problem: The Crucial Need of Limiting Manufacture Largely Overlooked," *New York Times*, June 25, 1925; see also John Palmer Gavit, *Opium* (New York: Brentano, 1927).

75. Caroline Jean Acker, "Addiction and the Laboratory: The Work of the National Research Council's Committee on Drug Addiction, 1928–1939," *Isis* 86, no. 2 (1995): 167–193.

76. Ibid., and Lyndon F. Small et al., *Studies on Drug Addiction: With Special Reference to Chemical Structure of Opium Derivatives and Allied Synthetic Substances and Their Physiological Action, United States.* Public Health Service. Public Health Reports. Supplement no. 138 (Washington, DC: U.S. Government Printing Office, 1938).

77. Nathan Adams, "Desomorphine." Produced by Meera Senthilingam. *Chemistry in Its Element*, July 9, 2014. Podcast, MP3 audio, https://www.chemistryworld.com/podcasts/desomorphine/7536.article.

78. "Memorandum for the Files," August 11, 1932; Walsh to Oyler, November 22, 1932; Eli Lilly & Co. to Anslinger, January 16, 1933; König to Fanham, February 13, 1933; Campbell to Commissioner of Customs, April 19, 1933; Wood to Shamhart, May 29, 1933; Woodward to Anslinger, May 5, 1934, RG 170/Subject Files, 1916–1970/Synthetic Narcotics, United States National Archives (henceforth USNA).

CHAPTER 4

1. Mümtaz Ziya, "Afyon Meselesi [The opium issue]," *Kadro: Aylık Fikir Mecmuası*, April 1932, 18–25; Fatih Demirci, "Kadro Hareketi ve Kadrocular [Kadro movement and Kadro members]," *Dumlupınar Üniversitesi Sosyal Bilimler Dergisi*, no. 15 (August 2006): 35–54.

2. Diana Kim, "The 'Evil Spectators?': Opium and Empire's Stakeholders in Twentieth-Century Southeast Asia," *The American Historical Review* 129, no. 1 (March 1, 2024): 53–83. See also Miriam Kingsberg, *Moral Nation: Modern Japan and Narcotics in Global*

History (University of California Press, 2013), 104–114; and Peter Thilly, *The Opium Business: A History of Crime and Capitalism in Maritime China* (Stanford, CA: Stanford University Press, 2022).

3. Only recently have historians of the opium trade, primarily in Southeast Asia, begun to grapple with the fractured and disparate arguments that pro-opium forces in Asia were making in the waning decades of European empire. Diana Kim has made the argument most clearly: "It is common to note the defensive positions of colonial governments or metropolitan authorities, but less so to specify their ties and tensions with the financial backers, physical transporters, and local sellers and buyers who personified the supply and demand for a global commerce in legalized opium" (Kim, ibid., 56). In doing so in the context of Southeast Asia, where pro-opium forces advanced deeply contradictory interpretations of how the commodity fit into wider imperial political economies, she instead analyzes the rise of global prohibition through the organizational weakness of opium's defenders.

4. Ryan Gingeras, *Heroin, Organized Crime, and the Making of Modern Turkey* (Oxford: Oxford University Press, 2014), 12–14. On this period, see also Suna Altan, *Osmanlı'dan Cumhuriyet'e Haşhaş: Sosyo-Ekonomik ve Dış Politik Boyutlarıyla (1909–1950)* [Poppy from the Ottoman Empire to the republic: socio-economic and foreign policy dimensions, 1909–1950] (Ankara: Sonçağ Yayınları, 2021); and James Windle, "A Very Gradual Suppression: A History of Turkish Opium Controls, 1933–1974," *European Journal of Criminology* 11 (2014): 195–212.

5. Zafer Toprak, *Türkiye'de Milli Iktisat, 1908–1918* [National economy in Turkey 1908–1918] (Ankara: Yurt Yaylari, 1982), 54–60; Ayhan Aktar, "Homogenising the Nation: Turkefying the Economy," in *Crossing the Aegean: An Appraisal of the 1923 Compulsory Population Exchange Between Greece and Turkey*, ed. Renée Hirschon (Oxford: Berghahn Books, 2003), 90–93.

6. Nissim Taranto, untitled dispatch in *Revue commerciale du Levant*, October 31, 1912, 501–502.

7. Nissim Taranto, untitled dispatch in *Revue commerciale du Levant*, September 15, 1919, 259–260.

8. "Opium," *American Druggist and Pharmaceutical Record* 69 (October 1, 1921): 35.

9. L.G. Nutt to Collector of Customs, New York, September 1, 1927; Mallinckrodt to Nutt, February 12, 1929; Mallinckrodt to Nutt, September 18, 1929; Mallinckrodt to Nutt, September 25, 1929; L.G. Nutt to Secretary of State, September 30, 1929; Mallinckrodt to Nutt, October 23, 1929; Wood to Mallinckrodt, April 25, 1932; "Declaration of Shipper of Food and Drug Products," May 8, 1932, RG 170—Correspondence of the Federal Narcotics Control Board Regarding Import Permits 1922–1932, USNA.

10. Schmidt, *From Anatolia to Indonesia*, 175–177.

11. Özgür Burçak Gürsoy, "Losing Wealth or Restricting the Poison? Changing Opium Policies in Early Republican Turkey, 1923–1945," *Historia Agraria* 61 (December 2013): 29.

12. Gingeras, *Heroin*, 70–71.

13. Daniel-Joseph Macarthur-Seal, "The Trans-Asian Pathways of 'Oriental Products': Navigating the Prohibition of Narcotics Between Turkey, China, and Japan, 1918–1938," *Modern Asian Studies* 56, no. 1 (January 2022): 207–249.

14. F. Cengiz Erdinç, *Overdose Turkiye: Türkiye'de eroin kaçakçılığı, bağımlılığı ve politikalar* (İstanbul: İletişim Yayınları, 2004), 53–70.

15. Eczayı Tıbbiye ve Kimyeviye—"The Medical and Chemical Products Factory"—took funding from Paris's Comptoir Central Des Produits Chimiques. It also enjoyed particular patronage from Yunus Nadi, the founder of the Republican People's Party's mouthpiece, *Cumhuriyet*; Nadi's Nazi sympathies and anti-Semitic broadsides did not preclude investment in the Tarantos' new enterprise; Gingeras, *Heroin*, 71.

16. Hariciye Vekâleti [Department of State], Republic of Turkey, "Control of Narcotic Drugs in Turkey" (Geneva, 1931).

17. Vladan Jovanović, "Jugoslavensko-američka opijumska suradnja, 1929–1941 godine [Yugoslav-American opium cooperation, 1929–1941]," *Časopis za suvremenu povijest* 50, no. 1 (May 25, 2018): 35–65.

18. James Kerrigan to Anslinger, December 5, 1931, RG 59/Records Relating to Narcotics/Turkey—1943 to 1944, USNA.

19. Taranto would rail for decades against what he viewed as the United States' destruction of his wholly legitimate business, saying that Washington owed him a debt of more than $100,000.

20. Gingeras, *Heroin*, 73–74. The facilities opened again later in the year, ostensibly for the purposes of processing old stock.

21. The "Türkiye Afyon Yetiştiriciler Satış Birliği" was constituted by Law No. 2061 on July 10, 1932. See Altan, "Cenevre Afyon Konferansları," and Ihno J. Bensussan, "La Turquie," in *L'Opium: Considérations Générales, Histoire, Géographie, Chimie, Fabrication et Usage de l'Opium et Études Économiques, Sociales et Législatives* (Paris: Vigot Freres, 1946), 147–158.

22. H. Nezihi, "Afyon ve Cemiyetiakvam [Opium and the League of Nations]," *İstanbul Ticaret ve Sanayi Odası Mecmuası* [Journal of the Istanbul Chamber of Commerce and Industry], no. 2 (January 1931): 50–53.

23. Mehmet Işık, *Madde Kullanımı ve Stratejik İletişim* [Substance use and strategic communication] (Ankara: Sage Yayıncılık, 2013), 61.

24. Özel Şahingiray, *Celal Bayar'ın Söylev ve Demeçleri* (Türkiye İş Bankası Kültür Yayınları, İstanbul 1999), 313.

25. The Uyuşturucu Maddeler Inhisarı was created by Law No. 2253.

26. The collaboration was short-lived, and frustrating for Yugoslav exporters: the Constantinople-based Turkish-Yugoslav Central Bureau for Raw Opium Export capped the amount of Yugoslav opium at around a fourth of the total exports. Jovanović, "Jugoslavensko-američka opijumska suradnja."

27. "Çok Modern Bir Daire Görmek İsterseniz Uyuşturucu Maddeler İnhisarı Umumi Müdürlük Merkezini Ziyaret Ediniz [If you want to see a very modern office, visit the general directorate of the Narcotic Substances Monopoly]," December 2, 1933.

28. "Uyuşturucu Maddeler Inhisar Idaresinden [From the Narcotic Substances Monopoly]," *Vakit*, June 16, 1933; H. Nezihi, "Uyusturucn Maddeler Inhisars Hakkmnda Kanun [Law on the monopoly of narcotic substances]," *İstanbul Ticaret ve Sanayi Odası Mecmuası* [Journal of the Istanbul Chamber of Commerce and Industry], no. 7 (July 1933): 284–286.

29. Kâmran Serif, *Afyon Türkiyede ve dünyada* [Opium in Turkey and the world] (Ankara: Devlet Matbaası, 1934).

30. "Milletler Cemiyeti Afyon Komisyonu Müzakereleri [Discussions of the League of Nations Opium Commission]," *Cumhuriyet*, July 4, 1938. Law No. 3491, which transferred the monopoly, saw it administered by a council of five members. See "Turkey

Establishes Office of Products of the Soil," *Foreign Agriculture* III, no. 1 (January 1939): 39–40.

31. Some of the Monopoly's work in its early years involved studying and increasing the levels of alkaloids in Turkish varieties of poppy; see Galip Bahtiyar Göker, *Afyon: Türkiye istihsalatı: haşhaş ziraatı, ziraat mıntıkaları, Afyon istihsalî, istatistik, ahdî ve kanunî mevzuat* [Opium: Turkey's production: poppy cultivation, agricultural regions, opium production, statistics, contractual and legal legislation] (İstanbul: Matbaacılıkve Neşriyat Türk Anonim Şirketi, 1933); and Ali Kürçay, *Hasbaslarin Kültür Sekline Girmesinde Türk Çesitlerinin Mevki ve Rolü* [The role and importance of Turkish varieties for opium-poppy growing] (Ankara: Çankaya Printing Works, 1946).

32. One economist saw Turkish opium as important in the national economy, but perhaps no more so than tobacco, hazelnuts, raisins, cotton, and wool in terms of overall economic significance. Salahaddin Ahmet Kurttepeli, "The Principal Export Articles of Turkey from the Commercial Point of View" (MA thesis, University of Southern California, 1939).

33. Bensussan, "La Turquie"; Paris Papamichos, "Mediterranean Jews and the Politics of Contraband Trade in World War I," in *The Macedonian Front, 1915–1918: Politics, Society and Culture in Time of War*, ed. Basil Gounaris, Michael Llewellyn-Smith, and Ioannis Stefanidis (London: Routledge, 2022), 134–142.

34. R.K. Newman, "India and the Anglo-Chinese Opium Agreements, 1907–14," *Modern Asian Studies* 23, no. 3 (July 1989): 525–560.

35. "Opium Trade Doomed; Anglo-Chinese Treaty Provides for Cessation of Traffic in Two Years," *New York Times*, May 28, 1911, C3.

36. E. Ralph Perkins, S. Everett Gleason, and Fredrick Aandahl, eds., "The Secretary of State to the Ambassador in the United Kingdom (Winant)," in *Foreign Relations of the United States: Diplomatic Papers, 1944, General: Economic and Social Matters, Volume II* (Washington, DC: U.S. Government Printing Office, 1967), 511.4A5/8–2144.

37. "Correspondence Between the Finance Dept. and the Punjab Government Regarding the Definition of the Terms 'Poppy Opium' and 'Poppy Heads' Under the Opium and Excise Acts: Amendment of the Notifications of the Punjab Government on the Subject," 1905, Foreign—Frontier-B; "Prohibition of the Cultivation of the Poppy and Hemp Plants in the Manipur State," January 3, 1905, Foreign—External-B, National Archives of India; "Allotment of Malwa Opium to the Malerkotla, Faridkot, and Kapurthala State," 1907, Punjab State Agency-Residency—General, NAI.

38. "Reduction of the Area Under Poppy Cultivation in the Bengal Opium Agencies to 600,000 Bighas During 1909–10," April 1909, Finance—Separate Revenue—A, NAI.

39. Pramathanath Banerjea, *Study of Indian Economics* (London: MacMillan, 1911), 171.

40. "Opium Convention Signed at The Hague in July 1912 and Modification of Laws, Regulations, Etc., Dealing with Opium, Morphia, and Other Substances in the States and Chiefships," 1924, Rajputana State Agency—Residency—Excise and Opium, NAI. This work continued until the abolition of the advisory role in 1936; see "Continuance of the Appointment of Excise Commissioner in Central India and Adviser on Opium Affairs for Central India and Rajputana," 1929, Foreign and Political—Establishment; "Continuation of the Appointment of a Central India Excise Commissioner and a Central India and Rajputana Opium Affairs Adviser for a Three-Year Term, Effective as of November 6, 1931," 1931, Foreign and Political—Establishment; "The Positions of the Excise and Opium Commissioner in Central India and the Adviser

on Excise and Opium Affairs in Rajputana Will Be Abolished, and Plans Will Be Made for the Commissioner's Duties in the Future," 1936, Rajputana State Agency—Residency—Jaipur Agency—Jagirdars, NAI.

41. "Adoption of the Measures Necessary to Give Effect to the Provisions of the Opium Convention Signed at The Hague," 1922, Punjab Hill State Agency—Residency—General, NAI. An earlier conference had been held in Indore in November 1915 for the rulers of states in Central India and Rajputana; see "Opium Papers," 1914, Rajputana State Agency—Residency—Jaipur Agency—Jagirdars, NAI.

42. "Annual Return of Opium Cultivation," 1920, Rajputana State Agency—Residency—Eastern Rajputana State Agency—Residency (Confidential); "Proposal to Conclude Reciprocal Arrangements with Indian States for the Extradition of Persons Concerned with the Traffic in Dangerous Drugs," 1931, Punjab State Agency—Residency—Judicial; "Opium Policy of Mewar Darbar and the Introduction of the State Monopoly System," 1934, Rajputana State Agency—Residency—Jaipur Agency—Jagirdars; "Abolition of Cultivation of Poppy in the Panjab Hill States," 1937, Punjab State Agency—Residency—Political, NAI.

43. Babu Ramprasad Saheb and Lala Ganeshdas Saheb, *Afeem ki Kheti* [Opium cultivation], trans. from Urdu (Neemuch, Gwalior Government, 1918).

44. "Cultivation of Malwa Opium on Behalf of Government," 1916, Rajputana State Agency—Residency—Mewar Residency; "Cultivation of Opium on Behalf of Government," 1924, Rajputana State Agency—Residency—Excise and Opium, NAI.

45. "Supply of Hard Ball and Biscuit Opium to S.R. States from the Indore Warehouse," 1931, Rajputana State Agency—Residency—Mewar Residency, NAI.

46. "Efforts to Stop the Smuggling of Opium out of Indian States," 1926, Rajputana State Agency—Residency—Mewar Residency; "Opium: Smuggling—Internal—Measures to Health," 1926, Central Board of Revenue—Excise—Opium; "The Process to Be Used in Situations of Opium Smuggling," 1926, Rajputana State Agency—Residency—Mewar Residency, NAI.

47. "Measures Adopted to Check the Smuggling of Opium," 1928, Rajputana State Agency—Residency—General, NAI; "Proposal for Enhancement of Selling Price of Opium to Prevent Smuggling," 1929, Rajputana State Agency—Residency—Jaipur Agency—Jagirdars; "Rules to Facilitate Cooperation in the Arrest of Opium Smugglers," 1935, Rajputana State Agency—Residency—Mewar Residency, NAI.

48. "Opium—Indian States—Discontinuance of Cultivation—Conference to Consider the States' Opium Problems—Committee to Investigate—Report Of," 1927, Central Board of Revenue—Excise—Opium; "Opium Cultivation in Indian States," 1927, Rajputana State Agency—Residency—Jaipur Agency—Jagirdars, NAI.

49. Anirudh Deshpande, "An Historical Overview of Opium Cultivation and Changing State Attitudes Towards the Crop in India, 1878–2000 A.D.," *Studies in History* 25, no. 1 (January 2009): 120–123. See also David M. Fahey and Padma Manian, "Poverty and Purification: The Politics of Gandhi's Campaign for Prohibition," *The Historian* 67, no. 3 (2005): 489–506.

50. Jawaharlal Nehru, "To Bishnu Ram Medhi," in *Selected Works of Jawaharlal Nehru*, ed. S. Gopal, vol. 8 (New Delhi: B.R. Publishing Corporation, 1976), 483–489. In a slightly later period, unfermented palm sap would be embraced by the Congress as an appropriate national temperance drink; see Darinee Alagirisamy, "The Problem with Neera: The (Un)Making of a National Drink in Late Colonial India," *The Indian Economic & Social History Review* 56, no. 1 (January 1, 2019): 77–97.

51. Maria Framke, "Internationalizing the Indian War on Opium: Colonial Policy, the Nationalist Movement and the League of Nations," in *A History of Alcohol and Drugs in Modern South Asia: Intoxicating Affairs*, ed. Harald Fischer-Tiné and Jana Tschurenev (London: Routledge, 2014), 155–171.

52. V.S. Srinivasa Sastri, "Speech at the League of Nations, 13th January, 1923," in *Speeches and Writing of the Rt. V.S. Srinivasa Sastri* (Madras: G.A. Natesan & Co., 1925), 401–425.

53. Framke, "Internationalizing," 158.

54. "Question of the Supply by Provincial Governments to States of Opium Duty-Free at a Fair Cost Price. Proposed Amendment of the Government of India Act, 1935 to Prevent a Provincial Government from Interfering with the Transport to and from Places Outside the Province of Opium Consigned to or from the Government Opium Factory and of Narcotics," 1937, Reform Office—Federation, NAI.

55. "Central Board of Revenue, Opium Administration 1937–1946," 1937, Military—Quarter Master General, NAI.

56. "Proposed Employment in the Laboratory of the Opium Factory at Ghazipur of a Trained English Chemist Having Practical Experience in the Preparation of Opium Alkaloids," March 1908, Finance Department—Separate Revenue, NAI.

57. "Report of Further Experiments at the Ghazipur Opium Factory for the Extraction of Alkaloids from Waste Opium with Coal Tar Oil," April 1912, Finance Department—Separate Revenue, NAI.

58. "Giving the Government of the United Provinces at Allahabad, Samples of Poppy Seeds from Mesh and Ispahan for Testing," 1916, Foreign and Political—External (B), NAI.

59. "Report on the Opium Factory, Ghazipur, by Mr. W.A. Davis, Indigo Research Chemist, Pusa, and Proposals for the Appointment of an Advisory Chemist in London and of a Chief Works Chemist at the Ghazipur Opium Factory," September 1918, Finance Department—Separate Revenue; "Creation of a Research Branch in the Opium Department and the Reorganisation of the Opium Factory at Ghazipur," August 1919, Finance Department—Separate Revenue, NAI.

60. "Opium: Medical Opium, High-Testing Opium, Manufacture Of," 1925, Central Board of Revenue—Excise—Opium; "Opium—Special Medical Opium—Manufacture of at the Opium Factory, Ghazipur, for Supply to the United Kingdom," 1940, Central Board of Revenue—Excise—Opium, NAI.

61. On its first seasons of operations, see "A Report on the Working of the Neemuch Opium Factory for the Period from 1st April 1935 to the 31st March 1936," 1936; "A Report on the Working of the Neemuch Opium Factory for the Period from 1st April 1936 to the 31st March 1937," 1937, IOR/L/E/9/733, British Library.

62. "Conversion of the Old Opium Sale Room into an Opium Godown," July 1909, Finance Branch—Separate Revenue (Opium), file 16, 3B-12 Nos. 119, West Bengal State Archives, Kolkata. This collection more broadly offers a view into the complex administrative wind-down of the Bengal industry in the years immediately following the Anglo-Chinese agreement.

63. "The Secretary of State to the Ambassador in the United Kingdom (Winant)."

64. *Report on the Operations of the Opium Department for the Year Ending September 30, 1934* (Benares: Opium Department, United Provinces of Agra and Oudh, 135), 2; *The Combined Civil List for India and Burma No. 157* (Lahore: Civil and Military Gazette Ltd., 1946), 348(b).

65. "Manufactured Drugs—Thebaine—Manufacture of, at the Alkaloid Works, Ghazipur," 1946, Central Board of Revenue—Excise and Opium—Progs., Nos. 321-E. O., 1946, NAI.

66. For a relatively comprehensive accounting, see RG 170/Correspondence of the Federal Narcotics Control Board Regarding Import Permits, USNA. A smaller number of shipments went to other East Coast ports.

67. Paul A. Kramer, "Embedding Capital: Political-Economic History, the United States, and the World," *The Journal of the Gilded Age and Progressive Era* 15, no. 3 (July 2016): 331–362; see also Paul A. Kramer, "Power and Connection: Imperial Histories of the United States in the World," *American Historical Review* 116 (2011): 1348–1391. The earliest formulations of this approach include William Appleman Williams, *The Tragedy of American Diplomacy* (New York: W. W. Norton, 1972); Walter LaFeber, *The New Empire: An Interpretation of American Expansion, 1860–1898* (Ithaca, NY: Cornell University Press, 1963); and Lloyd C. Gardner, *Imperial America: American Foreign Policy Since 1898* (New York: Harcourt Brace Jovanovich, 1976). On American empire more generally two recent and influential interpretations are A.G. Hopkins, *American Empire: A Global History* (Princeton, NJ: Princeton University Press, 2018); Daniel Immerwahr, *How to Hide an Empire: A History of the Greater United States* (New York: Picador, 2019).

68. Suzanna Reiss, *We Sell Drugs: The Alchemy of US Empire* (Berkeley: University of California Press, 2014).

69. On Anslinger, see Douglas Clark Kinder, "Bureaucratic Cold Warrior: Harry J. Anslinger and Illicit Narcotics Traffic," *Pacific Historical Review* 50, no. 2 (1981): 169–191; Douglas Clark Kinder and William O. Walker, "Stable Force in a Storm: Harry J. Anslinger and United States Narcotic Foreign Policy, 1930–1962," *The Journal of American History* 72, no. 4 (1986): 908–927; John C. McWilliams, *The Protectors: Harry J. Anslinger and the Federal Bureau of Narcotics, 1930–1962* (Newark: University of Delaware Press, 1990). Anslinger's domestic campaigns are examined exhaustively in Kathleen J. Frydl, *The Drug Wars in America, 1940–1973* (Cambridge: Cambridge University Press, 2013); his role in international regulation is central in Suzanna Reiss, *We Sell Drugs: The Alchemy of US Empire* (Berkeley: University of California Press, 2014).

70. "Ample Opium, Other Drugs Stored, McNutt Declares," *Washington Post*, December 10, 1941; see Reiss, *We Sell Drugs*, 17. The State Department estimated a stockpile of 262,000 kilograms of opium in the United States and imagined consumption certain never to exceed 100,000 kilograms a year. George Morlock to Merchant, 1 June 1942, RG 59/Records Relating to Narcotics/Turkey—1943 to 1944, USNA.

71. McAllister, *Drug Diplomacy in the Twentieth Century*, 145–146.

72. "Summary Report on Studies and Projects in the Office of the General Counsel," November 1941, Diary/Book 502/February 27 and 28, 1942, Franklin D. Roosevelt Library; and *New York Quinine & Chemical Works, Inc; Merck & Co, Inc; and Mallinckrodt Chemical Works*. A fourth company, Hoffman-LaRoche, was allowed to import a small amount for the manufacture of Pantopon; four other firms—Parke-Davis of Detroit, Eli Lilly of Indianapolis, Sharp & Dome of Philadelphia, and E.R. Squibb & Sons of Brooklyn—were permitted to import small quantities for experimental or drug development purposes. Bureau of Narcotics, United States Treasury Department, *Traffic in Opium and Other Dangerous Drugs for the Year Ended December 31, 1939*.

73. Gingeras, *Heroin*, 80; William M. Franklin and E. B. Perkins, eds., *Foreign Relations of the United States: Diplomatic Papers, 1942, The Near East and Africa*, Volume IV (Washington, DC: United States Government Printing Office, 1963), Document 835. On Turkish

imports, see Morlock to Merchant, "Purchase of Opium by the United States as a Measure of Economic Warfare," June 1, 1942; Boelter, "Opium Purchased by Defense Supplies Corporation from Turkey," October 20, 1943; Spiro to Halsted, October 22, 1943; Morlock to Steinhardt, August 16, 1944; Morlock, "Purchases of Turkish Opium by United States Importers," August 17, 1944; Morlock, "Purchase of Turkish Opium," September 19, 1944; Bureau Central Turco-Yougoslave Pour L'Exportation de L'Opium Brut to Merck and Co., September 23, 1942; Steinhardt to Harris, November 24, 1944, RG 59/Records Relating to Narcotics/Turkey—1943 to 1944, USNA.

74. Merck's other agent in Turkey was Sarkis Touloukian. The Touloukians, Armenians from Eskişehir, had been involved in the opium trade since the 1920s: Haroutune Hagop Touloukian, a textile merchant, had immigrated to the United States and served as representative of the Turkish-Yugoslav Central Bureau for Raw Opium Export there. His brother, Edward Hagop Touloukian, had migrated to Boston, where in 1922 he founded the Massachusetts Importing Company, which imported opium alongside mohair and carpets. Jovanović, "Jugoslavensko-američka opijumska suradnja."

75. Horace Alexander, "Narcotics in India & South Asia," 1930, Harry J. Anslinger Papers, Box 8, Folder 23, Penn State University Library Special Collections. Anslinger's extensive correspondence with his Indian counterparts is held in in RG 170/Subject Files, 1916–1970/India 1924–1943, USNA.

76. "Opium," June 1929, RG 59/Records Relating to Narcotics/India—1937 and Previous; Telegram from Cordell Hull, September 30, 1939; Browne to Groth, October 14, 1939; Anslinger to Ewing, October 14, 1939, RG 170/Subject Files, 1916–1970/India 1924–1943, USNA; "Opium Department Review," *Times of India*, April 22, 1941; "Proposed Expansion in the Work of the Opium Factory, Ghazipur," 1941, DGIMS—Store—Progs. No. 1941/32/14/41-S, and "Supply of Opium and Its Products, Morphine and Codeine etc to Overseas States," 1941, DGIMS—Store—55—25/41-S, NAI.

77. See the reports in Bureau of Narcotics, United States Treasury Department, *Traffic in Opium and Other Dangerous Drugs for the Year Ended December 31, 1942* (Washington, DC: United States Government Printing Office, 1943); Bureau of Narcotics, United States Treasury Department, *Traffic in Opium and Other Dangerous Drugs for the Year Ended December 31, 1943* (Washington, DC: United States Government Printing Office, 1944); Bureau of Narcotics, United States Treasury Department, *Traffic in Opium and Other Dangerous Drugs for the Year Ended December 31, 1945* (Washington, DC: United States Government Printing Office, 1946); as well as Anslinger to Thornton, October 3, 1945; Gates to Anslinger, December 7, 1945, RG 170/Subject Files, 1916–1970/India #2, USNA.

78. Groth to Hull, March 8, 1941; Don C. Bliss, "Opium Department Increases Profit," April 10, 1941 RG 170/Subject Files, 1916–1970/India 1924–1943, USNA; Kerrigan to Anslinger, October 21, 1941; Guinness, Mahon & Co. to Merck & Co., February 4, 1943; Kerrigan to Anslinger, February 4, 1942; Anslinger to Goodloe, February 19, 1942; Blumenfeld to Anslinger, February 26, 1942; Gaston to Hull, April 16, 1942; Donovan to Hull, June 12, 1942; Breidenbach to Anslinger, June 22, 1942; Donovan to Hull, July 2, 1942; Kerrigan to Bureau of Narcotics, July 3, 1942, RG 170/Subject Files, 1916–1970/Indian Opium (1942–1954), USNA. The purchases continued into 1943, shipped from Bombay around the monsoon.

79. Norman Ohler, *Blitzed: Drugs in the Third Reich*, trans. Shaun Whiteside (Boston: Houghton Mifflin Harcourt, 2017).

80. "War Progress Notes: Opium Imports," *War Progress*, no. 137 (April 30, 1943); *New York Quinine & Chemical Works, Inc; Merck & Co, Inc; and Mallinckrodt Chemical Works*; See Hoffman-LaRoche to Anslinger, 16 June 1941, Mallinckrodt to Anslinger, 24 June 1941, and McDonough to Anslinger, 26 June 1941, RG 170/Subject Files, 1916–1970/ Opium Prices, USNA; Douglas Valentine, *The Strength of the Wolf: The Secret History of America's War on Drugs* (Brooklyn: Verso Books, 2013).

81. Quinten Jones, *History of Poppy Straw Production and Processing Research in the United States*, February 11, 1974, RG 170/Foreign Country Files Related to Medicinal Opium Derivatives 1969–1985/Opium Policy—12/73 Policy Paper Follow-Up, USNA.

82. Peter Hayes, *Industry and Ideology: IG Farben in the Nazi Era* (Cambridge: Cambridge University Press, 1987); J. Gimbel, "The American Exploitation of German Technical Know-How After World War II," *Political Science Quarterly* 105, no. 2 (1990): 295; Dominique A. Tobbell, *Pills, Power, and Policy: The Struggle for Drug Reform in Cold War America and Its Consequences* (Berkeley: University of California Press, 2012).

83. In 1949, Merck, New York Quinine & Chemical Works, and Mallinckrodt successfully argued that they were entitled to a refund from the Turkish opium monopoly for wartime imports which had arrived with a lower quantity of opium than had been contractually agreed upon. US Congress, House, Committee on the Judiciary, New York Quinine & Chemical Works, Inc.; Merck & Co., Inc.; and Mallinckrodt Chemical Works, 81st Cong., 1st sess., 1949, H. Rep. 992, 1–15.

84. Motilal Himmatlal Avashia, "Confidential: The Federation of India and Sitamau State," March 14, 1937, 8525, Shree Natnagar Shodh Sansthan, Sitamau, Madhya Pradesh, India.

CHAPTER 5

1. Nargolwala to Anslinger, July 6, 1956; Nargolwala to Anslinger, August 10, 1956; Nargolwala to Anslinger, September 18, 1956; Anslinger to Nargolwala, September 27, 1956; Nargolwala to Anslinger, October 22, 1956, RG 170/Subject Files, 1916–1970/India #3 (September 1950–1956), United States National Archives.

2. See the correspondence between S.D. Nargolawala and Harry Anslinger between July and October 1956 in RG 170/Subject Files, 1916–1970/India #3 (September 1950–1956), USNA. On Nargolawala, see S.D. Nargolwala, "Civil Servants had to be Generalists and Specialists," in *Memoirs of Old Mandarins of India: The Administrative Change as the ICS Administrators Saw in India*, ed. Raj Kumar Nigam (New Delhi: Documentation Centre for Corporate & Business Policy Research, 1985), 243; Raj Kumar Nigam, ed., *Memoirs of Old Mandarins of India: The Administrative Change as the ICS Administrators Saw in India* (New Delhi: Documentation Centre for Corporate & Business Policy Research, 1985), 363.

3. On the historiography of Indian development, see Daniel Klingensmith, *"One Valley and a Thousand": Dams, Nationalism, and Development* (New Delhi: Oxford University Press, 2007); Sunil Amrith, "Food and Welfare in India, c. 1900–1950," *Comparative Studies in Society and History* 50, no. 4 (2008): 1010–1035; Subir Sinha, "Lineages of the Developmentalist State: Transnationality and Village India, 1900–1965," *Comparative Studies in Society and History* 50, no. 1 (2008): 57–90; Nicole Sackley, "The Village as Cold War Site: Experts, Development, and the History of Rural Reconstruction," *Journal of Global History* 6, no. 3 (2011): 481–504; Nicole Sackley, "Village Models: Etawah, India, and the Making and Remaking of Development in the Early Cold War," *Diplomatic History* 37, no. 4 (2013): 749–778; Taylor C. Sherman,

"From 'Grow More Food' to 'Miss a Meal': Hunger, Development and the Limits of Post-Colonial Nationalism in India, 1947–1957," *South Asia: Journal of South Asian Studies* 36, no. 4 (2013): 571–588; Medha Kudaisya, "The Promise of Partnership: Indian Business, the State, and the Bombay Plan of 1944," *Business History Review* 88 (2014): 97–131; Ornit Shani, *How India Became Democratic: Citizenship and the Making of Universal Franchise* (Cambridge: Cambridge University Press, 2017); David C. Engerman, *The Price of Aid: The Economic Cold War in India* (Cambridge, MA: Harvard University Press, 2018); Benjamin Robert Siegel, *Hungry Nation: Food, Famine, and the Making of Modern India* (Cambridge: Cambridge University Press, 2018); Rohit De, *The People's Constitution: The Everyday Life of Law in the Indian Republic* (Princeton, NJ: Princeton University Press, 2018); Uditi Sen, *Citizen Refugee: Forging the Indian Nation After Partition* (Cambridge: Cambridge University Press, 2018); Benjamin Siegel, "The Kibbutz and the Ashram: Sarvodaya Agriculture, Israeli Aid, and the Global Imaginaries of Indian Development," *The American Historical Review* 125, no. 4 (2020): 1175–1204; Mircea Raianu, *Tata: The Global Corporation That Built Indian Capitalism* (Cambridge, MA: Harvard University Press, 2021); Nikhil Menon, *Planning Democracy: Modern India's Quest for Development* (Cambridge: Cambridge University Press, 2022); Taylor C. Sherman, *Nehru's India: A History in Seven Myths* (Princeton, NJ: Princeton University Press, 2022); Aditya Balasubramanian, *Toward a Free Economy: Swatantra and Opposition Politics in Democratic India* (Princeton, NJ: Princeton University Press, 2023). An excellent review essay is Nikhil Menon, "Developing Histories of Indian Development," *History Compass* 19, no. 10 (2021): 1–14.

4. Reiss, *We Sell Drugs*.

5. Nils Gilman, *Mandarins of the Future: Modernization Theory in Cold War America* (Baltimore: Johns Hopkins University Press, 2003); David C. Engerman, *Modernization from the Other Shore: American Intellectuals and the Romance of Russian Development* (Cambridge, MA: Harvard University Press, 2003); David C. Engerman, ed., *Staging Growth: Modernization, Development, and the Global Cold War* (Amherst: University of Massachusetts Press, 2003); Michael E. Latham, *Modernization as Ideology: American Social Science and "Nation Building" in the Kennedy Era* (Chapel Hill: University of North Carolina Press, 2006); David Ekbladh, *The Great American Mission: Modernization and the Construction of an American World Order* (Princeton, NJ: Princeton University Press, 2010); Michael E. Latham, *The Right Kind of Revolution: Modernization, Development, and U.S. Foreign Policy from the Cold War to the Present* (Ithaca, NY: Cornell University Press, 2011).

6. On Turkey's constitutive role in making modernization theory, see Begüm Adalet, *Hotels and Highways: The Construction of Modernization Theory in Cold War Turkey* (Stanford, CA: Stanford University Press, 2020); see also Özge Sezer, *Forming the Modern Turkish Village: Nation Building and Modernization in Rural Turkey During the Early Republic* (Bielefeld, Germany: Transcript, 2023).

7. Black, *The Global Interior*, 6.

8. David Engerman makes a similar argument in Indian actors' leveraging Cold War powers against each other; David C. Engerman, *The Price of Aid: The Economic Cold War in India* (Cambridge, MA: Harvard University Press, 2018).

9. On Indian networks of science and technology, see Robert S. Anderson, *Nucleus and Nation: Scientists, International Networks, and Power in India* (Chicago: University of Chicago Press, 2010); David Arnold, "Nehruvian Science and Postcolonial India," *Isis*

104, no. 2 (June 2013): 197–428; Ross Knox Bassett, *The Technological Indian* (Cambridge, MA: Harvard University Press, 2016); and Jayita Sarkar, *Ploughshares and Swords: India's Nuclear Program in the Global Cold War* (Ithaca, NY: Cornell University Press, 2022).

10. Srijut Bijoy Chandra Bhagawati, "Assam's Opium Prohibition Drive," *Assam Information*, October 16, 1948, RG 170/Subject Files, 1916–1970/India #2, United States National Archives.

11. Assam had passed the near-total ban some months prior to independence; "The Assam Opium Prohibition Act, 1947," *Assam Gazette*, December 24, 1947.

12. Merrell to Secretary of State, April 12, 1946, RG 59/Records Relating to Narcotics/India—1938 to 1942.

13. Raghubir Sinh, "The Draft Constitution for the Proposed Malwa Union," April 1946, Shree Natnagar Shodh Samsthan, Sitamau, Madhya Pradesh, India.

14. Merrell to Secretary of State, February 12, 1947, RG 170/Subject Files, 1916–1970/India #2, USNA. "Opium, Safety in Black Market," *The Detroit Times*, December 4, 1947. Pakistan's opium situation, in the years after independence, was complicated by the fact that no legal opium-growing regions fell within the new nation's boundaries. Its annual requirement of 500 maunds was theoretically supposed to be supplied by India, but with relations uncertain, Pakistan embarked upon a series of experimental plantings between 1948 and 1952. After a number of failed experiments undertaken by former Indian Opium Department officials in Punjab's Montgomery District and elsewhere, adjoining districts in the Northwest Frontier Provinces and Punjab were selected as domestic cultivation sites. An opium factory was established in Lahore in 1950, and experiments on breed improvements were subsequently carried out at the Government Forest College in Abbottabad and at the Punjab University. A.E. Wright, "Opium in Pakistan," *Bulletin on Narcotics* 6 (1954): 11–15.

15. "All-India Narcotics Board to Meet," June 29, 1949, IOR/L/E/8/7522, British Library; "All-India Opium Conference," 1949, Western India States Agency—General—Progs., Nos. 12-20-G, 1949, NAI; "Opium Conference in Progress," August 4, 1949, IOR/L/E/9/736, British Library; "Resolutions Adopted at the All-India Opium Conference, 1949," September 27, 1949, RG 59/Records Relating to Narcotics/India—1938 to 1942, USNA.

16. A.N. Sattanathan, *Plain Speaking: A Sudra's Story*, ed. Uttara Natarajan (New Delhi: Permanent Black, 2007).

17. B.K. Mukhupadhyay, "Opium Alkaloids: Recent Developments in India," *Journal of Scientific & Industrial Research* VIII, no. 4 (April 1949): 118–121.

18. M. Emdad-ul Haq, *Drugs in South Asia: From the Opium Trade to the Present Day* (Basingstoke, UK: Palgrave Macmillan, 2000), 106–119. See the statements of Alladi Krishnaswami Ayyar, Biswanath Das, Shibban Lal Saksena, Rohini Kumar Caudhuri, and John Matthai in the Constituent Assembly Debates. On export numbers and values in this period, see *Explanatory Memorandum on the Budget of the Central Government for 1949–50* (New Delhi: Government of India Press, 1949); "Government of India's Reports on Sale of Opium Abroad—1950," 1950, Ministry of External Affairs—Lisbon, Legation of India—LIL. COM/7- (4)/50, NAI; Revenue from the Export of Opium, Rajya Sabha Debates, November 25, 1952, 303–304; Total Prohibition of Opium, Rajya Sabha Debates, November 26, 1952, 303–304; "Production of Opium in India," Rajya Sabha Debates, May 13, 1953, 5675–5676.

19. Ramesh Chandra Srivastava, "Human Resource Development as a Tool of Effectiveness: A Case Study of Government Opium Alkaloid Works Undertaking, Ghazipur, U.P." PhD dissertation (Veer Bahadur Singh Purvanchal University, 2002), 63.

20. The two facilities were in various states of physical decline: the older, located at Ghazipur, had been largely unrenovated since its construction in 1820, while the plant in Neemuch had been built in 1935 as part of the interwar effort to increase alkaloid production but had been poorly maintained during the war; the new state's representatives debated the merits of demolishing the factory and relocating its operations to the Rajasthani town of Ajmer instead. "Proposed Transfer of the Opium Factory at Neemuch to Ajmer," 1947, Gwalior Agency—Confidential—Progs., Nos. 51–55, 1947, NAI; Paul G. Mahlberg, *Upgrading of Technology in India for the Extraction of Alkaloids from Opium* (United Nations Industrial Development Organization, February 14, 1986); "Neemuch Opium Factory," *Times of India*, March 18, 1938.

21. "Development of Opium Industry," August 15, 1953, Press Information Bureau, Government of India; S.N. Asthana, "A Brief Digest on the Administrative Practice of the Monopoly System for Opium in India," *Narcotics Bulletin*, 1956, 31–34.

22. "Prohibition on Opium Cultivation," Rajya Sabha Debates, September 9, 1953, 1665–1666.

23. See Jay Sinha, "The History and Development of the Leading International Drug Control Conventions" (report prepared for the Senate Special Committee on Illegal Drugs, Library of Parliament, Ottawa, Canada, February 21, 2001).

24. Failing in this effort, he contented himself with a successful agreement with Harry Greenfield, the Indian Central Board of Revenue member in charge of opium policy. Anslinger to Thornton, October 3, 1945; Gates to Anslinger, December 7, 1945, RG 170/ Subject Files, 1916–1970/India #2, USNA; Anslinger to Greenfield, January 10, 1946; Greenfield to Anslinger, April 5, 1946, RG 170/Subject Files, 1916–1970/Opium in India, American Troops (#2, 1945–1947), USNA. See also Bureau of Narcotics, *United States Treasury Department, Traffic in Opium and Other Dangerous Drugs for the Year Ended December 31, 1946* (Washington, DC: United States Government Printing Office, 1947).

25. American officials would continue to take careful note of which Indian states had prohibited the smoking of opium as well. Withers, "Prohibition Plan for Bombay," January 16, 1947; see Anslinger to Timmons, January 30, 1947; Wilcox to Merrell, September 11, 1946, RG 170/Subject Files, 1916–1970/India #2, USNA. "Seizure of Indian Cakes of Raw Opium in New York on the British SS Adrastus Bearing the Stamped Impression of the Gwalior Government Opium Godown," 1946, External Affairs—Far East— Progs., Nos. 62-F.E, 1946, NAI.

26. Moorhead to Morley, December 8, 1945; Morley to Moorhead, December 1945; Moorhead to Henderson, March 7, 1946; Henderson to Moorhead, April 6, 1946; Henderson to Moorhead, June 17, 1946, RG 170/Subject Files, 1916–1970/India #2, USNA; Morlock to Thurston, "U.S. Policy Relating to Opium in India," July 19, 1946, RG 59/Records Relating to Narcotics/India—1938 to 1942.

27. The bill, HR-4795, was advanced by Arkansas representative Wilbur Mills; US House of Representatives, "H.R. 4795," November 26, 1945, RG 170/Subject Files, 1916–1970/ Indian Opium (1942–1954), USNA. See also the discussion in Bureau of Narcotics, United States Treasury Department, *Traffic in Opium and Other Dangerous Drugs for the Year Ended December 31, 1945* (Washington, DC: United States Government Printing

Office, 1946); and a wider discussion in Harry J. Anslinger and William F. Tompkins, *The Traffic in Narcotics* (New York: Funk & Wagnalls, 1953). The proposal was revised some years later; see "Sabath Offers Bill to Control Dope at Source," *Chicago Tribune*, February 11, 1952.

28. Sattanathan to Anslinger, December 29, 1950; Consul General of India to Anslinger, January 30, 1951, RG 170/Subject Files, 1916–1970/India #3 (September 1950–1956), USNA.

29. Morlock to Anslinger, May 28, 1952; Anslinger to Krishnamoorthy, September 11, 1952; Krishnamoorthy to Anslinger, September 18, 1952, RG 170/Subject Files, 1916–1970/India #3 (September 1950–1956), USNA.

30. Morlock to Thurston, February 1, 1946, RG 59/Records Relating to Narcotics/India—1938 to 1942, USNA; Nind to Tomkins, April 1, 1946; Kerrigan to Anslinger, March 7, 1946; Anslinger to Morlock, March 13, 1946; London to Byrnes, April 1, 1946; Gallman to Byrnes, April 1, 1946, RG 170/Subject Files, 1916–1970/Indian Opium (1942–1954), USNA. "Opium (Raw)—United States of America—Supply of, to—Request for (Refused)," 1946, Central Board of Revenue—Excise and Opium—Progs., Nos. 112-E. O., 1946, NAI; Guinness Mahon & Co. to High Commissioner for India, January 25, 1946; Guinness, Mahon & Co. to the High Commissioner for India, May 17, 1946; Marlow to Nind, May 28, 1946; France to Marlow, June 12, 1946, IOR/L/E/9/734.

31. Morlock to Anslinger, July 13, 1946, RG 170/Subject Files, 1916–1970/Indian Opium (1942–1954), USNA.

32. See their extensive personal correspondence; Anslinger to Sattanathan, December 20, 1947; Anslinger to Sattanathan, June 30, 1948; Anslinger to Saldanha, March 7, 1949; Glaser to Supervising Customs Agent, August 30, 1949; Gardner to Anslinger, September 26, 1949, RG 170/Subject Files, 1916–1970/India #2, USNA. Together, they worked to seize of a carload of opium found in Chandigarh that ultimately led investigators to a cache of 550 maunds in the Shimla Hills, earmarked for China, Mexico, and the United States. "World Gang of Opium Smugglers Active in Simla Hills," *Indian News Chronicle*, June 13, 1949, RG 170/Subject Files, 1916–1970/India #2, USNA.

33. Bureau of Narcotics, United States Treasury Department, *Traffic in Opium and Other Dangerous Drugs for the Year Ended December 31, 1953* (Washington, DC: United States Government Printing Office, 1954); "U.N. Pact Limits Opium Production," *New York Times*, June 28, 1953; Adolf Lande, "The Single Convention on Narcotic Drugs, 1961," *International Organization* 16, no. 4 (1962): 776–797; Taylor, *American Diplomacy*, 326; McAllister, *Drug Diplomacy*, 179–182. Sattanathan had expressed his willingness to accept similar terms from early in his tenure as Narcotics Commissioner; see Sattanathan to Anslinger, December 29, 1950; Consul General of India to Anslinger, January 30, 1951, RG 170/Subject Files, 1916–1970/India #3 (September 1950–1956), USNA.

34. India's pharmaceutical exports jumped from 4,893 maunds (approximately 182.65 metric tons) in the 1953–1954 season to 6,732 maunds (about 251.15 metric tons) the year after. Merck in particular was optimistic about Indian opium. *Income on Opium Export*, Rajya Sabha Debates, March 3, 1955, 1058–1059; *Export of Opium*, Rajya Sabha Debates, April 15, 1955, 4834–4835; Mills, "Telegram to John Foster Dulles," May 20, 1954, RG 170/Subject Files, 1916–1970/India—1954 and 1955.

35. "India's Opium Drugs Are in Great Demand," *Times of India*, August 15, 1953.

36. "Fresh Bid to Recapture World Opium Market: Ghazipur Factory's Plan," *Times of India*, June 16, 1955; Archibald R. Randolph, "Ghazipur Opium Factory," June 21, 1955, RG 170/Subject Files, 1916–1970/India—1954 and 1955.

37. "Profit from the Sale of Opium," Rajya Sabha Debates, April 26, 1956, 387–389.

38. McAllister, *Drug Diplomacy in the Twentieth Century*, 196.

39. Anslinger to Raj, December 8, 1958, RG 170/Subject Files, 1916–1970/India (1957–1965), USNA.

40. S.N. Asthana, "The Cultivation of the Opium Poppy in India," *Narcotics Bulletin*, 1954, 1–10.

41. Williams to Anslinger, March 8, 1949, RG 59/Records Relating to Narcotics/Turkey—1948 to 1949, USNA. On Taranto, see Devi Mays, "Becoming Illegal: Sephardi Jews in the Opiates Trade," *Jewish Social Studies* 25, no. 3 (Spring/Summer 2020): 1–34.

42. "Opium Production," 1945; "Opium Situation," January 1945, RG 59/Records Relating to Narcotics/Turkey—1943 to 1944, USNA; Morlock to Jones, "Turkish Opium," February 21, 1945; Jackson to Jackling, March 31, 1945; Acheson to Merck, April 2, 1946; S.A. & H. Touloukian to Merck, July 10, 1946, RG 59/Records Relating to Narcotics/Turkey—1945 to 1946, USNA.

43. Kross, "Turkey's 1946 Opium Crop—General Summary of the Opium Industry," July 18, 1946; "Report No. 163 (Ankara, Turkey)," August 6, 1946; American Embassy, Ankara, "Report No. 28," March 6, 1947, RG 59/Records Relating to Narcotics/Turkey—1945 to 1946, USNA. The Americans' British counterparts were even blunter in their assessment that Turkish opium farmers' resentment of the opium monopoly's prices made them unlikely to surrender their crops; see Lovett to Ankara, September 19, 1947, RG 59/Records Relating to Narcotics/Turkey—1945 to 1946, USNA.

44. Istanbul to Secretary of State, May 29, 1948, RG 59/Records Relating to Narcotics/Turkey—1948 to 1949, USNA.

45. "The Cultivation of the Opium Poppy in Turkey," *Bulletin on Narcotics*, 1950, 13–25.

46. Merrill, "Acting Director-General of Security Discusses the Illicit Traffic in Narcotics," September 12, 1952; Merrill, "Narcotics Report—Turkey," September 17, 1952; Merrill, "Narcotics and Opium Report: Turkey," January 23, 1953; Merrill, "Opium and Narcotics Report—Turkey," November 14, 1952, RG 59/Records Relating to Narcotics/Turkey—1943 to 1944, USNA.

47. Hoover to Ankara, November 10, 1955, RG 59/Records Relating to Narcotics/Turkey—1943 to 1944, USNA.

48. Reşat Saka, *Uyuşturucu maddeler: afyon, morfin, eroin, esrar, kokain hakkinda millî ve milletler arasi hukukî ve sosyal durum* [Narcotic substances: the national and international legal and social status of opium, morphine, heroin, cannabis, and cocaine] (İstanbul: Cumhuriyet Matbaasi, 1948).

49. Williams to Necati Bey, February 18, 1949; Toprak General Director to Williams, February 21, 1949; "Report by Mr. Maurice Ash to Merck," May 4, 1950; RG 59/Records Relating to Narcotics/Turkey—1948 to 1949, USNA.

50. Williams to Anslinger, February 25, 1949; Williams to Harney, February 25, 1949, RG 59/Records Relating to Narcotics/Turkey—1948 to 1949, USNA.

51. Anslinger to Morlock, July 13, 1950; Siragusa to Anslinger, August 25, 1950, C.A. Emerick, September 17, 1952, RG 59/Records Relating to Narcotics/Turkey—1948 to 1949, USNA.

52. Turkish opium also went to England and the Middle East; see "Ingilterede Afyon Kaçakciligi [Opium smuggling in England]," *Cumhuriyet*, June 14, 1954; and "Opium Production," March 24, 1959, RG 170/Subject Files, 1916–1970/Turkey 1957–1959, USNA.

53. Hadraba, "Turkey Adopts a New Opium Control Law," May 23, 1950; "An Act, Amending Code No. 5621 Which Amended Certain Articles of the Code of the Office of Soil Products," April 25, 1951, RG 59/Records Relating to Narcotics/Turkey—1943 to

1944, USNA; "Turkey—Policy Statement Relating to Opium," March 30, 1949; Morlock to Duffus, "Activities in Africa and the Near East," February 8, 1950, RG 59/ Records Relating to Narcotics/Turkey—1948 to 1949, USNA.

54. Anslinger to Harriman, August 20, 1952; Whittet, "Opium Alkaloid Factory," September 23, 1952; Dayton, "Opium Alkaloid Factory," September 29, 1952, RG 59/Records Relating to Narcotics/Turkey—1943 to 1944, USNA. A proposal for an alkaloid factory was eventually advanced but made limited progress; Fitzgerald, "Opium Alkaloid Factory," February 6, 1953, RG 59/Records Relating to Narcotics/Turkey—1943 to 1944, USNA.

55. E.P. Gross, "Turkish Opium Control," July 23, 1955, RG 59/Records Relating to Narcotics/Turkey—1943 to 1944, USNA.

56. See the extensive correspondence in RG 59/Records Relating to Narcotics/Turkey— 1943 to 1944. (The folder name notwithstanding, the files within span the years 1942 to 1956.)

57. John L. Wann, "Recent Competitive Aspects of Turkish Agriculture," *Foreign Agriculture* XIX, no. 10 (October 1955): 206.

58. Mackinnon to Anslinger, March 18, 1960; Spiro to Anslinger, March 21, 1960; Bradshaw to Anslinger, March 23, 1960; Gaffney to Anslinger, March 28, 1960, RG 170/Subject Files, 1916–1970/Turkey 1960–1961, USNA.

59. Heinrich Hartmann, "Meeting Again at Tahirova: German Expertise in Turkish Agriculture in the 20th Century," *Contemporary European History* 32, no. 4 (2023): 441–458.

60. Fethi Incekara, *Türkiye Haşhaş Çeşitleri ve Bunların Tohum ve Afyon Bakımından Değerleri* [Turkey hashish varieties and their values in terms of seeds and opium] (Ankara: Cankaya, 1949); Celal Tarman and Fethi İncekara, *Haşhaş Ziraati Nasıl Kazançli Olur?* [How can opium poppy cultivation be profitable?] (Ankara: İstiklal Matbaası, 1954).

61. S.A., "Memlekette Afyon Haşhaş Ziraatinden Vazgeçemez Miyiz? [Can we give up poppy cultivation in our country?]," *Cumhuriyet*, December 29, 1955; Siragusa to Knight, December 12, 1955; Bracken to Secretary of State, December 30, 1955, RG 59/ Records Relating to Narcotics/Turkey—1943 to 1944, USNA.

62. L.D. Kapoor, "Poppy Cultivation Is Paying," *Indian Farming* 11, no. 7 (October 1961): 8; *Report on the Operations of the Narcotics Department for the Year Ending September 30, 1959* (New Delhi: Ministry of Finance, Government of India, 1960); "Supply of Opium to Foreign Countries," Rajya Sabha Debates, June 19, 1962, 735–738; *Report on the Operations of the Narcotics Department for the Year Ending September 30, 1961* (New Delhi: Ministry of Finance, Government of India, 1961); *Indian Trade Journal* 216, no. 5 (1961): 264. Poppy farming was also possible briefly in certain districts in Himachal Pradesh.

63. V.S. Ramanathan, K. Prasad, and R.M. Gupta, "Absorption of Morphine from Opium by Porous Earthen Pots," *Narcotics Bulletin* 17, no. 4 (1965): 21–25; V.S. Ramanathan, J.C. Pal, and C. Ramachandran, "Narcotine in Indian Opium," *Bulletin on Narcotics* 4 (1966): 25–29; G.S. Shekhawat, "Cultivation Studies in Poppy," *Indian Journal of Agronomy* 12, no. 1 (1967): 83–85.

64. "The Abolition of Opium Smoking in India," *Bulletin on Narcotics* 9, no. 1 (1957): 1–7.

65. "Confirmed and registered addicts" were still able to purchase opium upon presentation of a physician's note. "Prohibition of Opium Consumption: Half a Century of Effort,"

Times of India, January 26, 1960; "Narcotics Conference Opens on Saturday: Consumption of Opium to Stop from April," March 15, 1959, Press Information Bureau, Government of India.

66. G. Borkar, *Health in Independent India* (New Delhi: Ministry of Health, Government of India, 1961), 59–60; see also B.G. Verghese, "Promising Trend in Drugs and Chemicals," *Times of India*, April 20, 1964.

67. Anslinger to Flues, October 21, 1959; Anslinger to Mackinnon, October 22, 1959, RG 170/Subject Files, 1916–1970/India (1957–1965), USNA.

68. Hayward to Giordano, May 12, 1966, RG 170/Subject Files, 1916–1970/Turkey—December 1965.

69. Cusack to Anslinger, March 2, 1962, RG 170/Subject Files, 1916–1970/India (1957–1965), USNA.

70. Giordano to Kohli, July 1, 1964; "Visit of Mr. Singh, High Indian Official, at Rome, Italy, on July 14, 1965," June 19, 1965; Arthur R. Doll, "Visit of Jasjit Singh," August 2, 1965, RG 170/Subject Files, 1916–1970/India (1957–1965), USNA.

71. McCann to Douglas, August 28, 1967, RG 170/Subject Files, 1916–1970/India (1957–1965), USNA.

72. "The Work of the Permanent Central Opium Board in 1960," *Narcotics Bulletin*, 1961, 39–41. Slightly lower figures are given in "Indian Opium and Foreign Exchange Earnings," Rajya Sabha Debates, August 28, 1959. A similar figure is given in Haq, *Drugs in South Asia*, 116.

73. "Central Revenue Collection for August 1961," October 11, 1961, Press Information Bureau, Government of India; "Licenses for the Production of Opium," Rajya Sabha Debates, June 19, 1962; "Supply of Opium to Foreign Countries," Rajya Sabha Debates, June 19, 1962; "Purchase and Sale of Opium," Rajya Sabha Debates, August 7, 1962; "Central Revenue Collections for June 1962," August 14, 1962, Press Information Bureau, Government of India; "Narcotics Department: Increase in Profit of Government Factories," September 29, 1962, Press Information Bureau, Government of India; "Licensing Policy for Poppy Cultivation for 1963–64: Performance of Yield Criterion of Eligibility," September 30, 1963, Press Information Bureau, Government of India; "Conversion of Opium of 70 Degree Density into Opium of 90 Degree Density," Rajya Sabha Debates, November 18, 1964. See also *Report on the Operations of the Narcotics Department for the Half Year Ending the 31st March 1965* (New Delhi: Ministry of Finance, Government of India, 1965); *Report on the Operations of the Narcotics Department for the Year Ending the 31st March 1966* (New Delhi: Ministry of Finance, Government of India, 1966).

74. *Report on the Operations of the Narcotics Department for the Year Ending September 30, 1959* (New Delhi: Ministry of Finance, Government of India, 1960); *Report on the Operations of the Narcotics Department for the Year Ending September 30, 1960* (New Delhi: Ministry of Finance, Government of India, 1960); *Report on the Operations of the Narcotics Department for the Year Ending September 30, 1961* (New Delhi: Ministry of Finance, Government of India, 1961); *Report on the Operations of the Narcotics Department for the Year Ending September 30, 1962* (New Delhi: Ministry of Finance, Government of India, 1962); *Report on the Operation of the Narcotics Department for the Year Ending the 30th September 1963* (New Delhi: Ministry of Finance, Government of India, 1963); *Report on the Operations of the Narcotics Department for the Half Year Ending the 31st March 1965* (New Delhi: Ministry of Finance, Government of India,

1965); *Report on the Operations of the Narcotics Department for the Year Ending the 31st March 1966* (New Delhi: Ministry of Finance, Government of India, 1966).

75. Giordano to Director of Intelligence Bureau, September 20, 1961; Director, Intelligence Bureau to Anslinger, October 8, 1961; Long to Emerick, October 31, 1961; Director, Intelligence Bureau to Anslinger, November 8, 1961; Anslinger to Director of Intelligence Bureau, November 17, 1961; Giordano to Director of Intelligence Bureau, December 1, 1961; Wu to Treasury Department, December 12, 1961; Director, Intelligence Bureau to Anslinger, December 26, 1961; Intelligence Bureau to Anslinger, March 4, 1962; Giordano to Banerjee, March 12, 1962; Giordano to Intelligence Bureau, April 3, 1962; Ziesnitz to Emerick, March 20, 1962; Giordano to Director of Intelligence Bureau, April 3, 1962, RG 170/Subject Files, 1916–1970/India (1957–1965), USNA.

76. Śrīlāla Śukla, *Raag Darbari*, trans. Gillian Wright (New Delhi: Penguin Books India, 1992), 40–41.

77. Reşat Enis, "Despot," *Cumhuriyet*, February 25, 1957. The novel was published later that year as Reşat Enis, *Despot* (İstanbul: Remzi Kitabevi, 1957).

78. Adalet, *Hotels and Highways*.

79. On the peasantry in this earlier period, see M. Asim Karaömerlioğlu, "Elite Perceptions of Land Reform in Early Republican Turkey," *The Journal of Peasant Studies* 27, no. 3 (April 1, 2000): 115–141.

80. For perspectives on opium in the 1950s with economic data, see "Memleketimizde Afyon Ticareti [Opium trade in our country]," *İstanbul Ticaret Odası Mecmuası* [Journal of the Istanbul Chamber of Commerce] 41, no. 3 (1956): 779–780; "Afyon-Opium [Opium-Opium]," *Farmakoloğ* [Pharmacologist] 3, no. 5 (1957): 661–667; Mehmet Ali Kağıtçı, *Afyon* [Opium] (Istanbul: Vakit Matbaası, 1960); and Ali Kürçay, *Haşhaş Yetiştirilmesi* (Ankara: Tarım Bakanlığı, 1962).

81. Hadary, "Opium Production, Limitation and Control in Turkey," July 28, 1953, RG 59/Records Relating to Narcotics/Turkey—1943 to 1944, USNA.

82. "Information Regarding Cultivation of Opium in Provinces Throughout Turkey, November 5, 1963; Giordano to Betts, "Increase in Staff at Istanbul, Turkey," October 13, 1965, RG 170/Subject Files, 1916–1970/Turkey 1964–1965.

83. *Comments on Opium Production for Export Under Existing International Narcotics Treaties and the G.O.T. Program*, 1963, RG 170/Subject Files, 1916–1970/Turkey—December 1965.

84. J.T. Cusack, "Memorandum for Gaffney Re: Opium Production Turkey," July 7, 1965, RG 170/Subject Files, 1916–1970/Turkey 1964–1965.

85. *Proposal for Eradication of Opium Poppy Cultivation in Turkey*, May 26, 1966, RG 170/Subject Files, 1916–1970/Turkey—December 1965.

86. Acheson to Macomber, "Control of Illegal Diversion of Turkish Opium," December 13, 1965; Acheson to Farr, December 30, 1965; Cusack to Giordano, "Opium Control Project—Turkey," May 10, 1966; "Proposal for Eradication of Opium Poppy Cultivation in Turkey," May 26, 1966, RG 170/Subject Files, 1916–1970/Turkey—December 1965; Komer to Hart, February 26, 1966, RG 170/Subject Files, 1916–1970/Turkey—December 1965.

87. McAllister, *Drug Diplomacy*, 156–211.

88. "The International Narcotics Control Board Enters upon Its Functions." *Bulletin on Narcotics*, January 1968, 49–50.

CHAPTER 6

1. Richard Tuhoy, "Opium Fields: Bumper Crop May Be Last," *Los Angeles Times*, July 1, 1971.

2. Charles Siragusa, "Letter to Paul E. Knight," December 12, 1955, RG 59/Records Relating to Narcotics/Turkey—1943 to 1944, USNA.

3. Cusack to Gaffney, "Opium Production in Turkey," July 7, 1965, RG 170/Subject Files, 1916–1970/Turkey 1964–1965, USNA.

4. Ahmet Gülen, "Nihat Erim Hükûmetleri'nin Haşhaş Politikası [The poppy policy of Nihat Erim's governments]," *Cumhuriyet Tarihi Araştırmaları Dergisi* 15, no. 30 (Fall 2019): 363–389. On the Turkish ban, see also Gingeras, *Heroin*, 190–199; and James W. Spain, "The United States, Turkey and the Poppy," *Middle East Journal* 29, no. 3 (1975): 295–309. See also Ayhan Songar, *Haşhaş Meselesi ve* Türkiye [Turkey and the opium poppy problem] (Istanbul: Hareket Yayınları, 1974).

5. *Dışişleri Bakanlığı Belleteni* [Ministry of Foreign Affairs bulletin], no. 81 (June 1971): 141.

6. Kyle T. Evered, "'Poppies Are Democracy!' A Critical Geopolitics of Opium Eradication and Reintroduction in Turkey," *Geographical Review* 101, no. 3 (2011): 306.

7. Şevket Süreyya Aydemir, "Olaylar ve Görüşler: Haşhaşın Ardından! [Events and opinions: in the wake of the poppy]," *Cumhuriyet*, July 5, 1961, 2.

8. Gülen, "Nihat Erim Hükûmetleri'nin Haşhaş Politikası," 379.

9. Susan K. Holly and William B. McAllister, "Telegram 4337 from the Embassy in Turkey to the Department of State, June 23, 1971," in *Foreign Relations of the United States, 1969–1976*, vol. E-1, *Documents on Global Issues, 1969–1972* (Washington DC: United States Government Printing Office, 2005).

10. *Haşhaş Ekim Bölgelerinde Tarımsal Gelirin Geliştirilmesi: Yapılacak Acil İşler Programı : Türk-Amerikan Müşterek Tarım Grubunun Tavsiyeleri* [Improving farm income in the poppy region: a program for action: recommendations of the Joint Turkish/American Agricultural Team] (Ankara: Grup, 1972); "Yurtta Haşhaş Yerine Kolza Üretmek Mümkün," *Milliyet*, August 6, 1973; Çağrı Erhan, *Beyaz Savaş: Türk-Amerikan İlişkilerinde Afyon Sorunu* [White war: the opium problem in Turkish-American relations] (İstanbul: Altınbaş Üniversitesi, 2018), 106–111.

11. United States Congress House Committee on Foreign Affairs, *The Politics of the Poppy: Report of a Study Mission to Turkey, March 14–16, 1974* (Washington, DC: United States Government Printing Office, 1974).

12. Henry Kamm, "Turkish Farmers See Poverty in Ban on the Poppy," *New York Times*, October 3, 1972.

13. Adalet, *Hotels and Highways*, 216.

14. Edward Jay Epstein, *Agency of Fear: Opioids and Political Power in America* (New York: Verso, 1990), 288.

15. Reiss, *We Sell Drugs*; Kathleen J. Frydl, *The Drug Wars in America, 1940–1973* (Cambridge: Cambridge University Press, 2013); Anne L. Foster, *The Long War on Drugs* (Durham, NC: Duke University Press, 2023).

16. Two years later, several different narcotics agencies would be merged into a new group, the Drug Enforcement Administration. Frydl, *The Drug Wars in America*, 384–388; McCoy, *The Politics of Heroin*, 389–395.

17. The head of that office, Jerome Jaffe, was a young and progressive thinker on drug use and abuse. A well-respected psychiatrist, Jaffe had long advocated for methadone

treatment for heroin users—a paradigm that was still controversial in many circles. Jaffe's employment nonetheless largely gave cover to a draconian program of policing and politicking.

18. Richard Nixon, "Special Message to the Congress on Drug Abuse Prevention and Control" (speech, Washington, DC, June 17, 1971).

19. Nathan B. Eddy, *The National Research Council Involvement in the Opiate Problem* (Washington, DC: National Academies Press, 1973); Nathan B. Eddy and Everette L. May, "The Search for a Better Analgesic," *Science* 181, no. 4098 (1973): 407–414; Caroline Jean Acker, "Addiction and the Laboratory: The Work of the National Research Council's Committee on Drug Addiction, 1928–1939," *Isis* 86, no. 2 (1995): 167–193; Caroline Jean Acker, "Planning and Serendipity in the Search for a Nonaddicting Opiate Analgesic," in *Medicines: The Inside Story*, ed. Gregory J. Higby and Elaine C. Stroud (Madison: American Institute for the History of Pharmacy, 1997), 139–159; David Herzberg, *White Market Drugs: Big Pharma and the Hidden History of Addiction in America* (Chicago: University of Chicago Press, 2020).

20. Herzberg, *White Market Drugs*, 96.

21. Nancy D. Campbell et al., *The Narcotic Farm: The Rise and Fall of America's First Prison for Drug Addicts* (Lexington: South Limestone, 2021).

22. On Demerol, see A.E. Ratelle and M.K. Kim, "Demerol as an Anesthetic Agent Used in 9,000 Surgical Cases," *Minnesota Medicine* 43 (January 1960): 22–24; B.W. Jones, "The Use of Demerol as an Anesthetic Agent," *AANA Journal* 42, no. 5 (October 1974): 439–446.

23. Musto, *The American Disease*, 238–250; Samuel Roberts and Helena Hansen, "Two Tiers of Biomedicalization: Buprenorphine, Methadone and the Biopolitics of Addiction Stigma and Race," in *Critical Perspectives on Addiction*, ed. Julie Netherland (Bingley: Emerald, 2012); Mical Raz, "Treating Addiction or Reducing Crime? Methadone Maintenance and Drug Policy Under the Nixon Administration," *Journal of Policy History* 29, no. 1 (2017): 58–86.

24. McNeil Laboratories Inc., "Fentanyl (Sublimaze)," *Clinical Pharmacology & Therapeutics* 9, no. 5 (1968): 704–706.

25. Herzberg, *White Market Drugs*, 247.

26. World Health Organization Scientific Group on Opiates and Their Alternates for Pain and Cough Relief, *Opiates and Their Alternates for Pain and Cough Relief: Report of a WHO Scientific Group* (Geneva: World Health Organization, 1972).

27. "Manufactured Drugs—Thebaine—Manufacture of, at the Alkaloid Works, Ghazipur," NAI.

28. Robert J. Bryant, "The Manufacture of Medicinal Alkaloids from the Opium Poppy—a Review of a Traditional Biotechnology," *Chemistry and Industry* 5 (January 1, 1988): 146–153.

29. André Barbier, *Annales Pharmaceutiques Françaises* 5 (1947): 121; André Barbier, "The Extraction of Opium Alkaloids," *United Nations Office on Drugs and Crime*, 1951.

30. Dawson to Weiner, April 5, 1954; Klein to Anslinger, November 5, 1954; Klein to Anslinger, December 3, 1954, RG 170/Subject Files, 1916–1970/Synthetic Narcotics, USNA.

31. *Journal de Pharmacie et des Sciences Accessoires* 13 (1827): 31–32; M. Magendie, "Formulary for the Preparation and Employment of Several New Remedies," trans. Charles Wilson Gregory, 8th ed. (London: E. Cox, 1835), 21.

32. A Buchner, "Über die Versuche zur Beantwortung der Frage, ob die unreifen oder die reifen Mohnköpfe zum Arzneigebrauche den Vorzug verdienen?" *Annalen der Chemie und Pharmacie* (1851): 255–259.

33. János Kabay, Improved Process for Obtaining Opium Alkaloids, More Particularly from Poppy-Plants, GB Patent GB406107 (A), issued February 22, 1934; Istvan Bayer, "Manufacture of Alkaloids from the Poppy Plant in Hungary," *Bulletin on Narcotics* 13, no. 1 (January 1, 1961): 21–28; Istvan Bayer, "János Kabay and the Poppy Straw Process: Commemoration on the 50th Anniversary of His Death," *Acta pharmaceutica Hungarica* 57, nos. 3–4 (1987): 105–110.

34. Willi Küssner, "Poppy Straw," *Bulletin on Narcotics* 13, no. 1 (1961): 12–21.

35. Cusack would later become Chief of the International Operations Division of the Drug Enforcement Administration when it was founded in 1973.

36. John T. Cusack, "Poppy Straw Extract," undated (most likely 1970 or 1971), RG 170/ Foreign Country Files Related to Medicinal Opium Derivatives 1969–1985/Poppy Straw Extract, USNA.

37. RG 170/Foreign Country Files Related to Medicinal Opium Derivatives 1969–1985/ Poppy Straw Extract, USNA.

38. "Poppy Straw Production in the United States: Arguments for and Against," undated (most likely 1971 or 1972), RG 170/Foreign Country Files Related to Medicinal Opium Derivatives 1969–1985/Poppy Straw Extract, USNA.

39. N. Sharghi and I. Lalezari, "Papaver Bracteatum Lindl., a Highly Rich Source of Thebaine," *Nature* 213, no. 5082 (March 1967): 1244.

40. J.W. Fairbairn and F. Hakim, "Papaver Bracteatum Lindl.: A New Plant Source of Opiates," *The Journal of Pharmacy and Pharmacology* 25, no. 5 (May 1973): 353–358.

41. "*Bracteatum*: A Potential Domestic Source of Codeine," May 15, 1975, RG 170/Foreign Country Files Related to Medicinal Opium Derivatives 1969–1985/Opium Policy— Bracteatum, Industry Papers, USNA. The idea that this was a "heroin-free" process was not a consensus view. Sidney Archer, a highly respected professor of chemistry at Rensselaer Polytechnic, warned that the process of making thebaine into a drug of abuse was available to an average undergraduate with a year's training in organic chemistry. Pharmaceutical manufacturers like Burroughs Wellcome were also writing to Washington to lend their support for the project; see Baker to Lawton, June 11, 1975, RG 170/Foreign Country Files Related to Medicinal Opium Derivatives 1969–1985/Opium Policy—Congressional, USNA.

42. Miller to Members of Committee on Opium Shortage, April 13, 1973, RG 170/Foreign Country Files Related to Medicinal Opium Derivatives 1969–1985/Narcotics Raw Materials [Folder 2 of 2], USNA; Reed to Ingersoll, February 14, 1973, RG 170/Foreign Country Files Related to Medicinal Opium Derivatives 1969–1985/Policy Review Committee Matters, USNA.

43. "Codeine Shortage Seen in Opium War," *Atlanta Constitution*, June 13, 1973; Jonathan Spivak, "Nixon's Bid to End Opium Output Is Succeeding but May Cause Shortages of Legal Pain-Killers," *Wall Street Journal*, November 26, 1973.

44. Secretary of State to New Delhi re: Indian Opium Policy, May 18, 1973, RG 59/Electronic Telegrams, 1973, USNA.

45. American Medical Association, "Press Release: AMA Meeting Will Seek Answers to Pending Shortage of Codeine," February 1975; American Medical Association,

"Program: AMA Symposium on Supplies of Opium for Medical Use," March 3, 1975; "Poppy Ban Didn't End Addiction," *Bakersfield Californian*, March 4, 1975; William Hines, "No Codeine Shortage, but Poppy-Growing Still Eyed," *Chicago Sun-Times*, March 15, 1975; Lydia Woods Schindler, "Codeine Shortage Downplayed in U.S. Government Turnabout," *The Journal* 4, no. 4 (April 1, 1975): 1, 4. On the changing priorities of the American Medical Association, see Keith Wailoo, *Pain: A Political History* (Baltimore: Johns Hopkins University Press, 2014), 20–27, 46–47, 156–157, 166.

46. McGrew to Bartels, October 15, 1974, RG 170/Foreign Country Files Related to Medicinal Opium Derivatives 1969–1985/Opium Supply—Drug Companies, USNA.

47. Todd to Ford, October 18, 1974; Barclay to Editor, *Wall Street Journal*, October 31, 1974, RG 170/Foreign Country Files Related to Medicinal Opium Derivatives 1969–1985/ Opium Production, USNA.

48. Jack Anderson, "U.S. Eyes Poppy-Growing for Drugs," *Washington Post*, December 18, 1974; Secretary of State to Ankara re: Misleading *Gunaydin* Report on U.S. Poppy Seed Production, September 9, 1975, RG 59/Electronic Telegrams, 1975, USNA.

49. Juan de Onis, "Opium Poppy Gone, Turkish Farmers Ask Why Has U.S. Done This to Us?," *New York Times*, August 9, 1973; "Amerika Yılda 335 Yerine 170 Milyon Veriyor [America gives $170 million instead of $335 million annually]," *Milliyet*, November 5, 1971; "Haşhaş Ekçisine 6 Aralık'tan Itibaren Tazminat Ödenecek [Compensation for poppy farmers to begin December 6th]," *Milliyet*, December 2, 1971; "Haşhaşta Gizlilik [Secrecy in poppy affairs]," *Milliyet*, February 11, 1972.

50. Secretary of State to Ankara re: U.S. Firms' Interest in Turkish Opium Stocks, August 16, 1973, RG 170/Foreign Country Files Related to Medicinal Opium Derivatives 1969–1985/Opium Supply—Drug Companies, USNA.

51. Ankara to Secretary of State, March 14, 1974; March 21, 1974, RG 59/Electronic Telegrams, 1974, USNA; "Polis Örgütleri Pusuda," *Milliyet*, November 19, 1973; "Türkiye'de Üretimin Yasaklanmasi, Soruna Hiç Bir Çozüm Getirmedi," *Milliyet*, November 20, 1973.

52. "Rep. Rangel Warns U.S. of Opium Crops from Turkey," *Jet*, May 16, 1974; Secretary of State to Ankara re: Opium Production in Turkey, March 22, 1974; Ankara to Washington re: Background for Secretary's Discussion with Turkish Foreign Minister, April 12, 1974, RG 59/Electronic Telegrams, 1974, USNA; United States Congress House Committee on Foreign Affairs, *The Politics of the Poppy: Report of a Study Mission to Turkey, March 14–16, 1974* (Washington, DC: United States Government Printing Office, 1974).

53. Ankara to Secretary of State re: Indian Poppy Growing, April 4, 1974; Ankara to Secretary of State, April 8, 1974, RG 59/Electronic Telegrams, 1974, USNA.

54. Jack Anderson, "Lifting the Turkish Opium Ban," *Washington Post*, April 14, 1974; Steven V. Roberts, "Turkish Farmers Insist the Opium Poppy Is Still Staff of Life," *New York Times*, May 11, 1974.

55. Horan to Kennedy re: Turkish Opium Production, July 1, 1974, CIA Declassified Document LOC-HAK-258-3-5-7; "Turks Lift Ban on Poppy Culture Imposed in 1971 at U.S. Request," *New York Times*, July 2, 1974; Bernard Gwertzman, "U.S. Calls Back Its Envoy in Turkish Opium Dispute," *New York Times*, July 6, 1974; Istanbul to Secretary of State re: *Milliyet* Editor Abdi İpekçi's Questions on Poppy Ban, July 9, 1974, RG 59/ Electronic Telegrams, 1974, USNA.

56. TMO to Penick, August 9, 1974, RG 170/Foreign Country Files Related to Medicinal Opium Derivatives 1969–1985/Opium Supply—Drug Companies, USNA.

57. *Rescission of the Opium Poppy Growing Ban by Turkey* (Department of State Agency for International Development, September 9, 1974).

58. Armağan Emre Çakır, *The United States and Turkey's Path to Europe: Hands Across the Table* (Abingdon, UK: Routledge, 2015), 61–62; William B. McAllister, ed., "Memorandum of Conversation, the Ambassador's Residence, Helsinki, Finland, July 31, 1975, 8 a.m.," in *Foreign Relations of the United States, 1969–1976*, vol. E–3, *Documents on Global Issues, 1973–1976* (Washington DC: United States Government Printing Office, 2009); Secretary of State to Ankara re: Misleading Gunaydin Report on U.S. Poppy Seed Production, September 9, 1975, RG 59/Electronic Telegrams, 1975, USNA.

59. "Turkey Keeps Tight Clamp on Opium Traffic," *The Austin American Statesman*, October 3, 1975.

60. Bob Wiedrich, "Turkish Dope Peril Renewed," *Chicago Tribune*, August 31, 1975. Authorities insisted that these stocks were holdovers from the last legal harvest; Secretary of State to Dar Es Salaam re: 5th UN Congress on the Prevention of Crime and the Treatment of Offenders, September 5, 1975, RG 59/Electronic Telegrams, 1975, USNA.

61. Emel Anil, "Turkey Vows to Keep New Opium Crop Legal," *Washington Post*, August 18, 1975.

62. Numan Baycin and Sadi Özgen, "Contract for the Sale of 1500 Metric Tons Net Weight Unlanced Poppy Capsules," December 25, 1976, RG 170/Foreign Country Files Related to Medicinal Opium Derivatives 1969–1985/FEMA Turkish Concentrate Poppy Straw Stockpile Purchase, USNA. Secretary of State to Ankara re: Bids on Poppy Straw, September 8, 1976, RG 59/Electronic Telegrams, 1976, USNA.

63. Ankara to Secretary of State, February 13, 1979, RG 170/Foreign Country Files Related to Medicinal Opium Derivatives 1969–1985/Confidential Opium Info, USNA.

64. Miller to Bensinger re: Concentrate of Poppy Straw Importation, November 24, 1978, RG 170/Foreign Country Files Related to Medicinal Opium Derivatives 1969–1985/ Report Files, USNA.

65. Ankara to Secretary of State, February 16, 1979, RG 170/Foreign Country Files Related to Medicinal Opium Derivatives 1969–1985/Confidential Opium Info, USNA. Ultimately, Diosynth agreed to import 6,060 tons of Turkish poppy capsules, while providing Turkey with six tons of finished product for domestic use; Ankara to Secretary of State, May 14, 1979, RG 170/Foreign Country Files Related to Medicinal Opium Derivatives 1969–1985/Confidential Opium Info, USNA.

66. Krishna Kumar, Ernest Carter, and Stan Samuelson, *A Review of AID's Narcotics Control Development Assistance Programme*, Special Study 29 (Washington DC: United States Agency for International Development Evaluation, 1996); Ankara to Secretary of State, April 19, 1979, RG 170/Foreign Country Files Related to Medicinal Opium Derivatives 1969–1985/Confidential Opium Info, USNA; Samuelson to Merck, April 20, 1979; Samuelson to Durrin, April 20, 1979, RG 170/Foreign Country Files Related to Medicinal Opium Derivatives 1969–1985/Articles, USNA.

67. Ankara to Secretary of State, "Visit of Assistant Secretary Falco," June 28, 1979; Ankara to Secretary of State, "GOT Concerns about US Policy Regarding DEA Regulations Governing Importation of Narcotic Raw Materials into US," June 28, 1979; Ankara to Secretary of State, "Opium Poppy Capsule Stocks and the Bolvadin Alkaloid Factory," August 20, 1979, RG 59/Electronic Telegrams, 1979; "Status of 1979–1980 Turkish Poppy Crop and 1980–1981 Prospects," June 10, 1980, RG 170/Foreign Country Files Related to Medicinal Opium Derivatives 1969–1985/Articles, USNA.

68. Falco to Bensinger, April 28, 1980, RG 170/Foreign Country Files Related to Medicinal Opium Derivatives 1969–1985/NRM Policy—1980 Replies, USNA.

69. Kenneth A. Durrin, "Meeting with Turkish IVP Group," November 2, 1979, RG 170/Foreign Country Files Related to Medicinal Opium Derivatives 1969–1985/ Articles, USNA.

70. F. Cengiz Erdinç, *Overdose Turkiye: Türkiye'de Eroin Kaçakçılığı, Bağımlılığı ve Politikalar* [Overdose Turkey: heroin trafficking, addiction, and policies in Turkey] (İstanbul: İletişim Yayınları, 2004), 190–191.

71. *IMS Pharmaceutical Marketletter*, February 2, 1976, 6; Minutes of the Cabinet Committee on International Narcotics Working Group Meeting, October 18, 1976.

72. Ankara to Secretary of State, March 9, 1979, RG 59/Electronic Telegrams, 1979, USNA.

73. Robert W. Pearson, "Visit to Turkish CPS Processing Plant by U.S. Pharmaceutical Industry Representative," May 9, 1979, RG 170/Foreign Country Files Related to Medicinal Opium Derivatives 1969–1985/Articles, USNA.

74. "Letter to Robert W. Pearson Re: Administrator's Visit to Bolvadin," July 9, 1980, RG 170/Foreign Country Files Related to Medicinal Opium Derivatives 1969–1985/ Articles, USNA.

75. Smith, "Turkish LC Assay Method for Poppy Straw," May 29, 1979; Nystrom to Samuelson, June 4, 1979, RG 170/Foreign Country Files Related to Medicinal Opium Derivatives 1969–1985/P. Bracteatum Processing by Penick, USNA; R.W. Pearson, "Debriefing of Dr. Chuck Gerfen, Mallinckrodt, upon His Return from Turkey and India," August 8, 1980, RG 170/Foreign Country Files Related to Medicinal Opium Derivatives 1969–1985/Articles, USNA.

76. "Official Opening of Bolvadin Alkaloid Factory," August 1980, RG 170/Foreign Country Files Related to Medicinal Opium Derivatives 1969–1985/Articles, USNA.

77. "Discussion Items for Meeting of June 10, 1981 with Guliani," 1981, RG 170/Foreign Country Files Related to Medicinal Opium Derivatives 1969–1985/General Files on Opium, USNA; Ankara to Secretary of State, August 6, 1981; Ankara to Secretary of State, October 16, 1981, RG 170/Foreign Country Files Related to Medicinal Opium Derivatives 1969–1985/Confidential Opium Info, USNA.

78. Robert L. Dupont, "The Drug Abuse Decade," *Journal of Drug Issues* 8, no. 2 (1978), 173–187. For wider context, see Claire D. Clark, *The Recovery Revolution: The Battle over Addiction Treatment in the United States* (New York: Columbia University Press, 2017), 116.

79. William B. McAllister, ed., "Minutes of a Joint Meeting of the Cabinet Committees on Drug Abuse, Washington, November 27, 1973," and "Memorandum from the Counselor to the President (Laird), the Director of the Office of Management and Budget (Ash), Secretary of Health Education and Welfare Weinberger, and Secretary of the Treasury Shultz to President Nixon, Washington, December 15, 1973," in *Foreign Relations of the United States, 1969–1976*, vol. E-3, *Documents on Global Issues, 1973–1976* (Washington DC: United States Government Printing Office, 2009).

80. Jaffe to Hinnick, July 17, 1973, RG 170/Foreign Country Files Related to Medicinal Opium Derivatives 1969–1985/Opium Policy—Synthetics, USNA.

81. "Testimony of Jerome H. Jaffe re: Investigate Juvenile Delinquency Hearings on Cultivation, Use & Control of Opium," March 26, 1975, RG 170/Foreign Country Files Related to Medicinal Opium Derivatives 1969–1985/Bayh Hearings 3/75, USNA.

82. "Statement of Robert L. Dupont, M.D. Before the Juvenile Delinquency Subcommittee," March 5, 1975, RG 170/Foreign Country Files Related to Medicinal Opium Derivatives 1969–1985/Opium Policy—Congressional, USNA; United States Congress Senate Committee on the Judiciary Subcommittee to Investigate Juvenile Delinquency, *Poppy Politics: Hearings Before the Subcommittee to Investigate Juvenile Delinquency of the Committee on the Judiciary, United States Senate*, vol. 1 (Washington, DC: United States Government Printing Office, 1977), 284.

83. David Zimmerman, "Codeine Crisis: Does One Exist? An In-Depth Report," *The Journal* 4, no. 4 (April 1, 1975): 16.

84. "Synthetic Opiates May Be Worse," *Baltimore News American*, March 14, 1975; "Statement of Senator Birch Bayh re: At Hearings on Cultivation, Use, Abuse & Control of the Opium Poppy," March 26, 1975, RG 170/Foreign Country Files Related to Medicinal Opium Derivatives 1969–1985/Bayh Hearings 3/75, USNA.

85. Secretary of State to US Embassies, "USG Review of Definition of Concentrate of Poppy Straw," August 23, 1979, RG 170/Foreign Country Files Related to Medicinal Opium Derivatives 1969–1985/Confidential Opium Info, USNA.

86. Johnson, "Poppy Cultivation for Medical Use," February 10, 1975; Johnson to Bonitati, February 13, 1975; Johnson to O'Neill, February 28, 1975, RG 170/Foreign Country Files Related to Medicinal Opium Derivatives 1969–1985/Bayh Hearings 3/75; Willette to Beckenheimer, February 20, 1975; Johnson to Cavanaugh, [n.d.], RG 170/Foreign Country Files Related to Medicinal Opium Derivatives 1969–1985/Opium Policy—Bracteatum Evaluation; Geneva to Secretary of State re: Commission on Narcotic Drugs Agenda Item 11, February 27, 1975; "Papaver Bracteatum, Prospects for Commercialization in the USA," April 12, 1975, RG 170/Foreign Country Files Related to Medicinal Opium Derivatives 1969–1985/Bracteatum Cost; Johnson to O'Neill re: Opium Policy, June 4, 1976, RG 170/Foreign Country Files Related to Medicinal Opium Derivatives 1969–1985/Opium Policy—Bracteatum Agency Positions, USNA; "*Papaver bracteatum*: Production and Control," *Federal Register* 41, no. 225 (November 19, 1976): 51036–51039.

87. "US Is Divided on Question of Scarlet Poppy," *The Journal* 6, no. 5 (May 1, 1977): 1, 3.

88. Bourne to Bergland, May 25, 1977, RG 170/Foreign Country Files Related to Medicinal Opium Derivatives 1969–1985/Opium Policy—Bracteatum Evaluation, USNA; Sammons to Bensinger, July 5, 1977, RG 170/Foreign Country Files Related to Medicinal Opium Derivatives 1969–1985/Comments on A.N.P.R., USNA.

89. Secretary of State, "Acquisition of Opium for Medicinal Purposes: Necessity for Waiver Under 1953 Protocol," September 30, 1974; Secretary of State to Vientiane re: Acquisition of Seized Opium for Medicinal Purposes, February 13, 1975, RG 59/Electronic Telegrams, 1975, USNA.

90. Kabul to Secretary of State re: US Firm to Submit Revised Bid for Purchase Seized Opium from Afghanistan, September 23, 1974, RG 59/Electronic Telegrams, 1974, USNA; "Proposed Drug Deal," *Congressional Record*, November 10, 1975; Secretary of State to All East Asian and Pacific Diplomatic Posts re: May 6 East Asia Press Summary, May 6, 1975, RG 59/Electronic Telegrams, 1975, USNA. On the eventual failure of the plan, see John Jacobs, "2 Carter Aides Reject Opium-Buying Proposal," *Washington Post*, July 13, 1977.

91. "Halt in Turkish Poppy Output Backfires in Opiates Pinch," *Hospital Tribune*, January 7, 1974.

CHAPTER 7

1. "Minister Addresses Conference of Poppy Growers," *Times of India*, August 25, 1981.

2. Shree Sondhi, "Big Godowns Being Built to Store Unsold Opium," *Economic Times*, November 11, 1981.

3. Benjamin Siegel, "Woven, Mined, Milled, and Packed: The Global Destinies of Indian Commodities, 1500–2023," in *India in the World: 1500 to the Present*, ed. Rajeshwari Dutt and Nico Slate (New York: Routledge, 2023), 33–54.

4. Prakash Kumar, *Indigo Plantations and Science in Colonial India* (Cambridge: Cambridge University Press, 2012).

5. Tariq Omar Ali, *A Local History of Global Capital: Jute and Peasant Life in the Bengal Delta* (Princeton, NJ: Princeton University Press, 2018).

6. Edward D. Melillo, "Global Entomologies: Insects, Empires, and the 'Synthetic Age' in World History," *Past & Present*, no. 223 (2014): 233–270.

7. "Concern Expressed Over Glut in International Opium Market," *Working People's Daily*, March 11, 1981; Opium to Be Exported at Reduced Rates," *Times of India*, August 25, 1981; "Opium Demand," *Times of India*, September 9, 1981.

8. William B. Spong, *Heroin: Can the Supply Be Stopped?* (Washington, DC: United States Congress Senate Committee on Foreign Relations, 1972), 3.

9. Susan K. Holly and William B. McAllister, "Telegram 4337 From the Embassy in Turkey to the Department of State, June 23, 1971," in *Foreign Relations of the United States, 1969–1976*, vol. E–1, *Documents on Global Issues, 1969–1972* (Washington DC: United States Government Printing Office, 2005).

10. Secretary of State to Geneva re: Opium Policy at Geneva Meeting, January 28, 1974; Washington to Geneva re: Opium Policy at Geneva Meeting, February 2, 1974; Secretary of State to Mexico City re: Meeting with Prime Minister, Opium Poppy Ban, February 23, 1974, RG 59/Electronic Telegrams, 1974, USNA; William B. McAllister, ed., "Telegram 1310 from the Embassy in Ankara to the Department of State, February 21, 1974, 1700Z," in *Foreign Relations of the United States, 1969–1976*, vol. E–3, *Documents on Global Issues, 1973–1976* (Washington DC: United States Government Printing Office, 2009). Süleyman Demirel upbraided Gerald Ford over India's role in a meeting in Helsinki the year after. William B. McAllister, ed., "Memorandum of Conversation, the Ambassador's Residence, Helsinki, Finland, July 31, 1975, 8 a.m.," in *Foreign Relations of the United States, 1969–1976*, vol. E–3, *Documents on Global Issues, 1973–1976* (Washington DC: United States Government Printing Office, 2009).

11. Susan K. Holly and William B. McAllister, eds., "Memorandum from the Executive Secretary of the Department of State (Eliot) to the President's Assistant for National Security Affairs (Kissinger), January 29, 1972," in *Foreign Relations of the United States, 1969–1976*, vol. E–1, *Documents on Global Issues, 1969–1972* (Washington DC: United States Government Printing Office, 2005).

12. Central Intelligence Agency, "The World Opium Situation," Intelligence Memorandum, ER IM 70–148 (Washington, DC, October 1970).

13. Central Intelligence Agency, "South Asia: A Potential Source of Illicit Opium for the US Market," Intelligence Memorandum, ER IM 72–105 (Washington, DC, June 28, 1972).

14. "U.S. Team Satisfied with Talks on Drug Control," *Statesman*, September 28, 1971; Schneider to Gross, October 5, 1971; Ernst to Tiger, October 12, 1971, RG 59/Records

Relating to India, 1966–1975/Social Conditions Non India—1971—Traffic in Narcotics, USNA.

15. Ernst to Tiger, October 6, 1971, RG 59/Records Relating to India, 1966–1975/Social Conditions in India—1971—Traffic in Narcotics, USNA.

16. Peter N. Kyros, James F. Hastings, and Lou Frey Jr., *Report by Members of the Committee on Interstate and Foreign Commerce, Concerning Narcotic Enforcement Efforts in Hong Kong, Thailand, Burma, India, Lebanon, Greece, Turkey, France, and the Netherlands* (Washington, DC: United States Government Printing Office, 1973), 29–34.

17. Secretary of State to Geneva re: Narcotics Seizure in Bombay, September 6, 1973; Colombo to Secretary of State re: Narcotics Control Action Plan for Sri Lanka, September 18, 1973; New Delhi to Secretary of State re: Consultation with India on CND Agenda, December 17, 1973, RG 59/Electronic Telegrams, 1973, USNA.

18. New Delhi to Secretary of State re: Consultation with India on Disposal of Stockpiled Opium, September 11, 1973, RG 59/Electronic Telegrams, 1973, USNA.

19. New Delhi to Secretary of State re: Codel Frey Report on Narcotics Enforcement Efforts, April 24, 1973; New Delhi to Secretary of State re: Request by GOI for Codel Frey Report on Narcotics Enforcement Efforts, September 29, 1973; New Delhi to Secretary of State re: Other Countries' Evaluation of India's Control System, November 5, 1973, RG 59/Electronic Telegrams, 1973, USNA.

20. Secretary of State to Beirut re: Visit of Shanley/Lacy Enroute to New Delhi, March 27, 1973; New Delhi to Ankara, June 15, 1973; Secretary of State to Geneva re: Notice of Visit and Security Clearance, November 5, 1973; RG 59/Electronic Telegrams, 1973, USNA; Schneider to Laingen, June 28, 1973, RG 59/Records Relating to India, 1966–1975/ Social Conditions/Pol-India 1973—Correspondence with New Delhi, USNA.

21. New Delhi to Ankara re: Narcotics Seizure in Bombay, September 4, 1973, RG 59/ Electronic Telegrams, 1973, USNA.

22. New Delhi to Secretary of State re: Opium Racket, August 29, 1974, RG 59/Electronic Telegrams, 1974, USNA; *Rajya Sabha Debates*, "Smuggling of Opium Out of India," November 19, 1974, cols. 37–38. See also Chand Joshi, "Mafia Enters Indian Dope Scene," *Hindustan Times*, December 9, 1973; "Growing Black Market in Opium?," *Hindustan Times*, December 9, 1973.

23. New Delhi to Islamabad re: Indian Opium Smuggling to Persian Gulf, January 22, 1974; New Delhi to DEA re: Indian Opium Seizures in U.S., January 25, 1974; New Delhi to Secretary of State re: Reports of Opium Smuggling from India, January 29, 1974, RG 59/Electronic Telegrams, 1974, USNA.

24. "Congressman Wolff Interview," April 15, 1974, RG 59/Electronic Telegrams, 1974, USNA.

25. An authoritative recent account is Gyan Prakash, *Emergency Chronicles: Indira Gandhi and Democracy's Turning Point* (Princeton, NJ: Princeton University Press, 2019). On the Emergency's international dimensions, see Edward Anderson and Patrick Clibbens, "'Smugglers of Truth': The Indian Diaspora, Hindu Nationalism, and the Emergency (1975–77)," *Modern Asian Studies*, June 2018, 1729–1773.

26. M. Rajangam, "Junkie," *Times of India*, October 26, 1975.

27. New Delhi to Secretary of State re: Subcommission on Education and Culture, September 30, 1975, RG 59/Electronic Telegrams, 1975, USNA.

28. New Delhi to Colombo re: Khalildad Khan, April 1, 1975; New Delhi to Colombo re: Khalildad Khan, June 10, 1975, RG 59/Electronic Telegrams, 1975, USNA.

29. K.L. Chadha and B. Choudhury, eds., *Ornamental Horticulture in India: Commemorative Volume Released on the Eightieth Birthday of Dr B.P. Pal* (New Delhi: Indian Council of Agricultural Research, 1986), 44.

30. U.S. Kaicker, H.C. Saini, H.P. Singh, and B. Choudhury, "Environmental Effects on Morphine Content in Opium Poppy (*Papaver somniferum L.*)," *Bulletin on Narcotics* 30, no. 3 (1978): 69–74.

31. US. Kaicker and B. Choudhury, "Hybrids of Opium Poppy (*Papaver somniferum L.*) with Changed Morphine Alkaloid Content," *Acta Horticulturae* 132 (1983): 197–202; H.C. Saini and U.S. Kaicker, "Combining Ability in Opium Poppy," *Indian Journal of Genetics and Plant Breeding* 43, no. 2 (1983): 252–256.

32. H.C. Saini and U.S. Kaicker, "Genetic Diversity in Opium Poppy," *Indian Journal of Genetics and Plant Breeding* 47, no. 3 (1987): 291–296.

33. U.S. Kaicker, B. Singh, and B. Choudhury, "Try Your Hand at Black Gold-Opium Poppy," *Indian Horticulture* 20, no. 3 (October/December 1975): 7, 9, 23.

34. See Benjamin Robert Siegel, *Hungry Nation: Food, Famine, and the Making of Modern India* (Cambridge: Cambridge University Press, 2018).

35. Jaisukhlal Hathi, ed., *Report of the Committee on Drugs and Pharmaceutical Industry* (New Delhi: Ministry of Petroleum & Chemicals, Government of India, 1975); W.S. Titus, "Drug Industry in the Doldrums," *India Today*, June 30, 1976.

36. Geneva to Secretary of State re: UN Narcotics Laboratory Poppy Research Project, August 29, 1974, RG 59/Electronic Telegrams, 1974, USNA; "Mission to India of Dr. Quentin Jones and Dr. Olav J. Brænden, 13 to 17 November 1974," 1974, RG 170/Foreign Country Files Related to Medicinal Opium Derivatives 1969–1985/Opium Policy—India, USNA.

37. *All India Coordinated Improvement Project on Medicinal and Aromatic Plants, Proceedings of Second Workshop Held at Gujarat Agricultural University, Anand Campus, Anand, from November 1st to 4th, 1976* (New Delhi: Indian Agricultural Research Institute, 1976); "25 Percent of India's Opium Output Comes from Chittorgarh District," *Times of India*, December 11, 1976.

38. Rajya Sabha, "Written Answers to Starred Questions: Poppy Cultivation in States," Rajya Sabha Official Debates, Part 1 (Question and Answer), 106th Session, July 25, 1978, 41–43.

39. Donald E. Miller, "Memorandum from the Chief Counsel of the Bureau of Narcotics and Dangerous Drugs (Miller) to Members of the Opium Shortage Committee," April 13, 1973, in *Foreign Relations of the United States, 1969–1976*, vol. E–3, *Documents on Global Issues, 1973–1976*, ed. Office of the Historian (Washington, DC: Government Printing Office, 2009).

40. Harold Eugene Thayer, interview by James J. Bohning, transcript, December 1, 1994, Chemical Heritage Foundation, St. Louis, Missouri; Henry W. Berger, *St. Louis and Empire: 250 Years of Imperial Quest and Urban Crisis* (Carbondale: Southern Illinois University Press, 2015), 203–205.

41. Secretary of State to Ankara re: Visit of Mallinckrodt Official for Opium Discussion, September 11, 1973; New Delhi to Secretary of State, September 20, 1973; Secretary of State to New Delhi re: Indian Opium Prospects, October 17, 1973, RG 59/Electronic Telegrams, 1973, USNA.

42. New Delhi to Secretary of State re: Opium Availability in 1974 and 1975, May 15, 1974. RG 59/Electronic Telegrams, 1974, USNA.

43. New Delhi to Secretary of State re: Indian Opium Exports, June 14, 1974, RG 59/ Electronic Telegrams, 1974, USNA.

44. New Delhi to Secretary of State re: Consultation with India on Article 9 of CND Agenda Item, December 17, 1973, RG 59/Electronic Telegrams, 1973, USNA.

45. New Delhi to Secretary of State re: Desirable Level of Indian Opium Production, July 27, 1973; Geneva to Secretary of State re: Opium Requirements for Medical Purposes, July 17, 1973; Geneva to Secretary of State, July 20, 1973, RG 59/Electronic Telegrams, 1973, USNA.

46. New Delhi to Secretary of State re: Opium Production for World Medical Use, June 26, 1974, RG 59/Electronic Telegrams, 1974, USNA.

47. New Delhi to Secretary of State re: Prospects for Increasing Opium Production, August 23, 1974, RG 59/Electronic Telegrams, 1974, USNA.

48. See New Delhi to Secretary of State re: Future US Opium Requirements, August 1, 1974; Secretary of State to New Delhi re: Narcotics Country Assessment for India, October 15, 1974; *Rajya Sabha Debates*, "Opium Production and Export," August 26, 1976, cols. 93–94; New Delhi to Secretary of State re: Indian Opium Production for 1975, May 9, 1975, RG 170/Foreign Country Files Related to Medicinal Opium Derivatives 1969–1985/ Opium Policy—India, USNA. India had enjoyed a good year, producing around 1,050 tons of opium and reserving 850 of them for export; American firms were allocated to receive a shared 200 tons. India was also exporting close to 15,000 tons of bulk poppy straw to countries with the ability to process it, like the Netherlands, Hungary, and East Germany.

49. American Embassy, New Delhi. "Telegram to Secretary of State Re: Visit of Mr. Jasjit Singh," May 7, 1975. RG 59/Electronic Telegrams, 1975, USNA.

50. Secretary of State to New Delhi re: Indian Opium Allocations, May 2, 1975; New Delhi to Secretary of State re: Indian Opium Allocations, May 8, 1975, RG 59/Electronic Telegrams, 1975, USNA.

51. New Delhi to Secretary of State re: Visit to US of Mr. Jasjit Singh, April 21, 1975; Department of State to American Embassy, New Delhi re: Visit of Mr. Jasjit Singh, May 2, 1975; New Delhi to Secretary of State re: Visit of Mr. Jasjit Singh, May 7, 1975; New Delhi to Secretary of State re: Visit of Mr. Jasjit Singh, May 9, 1975; Department of State to American Embassy, New Delhi re: Visit of Jasjit Singh, May 9, 1975; New Delhi to Secretary of State re: Visit of Jasjit Singh, May 12, 1975, RG 59/Electronic Telegrams, 1975, USNA.

52. Secretary of State to New Delhi re: Indian Opium Allocations, May 2, 1975; New Delhi to Secretary of State re: Indian Opium Allocations, May 8, 1975, RG 59/Electronic Telegrams, 1975, USNA.

53. New Delhi to Secretary of State re: US Views on Item 9 of CND Agenda: Supply of Opiates for Medical Purposes, February 14, 1974; Department of State to New Delhi et al. re: Narcotics Production for World Medical Use, June 24, 1974; New Delhi to Secretary of State re: Prospects for Increasing Opium Production, August 23, 1974; New Delhi to Secretary of State re: Narcotics Country Assessment for India, October 17, 1974; RG 59/Electronic Telegrams, 1974, USNA.

54. American Embassy, New Delhi. "Telegram to Secretary of State re: Narcotics: Consultation with India on Article 9 of CND Agenda Item," December 17, 1973. RG 59/Electronic Telegrams, 1973; American Embassy, New Delhi. "Telegram to Secretary of State re: US Views on Item 9 of CND Agenda: Supply of Opiates for Medical

Purposes," February 14, 1974; Department of State to New Delhi et al. re: Narcotics Production for World Medical Use, June 24, 1974, Electronic Telegrams, 1974, USNA.

55. New Delhi to Secretary of State re: Indian Opium Production, March 27, 1974, RG 59/ Electronic Telegrams, 1974, USNA; *Rajya Sabha Debates*, "Proposal to Set Up an Alkaloid Project in M.P.," November 26, 1974, cols. 149–150. V.T. Joshi, "Alkaloid Unit Will Boost Exports," *Times of India*, October 26, 1976; "Plans for Increasing Opium Production, Exports Outlined," *Indian Express*, November 24, 1976; "Papers Regarding Opium Factory & Alkaloid Works," 1979, Prime Minister Office—PMS—37/686/1979 PMS, National Archives of India; "Opium, Alkaloid Exports," *Hong Kong AFP*, September 7, 1979.

56. New Delhi to Secretary of State re: Opium Allocation, May 6, 1976, RG 59/Electronic Telegrams, 1976, USNA.

57. New Delhi to Secretary of State re: Indian Candidate for International Narcotics Control Board Jasjit Singh, October 27, 1978; Geneva to Secretary of State re: Elections to International Narcotics Control Board February—May 1979, November 8, 1978. RG 59/Electronic Telegrams, 1978, USNA; New Delhi to Secretary of State re: Elections to INCB: Indian Candidacy," February 6, 1979, RG 59/Electronic Telegrams, 1979, USNA.

58. New Delhi to Secretary of State re: Authorizing Growth of Bracteatum Poppy in the US, November 26, 1976, RG 59/Electronic Telegrams, 1976, USNA.

59. Robert Goheen to Secretary of State, "Indian Opium Production," October 27, 1978, RG 59/Electronic Telegrams, 1978, USNA; Robert Goheen to Secretary of State, "Possible US Import Ban on Poppy Straw Concentrate," January 12, 1979; Robert Goheen to Secretary of State, "Possible Changes to US Legal Provisions for Importation of Narcotic Raw Materials," March 1, 1979; Robert Goheen to Secretary of State, "Indo-US Cooperation on Narcotics Matters: US Imports of Narcotic Raw Materials; Enforcement Activities," March 13, 1979; Robert Goheen to Secretary of State, "Indian Alkaloids Plant," October 26, 1979; Robert Goheen to Secretary of State, "Indian Licit Opium Production; General Review and Projection October 1979," November 2, 1979, RG 59/Electronic Telegrams, 1979, USNA.

60. Robert Goheen to Secretary of State, "Indo-US Cooperation on Narcotics Matters," March 13, 1979, RG 59/Electronic Telegrams, 1979, USNA.

61. New Delhi to Secretary of State, "Indian Opium Exports to the United States," June 26, 1979; New Delhi to Secretary of State, "Indian Licit Opium Production; General Review and Projection October 1979," November 2, 1979, RG 59/Electronic Telegrams, 1979, USNA.

62. R.W. Pearson, "Debriefing of Dr. Chuck Gerfen, Mallinckrodt, upon His Return from Turkey and India," August 8, 1980, RG 170/Foreign Country Files Related to Medicinal Opium Derivatives 1969–1985/Articles, USNA.

63. "Press Agency Reports Crisis in Opium Export Trade," *Patriot*, March 16, 1981. The crop was particularly strong in Rajasthan, whose per hectare average was far beyond those of cultivators in Madhya Pradesh and U.P.; "Rajasthan Opium Production," *Patriot*, June 9, 1981; "Opium Imports from India," December 11, 1980, RG 170/Foreign Country Files Related to Medicinal Opium Derivatives 1969–1985/Narcotics Raw Materials—Mallinckrodt, Inc., USNA; "Fall in Opium Exports Affects Foreign Earnings," *Patriot*, March 11, 1981. On this period, see M. Emdad-ul Haque, "The Politics of Medicinal Opium: Resurgence of Indian International Drug Trafficking in the 1980s," *South Asia: Journal of South Asian Studies* 21, no. 2 (December 1, 1998): 121–143.

64. "Fall in Opium Exports Affects Foreign Earnings," *Patriot*, March 11, 1981; "Opium Glut," *Patriot*, December 6, 1981.

65. "Aid in Reduction of Opium Stockpile Seen," *Patriot*, February 15, 1982.

66. Ravi Bhatia, "Varanasi Drugs Haul Tip of the Iceberg," *Times of India*, April 17, 1981.

67. "Morphine Lab Unearthed in Delhi," *Times of India*, August 1, 1981.

68. New Delhi to Secretary of State "US Goals, Objectives and Resource Management for FY-81," March 1, 1979; New Delhi to Secretary of State, "Customs International Training for FY 80," March 16, 1979, RG 59/Electronic Telegrams, 1979, USNA.

69. "Mandsaur: Where Opium Trail Ends," *Statesman*, October 11, 1979.

70. "Policeman with Opium," *Patriot*, January 10, 1981; "Morphine Lab Unearthed in Delhi," *Times of India*, August 1, 1981; "'Narcotics King' Arrested," *Times of India*, August 14, 1981; "Delhi Opium Seizure," *Patriot*, August 22, 1981; "Opium Seized in Delhi," *National Herald*, November 24, 1981; "Bareilly Drug Arrests," *Patriot*, April 11, 1982.

71. "Trading in Illicit Opium Reported," *Muslim [Islamabad]*, December 11, 1981.

72. "Heroin Smuggler Arrested," *Patriot*, February 16, 1982; "Palam Heroin Haul," *Patriot*, April 23, 1982; "Heroin Laboratories Uncovered in Varanasi," *India Today*, April 30, 1982; Asoka Raina, "Narcotics: The Test Tube Terror," *India Today*, April 30, 1982; Asoka Raina, "Narcotics: The Golden Goose," *India Today*, August 31, 1982; Asoka Raina, "Narcotics: Traffic on the Border," *India Today*, December 15, 1982.

73. "Poppy Cultivation in Rajasthan," *Economic Times*, November 11, 1981.

74. *Report 1981–1982* (New Delhi: Ministry of Finance, Government of India, 1982).

75. Tavleen Singh, "Delhi a Haven for Drug Smugglers," *Telegraph*, November 21, 1982.

76. Flanagan to Hatfield, June 22, 1982, RG 170/Foreign Country Files Related to Medicinal Opium Derivatives 1969–1985/P. Bracteatum, USNA.

77. Murtha to Durrin, May 15, 1979; Murtha to Durrin, June 4, 1979; Nystrom to McClain, June 4, 1979; Durrin to Murtha, July 3, 1979; Durrin to Nystrom, July 6, 1979; Adams to McClain, July 6, 1979; Adams to McClain, November 13, 1979, RG 170/Foreign Country Files Related to Medicinal Opium Derivatives 1969–1985/P. Bracteatum Processing by Penick, USNA.

78. Ricks to Mullen re: Domestic Cultivations of Papaver Bracteatum, July 12, 1982; Mullen to Morrison, August 9, 1982; Mullen to Hatfield, August 10, 1982; Mullen to Packwood, August 16, 1982, RG 170/Foreign Country Files Related to Medicinal Opium Derivatives 1969–1985/P. Bracteatum, USNA.

79. "Bracteatum Poppy Yields Valuable Codeine, but Not Heroin," *Chemical Week*, July 2, 1980, 34.

80. League of Nations, *Traffic in Opium and Other Dangerous Drugs: Annual Reports of Governments for the Year 1942* (Geneva, 1946), 25; Gérard Badou, "Opium: The French 'Golden Triangle,'" *L'Express*, May 18, 1995; Raymond H. A. Carter, *Pharmacodépendance et pharmacodélinquance* (Paris: Chiron, 1990), 66–71; Ivan Drapeau and Sandrine Cabut, "En France, 12 000 hectares de pavot cultivés," *Le Monde*, September 9, 2013; Alexandre Marchant, *L'Impossible prohibition: Drogues et toxicomanie en France 1945–2017* (Paris: Perrin, 2018); Sébastien Hervier, "En Charente-Maritime, le pavot somnifère, destiné à l'industrie pharmaceutique, se cultive en toute discrétion," *Sud Ouest*, July 3, 2024.

81. At a smaller scale, Spain opted for a similar approach. In 1972, Spain began growing poppy for pharmaceutical use domestically; in 1986, the work was taken over by a private

firm, Alcaliber, which was tasked with producing alkaloids by the Ministry of Health. *Demand and Supply of Opiates for Medical and Scientific Needs: Report of the International Narcotics Control Board for 1980* (Vienna: International Narcotics Control Board, 1981), 173; Manuel Ansede and Olivia López Bueno, "Los vampiros del opio: un temerario turismo por los pueblos de España en busca de morfina [Opium vampires: a wild tour through Spain's towns in search of morphine]," *El País*, June 1, 2022.

82. The INCB was also decidedly old-fashioned. Its focus on supply meant that it ignored changing understandings of narcotics consumption, both licit and illicit. Focused on opium, coca, and cannabis, it had little to say about the emergence of new synthetic drugs and the increasing popularity of psychotropic substances and had made little impact on informal production.

83. International Narcotics Control Board, *Report of the International Narcotics Control Board for 1978* (New York: United Nations, 1978).

84. International Narcotics Control Board, *Report of the International Narcotics Control Board for 1979* (New York: United Nations, 1979).

85. United Nations Economic and Social Council Resolution 1979/8, "Maintenance of a World-Wide Balance Between the Supply of Narcotic Drugs and the Legitimate Demand for Those Drugs for Medical and Scientific Purposes" (May 9, 1979).

86. Varsha Shah, "Economic Analysis of India's Exports to U.S.A." (PhD diss., Gujarat University, 1978); Lynn Gray-Schofield, "Trends in Wildlife Trade from India to the United States," World Wildlife Fund, 1983.

87. Secretary of State to Ankara, "Possible Changes to US Legal Provisions for Importation of Narcotic Raw Materials," February 8, 1979, RG 59/Electronic Telegrams, 1979, USNA.

88. Pearson to Miller, "Narcotics Raw Materials Supply Options Paper," January 16, 1979; "Minutes," January 19, 1979; Freedman to Miller, "Narcotic Raw Materials," January 30, 1979, RG 170/Foreign Country Files Related to Medicinal Opium Derivatives 1969–1985/Opium Options, USNA.

89. "Narcotic Raw Materials: Justice/DEA Request Comments on Advanced Noticed of Proposed Rulemaking on Limiting Importation; Comments by 7-12-79," *Federal Register* 44, no. 114 (June 12, 1979): 33695–33697.

90. Charles Storch, "Drugs Firms Waging Opium War with U.S.," *Chicago Tribune*, October 28, 1979; Charles Storch, "Plan to Close Opium Marts Brings Withdrawal Pains," *Chicago Tribune*, October 29, 1979.

91. Turkish Embassy, Washington DC, "Turkish Views on the 'Proposed Limitations on Imports of Narcotic Raw Materials,'" July 11, 1979, RG 170/Foreign Country Files Related to Medicinal Opium Derivatives 1969–1985/Comments on A.N.P.R., USNA.

92. Anderson to DEA Federal Register Representative, July 6, 1979, RG 170/Foreign Country Files Related to Medicinal Opium Derivatives 1969–1985/Comments on A.N.P.R., USNA.

93. American Medical Association to the Administrator, Drug Enforcement Administration, July 27, 1979, RG 170/Foreign Country Files Related to Medicinal Opium Derivatives 1969–1985/Comments on A.N.P.R., USNA.

94. Pietraszek to DEA Federal Register Representative, July 9, 1979; Budapest to Secretary of State, "Proposed US Rules on Imports of Narcotic Raw Materials," August 7, 1979; Ferenc Toldi, "Advance Notice of Proposed Rulemaking on Narcotic Importation Policy," August 9, 1979, RG 170/Foreign Country Files Related to Medicinal Opium Derivatives 1969–1985/Comments on A.N.P.R., USNA.

95. Government of Australia, "Aide-Memoire," July 13, 1979, RG 170/Foreign Country Files Related to Medicinal Opium Derivatives 1969–1985/NRM Policy—1979 Replies, USNA.

96. Stratmeyer to Bensinger, July 10, 1979, RG 170/Foreign Country Files Related to Medicinal Opium Derivatives 1969–1985/NRM Policy—1979 Replies, USNA.

97. Lee to Bensinger, "Advance Notice of Proposed Rulemaking on Narcotic Importation Policy," July 6, 1979, RG 170/Foreign Country Files Related to Medicinal Opium Derivatives 1969–1985/NRM Policy—1980 Replies, USNA.

98. Percy to Bensinger, September 12, 1979; Bayh to Bensinger, October 5, 1979, RG 170/Foreign Country Files Related to Medicinal Opium Derivatives 1969–1985/NRM Policy—1979 Replies, USNA.

99. "Proposed Limitations on Import of Narcotic Raw Materials," *Federal Register* 45, no. 30 (February 12, 1980): 9289–9293.

100. Embassy of India, Washington DC, "Comments on Regulation Proposed by the US Drug Enforcement Agency," November 3, 1980, RG 170/Foreign Country Files Related to Medicinal Opium Derivatives 1969–1985/NRM Policy—1980 Replies, USNA.

101. Bensinger to Young, June 23, 1980, RG 170/Foreign Country Files Related to Medicinal Opium Derivatives 1969–1985/NRM Policy—1980 Replies, USNA; "Comments on Submission of Glaxo Australia" October 8, 1980, RG 170/Foreign Country Files Related to Medicinal Opium Derivatives 1969–1985/Narcotics Raw Materials—Mallinckrodt, Inc., USNA.

102. "Limitations on Imports of Narcotic Raw Materials," *Federal Register* 46, no. 159 (August 18, 1981): 41775–41776.

103. "Too Many Poppies," *Times of India*, April 22, 1984.

104. "Narcotics: The Drug Debate," *India Today*, May 15, 1984.

105. Secretary of State, "India: Licit Opium," January 31, 1984, RG 170/Foreign Country Files Related to Medicinal Opium Derivatives 1969–1985/General Files on Opium, USNA.

106. Paul G. Mahlberg, *Upgrading of Technology in India for the Extraction of Alkaloids from Opium* (United Nations Industrial Development Organization, February 14, 1986).

107. Haislip to New Delhi, August 8, 1987, RG 170/Foreign Country Files Related to Medicinal Opium Derivatives 1969–1985/Articles, USNA.

108. "Delhi Response to Concern Over Drug Abuse Scored," *Hindu*, December 5, 1981.

109. Shrabani Basu, "The Drug Street Beat," *Times of India*, October 7, 1984.

110. Rajiv Tiwari, "Crude Heroin Takes Over Bombay," *Times of India*, June 3, 1983; "Heroin Takes Delhi Market by Storm," *Times of India*, October 15, 1984; "Sayed—A Life of Dodging the Law," *Times of India*, June 23, 1985.

111. Raju Santhanam and Sumit Mitra, "Narcotics: The Growing Threat," *India Today*, July 15, 1985.

112. "Drug-Peddling Up in Varanasi," *Times of India*, October 23, 1983.

113. Nameirakpam Bisheswar, *Down with Heroin War* (Imphal: Pax Publications, 1985).

114. William K. Stevens, "India Called Key Staging Area for Heroin Sent to U.S.," *New York Times*, April 12, 1984.

115. By 1990, that number was said to be closer to half. "Forty Percent of Opium Production Smuggled out of Country," *Working People's Daily*, November 24, 1981; "40 p.c. of

Opium Yield Smuggled Out," *Business Standard*, November 20, 1981; *India's Antinarcotics Initiatives: Can New Delhi Control Drug Trafficking?* (Directorate of Intelligence, Central Intelligence Agency, September 17, 1986); Andrew Giarelli, "India's Drug Byways," *World Press Review*, January 1989, 45; Douglas Jehl, "'Indian Connection' Poppies Throw a Curve at U.S. Drug Policy," *Los Angeles Times*, March 19, 1990.

116. Stevens, "India Called Key Staging Area"; the *New York Times* later described India as "a major transit point for narcotics shipments to the United States and Europe." Steven R. Weisman, "Problem of Drugs Growing in India," *New York Times*, March 16, 1986.

117. Anirudhya Mitra, "Making a Killing," *India Today*, November 15, 1991.

118. "Narcotics: The Drug Debate," *India Today*, May 15, 1984.

119. "The Narcotic Drugs and Psychotropic Substances Act, 1985," September 16, 1985, Narcotics Control Bureau, Ministry of Home Affairs, Government of India.

CHAPTER 8

1. Suresh's poetic phrase was "*jaise ma bacche ki dekhbhal karti hai.*"

2. These are the values reported in conversation with Suresh Patidar, whose name has been changed here. Elsewhere, the numbers have been reported at around $28 a kilogram in the licit market, and $920–1,850 in the black market.

3. Sayantan Bera, "The Opium Trap," *Livemint*, September 8, 2017.

4. International Narcotics Control Board, "Narcotic Drugs: Estimated World Requirements for 2024; Statistics for 2022," United Nations (Vienna, 2024), 169–197.

5. Donald J. Frederick, "Dull Brown Tasmanian Poppies Bring in Green," *National Geographic*, February 20, 1994; Michael Richardson, "Tasmania Brings Opiates to the Masses," *The Australian*, December 12, 1995; Keith Bradsher, "Shake-Up on Opium Island: Tasmania, Big Supplier to Drug Companies, Faces Changes," *New York Times*, July 19, 2014; "How Australia's Smallest State Wound Up in the Middle of America's Biggest Drug Crisis," ABC News, October 12, 2019; Peter Whoriskey, "How Johnson & Johnson Companies Used a 'Super Poppy' to Make Narcotics for America's Most Abused Opioid Pills," *Washington Post*, March 26, 2020.

6. "Comments on Submission of Glaxo Australia Pty. Ltd., Docket No. 80—18," October 8, 1980, RG 170/Foreign Country Files Related to Medicinal Opium Derivatives 1969–1985/Narcotics Raw Materials—Mallinckrodt, Inc., USNA; A.J. Fist, "The Tasmanian Poppy Industry: A Case Study of the Application of Science and Technology," in *10th AAC* (presented at the Australian Agronomy Conference, Westbury, Tasmania, 2001); Brian Frappell, "Fifty Years of Poppies in Tasmania: The First Ten Years, 1960 to 1970," *Papers and Proceedings: Tasmanian Historical Research Association* 57, no. 2 (2010): 73–79; David Jack, "Obituary: Frederick ('Eric') Randall Smith" (Royal Society of Edinburgh, 1994); John Watson, *Tasmanian Poppy Industry* (Canberra: Commonwealth of Australia, 1999); Stewart Williams, "On Islands, Insularity, and Opium Poppies: Australia's Secret Pharmacy," *Environment and Planning D: Society and Space* 28, no. 2 (2010): 302; L.J. Wood, "Poppies in Tasmania," *Geography* 63, no. 3 (1978): 213–217.

7. János Kabay, "Improved Process for Obtaining Opium Alkaloids, More Particularly from Poppy-Plants," UK Patent GB406107 (A), filed November 29, 1932, and issued February 22, 1934.

8. Quentin Jones and Olav J. Braenden, Report on Mission to Australia, March 1976, RG 170/Foreign Country Files Related to Medicinal Opium Derivatives 1969–1985/Opium Policy—Australia, USNA.

9. Government of Australia, "Aide-Memoire."

10. L.J. Wood, "The Legal Production of Narcotic Materials in Australia," *Australian Geographer* 17–18 (November 1987): 161–165.

11. L.J. Wood, "Not Ordinary Merchandise: World Trends in the Licit Production of Opiates," *Geography* 73, no. 2 (April 1988): 149–151.

12. United States Congress House Committee on Foreign Affairs, *U.S. Licit Opium Imports: Foreign Policy Issues: Report of a Staff Study Mission to Turkey, India, and Australia to the Committee on Foreign Affairs, U.S. House of Representatives* (Washington, DC: United States Government Printing Office, 1989).

13. "U.S. Policy May Hit Indian Opium Sales," *Times of India*, June 2, 1989.

14. Anti-Drug Abuse Act of 1988, Public Law 100–690, § 4307, U.S. Statutes at Large 102 (1988): 4181.

15. United States Congress House Committee on the Judiciary, Subcommittee on Crime, *The Licit Importation of Opium: Hearing Before the Subcommittee on Crime of the Committee on the Judiciary, House of Representatives, One Hundred First Congress, Second Session, February 27, 1990* (Washington, DC: United States Government Printing Office, 1990); Kathleen Frydl, "The Pharma Cartel," in *The War on Drugs: A History*, ed. David Farber (New York: New York University Press, 2021), 303–342.

16. "UN Call to Lift Opium Stocks from India," *Times of India*, February 4, 1990.

17. "Opium for America," *Far Eastern Economic Review*, October 22, 1992, 44.

18. Paul G. Mahlberg, *Upgrading of Technology in India for the Extraction of Alkaloids from Opium* (United Nations Industrial Development Organization, February 14, 1986).

19. See *State of Punjab v. Nachhattar Singh*, 1982 CRILJ 1197 (Punjab and Haryana High Court 1982).

20. Ramesh Menon, "Opium Addiction: A Dangerous Dependence," *India Today*, November 15, 1984.

21. M. Emdad-ul Haque, "The Politics of Medicinal Opium: Resurgence of Indian International Drug Trafficking in the 1980s," *South Asia: Journal of South Asian Studies* 21, no. 2 (December 1, 1998): 121–143.

22. William K. Stevens, "India Called Key Staging Area for Heroin Sent to U.S.," *New York Times*, April 12, 1984.

23. Anirudhya Mitra, "Making a Killing," *India Today*, November 15, 1991.

24. Pranab Basu, "Opium and Religion," *Times of India*, April 11, 1993.

25. Bulbul Pal, "Gone to Opium Everyone," *Times of India*, July 21, 1991. The government's purchasing price in 1992 was around 200 rupees a kilogram, compared with 6,000 rupees on the black market. Anil Sharma, "Mandsaur Thrives on Opium," *Times of India*, April 6, 1992.

26. US Department of State, Washington DC, "Memorandum Re: India-Licit Opium," January 31, 1984, RG 170/Foreign Country Files Related to Medicinal Opium Derivatives 1969–1985/General Files on Opium, USNA.

27. United States Congress House Committee on Foreign Affairs, *Review of United States Narcotics Control Efforts in the Middle East and South Asia: Hearings Before the Committee on Foreign Affairs, House of Representatives, Ninety-Ninth Congress, Second Session, May 13 and May 22, 1986* (Washington, DC: United States Government Printing Office, 1986), 85–89.

28. Chinu Panchal, "Severe Curbs on Poppy Cultivation," *Times of India*, February 10, 1987.

29. Anil Saxena, "US Threatens Aid Cuts," *Times of India*, February 14, 1992.

30. Haque, "The Politics of Medicinal Opium," 131.

31. Vinay Srivastava, *Aphīm kṛṣhi kā itihās: Mālvā ke viśesh sandarbha mem* [The history of opium cultivation with special reference to Malwa] (Sitamau: Shree Natnagar Shodh Samsthan, 2007), 180–181.

32. Ramesh Chandra Srivastava, "Human Resource Development as a Tool of Effectiveness: A Case Study of Government Opium Alkaloid Works Undertaking, Ghazipur, U.P." (Veer Bahadur Singh Purvanchal University, 2002); Pranab Dhal Samanta, "India's Own Golden Triangle," *The Hindu*, April 7, 2002; "Fort Knox Vaults Harbor Millions in Opium, Morphine—Stockpile Held for Emergencies," *Seattle Times*, September 16, 1993.

33. Angela S. Burger, "Narcotic Drugs: Security Threat or Interest to South Asian States?," in *South Asia Approaches the Millennium*, ed. Marvin G. Weinbaum and Chetan Kumar (San Francisco: Westview Press, 1995), 175.

34. A.J. Fist, "The Tasmanian Poppy Industry: A Case Study of the Application of Science and Technology" (presented at the Australian Agronomy Conference, Westbury, Tasmania, 2001); "Poppy Breeders' Breakthroughs in Medicinal Crops," ABC News, June 6, 2014, https://www.abc.net.au/news/rural/2014-06-06/tch-fist-poppy-legacy/5504514. The "Tasmanian angle" appeared in narratives of the United States opioid crisis as early as 2014 and has played an increasingly prominent role in supply-side accounts; see Keith Bradsher, "Shake-Up on Opium Island," *New York Times*, July 19, 2014; Peter Andrey Smith, "The Global Opioid Supply Chain Begins in Tasmania," *Pacific Standard*, July 11, 2019, https://psmag.com/ideas/opioids-limiting-the-legal-supply-wont-stop-the-overdose-crisis; Katie Thomas and Tiffany Hsu, "Johnson & Johnson's Brand Falters Over Its Role in the Opioid Crisis," *New York Times*, August 27, 2019; "How Australia's Smallest State Wound Up in the Middle of America's Biggest Drug Crisis," ABC News, October 12, 2019; Peter Whoriskey, "Johnson & Johnson Companies Used a Super Poppy to Make Narcotics for Popular Opioid Pills," *Washington Post*, March 26, 2020; Julian Morgans, "Welcome to the Australian Island That Fueled America's Opioid Crisis," *Vice*, October 19, 2020.

35. Haque, "The Politics of Medicinal Opium," 131.

36. Donald J. Frederick, "Dull Brown Tasmanian Poppies Bring in Green," *National Geographic*, February 20, 1994; Michael Richardson, "Tasmania Brings Opiates to the Masses," *The Australian*, December 12, 1995.

37. Susan Milius, "Morphinefree Mutant Poppies," *Science News* 166, no. 13 (September 25, 2004): 196; Celia Henry, "Morphine-Free Poppies," *Chemical & Engineering News* 82, no. 39 (September 27, 2004): 8.

38. Marcia L. Meldrum, "A Capsule History of Pain Management," *Journal of the American Medical Association* 290, no. 18 (November 12, 2003): 2470–2475; Marcia L. Meldrum, "Brief History of Multidisciplinary Management of Chronic Pain, 1900–2000," in *Chronic Pain Management: Guidelines for Multidisciplinary Program Development*, ed. Michael E. Schatman and Alexandra Campbell (Boca Raton, FL: CRC Press, 2007), 1–13; Keith Wailoo, *Pain: A Political History* (Baltimore: Johns Hopkins University Press, 2014), 57–97.

39. Candace Pert, *Molecules of Emotion: Why You Feel the Way You Feel* (New York: Simon & Schuster, 1999); Candace B. Pert and Solomon H. Snyder, "Opiate Receptor: Demonstration in Nervous Tissue," *Science* 179, no. 4077 (March 9, 1973): 1011–1014. See also Garrett Epps, "Brainstormer: Dr. Candace Pert," *Washington Post*, December 31, 1978; Garrett Epps, "Brains and Ambitions," *Washington Post*, November 11, 1979; Neil A. Campbell, "A Conversation with Candace Pert," *The American Biology Teacher* 54, no. 6 (September 1992): 357–360; Emily Langer, "Candace B. Pert, Neuroscientist Who Discovered Opiate Receptor, Dies at 67," *Washington Post*, September 18, 2013; John Schwartz, "Candace Pert, 67, Explorer of the Brain, Dies," *New York Times*, September 19, 2013; Thomas H. Maugh, "Scientist Discovered Opiate Receptor," *Los Angeles Times*, September 24, 2013; Linda S. Brady and Miles Herkenham, "Candace B. Pert," *Neuropsychopharmacology* 38, no. 13 (December 2013): 2730.

40. Herzberg, *White Market Drugs*, 265–258. See also David Herzberg, "From One Extreme to the Other? The Political Construction of Opioid Consensus in the U.S.'s Long 20th Century," *Cahiers Droit, Sciences & Technologies*, no. 12 (May 31, 2021): 117–134.

41. United States Congress House Committee on the Judiciary, Subcommittee on Crime, *The Licit Importation of Opium*, 138–140.

42. Milius, "Morphinefree Mutant Poppies."

43. Peter Whoriskey, "'Super Poppy.'"

44. "Opium for America," *Far Eastern Economic Review*, October 22, 1992, 44.

45. John Watson, "Tasmanian Poppy Industry," Australian Senate transcripts, September 28, 1999, 9076–9077.

46. Kathleen Frydl, "The Pharma Cartel," in *The War on Drugs: A History*, ed. David Farber (New York: New York University Press, 2021), 303–342.

47. "The World Today Archive—Poppy Industry Crosses Fingers Over Drug Enforcement Outcome," *The World Today*, November 23, 2000.

48. Gery P. Guy et al., "Vital Signs: Changes in Opioid Prescribing in the United States, 2006–2015," *Morbidity and Mortality Weekly Report* 66, no. 26 (2017): 697–704.

49. Kumar Saurav, "A Shop That Waits for 22 Deaths," *Mid-Day*, March 22, 2010; "Legal Opium Shop Alive till Old Patrons Are," *Deccan Herald*, October 28, 2014; Kundan Jha, "Customers Missing, Delhi's Lone Legal Opium Shop About to Shut," *Sunday Guardian*, November 18, 2017; R.V. Smith, "The Height of Addiction," *Hindu*, May 21, 2018.

50. Dinesh C. Sharma, "Non-Narcotic Poppy Developed," *Times of India*, January 22, 2000.

51. Satyabrata Maiti and K.A. Geetha, "Research Highlights of Opium Poppy Under AICRP," Technical Bulletin, All India Co-ordinated Research Project on Medicinal and Aromatic Plants, National Research Centre for Medicinal and Aromatic Plants, Boriavi, Anand, Gujarat, September 2000.

52. Ramesh Chandra Srivastava, "Human Resource Development as a Tool of Effectiveness: A Case Study of Government Opium Alkaloid Works Undertaking, Ghazipur, U.P." (PhD diss., Veer Bahadur Singh Purvanchal University, 2002).

53. Letizia Paoli, Victoria A. Greenfield, and Peter Reuter, *The World Heroin Market: Can Supply Be Cut?* (Oxford: Oxford University Press, 2009), 159–160, 260.

54. "No Move to Prevent Opium Farming," *Times of India*, May 15, 1993.

55. Law Kumar Mishra, "MP Police Get Tough on Opium Trade," *Times of India*, March 29, 1997.

56. "New Govt. Policy 'Vindicated,'" *Business Line (The Hindu)*, May 15, 1997; "Record Opium Production Signals New Policy Success," *Economic Times*, May 20, 1997.

57. International Narcotics Control Board, "Report of the International Narcotics Control Board for 1996" (Vienna: United Nations, 1997), 19.

58. Prakash Bhandari, "All Eyes Are Set on Opium Growers in Chittorgarh," *Times of India*, November 16, 1998.

59. Neeraj Mishra, "Sister Morphine Comes to Opium Country," *Outlook*, March 8, 1999; Adrian Levy, "Smugglers Reap Benefit of India's Legal Opium Harvest," *Sunday Times*, June 13, 1999. On the changing dynamics of drug use in this period, see Molly Charles, "The Drug Scene in India," *Seminar*, no. 504 (2001): 17–22.

60. On the dynamics of *doda* or poppy-husk trading, see Roeland M. de Wilde, "Opium Poppy Husk Traders in Rajasthan: The Lives and Work of Businessmen in the Contemporary Indian Opium Industry" (PhD diss., London School of Economics, 2014).

61. Manjari Mishra, "Opium Growing Area in UP to Double to 9000 Hectares," *Times of India*, January 29, 2000.

62. Pranab Dhal Samanta, "India's Own Golden Triangle," *The Hindu*, April 7, 2002.

63. Steve Stecklow and Jonathan Karp, "Opium Importers Assail U.S. Rule That Favors India and Turkey," *Wall Street Journal*, April 3, 2000; "India, U.S. to Jointly Survey Opium Crop," *Times of India*, June 11, 2000; Executive Office of the President, "Certification for Major Illicit Drug Producing and Drug Transit Countries," *Federal Register* 66, no. 49 (March 12, 2001): 14454–14474.

64. Only the relatively smaller Pirmal Group agreed to take a role in codeine extraction, and this process took until 2007. See "Centre Allows Pvt Players to Process Opium," *Times of India*, November 8, 2003; "Neemuch Factory to Manufacture Four New Drugs," *Hindustan Times*, May 19, 2005; "Govt's Morphine Monopoly to End," *Financial Express*, May 12, 2006; "Pharma Companies Make a Beeline for Private Entry into Opium," *Indian Pharmacist*, May 31, 2007; Sapana Dorga Singh, "Piramal to Be First Pvt Company to Process Opium," *Business Standard*, July 2, 2009; "Govt Opens Door for Private Sector in Opium Biz," *Indian Express*, November 18, 2010; "Opening up Opium Business," *Kashmir Monitor*, February 25, 2012; Tabassum Barnagarwala, "Central Govt. Opens Doors for Private Players in Opium Cultivation," *The Indian Express*, May 8, 2018; Divya Rajagopal, "Opium Trade Sluggish as Norms, Infra Beg for Upgrade," *The Economic Times*, May 18, 2019.

65. Marvine Howe, "Turkish Farmers Turn Bitterly from Opium Poppy; Traditions and Tasty Cuisine a Form of Punishment Significant Drop in Production," *New York Times*, November 28, 1980.

66. *Bulgarian-Turkish Narcotics Connection—United States-Bulgarian Relations and International Drug Trafficking—Hearings and Markup Before the House Committee on Foreign Affairs, June 7, July 24, September 26, 1984* (Washington DC: U.S. Government Printing Office, 1984).

67. "Turkey-McNeil Laboratories Procurement of Turkish Concentrated Poppy Straw," November 10, 1983, RG 170/Foreign Country Files Related to Medicinal Opium Derivatives 1969–1985/General Files on Opium, USNA; Ankara to Secretary of State, August 1987, RG 170/Foreign Country Files Related to Medicinal Opium Derivatives 1969–1985/Articles, USNA.

68. United States Congress House Committee on Foreign Affairs, *U.S. Licit Opium Imports*, 7.

69. Erhan, *Beyaz Savaş* [White war], 134–138. For quantitative accounts of Turkey's exports in this time, see the INCB annual reports from 1990 to 2000.

70. "The God of Opium Smugglers," *Times of India*, November 9, 2014; Archana Sharma, "Opium Growers and Traders Share Profit with Deity in Rajasthan," *National Herald*, September 19, 2021.

71. "Opium a Big Poll Issue in MP's Mandsaur," *United News of India*, March 9, 2014; "Possibilities of Industrial and Agricultural Development in Mandsaur District," *Business Standard*, July 15, 2014.

72. Padma Shastri, "A Breathtaking Waste," *Hindustan Times*, June 1, 2009.

73. "Afeem Kisaanon Ne Dilli Pahunch Diya Dharna [Opium farmers have reached Delhi and started a sit-in protest]," *Nai Dunia*, April 18, 2017; Hemender Sharma and Seema Gupta, "Mandsaur: Here's What Led to Madhya Pradesh Farmers Protest," *India Today*, June 7, 2017; "Mandsaur Protests: Three Men at the Forefront of MP Farmers' Agitation," *Hindustan Times*, June 8, 2017; Aman Sethi, "Mandsaur Stir Was Run on WhatsApp: How Social Media Created a New Indian Farmer," *Hindustan Times*, June 19, 2017; "UP Farmers Perform 'Shavasana' to Protest Mandsaur Killing, Govt Policies," *Livemint*, June 21, 2017; Vishwadeepak, "Local BJP Leader Who Brokered Shivraj Singh Chouhan's Mandsaur 'Deal' Is an Opium Smuggler," *National Herald*, August 7, 2017; "Apheem Kisaan Aaj Bataayenge Apni Samasyaaen [Opium farmers will share their problems today]," *Nai Dunia*, March 18, 2018; Milind Ghatwai, "Behind Madhya Pradesh Move to Buy Banned Poppy Husk, the Farmer Constituency of 2018," *The Indian Express*, March 19, 2018; Sumati Mehrishi, "Mandsaur's Story: One Year After Farmer Protests, How Is Madhya Pradesh's Spice Basket Faring?," *Swarajya Magazine*, May 31, 2018; Pallavi Rebbapragada, "Mandsaur Agitation: Poppy Husk Smuggling, Lack of Technical Knowledge Plague Opium Farmers in Madhya Pradesh," *Firstpost*, June 6, 2018; "Afeem Ko Lekar Kyon Bhadke Kisaan [Why are farmers enraged over opium?]," *Patrika*, September 17, 2018; "Aktoobar ke pahle saptaah mein aayegi nayi Afeem neeti, badhenge patte [New opium policy to come in the first week of October, licenses will increase]," *Dainik Bhaskar*, September 25, 2018; Lola Nayar, "In Poll-Bound Madhya Pradesh, Farmers' Anger Grows Despite a Good Harvest," *Outlook*, November 1, 2018; Sayantan Bera, "Farmers on a Short Fuse in Election-Bound Madhya Pradesh," *Livemint*, November 21, 2018; Punya Priya Mitra, "In Madhya Pradesh's Opium Hub, Farm Distress Trumps All," *Hindustan Times*, November 21, 2018; Sayantan Bera, "BJP Leading in Madhya Pradesh's Farm Unrest Hotspot Mandsaur," *Livemint*, December 11, 2018; Pallavi Rebbapragada, "Congress Grants Farm Loan Waivers in Madhya Pradesh: Party's Loss in Mandsaur Shows Its Policy Is Unproductive," *Firstpost*, December 18, 2018; Anand Mishra, "Of Marx, Modi and Morphine in Mandsaur," *Deccan Herald*, May 16, 2019; Dalip Singh, "BJP, Cong Face Test as Anger Among Ryots Persists in Mandsaur," *Economic Times*, May 16, 2019; "Mandsaur Moves on After 2017 Police Firing Incident," *Asian Age*, May 17, 2019; "Mandsaur: Farmers Protest Against Changes in Opium Policy," *Free Press Journal*, October 18, 2019.

EPILOGUE

1. K. Ajithakumari, K. Sureshkumar, and M.R. Rajagopal, "Palliative Home Care: The Calicut Experience," *Palliative Medicine* 11, no. 6 (November 1997): 451–454.

2. Aasems Jacob and Aju Mathew, "End-of-Life Care and Opioid Use in India: Challenges and Opportunities," *Journal of Global Oncology* 3, no. 6 (January 25, 2017): 683–686.

3. M.R. Rajagopal, David E. Joranson, and Aaron M. Gilson, "Medical Use, Misuses, and Diversion of Opioids in India," *The Lancet* 358, no. 9276 (July 14, 2001): 139–143.

4. Jacob and Mathew, "End-of-Life Care."

5. A good account is in Keith Humphreys et al., "Responding to the Opioid Crisis in North America and Beyond: Recommendations of the Stanford–Lancet Commission," *The Lancet* 399, no. 10324 (February 5, 2022): 555–604.

6. On the Mexican drug trade in transition, see Benjamin T. Smith, *The Dope: The Real History of the Mexican Drug Trade* (New York: W. W. Norton, 2021).

7. The initial estimation was made in Laxmaiah Manchikanti and Angelie Singh, "Therapeutic Opioids: A Ten-Year Perspective on the Complexities and Complications of the Escalating Use, Abuse, and Nonmedical Use of Opioids," *Pain Physician* 11, no. 2 Suppl (March 2008): S63–88; for a more recent update, see Johnathan H. Duff et al., *Consumption of Prescription Opioids for Pain: A Comparison of Opioid Use in the United States and Other Countries*, Congressional Research Service, June 2, 2021.

8. Humphreys et al., "Responding to the Opioid Crisis."

9. Holly Hedegaard et al., "Drug Overdose Deaths in the United States, 1999–2020," NCHS Data Brief, no. 428 (National Center for Health Statistics, 2021).

10. Jan Hoffman, "Overdose Deaths Plummeted in 2024. Will Trump's Cuts Slow the Momentum?," *New York Times*, May 14, 2025.

11. On Canada, where the impact has been blunted by a universal health care system, see See Lisa Belzak and Jessica Halverson, "Evidence Synthesis—The Opioid Crisis in Canada: A National Perspective," *Health Promotion and Chronic Disease Prevention in Canada: Research, Policy and Practice* 38, no. 6 (June 2018): 224–233; Hance Clarke et al., "Canada's Hidden Opioid Crisis: The Health Care System's Inability to Manage High-Dose Opioid Patients," *Canadian Family Physician* 65, no. 9 (September 2019): 612–614; Amanda My Linh Quan et al., "Reporting on the Opioid Crisis (2000–2018): Role of *The Globe and Mail*, a Canadian English-Language Newspaper in Influencing Public Opinion," *Harm Reduction Journal* 17, no. 1 (November 30, 2020): 93.

12. See Raj Patel, *Stuffed and Starved: The Hidden Battle for the World Food System* (Brooklyn: Melville House, 2008).

13. Felicia M. Knaul et al., "The Lancet Commission on Palliative Care and Pain Relief—Findings, Recommendations, and Future Directions," *The Lancet Global Health* 6 (March 1, 2018): S5–S6, https://www.thelancet.com/journals/langlo/article/PIIS2214-109X(18)30082-2/fulltext.

Select Bibliography

MAJOR ARCHIVAL COLLECTIONS CONSULTED

India Office Records, British Library, London (IOR)
National Archives of India, New Delhi (NAI)
Pennsylvania State University, Harry J. Anslinger Papers
Records of the United States Department of State (RG 59)
Records of the Bureau of Narcotics, United States Treasury Department (RG 170)
Salt Research, Istanbul
Shree Natnagar Shodh Sansthan, Sitamau, Madhya Pradesh
United States National Archives, College Park, Maryland (USNA)
West Bengal State Archives, Kolkata, India

NEWSPAPERS

Aligarh Institute Gazette [Aligarh]
Arizona Miner [Prescott]
Business Standard [New Delhi]
Chicago Daily Tribune
Connecticut Journal [New Haven]
Cumhuriyet [Istanbul]
Deccan Herald [Bangalore]
Economic Times [Mumbai]
Far Eastern Economic Review [Hong Kong]
Firstpost [Mumbai]
Free Press Journal [Bombay]
The Hindu [Chennai]
Hindustan Times [New Delhi]
The Hindustani [Lucknow]
India Today [New Delhi]
Indian Express [Chennai]
Indu Prakash [Bombay]
Jam-e-Jamshed [Bombay]
Livemint [New Delhi]
Los Angeles Times
Mid-Day [Mumbai]
Milliyet [Istanbul]
Muslim [Islamabad]

National Herald [New Delhi]
Native Opinion [Bombay]
New York Times
New York Tribune
Oudh Akhbar [Lucknow]
Outlook [New Delhi]
Patriot [New Delhi]
Poona Vaibhav
Rural Carolinian [Charleston]
Selections from the Vernacular Newspapers Published in the Panjab, North-Western Provinces, Oudh, Central Provinces and Berar
Şalom Dergi [Istanbul]
Statesman [Calcutta]
Suhodh Sindhu [Allahabad]
Swarajya Magazine [Coimbatore]
Telegraph [Calcutta]
Vrit Dhara [Dhar, Malwa]
Washington Post
World Press Review

MEDICAL, AGRICULTURAL, AND COMMERCIAL JOURNALS

American Druggist and Pharmaceutical Record [New York]
American Journal of Pharmacy [Philadelphia]
Boston Medical and Surgical Journal [Boston]
Chemist and Druggist [London]
DeBow's Review [New Orleans]
The Dispensatory of the United States of America [Philadelphia]
Druggists' Circular and Chemical Gazette [New York]
France médicale [Paris]
Gazette du commerce [Paris]
Indian Farming [New Delhi]
Indian Journal of Genetics and Plant Breeding [New Delhi]
Indian Medical Gazette [Calcutta]
Journal of the American Medical Association [Chicago]
The Lancet [London]
Le Moniteur industriel [Paris]
Levant Trade Review [Constantinople]
Medical and Surgical Reporter [Philadelphia]
Merck's Archives of Materia Medica and Drug Therapy [New York]
Monthly Consular and Trade Reports [Washington]
New England Farmer [Boston]
Pacific Medical Journal [San Francisco]
The Pharmaceutical Review [Baltimore]
Practical Druggist [New York]
Revue commerciale du Levant [Constantinople]
Scientific American [New York]
Scientific Monthly [New York]

PUBLISHED SOURCES IN INDIAN LANGUAGES

Ramprasad Saheb, Babu, and Lala Ganeshdas Saheb. *Afeem ki Kheti* [Opium cultivation]. Neemuch: Gwalior Government, 1918.

Shukla, Shrilal. *Raag Darbari* [The courtly raga]. Allahabad: Lokbharati Prakashan, 1968.

Srivastava, Vinay. *Aphīm kṛṣhi kā itihās: Mālvā ke viśesh sandarbha meṃ* [The history of opium cultivation with special reference to Malwa]. Sitamau: Shree Natnagar Shodh Samsthan, 2007.

PUBLISHED SOURCES IN OTTOMAN TURKISH
AND MODERN TURKISH

Altan, Suna. *Osmanlı'dan Cumhuriyet'e Haşhaş: Sosyo-Ekonomik ve Dış Politik Boyutlarıyla (1909–1950)* [Poppy from the Ottoman Empire to the republic: socio-economic and foreign policy dimensions (1909–1950)]. Ankara: Sonçağ Yayınları, 2021.

Amasyan Efendi. *Hüdâvendigâr Vilâyeti Celîlesi Ziraat ve Nafia Müdürü Rif'atlû Amasyan Efendi'nin Afyon Tohumu Zir'aine Dâir Kaleme Aldigi Lâyîhadir* [A treatise on opium poppy cultivation, authored by the esteemed director of agriculture and public works of the sublime province of Hüdavendigar, Amasyan Efendi]. Istanbul: La Turquie Matbaası/ Matbaa-yi Âmîre, 1870.

"Bir Vilâyet Daru'l-Muallimininde Mesut Temâşalar: Bursa Daru'l-Muallimini Talebesi Mübezzer Makinasıyla Haşhaş Zira' Ederlerken [Happy scenes at a provincial teacher training college: students of Bursa Teachers' College cultivating poppies with a sowing machine]." April 1330 (1914), İBB Atatürk Kitaplığı.

Dışişleri Bakanlığı Belleteni [Bulletin of the Ministry of Foreign Affairs], no. 81 (June 1971): 141.

Erdinç, F. Cengiz. *Overdose Türkiye: Türkiye'de Eroin Kaçakçılığı, Bağımlılığı ve Politikalar* [Overdose Turkey: heroin smuggling, addiction, and policies in Turkey]. İstanbul: İletişim Yayınları, 2004.

Erhan, Çağrı. *Beyaz Savaş: Türk-Amerikan Ilişkilerinde Afyon Sorunu* [White war: the opium problem in Turkish-American relations]. İstanbul: Altınbaş Üniversitesi, 2018.

Erkal, Abdulkadir. "Divan Şiirinde Afyon ve Esrar [Opium and cannabis in Ottoman court poetry]." *A.Ü. Türkiyat Araştırmaları Enstitüsü Dergisi* 33 (2007): 25–60.

Erkal, Abdulkadir. *Osmanlı toplumunda ve edebiyatında afyon ve esrar* [Opium and cannabis in Ottoman society and literature]. Ankara: Birleşik Yayınevi, 2016.

Göker, Galip Bahtiyar. *Afyon: Türkiye istihsalatı: haşhaş ziraatı, ziraat mıntıkaları, Afyon istihsalî, istatistik, ahdî ve kanunî mevzuat* [Opium: Turkey's production: poppy cultivation, agricultural regions, opium production, statistics, contractual and legal legislation]. İstanbul: Matbaacılık ve Neşriyat Türk Anonim Şirketi, 1933.

Gülen, Ahmet. "Nihat Erim Hükûmetleri'nin Haşhaş Politikası [The poppy policy of the Nihat Erim governments]" *Cumhuriyet Tarihi Araştırmaları Dergisi* 15, no. 30 (Fall 2019): 363–389.

Haşhaş Ekim Bölgelerinde Tarımsal Gelirin Geliştirilmesi: Yapılacak Acil Işler Programı: Türk-Amerikan Müşterek Tarım Grubunun Tavsiyeleri [Improving farm income in the poppy region: a program for action: recommendations of the Joint Turkish/American Agricultural Team]. Ankara: Grup, 1972.

Haydar, Ali. *Haşhaş Ziraatı* [Poppy cultivation]. Hudavandekâr: Vilayet Matbaası, 1908.

Hilmi, Ahmet. *Afyonculuk* [Opium production]. Kastamonu: Kastamonu Matbaası, 1913.

Hilmi, Ahmet. *Kastamonu Vilayeti Ziraat Müdürü Ahmet Hilmi* [Director of Agriculture of the Kastamonu Province]. Kastamonu: Kastamonu Matbaası, 1913.

Incekara, Fethi. *Türkiye Haşhaş Çeşitleri ve Bunların Tohum ve Afyon Bakımından Değerleri* [Turkey hashish varieties and their values in terms of seeds and opium]. Ankara: Cankaya, 1949.

Kağıtçı, Mehmet Ali. *Afyon* [Opium]. Istanbul: Vakit Matbaası, 1960.

Kürçay, Ali. *Hasbaslarin Kültür Sekline Girmesinde Türk Çesitlerinin Mevki ve Rolü* [The role and importance of Turkish varieties for opium-poppy growing]. Ankara: Çankaya Printing Works, 1946.

Kürçay, Ali. *Haşhaş Yetiştirilmesi* [Poppy cultivation]. Ankara: Tarım Bakanlığı, 1962.

Nezihi, H. "Afyon ve Cemiyetiakvam [Opium and the League of Nations]." *İstanbul Ticaret ve Sanayi Odası Mecmuası* [Journal of the Istanbul Chamber of Commerce and Industry], no. 2 (January 1931): 50–53.

Nezihi, H. "Uyusturucn Maddeler Inhisars Hakkmnda Kanun [Law on the monopoly of narcotic substances]." *İstanbul Ticaret ve Sanayi Odası Mecmuası* [Journal of the Istanbul Chamber of Commerce and Industry], no. 7 (July 1933): 284–286.

Pasha, Sari. "Afyon [Opium]." Hazîne-i Evrak, November 1881.

Şahingiray, Özel. *Celal Bayar'ın Söylev ve Demeçleri*. İstanbul: Türkiye İş Bankası Kültür Yayınları, 1999.

Saka, Reşat. *Uyuşturucu maddeler: afyon, morfin, eroin, esrar, kokain hakkinda millî ve milletler arasi hukukî ve sosyal durum* [Narcotic substances: The national and international legal and social status of opium, morphine, heroin, cannabis, and cocaine]. İstanbul: Matbaasi, 1948.

Songar, Ayhan. *Haşhaş Meselesi ve Türkiye* [The poppy question and Turkey]. Istanbul: Hareket Yayınları, 1974.

Toprak, Zafer. *Türkiye'de Milli Iktisat, 1908–1918* [National economy in Turkey, 1908–1918]. Ankara: Yurt Yaylari, 1982.

Yildirim, Mehmet Ali. "Osmanlı'da Modern Ziraatın Gelişimine Katkı Sunan İki Ermeni Mütehassis [Two Armenian experts who contributed to the development of modern agriculture in the Ottoman Empire]." *Kilis 7 Aralık Üniversitesi Sosyal Bilimler Dergisi* 6, no. 12 (December 2016): 126–143.

Ziya, Mümtaz. "Afyon Meselesi [The opium question]" Kadro: Aylık Fikir Mecmuası (April 1932): 18–25.

PUBLISHED SOURCES IN EUROPEAN LANGUAGES

Aubergier, H. *Des Préparations d'opium Indigène de H. Aubergier, Approuvées Par l'Académie Impériale de Médecine*. Clermont: Hubler et Dubos, 1855.

Barbier, André. *Annales Pharmaceutiques Françaises* 5 (1947): 121.

Bensussan. "La Turquie." in *L'Opium: Considérations Générales, Histoire, Géographie, Chimie, Fabrication et Usage de l'Opium et Études Économiques, Sociales et Législatives* (Paris: Vigot Freres, 1946), 147–158.

Bonnemain, Bruno. "L'industrie pharmaceutique en France: le tournant décisif de 1915." *Revue D'histoire De La Pharmacie* 63, no. 388 (December 2015): 399–422.

Buchner, A. "Über die Versuche zur Beantwortung der Frage, ob die unreifen oder die reifen Mohnköpfe zum Arzneigebrauche den Vorzug verdienen?" *Annalen der Chemie und Pharmacie* 79, no. 3 (1851): 255–259.

Castellanos, Guillermo Valdés. *Historia del narcotráfico en México*. Madrid: Aguilar, 2013.

Charkauy, Mohamed Effendy. *École supérieure de Pharmacie de Paris: Thèse sur l'opium, etc.* Paris: Henri Plon, 1856.

Decharmes, Constantin. *Memoire sur l'opium indigène*. Amiens, France: Duval ed Herments, 1855.

Della Sudda, Georges. *Monographie des opiums de l'empire ottoman envoyés à l'exposition universelle de Paris*. Paris: Imprimerie Poitevin, 1867.

Du Titrage de l'opium, lettre à M. Favrot, rédacteur de la partie pharmaceutique de la "France médicale." Paris: Dubuisson, 1859.

Georgiadēs, Demetrios. *Smyrne Et L'Asie Mineure: Au Point De Vue économique Et Commercial*. Paris: Imprimerie Chaix, 1885.

Guibourt, Nicolas Jean-Baptiste Gaston. *Mémoire Sur Le Dosage de l'opium et Sur La Quantité de Morphine Que l'opium Doit Contenir*. Paris: n.p., 1862.

Hager, Hermann. *Commentar zur Pharmacopoea germanica*. Berlin: Julius Springer, 1874.

Hassoun, Th. *Le Siècle de Sa Majesté Impériale Le Sultan Abd-Ul-Hamid II*. Constantinople: Imprimerie Zareh, 1892.

Klockgether-Radke, A.P. "F. W. Sertürner und die Entdeckung des Morphins." *Anasthesiol Intensivmed Notfallmed Schmerzther* 37, no. 5 (May 2002): 244–249.

Landerer, X. "Über den Opiumhandel in Smyrna." *Neues Repertorium für Pharmacie* I (1852): 473–476.

Magendie, F. *Formulaire pour la préparation et l'emploi de plusieurs nouveaux médicaments* [French version referenced by Gregory translation].

Mallouf, Nassif, and Clément Huart. *Grammaire élémentaire de la langue turque*. Paris: E. Guilmoto, 1890.

Marchant, Alexandre. *L'Impossible prohibition: Drogues et toxicomanie en France 1945–2017*. Paris: Perrin, 2018.

Millant, Richard. *La culture du pavot et le commerce de l'opium en Turquie. Bibliothèque d'agriculture coloniale*. Paris: Augustin Challamel, 1913.

Nicolas, Michèle. "Deux personnalités du monde pharmaceutique dans l'Empire Ottoman." *Revue d'Histoire de la Pharmacie* 84, no. 312 (1996): 429–432.

Nicolas, Michèle. "La pharmacie d'officine ottomane." In *Histoire économique et sociale de l'Empire Ottoman et de la Turquie: 1326–1960: actes du sixième congrès international tenu à Aix-en-Provence du 1er au 4 juillet 1992*, edited by Daniel Panzac, 235–242. Paris: Peeters, 1995.

Nicolas, Michèle. "La pharmacie ottomane à Istanbul." *Revue d'Histoire de la Pharmacie* 90, no. 334 (2002): 257–270.

Réveil, Oscar. *Sur la culture du pavot a oeillette et sur l'extraction de l'opium indigène*. Paris: L. Martinet, 1857.

Scherzer, Karl, ed. *Smyrna. Mit besonderer Rücksicht auf die geographischen, Wirthschaftlichen und Intellectuellen verhältnisse von Vorder-Kleinasien*. Wien: A. Hölder, 1873.

Schneider, Franz Coelestin. "Opium (Laudanum, Meconium, Opium, Mohnsaft)." In *Pharmacognostischer Theil*, 410–414. Wien: G.J. Manz'schen Buchhandlung, 1874.

Thibout, Georges. *La question de l'opium à l'époque contemporaine*. Paris: G. Steinheil, 1912.

Toprak, Zafer. *Türkiye'de Milli Iktisat, 1908–1918* [National economy in Turkey 1908–1918]. Ankara: Yurt Yaylari, 1982.

Virchow, Rudolf, ed. *Canstatt's Jahresbericht Über Die Fortschritte Der Gesammten Medicin in Allen Ländern Im Jahre 1855*, vol. 5. Würzburg: Stahel'schen Buchhandlung, 1856.

Winkler, Eduard. *Pharmazeutische Warenkunde oder Handatlas der Pharmakologie.* Leipzig: Winter, 1857.

Zambaco Pacha, Démétrius Alexandre. *De la morphéomanie.* Paris: G. Masson, 1883.

PUBLISHED MATERIALS IN ENGLISH

Aasems Jacob, and Aju Mathew. "End-of-Life Care and Opioid Use in India: Challenges and Opportunities." *Journal of Global Oncology* 3, no. 6 (December 2017): 683–686.

Abdullah, Muhammad Faisal. "Trade and Cultivation of Opium in Malwa and Rajasthan During 1750–1900." PhD diss., Aligarh Muslim University, 2008.

Acker, Caroline Jean. "Addiction and the Laboratory: The Work of the National Research Council's Committee on Drug Addiction, 1928–1939." *Isis* 86, no. 2 (1995): 167–193.

Acker, Caroline Jean. *Creating the American Junkie: Addiction Research in the Classic Era of Narcotic Control.* Baltimore: Johns Hopkins University Press, 2002.

Acker, Caroline Jean. "From All-Purpose Anodyne to Marker of Deviance: Physicians' Attitudes Toward Opiates from 1890 to 1940." In *Drugs and Narcotics in History*, edited by Roy Porter and Mikuláš Teich, 114–132. Cambridge: Cambridge University Press, 1995.

Acker, Caroline Jean. "Planning and Serendipity in the Search for a Nonaddicting Opiate Analgesic." In *Medicines: The Inside Story*, edited by Gregory J. Higby and Elaine C. Stroud, 139–159. Madison: American Institute for the History of Pharmacy, 1997.

Adalet, Begüm. *Hotels and Highways: The Construction of Modernization Theory in Cold War Turkey.* Stanford, CA: Stanford University Press, 2020.

"Afyon-Opium [Opium-Opium]." *Farmakoloğ* 3, no. 5 (1957): 661–667.

Ahmad, Diana L. *The Opium Debate and Chinese Exclusion Laws in the Nineteenth-Century American West.* Reno: University of Nevada Press, 2011.

Ajithakumari, K., K. Sureshkumar, and M.R. Rajagopal. "Palliative Home Care: The Calicut Experience." *Palliative Medicine* 11, no. 6 (November 1997): 451–454.

Aktar, Ayhan. "Homogenising the Nation: Turkefying the Economy." In *Crossing the Aegean: An Appraisal of the 1923 Compulsory Population Exchange Between Greece and Turkey*, edited by Renée Hirschon, 90–93. Oxford: Berghahn Books, 2003.

Alexander, Joseph Gundry. *India's Opium Revenue: What It Is, and How It Should Be Dealt With.* London: P.S. King and Son, 1890.

Ali, Tariq Omar. *A Local History of Global Capital: Jute and Peasant Life in the Bengal Delta.* Princeton, NJ: Princeton University Press, 2018.

All India Coordinated Improvement Project on Medicinal and Aromatic Plants. *Proceedings of Second Workshop Held at Gujarat Agricultural University, Anand Campus, Anand, from November 1st to 4th, 1976.* New Delhi: Indian Agricultural Research Institute, 1976.

American Medical Association. "Press Release: AMA Meeting Will Seek Answers to Pending Shortage of Codeine." February 1975.

Amrith, Sunil. "Food and Welfare in India, c. 1900–1950." *Comparative Studies in Society and History* 50, no. 4 (2008): 1010–1035.

Anderson, Edward, and Patrick Clibbens. "'Smugglers of Truth': The Indian Diaspora, Hindu Nationalism, and the Emergency (1975–77)." *Modern Asian Studies* 52, no. 5 (June 2018): 1729–1773.

Anderson, Robert S. *Nucleus and Nation: Scientists, International Networks, and Power in India.* Chicago: University of Chicago Press, 2010.

Anglo-Oriental Society for the Suppression of the Opium Trade. *The Opium Revenue: Sir William Muir's Minute.* London, 1874.

Anslinger, Harry J., and William F. Tompkins. *The Traffic in Narcotics*. New York: Funk & Wagnalls, 1953.

Arias, Enrique Desmond, and Thomas Grisaffi, eds. *Cocaine: From Coca Fields to the Streets*. Durham, NC: Duke University Press, 2021.

Arnold, David. "Agriculture and 'Improvement' in Early Colonial India: A Pre-History of Development." *Journal of Agrarian Change* 5, no. 4 (2005): 505–525.

Arnold, David. *Colonizing the Body: State Medicine and Epidemic Disease in Nineteenth-Century India*. Berkeley: University of California Press, 1993.

Arnold, David. "Nehruvian Science and Postcolonial India." *Isis* 104, no. 2 (June 2013): 360–370.

Avci, Ayşegül. "Yankee Levantine: David Offley and Ottoman-American Relations in the Early Nineteenth Century." PhD diss., Ekonomi ve Sosyal Bilimler Enstitüsü, Bilkent University, 2019.

Balasubramanian, Aditya. *Toward a Free Economy: Swatantra and Opposition Politics in Democratic India*. Princeton, NJ: Princeton University Press, 2023.

Baltzell, E. Digby. *Philadelphia Gentlemen: The Making of a National Upper Class*. Piscataway, NJ: Transaction Publishers, 2011.

Banerjea, Pramathanath. *Study of Indian Economics*. London: MacMillan, 1911.

Barakat, Nora. *Bedouin Bureaucrats: Mobility and Property in the Ottoman Empire*. Stanford, CA: Stanford University Press, 2023.

Barbier, André. "The Extraction of Opium Alkaloids." Vienna: United Nations Office on Drugs and Crime, 1951.

Barop, Helena. *Mohnblumenkriege: Die globale Drogenpolitik der USA 1950–1979* [Poppy wars: the global drug policy of the United States, 1950–1979]. Göttingen: Wallstein Verlag GmbH, 2021.

Barton, Patricia. "The Great Quinine Fraud: Legality Issues in the 'Non-Narcotic' Drug Trade in British India." *Social History of Alcohol and Drugs* 22, no. 1 (2007): 6–25.

Basset, Ross Knox. *The Technological Indian*. Cambridge, MA: Harvard University Press, 2016.

Baszanger, Isabelle. *Inventing Pain Medicine: From the Laboratory to the Clinic*. New Brunswick, NJ: Rutgers University Press, 1998.

Bauer, Rolf. *The Peasant Production of Opium in Nineteenth-Century India*. Leiden, the Netherlands: Brill, 2019.

Baumler, Alan. *The Chinese and Opium Under the Republic: Worse than Floods and Wild Beasts*. Albany: State University of New York Press, 2012.

Baumler, Alan. *Modern China and Opium: A Reader*. Ann Arbor: University of Michigan Press, 2001.

Bayer, Istvan. "János Kabay and the Poppy Straw Process: Commemoration on the 50th Anniversary of His Death." *Acta pharmaceutica Hungarica* 57, nos. 3–4 (1987): 105–110.

Bayly, C.A. *Indian Society and the Making of the British Empire*. Cambridge: Cambridge University Press, 1987.

Bayly, C.A. *Rulers, Townsmen, and Bazaars: North Indian Society in the Age of British Expansion, 1770–1870*. Oxford: Oxford University Press, 1988.

Beck, Charles R.R. "Novelties in Opium Farming and Commercial Values." *The Pharmaceutical Review* 1, no. 4 (April 1892): 79–80.

Beckert, Sven. *Empire of Cotton: A New History of Global Capitalism*. New York: Vintage, 2015.

Beckert, Sven, Ulbe Bosma, Mindi Schneider, and Eric Vanhaute. "Commodity Frontiers and the Transformation of the Global Countryside: A Research Agenda." *Journal of Global History* 16, no. 3 (November 2021): 435–450.

Bello, David. *Opium and the Limits of Empire: Drug Prohibition in the Chinese Interior, 1729–1850*. Cambridge, MA: Harvard University Asia Center, 2005.

Belzak, Lisa, and Jessica Halverson. "Evidence Synthesis—The Opioid Crisis in Canada: A National Perspective." *Health Promotion and Chronic Disease Prevention in Canada: Research, Policy and Practice* 38, no. 6 (June 2018): 224–233.

Berg, Maxine. "Commodity Frontiers: Concepts and History." *Journal of Global History* 16, no. 3 (November 2021): 451–455.

Berger, Henry W. *St. Louis and Empire: 250 Years of Imperial Quest and Urban Crisis*. Carbondale: Southern Illinois University Press, 2015.

Berger, Rachel. *Ayurveda Made Modern: Political Histories of Indigenous Medicine in North India, 1900–1955*. Basingstoke, UK: Palgrave Macmillan, 2013.

Berridge, Virginia, and Griffith Edwards. *Opium and the People: Opiate Use in Nineteenth-Century England*. New Haven, CT: Yale University Press, 1987.

Bewley-Taylor, David R. *The United States and International Drug Control, 1909–1997*. London: A&C Black, 2002.

Birdal, Murat. *The Political Economy of Ottoman Public Debt: Insolvency and European Financial Control in the Late Nineteenth Century*. London: Bloomsbury, 2010.

Bisheswar, Nameirakpam. *Down with Heroin War*. Imphal, India: Pax Publications, 1985.

Black, Megan A. *The Global Interior: Mineral Frontiers and American Power*. Cambridge, MA: Harvard University Press, 2018.

Booth, Martin. *Opium: A History*. New York: St. Martin's Griffin, 1999.

Borkar, G. *Health in Independent India*. New Delhi: Ministry of Health, Government of India, 1961.

Bourke, Joanna. *The Story of Pain: From Prayer to Painkillers*. Oxford: Oxford University Press, 2017.

Bradford, James Tharin. *Poppies, Politics, and Power: Afghanistan and the Global History of Drugs and Diplomacy*. Ithaca, NY: Cornell University Press, 2020.

Brady, Linda S., and Miles Herkenham. "Candace B. Pert." *Neuropsychopharmacology* 38, no. 13 (December 2013): 2730.

Bray, Francesca. *The Rice Economies: Technology and Development in Asian Societies*. Berkeley: University of California Press, 1986.

Breen, Benjamin. *The Age of Intoxication: Origins of the Global Drug Trade*. Philadelphia: University of Pennsylvania Press, 2021.

Britto, Lina. *Marijuana Boom: The Rise and Fall of Colombia's First Drug Paradise*. Berkeley: University of California Press, 2020.

Brook, Timothy, ed. *Opium Regimes: China, Britain, and Japan, 1839–1952*. Berkeley: University of California Press, 2000.

Brown, J.B. "Politics of the Poppy: The Society for the Suppression of the Opium Trade, 1874–1916." *Journal of Contemporary History* 8, no. 3 (1973): 97–111.

Brown, Shannon. "The Partially Opened Door: Limitations on Economic Change in China in the 1860s." *Modern Asian Studies* 12, no. 2 (April 1978): 177–192.

Bruun, Kettil, Lynn Pan, and Ingemar Rexed. *The Gentlemen's Club: International Control of Drugs and Alcohol*. Chicago: University of Chicago Press, 1975.

Burger, Angela S. "Narcotic Drugs: Security Threat or Interest to South Asian States?" In *South Asia Approaches the Millennium*, edited by Marvin G. Weinbaum and Chetan Kumar, 175. San Francisco: Westview Press, 1995.

Burhop, Carsten. "Pharmaceutical Research in Wilhelmine Germany: The Case of E. Merck." *Pharmacy in History* 51, no. 3 (2009): 104–124.

Çakır, Armağan Emre. *The United States and Turkey's Path to Europe: Hands Across the Table*. Abingdon: Routledge, 2015.

Calangutcar, Archana. "Marwaris in Opium Trade: A Journey to Bombay in the 19th Century." *Proceedings of the Indian History Congress* 67 (2006): 745–753.

Campbell, Nancy D., J.P. Olsen, and Luke Walden. *The Narcotic Farm: The Rise and Fall of America's First Prison for Drug Addicts*. Lexington, KY: South Limestone, 2021.

Campbell, Neil A. "A Conversation with Candace Pert." *The American Biology Teacher* 54, no. 6 (September 1992): 357–360.

Carney, Judith A. *Black Rice: The African Origins of Rice Cultivation in the Americas*. Cambridge, MA: Harvard University Press, 2002.

Carpenter, George W. "Observations and Experiments on Opium." *American Journal of Science and Arts* 13, no. 1 (January 1828): 17.

Carroll, Lucy. "The Temperance Movement in India: Politics and Social Reform." *Modern Asian Studies* 10, no. 3 (1976): 417–447.

Carter, Raymond H.A. *Pharmacodépendance et pharmacodélinquance*. Paris: Chiron, 1990.

Case, Anne, and Angus Deaton. *Deaths of Despair and the Future of Capitalism*. Princeton, NJ: Princeton University Press, 2020.

Central Intelligence Agency. *The World Opium Situation*. Washington, DC: Central Intelligence Agency, October 1970.

Cezar, Yavuz. "The Role of the Sarrafs in Ottoman Finance and Economy in the Eighteenth and Nineteenth Centuries." In *Frontiers of Ottoman Studies*, vol.1: *State, Province, and the West*, edited by Colin Imber and Keiko Kiyotaki, 62–76. London: I.B. Tauris, 2005.

Chadha, K.L., and B. Choudhury, eds. *Ornamental Horticulture in India: Commemorative Volume Released on the Eightieth Birthday of Dr B.P. Pal*. New Delhi: Indian Council of Agricultural Research, 1986.

Chang, Gordon H. *Ghosts of Gold Mountain: The Epic Story of the Chinese Who Built the Transcontinental Railroad*. Boston: Mariner Books, 2019.

Chapman, Michael E. "Taking Business to the Tiger's Gate: Thomas Handasyd Perkins and the Boston-Smyrna-Canton Opium Trade of the Early Republic." *Journal of the Royal Asiatic Society Hong Kong Branch* 52 (2012): 7–28.

Chen, Yong. *Chinese San Francisco, 1850–1943: A Trans-Pacific Community*. Stanford, CA: Stanford University Press, 2000.

Chesson, Frederick William. *The Opium Trade Between India and China in Some of Its Present Aspects*. London: William Tweedie, 1870.

Chung, Tan. "The Britain-China-India Trade Triangle (1771–1840)." *The Indian Economic & Social History Review* 11, no. 4 (January 1974): 411–431.

Clark, Claire D. *The Recovery Revolution: The Battle over Addiction Treatment in the United States*. New York: Columbia University Press, 2017.

Clarke, Hance, James Bao, Aliza Weinrib, Ruth E. Dubin, and Meldon Kahan. "Canada's Hidden Opioid Crisis: The Health Care System's Inability to Manage High-Dose Opioid Patients." *Canadian Family Physician* 65, no. 9 (September 2019): 612–614.

Collins, John. *Legalising the Drug Wars: A Regulatory History of UN Drug Control*. Cambridge: Cambridge University Press, 2021.

Colvard, Robert Eric. "A World Without Drink: Temperance in Modern India, 1880–1940." PhD diss., University of Iowa, 2013.

Courtwright, David T. *Dark Paradise: A History of Opiate Addiction in America*. Cambridge, MA: Harvard University Press, 2001.

Courtwright, David T. "The Hidden Epidemic: Opiate Addiction and Cocaine Use in the South, 1860–1920." *The Journal of Southern History* 49, no. 1 (February 1983): 57–72.

Coxe, John Redman, and E. Staples. "Papaver." In *The American Dispensatory, Containing the Natural, Chemical, Pharmaceutical and Medical History of the Different Substances Employed in Medicine*, edited by John Redman Coxe, 510–529. Philadelphia: Carey & Lea, 1831.

Cramer, Tobias. "Building the 'World's Pharmacy': The Rise of the German Pharmaceutical Industry, 1871–1914." *Business History Review* 89, no. 1 (April 2015): 43–73.

Crooke, William. *Materials for a Rural and Agricultural Glossary of the Northwestern Provinces and Oudh*. Allahabad, India: North-western provinces and Oudh government Press, 1879.

Daemmrich, Arthur. "Pharmaceutical Manufacturing in America: A Brief History." *Pharmacy in History* 59, no. 3 (2017): 63–72.

Das, Shinjini. *Vernacular Medicine in Colonial India: Family, Market and Homoeopathy*. Cambridge: Cambridge University Press, 2019.

De, Rohit. *The People's Constitution: The Everyday Life of Law in the Indian Republic*. Princeton, NJ: Princeton University Press, 2018.

Demirci, Fatih. "Kadro Hareketi ve Kadrocular [Kadro movement and Kadro members]." *Dumlupınar Üniversitesi Sosyal Bilimler Dergisi*, no. 15 (August 2006): 35–54.

Deora, Bharat. "Opium Smuggling into British India from Rajputana." *Proceedings of the Indian History Congress* 80 (2019): 749–757.

Derks, Hans. *History of the Opium Problem: The Assault on the East, ca. 1600–1950*. Leiden, the Netherlands: Brill, 2012.

Deshpande, Anirudh. "An Historical Overview of Opium Cultivation and Changing State Attitudes Towards the Crop in India, 1878–2000 A.D." *Studies in History* 25, no. 1 (January 2009): 120–123.

de Wilde, Roeland M. *Opium Poppy Husk Traders in Rajasthan: The Lives and Work of Businessmen in the Contemporary Indian Opium Industry*. PhD diss., London School of Economics, 2014.

Dietrich, Christopher R.W., ed. *Diplomacy and Capitalism: The Political Economy of U.S. Foreign Relations*. Philadelphia: University of Pennsylvania Press, 2022.

Dikötter, Frank, Lars Laamann, and Zhou Xun. *Narcotic Culture: A History of Drugs in China*. Chicago: University of Chicago Press, 2004.

Dolbee, Samuel. *Locusts of Power: Borders, Empire, and Environment in the Modern Middle East*. Cambridge: Cambridge University Press, 2023.

Dolin, Eric Jay. *When America First Met China: An Exotic History of Tea, Drugs, and Money in the Age of Sail*. New York: Liveright, 2013.

Dormandy, Thomas. *The Worst of Evils: The Fight Against Pain*. New Haven, CT: Yale University Press, 2006.

Duffy, John. *Epidemics in Colonial America*. Baton Rouge: Louisiana State University, 1953.

Dupont, Robert L. "The Drug Abuse Decade." *Journal of Drug Issues* 8, no. 2 (1978): 173–187.

Dutt, Romesh Chunder. *The Economic History of India in the Victorian Age*. London: K. Paul, Trench, Trübner, 1906.

Dyck, Erika, and Chris Elcock, eds. *Expanding Mindscapes: A Global History of Psychedelics*. Cambridge, MA: The MIT Press, 2023.

Eacott, Jonathan. *Selling Empire: India in the Making of Britain and America, 1600–1830*. Chapel Hill: University of North Carolina Press, 2016.

Eddy, Nathan B. *The National Research Council Involvement in the Opiate Problem*. Washington, DC: National Academies Press, 1973.

Eddy, Nathan B., and Everette L. May. "The Search for a Better Analgesic." *Science* 181, no. 4098 (1973): 407–414.

Ekbladh, David. *The Great American Mission: Modernization and the Construction of an American World Order*. Princeton, NJ: Princeton University Press, 2010.

Emdād-ul Haq, M. *Drugs in South Asia: From the Opium Trade to the Present Day*. Basingstoke, UK: Palgrave Macmillan, 2000.

Emre Erdinç, F. Cengiz. *Overdose Turkiye: Türkiye'de Eroin Kaçakçılığı, Bağımlılığı ve Politikalar* [Overdose Turkey: heroin trafficking, addiction, and policies in Turkey]. İstanbul: İletişim Yayınları, 2004.

Engerman, David C. *Modernization from the Other Shore: American Intellectuals and the Romance of Russian Development*. Cambridge, MA: Harvard University Press, 2003.

Engerman, David C. *The Price of Aid: The Economic Cold War in India*. Cambridge, MA: Harvard University Press, 2018.

Engerman, David C., ed. *Staging Growth: Modernization, Development, and the Global Cold War*. Amherst: University of Massachusetts Press, 2003.

Epstein, Edward Jay. *Agency of Fear: Opioids and Political Power in America*. New York: Verso, 1990.

Evered, Kyle T. "'Poppies Are Democracy!' A Critical Geopolitics of Opium Eradication and Reintroduction in Turkey." *Geographical Review* 101, no. 3 (2011): 306.

"Explanatory Memorandum on the Budget of the Central Government for 1949–50." New Delhi: Government of India Press, 1949.

Fahey, David M., and Padma Manian. "Poverty and Purification: The Politics of Gandhi's Campaign for Prohibition." *The Historian* 67, no. 3 (2005): 489–506.

Fairbairn, J.W., and F. Hakim. "Papaver Bracteatum Lindl.: A New Plant Source of Opiates." *The Journal of Pharmacy and Pharmacology* 25, no. 5 (May 1973): 353–358.

Farooqui, Amar. "The Global Career of Indian Opium and Local Destinies." *Almanack*, no. 14 (December 2016): 52–73.

Farooqui, Amar. "Opium as a Household Remedy in Nineteenth-Century Western India." In *The Social History of Health and Medicine in Colonial India*, edited by Biswamoy Pati and Mark Harrison, 229–237. Abingdon, UK: Routledge, 2008.

Federico, Giovanni. *An Economic History of the Silk Industry, 1830–1930*. Cambridge: Cambridge University Press, 1997.

Fichter, James. *So Great a Proffit: How the East Indies Trade Transformed Anglo-American Capitalism*. Cambridge, MA: Harvard University Press, 2010.

First Report of the Royal Commission on Opium: With Minutes of Evidence and Appendices. 6 vols. London: Eyre & Spottiswoode for HM Stationery Office, 1895.

Fischer-Tiné, Harald, and Jana Tschurenev, eds. *A History of Alcohol and Drugs in Modern South Asia: Intoxicating Affairs*. London: Routledge, 2014.

Fist, A.J. "The Tasmanian Poppy Industry: A Case Study of the Application of Science and Technology." Presented at the Australian Agronomy Conference, Westbury, Tasmania, 2001.

Foster, Anne L. *The Long War on Drugs*. Durham, NC: Duke University Press, 2023.

Foster, Anne L. "Prohibition as Superiority: Policing Opium in South-East Asia, 1898–1925." *The International History Review* 22, no. 2 (2000): 253–273.

Framke, Maria. "Internationalizing the Indian War on Opium: Colonial Policy, the Nationalist Movement and the League of Nations." In *A History of Alcohol and Drugs in*

Modern South Asia: Intoxicating Affairs, edited by Harald Fischer-Tiné and Jana Tschurenev, 155–171. London: Routledge, 2014.

Frappell, Brian. "Fifty Years of Poppies in Tasmania: The First Ten Years, 1960 to 1970." *Papers and Proceedings: Tasmanian Historical Research Association* 57, no. 2 (2010): 73–79.

Frydl, Kathleen J. *The Drug Wars in America, 1940–1973*. Cambridge: Cambridge University Press, 2013.

Frydl, Kathleen J. "The Pharma Cartel." In *The War on Drugs: A History*, edited by David Farber, 303–342. New York: New York University Press, 2021.

Fullilove, Courtney. *The Profit of the Earth: The Global Seeds of American Agriculture*. Chicago: University of Chicago Press, 2017.

Galanté, Abraham. *Les Juifs d'Izmir (Smyrne), Histoire des Juifs d'Anatolie*. Istanbul: Babok, 1937.

Gardner, Lloyd C. *Imperial America: American Foreign Policy Since 1898*. New York: Harcourt Brace Jovanovich, 1976.

Gavit, John Palmer. *Opium*. New York: Brentano, 1927.

Gery, P. Guy. "Vital Signs: Changes in Opioid Prescribing in the United States, 2006–2015." *Morbidity and Mortality Weekly Report* 66 (2017): 697–704.

Ghiabi, Maziyar. *Drugs Politics: Managing Disorder in the Islamic Republic of Iran*. Cambridge: Cambridge University Press, 2019.

Ghiabi, Maziyar, ed. *Power and Illicit Drugs in the Global South*. London: Routledge, 2020.

Gilman, Nils. *Mandarins of the Future: Modernization Theory in Cold War America*. Baltimore: Johns Hopkins University Press, 2003.

Gimbel, J. "The American Exploitation of German Technical Know-How After World War II." *Political Science Quarterly* 105, no. 2 (1990): 295.

Gingeras, Ryan. *Heroin, Organized Crime, and the Making of Modern Turkey*. Oxford: Oxford University Press, 2014.

Glen, Andrew. "What Attitudes About Opium Were Driving the Government of India's Policies Between 1857–1906?" PhD diss., University of Strathclyde, 2018.

Gootenberg, Paul. *Andean Cocaine: The Making of a Global Drug*. Chapel Hill: University of North Carolina Press, 2008.

Gootenberg, Paul, ed. *Cocaine: Global Histories*. Abingdon, UK: Routledge, 1999.

Gootenberg, Paul. "Introduction: A New Global History of Drugs." In *The Oxford Handbook of Global Drug History*, edited by Paul Gootenberg, 1–20. Oxford: Oxford University Press, 2022.

Gortler, Leon. "Merck in America: The First 70 Years from Fine Chemicals to Pharmaceutical Giant." *Bulletin for the History of Chemistry* 25, no. 1 (2000): 1–9.

Gratien, Chris. *The Unsettled Plain: An Environmental History of the Late Ottoman Frontier*. Stanford, CA: Stanford University Press, 2022.

Gray, Elizabeth Kelly. *Habit Forming: Drug Addiction in America, 1776–1914*. New York: Oxford University Press, 2022.

Gray-Schofield, Lynn. "Trends in Wildlife Trade from India to the United States." World Wildlife Fund, 1983.

Grisaffi, Thomas. *Coca Yes, Cocaine No: How Bolivia's Coca Growers Reshaped Democracy*. Durham, NC: Duke University Press, 2019.

Guibourt, Nicolas Jean-Baptiste Gaston. *Mémoire Sur Le Dosage de l'opium et Sur La Quantité de Morphine Que l'opium Doit Contenir*. Paris, 1862.

Gupta, Devyani. "'Black Mail': Networks of Opium and Postal Exchange in Nineteenth-Century India." *Literature & History* 29, no. 1 (May 2020): 78–96.

Gürsoy, Özgür Burçak. "Losing Wealth or Restricting the Poison? Changing Opium Policies in Early Republican Turkey, 1923–1945." *Historia Agraria* 61 (December 2013): 29–71.

Hariciye Vekâleti [Department of State]. Republic of Turkey. "Control of Narcotic Drugs in Turkey." Geneva: League of Nations, 1931.

Hartmann, Heinrich. "Meeting Again at Tahirova: German Expertise in Turkish Agriculture in the 20th Century." *Contemporary European History* 32, no. 4 (2023): 441–458.

Hathi, Jaisukhlal, ed. *Report of the Committee on Drugs and Pharmaceutical Industry*. New Delhi: Ministry of Petroleum & Chemicals, Government of India, 1975.

Hattox, Ralph S. *Coffee and Coffeehouses: The Origins of a Social Beverage in the Medieval Near East*. Seattle: University of Washington Press, 1985.

Hayes, Peter. *Industry and Ideology: IG Farben in the Nazi Era*. Cambridge: Cambridge University Press, 1987.

Hecht, Gabrielle. *Being Nuclear: Africans and the Global Uranium Trade*. Cambridge, MA: MIT Press, 2014.

Hedegaard, Holly, Arialdi M. Miniño, Merianne Rose Spencer, and Margaret Warner. "Drug Overdose Deaths in the United States, 1999–2020." *NCHS Data Brief*, no. 428. Hyattsville, MD: National Center for Health Statistics, 2021.

Herzberg, David. *White Market Drugs: Big Pharma and the Hidden History of Addiction in America*. Chicago: University of Chicago Press, 2020.

Hoganson, Kristin L., and Jay Sexton, eds. *Crossing Empires: Taking U.S. History into Transimperial Terrain*. Durham, NC: Duke University Press, 2020.

Hopkins, A.G. *American Empire: A Global History*. Princeton, NJ: Princeton University Press, 2018.

Hosie, Alexander. *On the Trail of the Opium Poppy: A Narrative of Travel in the Chief Opium-Producing Provinces of China*. Boston: Small Maynard & Co., 1914.

Husain, Faisal H. "In the Bellies of the Marshes: Water and Power in the Countryside of Ottoman Baghdad." *Environmental History* 19, no. 4 (2014): 638–664.

Husain, Faisal H. *Rivers of the Sultan: The Tigris and Euphrates in the Ottoman Empire*. New York: Oxford University Press, 2021.

Immerwahr, Daniel. *How to Hide an Empire: A History of the Greater United States*. New York: Picador, 2019.

IMS Pharmaceutical Marketletter, February 2, 1976, 6.

The Indian Opium Revenue: Its Nature and Effects. London: Yates and Alexander, 1874.

Indian Trade Journal 216, no. 5 (1961): 264.

Inglis, Lucy. *Milk of Paradise: A History of Opium*. New York: Pegasus, 2019.

International Narcotics Control Board. *Demand and Supply of Opiates for Medical and Scientific Needs: Report of the International Narcotics Control Board for 1980*. Vienna: International Narcotics Control Board, 1981.

International Narcotics Control Board. *Report of the International Narcotics Control Board for 1978*. New York: United Nations, 1978.

International Narcotics Control Board. *Report of the International Narcotics Control Board for 1979*. New York: United Nations, 1979.

International Narcotics Control Board. *Report of the International Narcotics Control Board for 1996*. Vienna: United Nations, 1997.

Işık, Mehmet. *Madde Kullanımı ve Stratejik İletişim* [Substance use and strategic communication]. Ankara: Sage Yayıncılık, 2013.

Issawi, Charles. *The Economic History of Turkey 1800–1914*. Chicago: University of Chicago Press, 1980.

Jack, David. "Obituary: Frederick ('Eric') Randall Smith." Edinburgh: Royal Society of Edinburgh, 1994.

Jeffreys, Julius. *The British Army in India*. London: Longman, Brown, Green, Longmans & Roberts, 1858.

Johnson, Kendall. *The New Middle Kingdom: China and the Early American Romance of Free Trade*. Baltimore: Johns Hopkins University Press, 2017.

Jones, B.W. "The Use of Demerol as an Anesthetic Agent." *AANA Journal* 42, no. 5 (October 1974): 439–446.

Jones, Geoffrey. *Merchants to Multinationals: British Trading Companies in the Nineteenth and Twentieth Centuries*. Oxford: Oxford University Press, 2000.

Jones, Jonathan S. *Opium Slavery: Civil War Veterans and America's First Opioid Crisis*. Chapel Hill: University of North Carolina Press, 2025.

Journal de Pharmacie et des Sciences Accessoires 13 (1827): 31–32.

Jovanović, Vladan. "Jugoslavensko-američka opijumska suradnja, 1929–1941 godine [Yugoslav-American opium cooperation, 1929–1941]." *Časopis za suvremenu povijest* 50, no. 1 (May 25, 2018): 35–65.

Kağıtçı, Mehmet Ali. *Afyon* [Opium]. Istanbul: Vakit Matbaası, 1960.

Kaicker, U.S., and B. Choudhury. "Hybrids of Opium Poppy (Papaver somniferum L.) with Changed Morphine Alkaloid Content." *Acta Horticulturae* 132 (1983): 197–202.

Kaicker, U.S., B. Singh, and B. Choudhury. "Try Your Hand at Black Gold-Opium Poppy." *Indian Horticulture* 20, no. 3 (October/December 1975): 7, 9, 23.

Kâmran Serif. *Afyon Türkiyede ve dünyada* [Opium in Turkey and the world]. Ankara: Devlet Matbaası, 1934.

Kane, Harry Hubbell. *Opium-Smoking in America and China: A Study of Its Prevalence, and Effects, Immediate and Remote, on the Individual and the Nation*. New York: G.P. Putnam's Sons, 1882.

Keefe, Patrick Radden. *Empire of Pain: The Secret History of the Sackler Dynasty*. New York: Doubleday, 2021.

Kim, Diana. *Empires of Vice: The Rise of Opium Prohibition Across Southeast Asia*. Princeton, NJ: Princeton University Press, 2020.

Kinder, Douglas Clark. "Bureaucratic Cold Warrior: Harry J. Anslinger and Illicit Narcotics Traffic." *Pacific Historical Review* 50, no. 2 (1981): 169–191.

Kinder, Douglas Clark, and William O. Walker. "Stable Force in a Storm: Harry J. Anslinger and United States Narcotic Foreign Policy, 1930–1962." *The Journal of American History* 72, no. 4 (1986): 908–927.

Klingensmith, Daniel. *"One Valley and a Thousand": Dams, Nationalism, and Development*. New Delhi: Oxford University Press, 2007.

Klinger, Julie Michelle. *Rare Earth Frontiers: From Terrestrial Subsoils to Lunar Landscapes*. Ithaca, NY: Cornell University Press, 2018.

Koram, Kojo, ed. *The War on Drugs and the Global Colour Line*. London: Pluto Press, 2019.

Kramer, Paul A. "Embedding Capital: Political-Economic History, the United States, and the World." *The Journal of the Gilded Age and Progressive Era* 15, no. 3 (July 2016): 331–362.

Kramer, Paul A. "Power and Connection: Imperial Histories of the United States in the World." *American Historical Review* 116 (2011): 1348–1391.

Kudaisya, Medha. "India's Merchant Communities." In *Oxford Research Encyclopedia of Asian History* (online), 2022. https://doi.org/10.1093/acrefore/9780190277727.013.606.

Kudaisya, Medha. "The Promise of Partnership: Indian Business, the State, and the Bombay Plan of 1944." *Business History Review* 88 (2014): 97–131.

Kumar, Krishna, Ernest Carter, and Stan Samuelson. *A Review of AID's Narcotics Control Development Assistance Programme, Special Study 29*. Washington, DC: United States Agency for International Development Evaluation, 1996.

Kumar, Prakash. *Indigo Plantations and Science in Colonial India*. Cambridge: Cambridge University Press, 2012.

Kurttepeli, Salahaddin Ahmet. "The Principal Export Articles of Turkey from the Commercial Point of View." MA thesis, University of Southern California, 1939.

Kyros, Peter N., James F. Hastings, and Lou Frey Jr. *Report by Members of the Committee on Interstate and Foreign Commerce, Concerning Narcotic Enforcement Efforts in Hong Kong, Thailand, Burma, India, Lebanon, Greece, Turkey, France, and the Netherlands*. Washington, DC: United States Government Printing Office, 1973.

LaFeber, Walter. *The New Empire: An Interpretation of American Expansion, 1860–1898*. Ithaca, NY: Cornell University Press, 1963.

Lamour, Catherine, and Michel R. Lamberti. *The International Connection: Opium from Growers to Pushers*. New York: Pantheon Books, 1974a.

Lamour, Catherine, and Michel R. Lamberti. *The Second Opium War*. London: Lane, 1974b.

Lande, Adolf. "The Single Convention on Narcotic Drugs, 1961." *International Organization* 16, no. 4 (1962): 776–797.

Lane, Edward William. *The Manners and Customs of the Modern Egyptians*. London: J.M. Dent, 1836.

Latham, Michael E. *Modernization as Ideology: American Social Science and "Nation Building" in the Kennedy Era*. Chapel Hill: University of North Carolina Press, 2006.

Latham, Michael E. *The Right Kind of Revolution: Modernization, Development, and U.S. Foreign Policy from the Cold War to the Present*. Ithaca, NY: Cornell University Press, 2011.

League of Nations. *Traffic in Opium and Other Dangerous Drugs: Annual Reports of Governments for the Year 1942*. Geneva: League of Nations, 1946.

Leigh, John. *An Experimental Inquiry into the Properties of Opium: And Its Effects on Living Subjects*. Edinburgh: C. Elliot, 1786.

Lembke, Anna. *Drug Dealer, MD: How Doctors Were Duped, Patients Got Hooked, and Why It's So Hard to Stop*. Baltimore: Johns Hopkins University Press, 2016.

Liebenau, Jonathan M. "Scientific Ambitions: The Pharmaceutical Industry, 1900–1920." *Pharmacy in History* 27, no. 1 (1985): 3–11.

Lin, Man-houng. "Late Qing Perceptions of Native Opium." *Harvard Journal of Asiatic Studies* 64, no. 1 (2004): 117–144.

Lindsay-Poland, John. *Plan Colombia: U.S. Ally Atrocities and Community Activism*. Durham, NC: Duke University Press, 2018.

Livingston, Julie. "Cattle/Beef." In *Self-Devouring Growth: A Planetary Parable as Told From Southern Africa*, 35–60. Durham, NC: Duke University Press, 2019.

Livingston, William Kenneth. *Pain and Suffering*. Seattle: IASP Press, 1998.

Lloyd, John Uri. *A Treatise on Opium and Its Compounds*. Cincinnati: Lloyd Brothers, 1908.

Lodwick, Kathleen L. *Crusaders Against Opium: Protestant Missionaries in China, 1874–1917*. Lexington: University Press of Kentucky, 1996.

Logan, Michael. *The Lessening Stream: An Environmental History of the Santa Cruz River*. Tucson: University of Arizona Press, 2006.

Lorenz, Fredrick Walter. "The 'Second Egypt': Cretan Refugees, Agricultural Development, and Frontier Expansion in Ottoman Cyrenaica, 1897–1904." *International Journal of Middle East Studies* 53, no. 1 (February 2021): 89–105.

Lowes, Peter. *The Genesis of International Narcotics Control*. Geneva: Librairie Droz, 1966.

Lurtz, Casey Marina. *From the Grounds Up: Building an Export Economy in Southern Mexico*. Stanford, CA: Stanford University Press, 2019.

MacArthur-Seal, Daniel-Joseph. "The Trans-Asian Pathways of 'Oriental Products': Navigating the Prohibition of Narcotics Between Turkey, China, and Japan, 1918–1938." *Modern Asian Studies* 56, no. 1 (January 2022): 207–249.

MacFarlane, Charles. *Constantinople in 1828: A Residence of Sixteen Months in the Turkish Capital and Provinces: With an Account of the Present State of the Naval and Military Power, and of the Resources of the Ottoman Empire*, vol. 2. London: Saunders and Otley, 1829.

Macy, Beth. *Dopesick: Dealers, Doctors, and the Drug Company That Addicted America*. New York: Little, Brown and Company, 2018.

Magendie, F. *Formulary for the Preparation and Employment of Several New Remedies*. 8th ed. Translated by Charles Wilson Gregory. London: E. Cox, 1835.

Maiti, Satyabrata, and K.A. Geetha. "Research Highlights of Opium Poppy Under AICRP." Technical Bulletin, All India Co-ordinated Research Project on Medicinal and Aromatic Plants, National Research Centre for Medicinal and Aromatic Plants, Boriavi, Anand, Gujarat, September 2000.

Maltass, Sidney H. "On the Production of Opium in Asia Minor." *London Pharmaceutical Journal* 14 (March 1855): 395–400.

Manchikanti, Laxmaiah, and Angelie Singh. "Therapeutic Opioids: A Ten-Year Perspective on the Complexities and Complications of the Escalating Use, Abuse, and Nonmedical Use of Opioids." *Pain Physician* 11, no. 2 Suppl (March 2008): S63–88.

Markovits, Claude. "The Political Economy of Opium Smuggling in Early Nineteenth Century India: Leakage or Resistance?" *Modern Asian Studies* 43, no. 1 (January 2009): 89–111.

Maxwell, James L. *Questions on Opium Answered*. London, 1892.

Mays, Devi. "Becoming Illegal: Sephardi Jews in the Opiates Trade." *Jewish Social Studies* 25, no. 3 (Spring/Summer 2020): 1–34.

McAllister, William B. *Drug Diplomacy in the Twentieth Century: An International History*. London: Routledge, 2004.

McCook, Stuart. *Coffee Is Not Forever: A Global History of the Coffee Leaf Rust*. Illustrated edition. Athens: Ohio University Press, 2019.

McCoy, Alfred W. *The Politics of Heroin: CIA Complicity in the Global Drug Trade*. New York: Harper & Row, 1972.

McGreal, Chris. *American Overdose: The Opioid Tragedy in Three Acts*. New York: PublicAffairs, 2019.

McMurtrie, William. "American Opium." In *Monthly Report of the U.S. Department of Agriculture, January and February, 1876*, 39. Washington, DC Government Printing Office, 1876.

McNeil Laboratories, Inc. "Fentanyl (Sublimaze)." *Clinical Pharmacology & Therapeutics* 9, no. 5 (1968): 704–706.

McTavish, Betsy. "What Did Bayer Do Before Aspirin? Early Pharmaceutical Research at Bayer." *History of Pharmacy and Pharmaceuticals* 41, no. 1 (1999): 17–29.

McWilliams, John C. *The Protectors: Harry J. Anslinger and the Federal Bureau of Narcotics, 1930–1962*. Newark: University of Delaware Press, 1990.

Meier, Barry. *Pain Killer: An Empire of Deceit and the Origin of America's Opioid Epidemic*. New York: Random House, 2003.

Meldrum, Marcia L. "Brief History of Multidisciplinary Management of Chronic Pain, 1900–2000." In *Chronic Pain Management: Guidelines for Multidisciplinary Program Development*, edited by Michael E. Schatman and Alexandra Campbell, 1–13. Boca Raton, FL: CRC Press, 2007.

Melillo, Edward D. "Global Entomologies: Insects, Empires, and the 'Synthetic Age' in World History." *Past & Present*, no. 223 (2014): 233–270.

Melzack, Ronald, and Patrick D. Wall. *The Challenge of Pain*. New York: Penguin, 2008.

Melzack, Ronald. *The Puzzle of Pain*. Harmondsworth, England: Penguin Education, 1977.

"Memleketimizde Afyon Ticareti [Opium trade in our country]." *İstanbul Ticaret Odası Mecmuası* 41, no. 3 (1956): 779–780.

Menon, Nikhil. "Developing Histories of Indian Development." *History Compass* 19, no. 10 (2021): 1–14.

Menon, Nikhil. *Planning Democracy: Modern India's Quest for Development*. Cambridge: Cambridge University Press, 2022.

Meyer, Kathryn, and Terry M. Parssinen. *Webs of Smoke: Smugglers, Warlords, Spies, and the History of the International Drug Trade*. Lanham, MD, and Oxford: Rowman & Littlefield, 2002.

Mikhail, Alan. *Nature and Empire in Ottoman Egypt: An Environmental History*. Cambridge: Cambridge University Press, 2013.

Milius, Susan. "Morphinefree Mutant Poppies." *Science News* 169, no. 2 (January 28, 2006): 26.

Minutes of Evidence Taken Before the Royal Commission on Opium from 3rd to 27th January 1894, Volume III. London: Her Majesty's Stationery Office, 1894.

Mir Munshi Sultan Mahomed Khan, ed. *The Life of Abdur Rahman: Amir of Afghanistan*. London: John Murray, 1900.

Mitman, Gregg. *Empire of Rubber: Firestone's Scramble for Land and Power in Liberia*. New York: The New Press, 2023.

"Morphine and Its Salts." In *American Druggist*, vol. 36. American Druggist Publishing Company, 1900.

Mukharji, Projit Bihari. *Doctoring Traditions: Ayurveda, Small Technologies, and Braided Sciences*. Chicago: University of Chicago Press, 2016.

Mukhupadhyay, B.K. "Opium Alkaloids: Recent Developments in India." *Journal of Scientific & Industrial Research* 8, no. 4 (April 1949): 118–121.

Musto, David F. *The American Disease: Origins of Narcotic Control*. New York: Oxford University Press, 1973.

Nehru, Jawaharlal. "To Bishnu Ram Medhi." In *Selected Works of Jawaharlal Nehru*, vol. 8, edited by S. Gopal, 483–489. New Delhi: B.R. Publishing Corporation, 1976.

Nencini, Paolo. "Facts and Factoids in the Early History of the Opium Poppy." *The Social History of Alcohol and Drugs: An Interdisciplinary Journal* 36, no. 1 (Spring 2022): 45–71.

Nevill, H.R. *Ghazipur: A Gazetteer, Being Volume XXIX of the District Gazetteers of the United Provinces of Agra and Oudh*. Allahabad, India: Government Press, United Provinces, 1909.

Newman, R.K. "India and the Anglo-Chinese Opium Agreements, 1907–14." *Modern Asian Studies* 23, no. 3 (July 1989): 525–560.

Nigam, Raj Kumar. *Memoirs of Old Mandarins of India: The Administrative Change as the ICS Administrators Saw in India*. New Delhi: Documentation Centre for Corporate & Business Policy Research, 1985.

Ohler, Norman. *Blitzed: Drugs in the Third Reich.* Translated by Shaun Whiteside. Boston: Houghton Mifflin Harcourt, 2017.

Osseo-Asare, Abena Dove. *Bitter Roots: The Search for Healing Plants in Africa.* Chicago: University of Chicago Press, 2014.

Owen, David. *British Opium Policy in China and India.* New Haven, CT: Yale University Press, 1934.

Paoli, Letizia, Victoria A. Greenfield, and Peter Reuter. *The World Heroin Market: Can Supply Be Cut?* Oxford: Oxford University Press, 2009.

Papamichos, Paris. "Mediterranean Jews and the Politics of Contraband Trade in World War I." In *The Macedonian Front, 1915–1918: Politics, Society and Culture in Time of War,* edited by Basil Gounaris, Michael Llewellyn-Smith, and Ioannis Stefanidis, 134–142. London: Routledge, 2022.

Patel, Raj. *Stuffed and Starved: The Hidden Battle for the World Food System.* Brooklyn: Melville House, 2008.

Pati, Biswamoy, and Mark Harrison. *The Social History of Health and Medicine in Colonial India.* London: Routledge, 2009.

Pembleton, Matthew R. *Containing Addiction: The Federal Bureau of Narcotics and the Origins of America's Global Drug War.* Amherst: University of Massachusetts Press, 2017.

Perkins, E. Ralph, S. Everett Gleason, and Fredrick Aandahl, eds. "The Secretary of State to the Ambassador in the United Kingdom (Winant)." In *Foreign Relations of the United States: Diplomatic Papers, 1944, General: Economic and Social Matters,* vol. II, 511. Washington, DC: U.S. Government Printing Office, 1967.

Perramond, Eric. "The Dynamics of the Drug Trade in Northwestern Mexico." In *Dangerous Harvest: Drug Plants and the Transformation of Indigenous Landscapes,* edited by Michael K. Steinberg, Joseph J. Hobbs, and Kent Mathewson, 209–217. Oxford: Oxford University Press, 2004.

Pert, Candace. *Molecules of Emotion: Why You Feel the Way You Feel.* New York: Simon & Schuster, 1999.

Pilcher, Jeffrey M. *Food in World History.* London: Routledge, 2006.

Pletcher, David. *The Diplomacy of Involvement: American Economic Expansion Across the Pacific, 1784–1900.* Columbia: University of Missouri Press, 2001.

Poroy, Ibrahim Ihsan. "Expansion of Opium Production in Turkey and the State Monopoly of 1828–1839." *International Journal of Middle East Studies* 13, no. 2 (1981): 191–211.

Powar, Soonderbai H. *Opium Crime of the British Government: An Indian Woman's Impeachment.* London: Dyer Brothers, 1892.

Prakash, Gyan. *Emergency Chronicles: Indira Gandhi and Democracy's Turning Point.* Princeton, NJ: Princeton University Press, 2019.

Prioreschi, Plinio. "Medieval Anesthesia: The Spongia Somnifera." *Medical Hypotheses* 61, no. 2 (August 2003): 213–219.

Quinones, Sam. *Dreamland: The True Tale of America's Opiate Epidemic.* New York: Bloomsbury, 2015.

Raianu, Mircea. *Tata: The Global Corporation That Built Indian Capitalism.* Cambridge, MA: Harvard University Press, 2021.

Ram, Haggai. *Intoxicating Zion: A Social History of Hashish in Mandatory Palestine and Israel.* Stanford, CA: Stanford University Press, 2020.

Rana, Subir. "The Metahistory and Afterlife of a Public Institution: Natnagar Shodh Sansthan, Madhya Pradesh." *India International Centre Quarterly* 47, nos. 1/2 (2020): 188–204.

Ratelle, A.E., and M.K. Kim. "Demerol as an Anesthetic Agent Used in 9,000 Surgical Cases." *Minnesota Medicine* 43 (January 1960): 22–24.

Raz, Mical. "Treating Addiction or Reducing Crime? Methadone Maintenance and Drug Policy Under the Nixon Administration." *Journal of Policy History* 29, no. 1 (2017): 58–86.

Recio, Gabriela. "Drugs and Alcohol: US Prohibition and the Origins of the Drug Trade in Mexico, 1910–1930." *Journal of Latin American Studies* 34, no. 1 (February 2002): 21–42.

Reiss, Suzanna. *We Sell Drugs: The Alchemy of US Empire*. Berkeley: University of California Press, 2014.

Report 1981–1982. New Delhi: Ministry of Finance, Government of India, 1982.

Report on the Experimental Culture of the Opium Poppy for the Season 1876–77. Calcutta: Bengal Secretariat Press, 1877.

Report on the Experimental Culture of the Opium Poppy for the Season 1877–78. Calcutta: Bengal Secretariat Press, 1878.

Report on the Operation of the Narcotics Department for the Year Ending the 30th September, 1963. New Delhi: Ministry of Finance, Government of India, 1963.

Report on the Operations of the Narcotics Department for the Half Year Ending the 31st March 1965. New Delhi: Ministry of Finance, Government of India, 1965.

Report on the Operations of the Narcotics Department for the Year Ending the 31st March, 1966. New Delhi: Ministry of Finance, Government of India, 1966.

Return of an Article on Opium by Dr. Watt. Reporter on Economic Products with the Government of India, Recently Written by Him, and Intended to be Published in the Sixth Volume of the Dictionary of Economic Products of India. London: Her Majesty's Stationery Office, 1892.

Rey, Roselyne. *The History of Pain*. Cambridge, MA: Harvard University Press, 1998.

Richards, J.F. "The Indian Empire and Peasant Production of Opium in the Nineteenth Century." *Modern Asian Studies* 15 (1981): 59–82.

Richert, Lucas, and James H. Mills. *Cannabis: Global Histories*. Cambridge, MA: MIT Press, 2021.

Ricketson, Shadrach. "On the Cultivation of the Poppy-Plant, and the Method of Procuring Opium, Etc." In *Transactions of the Society for the Promotion of Agriculture, Arts and Manufactures*, vol. 1, 264–266. Albany: Charles R. and George Webster, 1801.

Rimner, Steffen. *Opium's Long Shadow: From Asian Revolt to Global Drug Control*. Cambridge, MA: Harvard University Press, 2018.

Roberts, Samuel, and Helena Hansen. "Two Tiers of Biomedicalization: Buprenorphine, Methadone and the Biopolitics of Addiction Stigma and Race." In *Critical Perspectives on Addiction*, edited by Julie Netherland, 79–103. Bingley, England: Emerald, 2012.

Roberts, Timothy M. "Commercial Philanthropy: American Missionaries and the American Opium Trade in Izmir During the First Part of the Nineteenth Century." *Journal of Mediterranean Studies* 19, no. 2 (2010): 371–388.

Robins, Jonathan E. *Oil Palm: A Global History*. Chapel Hill: University of North Carolina Press, 2021.

Rosenberg, Emily S., and Shanon Fitzpatrick, eds. *Body and Nation: The Global Realm of U.S. Body Politics in the Twentieth Century*. Durham, NC: Duke University Press, 2014.

Rothermund, Dietmar. *An Economic History of India: From Pre-Colonial Times to 1991*. London: Routledge, 2003.

Roy, Tirthankar. "The Mutiny and the Merchants." *The Historical Journal* 59, no. 2 (June 2016): 393–416.

Royal Botanic Garden, Calcutta. *Annals of the Royal Botanic Garden, Calcutta*. Calcutta: Bengal Secretariat Book Depot, 1888.

Rush, James R. "Opium in Java: A Sinister Friend." *The Journal of Asian Studies* 44, no. 3 (1985): 549–560.

Sackley, Nicole. "The Village as Cold War Site: Experts, Development, and the History of Rural Reconstruction." *Journal of Global History* 6, no. 3 (2011): 481–504.

Sackley, Nicole. "Village Models: Etawah, India, and the Making and Remaking of Development in the Early Cold War." *Diplomatic History* 37, no. 4 (2013): 749–778.

Sandos, James. "Northern Separatism During the Mexican Revolution: An Inquiry into the Role of Drug Trafficking, 1910–1920." *The Americas* 41, no. 2 (1984): 191–214.

Sarkar, Jayita. *Ploughshares and Swords: India's Nuclear Program in the Global Cold War*. Ithaca, NY: Cornell University Press, 2022.

Sassoon, Joseph. *The Sassoons: The Great Global Merchants and the Making of an Empire*. New York: Pantheon Books, 2022.

Sastri, V.S. Srinivasa. "Speech at the League of Nations, 13th January, 1923." In *Speeches and Writing of the Rt. V.S. Srinivasa Sastri*, 401–425. Madras: G.A. Natesan & Co., 1925.

Sattanathan, A.N. *Plain Speaking: A Sudra's Story*. Edited by Uttara Natarajan. New Delhi: Permanent Black, 2007.

Scarry, Elaine. *The Body in Pain: The Making and Unmaking of the World*. Oxford: Oxford University Press, 1985.

Scheltema, J.F. "The Opium Trade in the Dutch East Indies." *American Journal of Sociology* 13, no. 1 (1907): 79–112.

Schmidt, Jan. *From Anatolia to Indonesia: Opium Trade and the Dutch Community of Izmir, 1820–1940*. Istanbul: Nederlands Historisch-Archaeologisch Instituut te Istanbul, 1998.

Schmitz, Rudolf. "Friedrich Wilhelm Sertürner and the Discovery of Morphine." *Pharmacy in History* 27, no. 2 (1985): 61–74.

Schneider, Eric C. *Smack: Heroin and the American City*. Philadelphia: University of Pennsylvania Press, 2013.

Sen, Uditi. *Citizen Refugee: Forging the Indian Nation After Partition*. Cambridge: Cambridge University Press, 2018.

Sezer, Özge. *Forming the Modern Turkish Village: Nation Building and Modernization in Rural Turkey During the Early Republic*. Bielefeld, Germany: Transcript, 2023.

Shah, Varsha. "Economic Analysis of India's Exports to U.S.A." PhD diss., Gujarat University, 1978.

Sharghi, N., and I. Lalezari. "Papaver Bracteatum Lindl., a Highly Rich Source of Thebaine." *Nature* 213, no. 5082 (March 1967): 1244.

Shekhawat, G.S. "Cultivation Studies in Poppy." *Indian Journal of Agronomy* 12, no. 1 (1967): 83–85.

Sherman, Taylor C. "From 'Grow More Food' to 'Miss a Meal': Hunger, Development and the Limits of Post-Colonial Nationalism in India, 1947–1957." *South Asia: Journal of South Asian Studies* 36, no. 4 (2013): 571–588.

Sherman, Taylor C. *Nehru's India: A History in Seven Myths*. Princeton, NJ: Princeton University Press, 2022.

Siegel, Benjamin Robert. *Hungry Nation: Food, Famine, and the Making of Modern India*. Cambridge: Cambridge University Press, 2018.

Siegel, Benjamin Robert. "The Kibbutz and the Ashram: Sarvodaya Agriculture, Israeli Aid, and the Global Imaginaries of Indian Development." *The American Historical Review* 125, no. 4 (2020): 1175–1204.

Siegel, Benjamin Robert. "Woven, Mined, Milled, and Packed: The Global Destinies of Indian Commodities, 1500–2023." In *India in the World: 1500 to the Present*, edited by Rajeshwari Dutt and Nico Slate, 33–54. New York: Routledge, 2023.

Sinha, Subir. "Lineages of the Developmentalist State: Transnationality and Village India, 1900–1965." *Comparative Studies in Society and History* 50, no. 1 (2008): 57–90.

Slack, Edward. *Opium, State, and Society: China's Narco-Economy and the Guomindang, 1924–1937*. Honolulu: University of Hawaii Press, 2000.

Smith, Benjamin T. *The Dope: The Real History of the Mexican Drug Trade*. New York: W. W. Norton, 2021.

Snyder, Solomon. *Brainstorming: The Science and Politics of Opiate Research*. Cambridge, MA: Harvard University Press, 2013.

Soluri, John. *Banana Cultures: Agriculture, Consumption, and Environmental Change in Honduras and the United States*. Austin: University of Texas Press, 2006.

Soto Laveaga, Gabriela. *Jungle Laboratories: Mexican Peasants, National Projects, and the Making of the Pill*. Durham, NC: Duke University Press, 2009.

Souza, George Bryan. "Opium and the Company: Maritime Trade and Imperial Finances on Java, 1684–1796." *Modern Asian Studies* 43, no. 1 (January 2009): 113–133.

Spain, James W. "The United States, Turkey and the Poppy." *Middle East Journal* 29, no. 3 (1975): 295–309.

Specht, Joshua. *Red Meat Republic: A Hoof-to-Table History of How Beef Changed America*. Princeton, NJ: Princeton University Press, 2019.

Spillane, Joseph F. *Cocaine: From Medical Marvel to Modern Menace in the United States, 1884–1920*. Baltimore: Johns Hopkins University Press, 2000.

Spong, William B. *Heroin: Can the Supply Be Stopped?* Washington, DC: United States Congress Senate Committee on Foreign Relations, 1972.

Srivastava, Ramesh Chandra. "Human Resource Development as a Tool of Effectiveness: A Case Study of Government Opium Alkaloid Works Undertaking, Ghazipur, U.P." PhD diss., Veer Bahadur Singh Purvanchal University, 2002.

Starr, Paul. *The Social Transformation of American Medicine*. New York: Basic Books, 1982.

Stein, S.D. *International Diplomacy, State Administrators, and Narcotics Control: The Origins of a Social Problem*. Aldershot, UK: Gower, 1985.

Steinberg, Michael K., Joseph John Hobbs, and Kent Mathewson, eds. *Dangerous Harvest: Drug Plants and the Transformation of Indigenous Landscapes*. Oxford: Oxford University Press, 2004.

Śukla, Śrīlāla. *Raag Darbari*. Translated by Gillian Wright. New Delhi: Penguin Books India, 1992.

Swann, John P. "The Evolution of the American Pharmaceutical Industry." *Bulletin of the History of Medicine* 69, no. 2 (1995): 254–285.

Tarman, Celal, and Fethi İncekara. *Haşhaş Ziraati Nasıl Kazançli Olur?* [How can opium poppy cultivation be profitable?]. Ankara: İstiklal Matbaası, 1954.

Taylor, Arnold H. *American Diplomacy and the Narcotics Traffic, 1900–1958: A Study in International Humanitarian Reform*. Durham, NC: Duke University Press, 1969.

Temple, John. *American Pain: How a Young Felon and His Ring of Doctors Unleashed America's Deadliest Drug Epidemic*. Guilford, CT: Lyons Press, 2015.

Thacher, James. "On the Cultivation of the Papaver Somniferum, or Poppy-Plant, and the Method of Preparing Opium." In *The American New Dispensatory*, 454–457. Boston: T.B. Wait, 1810.

Thilly, Peter. *The Opium Business: A History of Crime and Capitalism in Maritime China*. Stanford, CA: Stanford University Press, 2022.

Tinsman, Heidi. *Buying into the Regime: Grapes and Consumption in Cold War Chile and the United States*. Durham, NC: Duke University Press, 2014.

Tobbell, Dominique A. *Pills, Power, and Policy: The Struggle for Drug Reform in Cold War America and Its Consequences*. Berkeley: University of California Press, 2012.

Turgay, A. Üner. "The Nineteenth Century Golden Triangle: Chinese Consumption, Ottoman Production, American Connection, Part I: Opium Trade in International Perspective and Early American Opium Trade." *International Journal of Turkish Studies* 2, no. 2 (Winter 1981–1982): 105–125.

Turgay, A. Üner. "The Nineteenth Century Golden Triangle: Chinese Consumption, Ottoman Production, American Connection, Part II: Ottoman Opium Production and Government Policies." *International Journal of Turkish Studies* 3, no. 1 (Winter 1984–1985): 65–92.

Turgay, A. Üner. "Ottoman-American Trade During the 19th Century." *Osmanlı Araştırmaları* 3 (1982): 189–246.

Turgay, Bülent. "The Nineteenth Century Golden Triangle Part II." Ottoman Opium Production and Government Policies." *International Journal of Turkish Studies* 3, no. 1 (Winter 1984–1985): 65–91.

Tyrrell, Ian. "Opium and the Fashioning of the American Moral Empire." In *Reforming the World: The Creation of America's Moral Empire*, 146–165. Princeton, NJ: Princeton University Press, 2013.

Tyrrell, Ian. *Reforming the World: The Creation of America's Moral Empire*. Princeton, NJ: Princeton University Press, 2010.

U.S. Congress, House, Committee on the Judiciary. *New York Quinine & Chemical Works, Inc. Merck & Co., Inc. and Mallinckrodt Chemical Works*. 81st Cong., 1st sess., 1949, H. Rep. 992, 1–15.

United States Congress House Committee on Foreign Affairs. *The Politics of the Poppy: Report of a Study Mission to Turkey, March 14–16, 1974*. Washington, DC: United States Government Printing Office, 1974.

United States Congress House Committee on Foreign Affairs. *U.S. Licit Opium Imports: Foreign Policy Issues: Report of a Staff Study Mission to Turkey, India, and Australia to the Committee on Foreign Affairs, U.S. House of Representatives*. Washington, DC: United States Government Printing Office, 1989.

United States Congress House Committee on the Judiciary, Subcommittee on Crime. *The Licit Importation of Opium*, 138–140. Washington, DC: United States Government Printing Office, 1990.

United States Congress Senate Committee on the Judiciary Subcommittee to Investigate Juvenile Delinquency. *Poppy Politics: Hearings Before the Subcommittee to Investigate Juvenile Delinquency of the Committee on the Judiciary, United States Senate*, vol. 1. Washington, DC: United States Government Printing Office, 1977.

Valentine, Douglas. *The Strength of the Wolf: The Secret History of America's War on Drugs*. Brooklyn: Verso Books, 2013.

Vance, J.D. *Hillbilly Elegy: A Memoir of a Family and Culture in Crisis*. New York: Harper, 2016.

Wailoo, Keith. *Pain: A Political History*. Baltimore: Johns Hopkins University Press, 2014.

Walker, William O. *Drug Control in the Americas*. Albuquerque: University of New Mexico Press, 1981.

Walker, William O. *Opium and Foreign Policy: The Anglo-American Search for Order in Asia, 1912–1954*. Chapel Hill: University of North Carolina Press, 1991.

Wann, John L. "Recent Competitive Aspects of Turkish Agriculture." *Foreign Agriculture* 19, no. 10 (October 1955): 206.

"War Progress Notes: Opium Imports." *War Progress*, no. 137 (April 30, 1943): 10.

Weimer, Daniel. *Seeing Drugs: Modernization, Counterinsurgency, and U.S. Narcotics Control in the Third World, 1969–1976*. Kent, OH: The Kent State University Press, 2011.

Weiss, Emanuel. "Opium: Can We Compete with the East in Its Production?" *Agricultural, Commercial, Industrial Progress and Resources* 20, no. 1 (January 1856): 60a–66a.

Weiss, Emanuel, and Bayard Clarke. *The Cultivation of Opium in the United States of America: Being a Memorial to Congress, 1866*. Private copy in the Boston Athenæum.

Wertz, Daniel. "Idealism, Imperialism, and Internationalism: Opium Politics in the Colonial Philippines, 1898–1925." *Modern Asian Studies* 47, no. 2 (March 2013): 467–499.

Westhoff, Ben. *Fentanyl, Inc.: How Rogue Chemists Are Creating the Deadliest Wave of the Opioid Epidemic*. New York: Atlantic Monthly Press, 2019.

White, Sam. *The Climate of Rebellion in the Early Modern Ottoman Empire*. Studies in Environment and History. New York: Cambridge University Press, 2011.

Williams, Elizabeth R. *States of Cultivation: Imperial Transition and Scientific Agriculture in the Eastern Mediterranean*. Stanford, CA: Stanford University Press, 2023.

Williams, Stewart. "On Islands, Insularity, and Opium Poppies: Australia's Secret Pharmacy." *Environment and Planning D: Society and Space* 28, no. 2 (2010): 302.

Williams, William Appleman. *The Tragedy of American Diplomacy*. New York: W. W. Norton, 1972.

Wood, L.J. "The Legal Production of Narcotic Materials in Australia." *Australian Geographer* 17–18 (November 1987): 161–165.

Wood, L.J. "Not Ordinary Merchandise: World Trends in the Licit Production of Opiates." *Geography* 73, no. 2 (April 1988): 149–151.

Wood, L.J. "Poppies in Tasmania." *Geography* 63, no. 3 (1978): 213–217.

World Health Organization Scientific Group on Opiates and Their Alternates for Pain and Cough Relief. *Opiates and Their Alternates for Pain and Cough Relief: Report of a WHO Scientific Group*. Geneva: World Health Organization, 1972.

Wright, H.R.C. "The Abolition by Cornwallis of the Forced Cultivation of Opium in Bihar." *The Economic History Review* 12, no. 1 (1959): 112–119.

Wright, Hamilton. "The Opium Problem: Its History and Present Condition." In *China and the Far East*, edited by George Hubbard Blakeslee, 152. New York: T.Y. Crowell & Company, 1910.

Yang, Timothy M. *A Medicated Empire: The Pharmaceutical Industry and Modern Japan*. Ithaca, NY: Cornell University Press, 2021.

Zebroski, Bob. *A Brief History of Pharmacy: Humanity's Search for Wellness*. New York: Routledge, 2016.

Zheng, Yangwen. "The Social Life of Opium in China, 1483–1999." *Modern Asian Studies* 37, no. 1 (2003): 1–39.

Index

For the benefit of digital users, indexed terms that span two pages (e.g., 52–53) may, on occasion, appear on only one of those pages.